GUYS, DOLLS,
and
CURVEBALLS

—

Damon Runyon on Baseball

EDITED BY JIM REISLER

CARROLL & GRAF PUBLISHERS
NEW YORK

GUYS, DOLLS, AND CURVEBALLS
DAMON RUNYON ON BASEBALL

Carroll & Graf Publishers
An Imprint of Avalon Publishing Group Inc.
245 West 17th Street
New York, NY 10011

AVALON
publishing group incorporated

Compilation Copyright © 2005 by Jim Reisler
First Carroll & Graf edition 2005

Front photo: © Corbis
Chapter photos: © National Baseball Hall of Fame Library, Cooperstown, NY
Library of Congress Cataloging-in-Publication Data is available.

ISBN: 0-7867-1540-5

Printed in the United States of America
Book design by Jamie McNeely
Distributed by Publishers Group West

For Tobie and Julia, with love

Sincere thanks, as always, go to Tim Wiles, Gabe Schechter, Bill Burdick, and the rest of the crack staff at the National Baseball Hall of Fame for your guidance. Thanks as well to Leo Stanger, Peter Berger, and Philip Furgang for your legal help; and to Nate Knaebel of Carroll & Graf; D'Ann Van Arsdale; and Frank Scatoni and Greg Dinkin of Venture Literary for supporting this project. And finally, Marty Kounitz, Joe Sterling, Jim and Mike Gardner, and David Walk, thanks for your friendship.

CONTENTS

INTRODUCTION VII

1 — CHARACTERS & CRAFTSMEN 1

2 — MEMORABLE MOMENTS 105

3 — WORLD SERIES 139

4 — BLACK SOX 257

5 — SPRING TRAINING 289

6 — AROUND THE WORLD 331

7 — MUSINGS & (MOSTLY) ORDINARY
GAMES 361

Damon Runyon

INTRODUCTION

I have no fancy for returning to sports writing," Damon Runyon wrote late in life. "I would be no good at it any more, at least not in the tradition of sports writing that flourished in my day as a member of that branch of the newspaper game."

Perhaps not. But in his "day," Alfred Damon Runyon stood alone as the most distinctive, most unusual, and arguably best baseball voice of his era, starting in 1911 and enduring for nearly three decades. Runyon rewrote how the sport was covered and did so with a healthy, iconoclastic dose of humor and an eye out for the kind of characters that would later make him famous.

Long before Runyon created memorable Broadway wise guys like Nathan Detroit, Nicely Nicely Johnson and Dave the Dude, he wrote of real-life baseball legends like John McGraw, Christy Mathewson, Ty Cobb, and Babe Ruth. Long before he penned memorable short stories like *All Horse Players Die Broke* and *A Slight Case of Murder*, which spun the tales of Broadway bootleggers, bookies, and bums, he covered baseball with searing portraits of not just the best players, but also the most quotable and those at the margins. Included were all the flourishes of what later became known as "Runyonesque" prose — Runyon's thoughts on everything from what the gamblers were saying to the latest styles of women's hats in the stands, clubhouse gossip, occasional poetry, and, for a brief few weeks during spring training in 1920, the poignant saga of his pet alligator, Aloysius.

Baseball was Runyon's introduction to New York and the kind of characters who would come to embellish his fiction. Up to then, baseball journalism had all the color of chess coverage, with bland reports of who won, who had the hits, and who pitched. Not Runyon, who, depending on his mood, could be funny, introspective—and pretty damn funny. Yes, he was that good a writer—good enough to infuse his copy with, well, whatever was on his mind. Along the way, he became his generation's most distinctive sportswriter, helping usher in a truly golden age of sports.

Anything Was Game

Anything was game in Runyon's world. In the middle of the 1919 season, for no apparent reason, he wrote a month's worth of game stories in single sentence-paragraphs, which included coverage of a Giants-Pirates' game from the perspective of a five-year-old boy. Weather was a preoccupation, as were ladies' hats; fishing, which he disliked; and golf, which he disliked more. In 1920, he covered a spring-training eating contest with the drama of a prizefight, and once covered a rare deadball-era slugfest from the perspective of the ball: "If I wanted to be right chesty about it," Runyon wrote. "I might tell you that I am THE Home Run, and you would never know any better, but I am an honest Home Run, and as modest and unassuming as Ed Sweeney's batting average." As Jimmy Breslin put it in *Damon Runyon: A Life*: "He put a smile into a newspaper, which (at the time) . . . ha(d) as much humor as a bus accident. (In doing so,) "he beat the New York newspaper business, beat it to a pulp."

Runyon could be "laugh out loud" funny, as in describing the conversation of gamblers aboard a train headed to the 1911 World Series. He could be a soppy sentimentalist, pining for the old days of Boston's Royal Rooters or tenderly calling to attention the plight of an old ballplayer in need. The benchwarmers in the dugout and the fans in the cheap seats were of particular interest to Runyon: During the 1926 World Series, Runyon wondered just why it was that the big shots and not the real fans always ended up in the best seats. "This world, as I have long since discovered, is arranged all wrong," he wrote. "I do not know just how I would rearrange it if they left the job to me, but I would certainly make some provision for the regulars getting the best seats when the best seats are really worth having."

An eye for the eccentric and the unusual was a gift. When a simpleton named Charles "Victory" Faust presented himself to Giants' manager John McGraw, saying a fortune-teller had directed him to pitch the Giants to the pennant, Runyon took note, and by summer's end, had made Faust a living legend. In the tumult of the Yankees' World Series sweep of 1932, Runyon's lead focused on Yankee owner Jacob Ruppert's silk pajamas—yes, his pajamas, which the Yankees enjoyed ripping apart after a championship. For all his thousands of game stories, a few stood out, as in the day in 1926 when Grover Cleveland Alexander arose from a Times Square bar stool to pitch the Cardinals to a World Series triumph at Yankee Stadium, the sad saga of the 1919 Chicago White Sox, and the day Babe Ruth pointed to outfield fence in the World Series at Wrigley Field—or didn't—and drilled a home run.

Runyon was different from the get-go. Arriving in New York in 1911 at the age of 30 as William Randolph Hearst's baseball man for the *American*, he accompanied the Giants that March to spring training in Marlin, Texas, where he immediately zeroed in on the life and times of a talented but troubled pitcher with a great nickname—Arthur "Bugs" Raymond. Later, Runyon was attracted to the garbled syntax of a Yankee outfielder named Ping Bodie, the Yogi Berra of his day; little that Bodie said was off the record and a lot of it was funny. The great Hall of Fame Giants' pitcher Christy Mathewson? Celebrated as much for wholesome ways as his devastating fadeaway pitch, Mathewson was a friend, but didn't interest Runyon much as a reporter; too bland.

Rainouts and off-days were a treat for Runyon's readers. Days when the field was too wet to play or there was no game sent

Runyon into hotel lobbies in search of baseball conversation, like John McGraw holding court on the *really* old days of baseball and Ruth predicting World Series glory. With copy to fill, Runyon ruminated with whatever was on this mind—from the state of the pennant race to the breakneck speeds of Pittsburgh cab drivers. "After the most evenly balanced expert in the world has journeyed from the railroad station to a hotel in a Pittsburgh taxicab, he is in no condition to give his best efforts to experting," Runyon wrote on the eve of the 1927 Yankees-Pirates World Series. "He is apt to be too badly frightened."

In the days when reporters seldom ventured into the locker room to quote the ballplayers or the manager, Runyon built up a small stable of people he'd commonly reference: not the stars, but people like Harry Stevens, the Polo Grounds' British-born concessions' king—'Arry, Runyon typically called him—along with groundskeeper Henry Fabian, Yankee business manager Harry Sparrow, and the former Giant-turned-actor, the flamboyant Mike Donlin, all friends. These were men on the fringe of the game—characters who added color and context to his stories—as well as shades of things to come: Years later, Runyon would use the same technique in his celebrated short stories, not featuring the big shots, but those on the edge.

Ruppert and the exquisitely named Tillinghast L'Hommedieu Huston, who jointly owned the Yankees for a time, were friends as well, and Runyon referred to them often—usually spelling out Huston's full name because, well, it was funny. Knowing that upbeat coverage could boost ticket sales, team owners cultivated the writers in those days—making sure they had all the booze and the food they could handle. That didn't stop Runyon from poking fun at those in charge, particularly the vain, blustery, and rotund American League president Ban Johnson—"Mr. Bancroft B. Johnson," he called him—and portly Brooklyn manager Wilbert Robinson, forever christened "your Uncle Wilbert" because, after all, he looked the part.

Yet Runyon's humor was gentle, hardly malicious nor overly critical. He never lost sight that baseball was entertainment—even on the bizarre day when Ty Cobb climbed into the stands at Hilltop Park in 1915 and beat a heckler senseless. In an era when most players had little education, the literate Runyon could have made fun of their humble roots, but he never did. Names and hometowns put a smile on his face, as in his report after the 1912 World Series of where the Giants were headed for the winter: "Otis Crandall will, of course, go to Wadina, Ind., for a Winter in Wadina without Otis would be a dreary social season, indeed." About the only time that baseball upset Runyon was in the wake of the 1919 World Series scandal.

Hearst loved every word from the moment he started receiving mail and phone messages barely weeks into Runyon's new beat in 1911 from readers praising the style of this quirky new reporter. Calling Runyon a few weeks later to his apartment on Riverside Drive in New York City, Hearst tripled his salary in appreciation. Within two years, Runyon was the newspaper's featured humorist, and in 1914, started a daily column, *Th' Mornin's Mornin'*, a collection of bits and pieces from boxing, horse racing, and Broadway. Hearst's early generosity may have been the reason that Runyon stayed loyal; years after he'd left the baseball beat and become a big deal in Hollywood, Runyon kept writing for the *American*.

Hearst recognized that Runyon sold papers—and within a year or two, he was habitually taking his star reporter off the baseball beat to cover political conventions, murder trials, heavyweight title fights, the Kentucky Derby, and other big events. With the Giants in 1916 at spring training in Marlin, Texas, Runyon was suddenly dispatched to Mexico to accompany General John J. Pershing's pursuit of Pancho Villa—and the reports he sent home became must reading. In 1918, Runyon went to Europe as a war correspondent, and a year later wrote a syndicated biographical series about heavyweight champion Jack Dempsey, a friend from Colorado days. By the early 1920s, he was a syndicated star—but seldom missed opening day at the Polo Grounds or the World Series, filing expansive World Series batter-by-batter game summaries that he'd write as the game went on, rarely changing a word.

At Home Elsewhere

The irony is Runyon felt more at home at boxing arenas and race-tracks than ballparks since they were stocked with the kinds of hangers-on and marginal characters he found so intriguing. Long-time colleague Fred Lieb says Runyon never bothered to learn how to compile a box score, and would ask to borrow them, saying "I never did learn to get up one of those damned things." Runyon not only covered boxing; he bet heavily on the sport, but instead of going with favorites like Gene Tunney or Joe Louis, he cast his lot among underdogs with great names like Napoleon Dorval and Wyoming Warner. Periodically, Runyon bought "pieces" of fighters and horses, but like the characters in his stories, seldom earned anything. The one exception was a horse named "Tight Shoes," a 1940 Kentucky Derby favorite, which suddenly became ill before the race and was never again a serious threat. Asked by a friend whether he'd rather own the great thoroughbred Seabiscuit or heavyweight champ Joe Louis, Runyon opted for the horse: No need to split the purse with a horse, he explained.

But Runyon still loved baseball, and its schedule suited him. He stuck mostly to New York, where at the Polo Grounds, most games started at 3 or 4 P.M., affording him the luxury to sleep late, head up to the ballpark early in the afternoon, and file his story by dinner. Runyon combined extraordinarily fast typing with the ability to writes most game stories as they happened—giving him plenty of time to hang out most of the night, soaking up the pulse of Broadway. By the 1920s, Runyon was spending most every night in clubs as a non-drinking, coffee-chugging (upwards of 40 cups a day!) correspondent who would then head home at dawn, and fortified by more coffee, write about what he had seen.

John McGraw was Runyon's entrée to the Broadway crowd, many of whom hung out at the Giant skipper's theatrical Lambs Club on 43rd Street, or at Lindy's, the well-known eatery at Broadway and 53rd Street—immortalized as "Mindy's" in his stories. It was at Lindy's that Runyon would occupy a seat for long hours as he hosted a steady stream of characters, many of whom would find themselves worked into a short story: "It ain't hard to spot the guys in the stories," said a regular after reading a Runyon piece.

Baseball also gave Runyon a rich source of friends—McGraw and Mathewson were genuine pals, as was Babe Ruth, with whom he enjoyed hunting in the winter. So were press box colleagues Lieb and Heywood Broun, who started the very same day as Runyon, creating a kind of golden class of '11—as well as the great Grantland Rice. All three—and Runyon—are enshrined in the Writers' Wing of the Baseball Hall of Fame.

Many considered Runyon a cynic and an iconoclast, a non-traditionalist, who enjoyed taking people down in print. But "that wasn't the Runyon that I knew," Lieb wrote in his memoirs. "He had a sharp sense of humor, liked fun, and was willing to go wherever it led him. He didn't smile or laugh much, but when he peered out at the world through glasses that made him look studious, there was a suggestion he was smugly amused at the foolishness he saw. I thought he liked most of all to stand quietly in the background watching and half laughing at the people who passed his vision. But destructive or bitter—never."

Manhattan to Manhattan

A native of Manhattan (Kansas, that is) and raised in Pueblo, Colorado, Runyon arrived in New York after a rackety youth, Army service in the Philippines, a decade's worth of writing for papers in Denver and San Francisco, and a serious addiction to the bottle. Runyon didn't have much of a childhood—his mother died when he was 7, and his alcoholic father, a printer and newspaper typesetter, kept odd hours and left the boy largely on his own. Runyon practically grew up on the streets, dropped out from school at 13, and became a messenger in Pueblo's red-light district before turning to journalism at 15 as a police reporter in Pueblo.

Encouraged by a friend to move to New York and pursue a more temperate life, Runyon did so, swearing off alcohol for the rest of the life, or as he called it, "getting the money," his phrase for staying sober enough to earn a living. "I just can't drink, and now

I'm smart enough to know it," he told Lieb. "I used to drink, hard. I frequently got stinking drunk. And when I was drinking, I was real mean." Lieb had a theory on why his friend quit: "He had a dread that he would follow in the footsteps of his father, whom he worshipped, who was usually broke because of his drinking."

In New York, Runyon resorted to a pedestrian life—for a time. In 1911, he married Ellen Egan, a former *Rocky Mountain News* society editor, and the couple had two children. But after Runyon took to spending his nights on Broadway and not at home, the couple separated. Ellen died in 1931, and a year later, Runyon married Patrice Amati del Grande, a dancer; they had no children. Along the way, Runyon kept covering baseball and politics and wrote columns while churning out a series of books of Kiplingesque poetry, and writing short stories about his drinking days to national periodicals such as *Collier's, Harper's Weekly,* and *McClure's.* He even became somewhat of a dude himself—developing a passion for fancy shoes and pin-striped suits, and with a cigarette dangling from his lips; he always changed the carnation in his lapel three times a day.

By the 1920s, Runyon was earning $30,000 a year—hefty wages in those days and way more than most ballplayers—with his continued newspaper work and turning out a blizzard of magazine stories. Many of the people he wrote about became his friends, from Arnold Rothstein, the notorious gambler and alleged financier of the 1919 Black Sox, to the ballplayers, boxers, bookies, loan sharks, con men, society swills and chorus girls who prowled Broadway. In time, Runyon was regularly selling many of his stories to the movies—17 plot sequences in all—for ever-mounting fees. In the 1930s, when his baseball writing was limited mostly to the World Series, Runyon enjoyed his greatest commercial success—peddling to Hollywood stories like *Lady for a Day,* based on *Guys and Dolls,* and *Little Miss Marker,* which made a star of Shirley Temple.

Forever Baseball

Runyon's affection for baseball endured, and wound its way into several of his stories. Take Runyon's 1936 *Cosmopolitan* story, "Baseball

Hattie": "It comes on springtime, and the little birdies are singing in the trees in Central Park, and the grass is green all around and about, and I am at the Polo Grounds on the opening day of the baseball season, when who do I behold but Baseball Hattie?" the story begins.

Turns out Hattie, a groupie or "Baseball Annie" of sorts, falls for and marries a hot left-hander of a dimwitted prospect named Haystack Duggeler. Haystack gets off to a grand start with the Giants, but falls in with a bad crowd led by a gambler named Armand Fibleman. Then comes his discovery of the racetrack and big debts are soon owed to Armand. After that, it gets real complicated, real fast. Downright Runyonesque too, which means baseball, betting, race tracks, numerous wise guys and all the familiar flourishes.

Early in 1944, Runyon was diagnosed with throat cancer, which sapped his voice. On December 10, 1946, he died at 66, and eight days later, in a Runyonesque flourish he would have enjoyed, Damon Runyons's ashes were scattered over Broadway from an airplane piloted by Eddie Rickenbacker. Columnist Walter Winchell created the Damon Runyon Cancer Fund to memorialize his close associate and friend.

Connie Mack called Runyon, "a master of characters and plots such as we see everyday in our grandstands," a tribute included in the commemoration of Runyon's 1967 election to the Writer's Wing at Cooperstown. Editor Herbert Bayard Swope, the first newspaperman to earn a Pulitzer Prize, ranked Runyon tops of any reporter or editor he'd ever seen. Fred Lieb agreed: "To Damon, there were no good guys and bad guys, no gracious ladies who promoted church fairs, no tawdry streetwalkers," he wrote. "They were all guys and dolls, and you judged them, if at all, by their inner qualities, not their outward circumstances."

And for a decade or so in the early part of the 20th century when giants like Babe Ruth and Ty Cobb roamed the ballparks of America, those "guys" were ballplayers, who Runyon wrote about in a way that has never been matched.

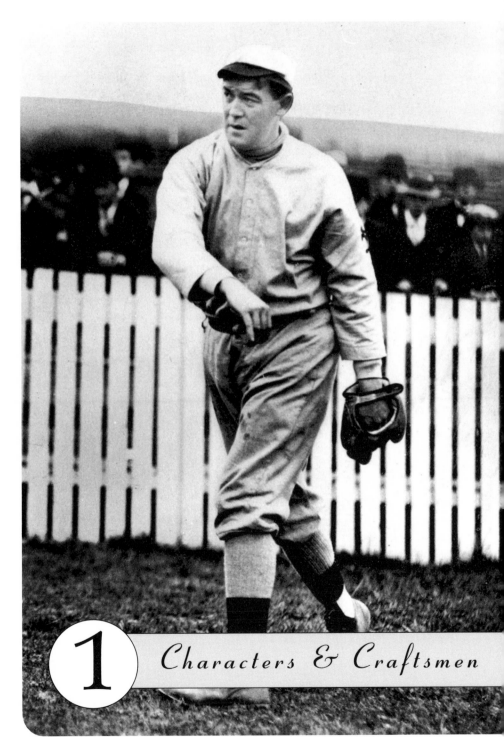

1 *Characters & Craftsmen*

Arthur "Bugs" Raymond

With an eye to the unusual and the eccentric, Damon Runyon profiled both the winners—and the losers.

BUGS RAYMOND

Shortly after arriving in New York, Runyon sought out the eccentric alcoholic Giants' pitcher Bugs Raymond, making him his real-life character. "One day I was pitching here, and a whole flock of these big fat grasshoppers and lightning bugs came swooping down upon the diamond," Raymond told Runyon. "I got a broom and swept 'em all back of first base and went on pitching, and ever since that they've called me 'Bugs.'" Back in New York, the columns became instant hits, particularly with Runyon's publisher, William Randolph Hearst.

Giants Have Batting Eyes Wide Open (Mar. 30, 1911)
McGraw's Regulars Trim Atlanta, 10–3—"Bugs" Raymond Reminiscent
ATLANTA, MARCH 29—Arthur, formerly "Bugs" Raymond, was moved to reminiscence this afternoon as he paused from time to time in his labor of devastating the Atlanta team of the Southern League, and showing the Giant regulars the way to an easy 10 to 3 victory.

The game was really incidental to the recollections of Raymond, the rejuvenated, and to his pitching efforts, but it served to show that the regulars have their batting eyes wide open for the start of the season. They accumulated thirteen hits off various grades of pitching. They also demonstrated that their teamwork is well nigh perfect.

Dick Rudolph followed Raymond, and the Bronx boy showed well. Five hits and one run was the best Atlanta could do with Raymond, and four hits and two runs were taken from Rudolph, but this was after McGraw had commenced to switch the line-up to give the youngsters a chance.

Getting back to that Raymond narrative, however, it was in this historic city that Raymond first acquired his famous title. There are other versions, of course, but after his work this afternoon Arthur is entitled to some place on the esteem of the credulous.

Why Raymond Is Called "Bugs"

"One day I was pitching here, and a whole flock of these big fat grasshoppers and lightning bugs came swooping down upon the diamond," says the veracious Raymond. "I got a broom and swept 'em all back of first base and went on pitching, and ever since that they've called me 'Bugs.'"

Simple, isn't it? Certainly much more simple than the revamped twirler's delivery proved for the Crackers. He got in trouble once or twice by his generosity, but arose nobly to each occasion, and when he had finished his labor the game was over so far as the result was concerned.

Chief Meyers and Red Murray were the hitting stars for the Regulars, getting three each. The Giants worked the hit and run from start to finish, and the score would have been larger if McGraw had not finally sent his men running bases recklessly to hurry the game.

Arthur Bell was a lonely figure at the turnstile throughout the afternoon, but the few Atlanta fans who turned out were noisy and personal in their conversation directed to the Giants. Most of the spectators were players on the Washington team of the American League, and they are all predicting that the Giants will win the National League race. Mathewson and Walter Johnson, Washington's star, met and hobnobbed around the hotel during the morning.

(Frank) Scanlon, a left-hander, started in for Atlanta, and the

Regulars liked him very much indeed. In the second inning, (Fred) Merkle tried to cave in a signboard in deep-center with a terrific drive, which went for a homer. In the fourth inning, the Giants landed all over the Cracker . . .

Mr. "Bugs" Raymond Assists in Slaughter of Greensboro "Mob" (Apr. 4, 1911)
Chilly Breezes Greet Giants in North Carolina —
Josh Devore Gets Home Run

GREENSBORO, N.C., APRIL 3—"Mid the silence of the soughing pines," writes "Bugs" Raymond, "in the presence of the wit and beauty of these parts, and also in an atmosphere three and a half degrees colder than a club treasurer's heart, we Giant regulars today tore off this here Greensboro mob of the Carolina Association by a score of 11 for us and nothing for the home boys. Good night all."

The celebrated entomologist assisted. He wheeled them over for three innings, during which time the locals only occasionally made a foul. Prior to the appearance of Mr. Raymond, Jeff Tesreau, the celebrated grizzly grabber of the Ozark hillocks, drove his elusive bear grease ball through the congealed air for three marches and the Greensboro batters were lost in the woods.

Big Jeff felt right at home in the piney environment. The breath of the surrounding forest was as the aroma of his native heath, and it is also likely that he sniffed afar the tracks of some itinerant grizzly. While warming up, he pounded one off Arthur Devlin's damask cheek, nearly putting the third baseman down for the count and raising a large lump on his face.

Hendrick's Slants Delight Natives
Following the great bruin snatcher came Hendricks, the Michigan gravy train, with a left-hand slant, which seemed to delight the natives. Anyway, they took two rather sickly-looking bings away from the Wolverine giant, which was the sum total of their afternoon's efforts.

Last, but by no means least, came our great relief pitcher, John J. McGraw, with his now famous crossfire and wave delivery. He pitched one inning, and in order that he might have support in which he could have absolute confidence he sent Jack Murphy to first, Lou Drucke, the "condiment kid," to the field, and shifted the line-up. Not a hit or run was collected while he looped them across.

The Boston Nationals beat the Greensboro team Saturday by a score of 34 to 0, but local authority assures the casual inquirer that the team, which represented Greensboro, was made up of amateurs. They had a better line-up today, including a catcher about the size of a pint flask, who has a really remarkable throwing arm.

It was too cold for much ball playing, and none of the Giant pitchers got really warmed up.

A local fan made a bet of $20 to $1 that the Giants would not put a ball over the fence today. The fellow who took the short end offered a $5 reward to the first man who accomplished the feat. It seems that it has been done just twice before in the history of the park. Josh Devore was told about the offer and he kept it a secret from the rest of the players, and on his second trip to the pan, he raised a warning hand to the stands and announced, "Here she goes."

Josh Devore Wins $5 Reward

Then he plucked a fast one right on the ear, and it sailed over into the pine trees beyond the fence, while Devore galloped hastily home to collect the five. As soon as he got it, Louis Drucke earnestly endeavored to jar a dollar out of him, claiming that he is Josh's creditor to that amount. Devore did not loosen, and he soon afterwards accepted relief in the field from Becker and hastened home to sew the five to his wishbone.

Al Bridwell was the umpire today, and he called the decisions in a high, throaty voice without reference to personal friendships. Hank Gowdy is still eying him with an injured air for calling him out on strikes.

This is the coldest weather the Giants have yet encountered.

The thermometer is flowing snowward, and the players were enveloped in clouds of steam from their own breath as they raced around, trying to keep warn. Both (Huck) Wallace and Rube Eldridge, the local pitchers, were easy for the Giants, Red Murray being the batting star, with a double and two singles.

In the first inning Merkle plucked himself a nice three-bagger, and scored on Fletcher's infield out. Devore's home run was next, and in the fourth inning, Murray drove (Fred) Snodgrass, who had singled, home with his three-bagger. Thereafter the Giants scored about as they pleased, the game being brought to a close with a general all-round workout for all hands, McGraw sending the players home as fast as possible to get them out of the cold.

Greensboro threatened to score just once, (Mark) Stewart driving one through Merkle for two bases, and getting the third on Wallace's single, but Raymond froze up the and the next men in line could not crack the score.

Bugs Raymond may have started his 1911 trail with the Giants with promise, but he was already doomed. Before the season, John McGraw had arranged for him to receive treatment for his alcoholism at the well-known Keeley Institute in Dwight, Illinois, but Raymond was tossed from the program for inappropriate behavior. He then had two lapses during spring training and another during the season—quite enough for McGraw, who hid the episodes from reporters, and waived Raymond after he appeared in only 17 games. Afterwards, when the team got back to New York from a road trip, Bugs's uniform was hanging in the window of a bar near the Polo Grounds with the sign, "Bugs Raymond Tending Bar Here."

But Raymond wasn't tending bar, and in 1912, by then separated from his wife and mourning the death of his five-year-old daughter from influenza, he drifted to Chicago, where he played semi-pro baseball and worked as a pressman. That September, the 30-year-old Raymond was found dead in the room of his run-down hotel. A coroner ruled he had died from a cerebral hemorrhage, from a fractured skull. Hearing of Raymond's passing, McGraw was terse: "That man took seven years off my life," he said.

—

Christy Mathewson

The great Christy Mathewson and Runyon were friends. But the writer rarely wrote much about Mathewson beyond the game, mainly because the 318-game winner with matinee-idol looks was religious, relatively quiet, and happily married to his college sweetheart—in short, not a Runyon type of guy. This column, written from Pittsburgh, was an exception. But the sportswriter admired the talents of the greatest pitcher of his generation, as this story attests.

Redlegs Give "Big Train" A Close Tussle (July 16, 1911)
Ninth Inning Rally by Cincinnati Comes Near to Disaster for Giants; The Final Count Is 4 to 3

Mathewson pitched against Cincinnati yesterday.

Another way of putting it is that Cincinnati lost a game of baseball. The first statement means the same as the second.

The score was 4 to 3. But that ninth inning rally by the Reds caused some chills to creep up the backs of the Giant fans.

After three straight defeats, Big Train rolled to Victory over the easy Redville route. The incident contains no news. If Cincinnati had won, it would have been a sensation for the Reds have not beaten Matty since 1908, which is too far back to remember.

Harry Gasper gave the big fellow a battle during the early stages of the game, and once a home run by (Dick) Hoblitzel put the Reds on even terms with the Giants, but Fred Merkle finally blazed the ball into the leftfield bleachers, with two on bases, and that was sufficient.

(Manager) Clarke Griffith's much-abused club looks about the same except that the Silver Fox introduced a brace of Cubans, playing one in center and putting the other in to bat against Mathewson in a pinch, with two out, and two on bases.

(One) youth looked Mr. Mathewson's fadeaway over three times and then resumed his seat.

(Bert) Humphries, recently of Philadelphia, succeeded Gasper after the Cuban had been made known. The contest dragged in spots, but both clubs fielded well. The Giants were wet-seated out of first place the day before, so they went in determined to make up all the ground possible.

Murray Given a Rest

Cincinnati is not much of an attraction the way it is going, and only about 15,000 people saw the game. Griffith used one of the Cubans, (Armando) Marsans, in centerfield in place of (Johnny) Bates, who has been suspended. Beals Becker appeared in rightfield for the Giants instead of Jack Murray, the regular being given a rest.

Mathewson started the game . . .

(With the Giants ahead 4-1), the Reds started a brief rally in the ninth, and had Matty in trouble for a time, but the second Cuban (Rafael Almeida) came up in the pinch and could not help.

(Tom) Downey opened the ninth inning by cracking a single off (third baseman Art) Fletcher's knees, and (Eddie) Grant followed by a hot drive, which (Al) Bridwell could not handle.

(Jimmy) Esmond forced Grant at second and Downey took third. Matty walked (Larry) McLean, apparently purposely filling the bases, and the big catcher was replaced by a runner by the name of (Herb) Juul. (Hank) Severeid was sent in to bat for Humphreys and popped to (Larry) Doyle. (Bob) Bescher singled, scoring Downey and Esmond, Juul taking third. Bescher stole second, without drawing a throw, and Marsans tapped weakly to Bridwell, and the game was over.

❊   ❊   ❊

Stop the presses! Christy Mathewson gambles! Okay, it's checkers at the Pittsburgh YMCA, but it's a story, and Runyon is on the scene.

Discuss Matty's Greatness (Sept. 18, 1911)

Players Say Big Train Never Had More Stuff Than He Displayed Saturday

PITTSBURGH, SEPT. 17—A big, blond, loose-gaited fellow, with a slight stoop to his shoulders, shambled into the headquarters of the Young Men's Christian Association of Pittsburgh last night, where a crowd of studious-looking men were gathered about tables littered with checker disks.

In quiet gray tweeds, with a soft felt hat pulled down over his light hair and with eyes as serious as a deacon's, the big chap seemed to somehow fit into the company at once.

A diamond flashing from his finger and a diamond blazing from his tie were the only touches incongruous with his surroundings. Quietly he accepted admiring introductions; quietly he listened to glowing expressions, and quietly he sat down before a checker board, and was soon engaged in a game in which he played a lone hand against a crowd.

While They Talked of Matty

This is how Christy Mathewson, the "Big Train" of the Gotham Giants, spent an evening which was devoted by his comrades to a discussion of nothing but the topic of how great he had appeared in the two short innings he worked against Pittsburgh Saturday afternoon.

Mathewson had been playing ball a long time with the Giants, but it is doubtful if he or any other individual member of the club was ever so thoroughly discussed by his fellow players after a game. Even the great Rube Marquard was never praised in such fashion, and the Rube is a new topic, while Mathewson is an old subject.

(John) McGraw himself remarked upon it; older members of the club like Arthur Devlin, Leon Ames and George Wiltse talked about it, while veteran followers of the Giants dwelt upon it at length.

Mathewson, As Advertised, Shows Up
Beaumont Laddies (Apr. 3, 1914)

"Big Six," However, Disappoints the Populace by Not Striking Out Every
Batter of the Opposition in His Six Innings—Giants Tango
Home with Game by 12 to 1

BEAUMONT, TEXAS—As per small bills in the barbershop window, Christy Mathewson, the well-known public spectacle, was exhibited here today, fresh from his unparalleled run of four weeks on live Oak Street, Marlin, Texas.

He was witnessed by a large crowd of some of the most prominent persons in this vicinity, and every promise made by the management concerning the celebrated sight was strictly fulfilled. Mr. Mathewson carried his "fadeaway (pitch)," and wore the very same expression of ennui that he will wear in the large league all this summer.

There seemed to be some disappointment because Mr. Mathewson did not strike out all the home boys, and a slight murmur of suspicion ran through the stands as the score gradually mounted up to 12 to 1 in favor of the Giants, but all in all, the show went very well and everything was absolutely on the level. We have "Sinister" Dick Kinsella's word for it.

In honor of Mr. Mathewson's appearance, "Sinister" Dick Kinsella arranged a "Ladies Day." Ladies were admitted at the gate free of charge. All they had to pay for was a seat in the grandstand. This magnificent bargain accounted for a great gathering of the fair sex and made Ferdinand Schupp pretty mad that he was not allowed to pitch awhile.

Chris Mathewson worked six innings against the Beaumont Oilers as they are called, and he allowed five hits and one run. Then, Bunny Hearn was admitted to the pitching enclosure by J. J. McGraw, but by that time some of the beauty and chivalry present had commenced to leak out of the yard. They had seen Mr. Mathewson personally steal a base, and felt that this act was the tip-off on the pastime.

—

CHARLES "VICTORY" FAUST

Told by a Kansas fortune-teller he was destined to pitch the Giants to greatness, Charles Faust introduced himself in late July 1911 to John McGraw. The Giant manager, anxious for anything to help his slumping team, gave him a look—and by season's end, Faust was thought to be responsible for the team's late-season charge to the pennant, and even appeared in two games. Runyon got on board in early August, and ushered the man he called "Victory" Faust into legend. The two men shared a curious similarity; both were born in Kansas one day apart— Runyon on October 8, 1880, and Faust a day later. But as quickly as Faust arrived to liven up the New York baseball scene, he was gone only months later; four years later, Victory Faust died in a Washington mental institution.

Matty Fans Luderus Exactly Four Times
(Aug. 12, 1911)
"Big Six," Although Battled Freely Throughout, Tightens Up in Pinches and Blanks Falling Phillies

Last night will be remembered ever in Milwaukee as the night of the big dry spell. There was nothing stirring down at Luderus. Only cash customers were welcomed by the peeved clerk.

Returns from all National League baseball games participated in by Philadelphia are received at Luderus' (Bar), ticker wise, according to reports, so that the friends and admirers of Fred Luderus, official fence breaker of the National League, and home runner extraordinary, may keep tab on his circuit slams.

And it is related every time that Freddie dings one, which is often, his estimable sire buys for the house.

Thus is paternal pride given manifestation and business encouraged.

Last evening, however, only mournful tidings went trickling

telegraphically into Luderus', for F. Luderus, champion of champions in the home-run hitting line, was struck out but four times in succession by Citizen Christy Mathewson, of New York.

FOUR TIMES—One, two, three, four (1-2-3-4).

There is no mistake about the matter, it was four.

When this shock was fully assimilated by Milwaukee, there fell a silence, which had been unbroken up to a late hour last night, and even the habitual calm of Philadelphia became more pronounced.

Striking out F. Luderus at any time is quite a trick, but when the count slowly tolls to four—well, Milwaukee and Philadelphia will always believe there was some error somewhere.

Matty's Departure Delayed

Citizen Christy Mathewson delayed that frequently rumored departure for Hasbeenville, or the Old Soldiers' Home or wherever else it is we have been led to believe he is going, long enough to lather the Falling Phillies with a goose-egg shampoo. The final score was 6 to 0, and as a result, John J. McGraw is seriously considering the retention of the Big Train on the Giant side tracks for next week at least.

Every time Matty has been supposed to have had his satchel packed and his ticket purchased for that gone-back place this season, he has bobbed up serenely with a gorgeous game like that of yesterday. He seemed to fairly revel in the humid going and he grinned widely whenever he got a crack at Luderus.

Each time that Luderus came to bat, he spanked the ozone with resounding whacks. In the third, with two men on, Matty spun the fadeaway before the young man's startled vision for his second strikeout. In the ninth, Big Six accomplished the trick with three pitched balls.

And all this was before the very eyes and in the very presence of Horace Fogel, owner of the Phillies.

All Indignities Avenged

All the indignities which have been heaped upon Mathewson and the Giants this season—and they have not been a few—were avenged by the big fellow yesterday. The Phillies hit him freely enough across the game, but could not slip in their punches consecutively, Matty being especially strong with men on bases.

J. Tortes Meyers, chief of the Hit-'Em-a-Heaps, only batted a thousand for himself yesterday, gathering a pair of notable drives in each of his two times at bat and getting on a third time through being hit by the pitcher. McGraw thought that this entitled the slugging Indian to a rest, so he sent "Pud" Wilson in at the opening of the eighth. Wilson was so tickled that he boosted a home run into the leftfield bleachers on his initial appearance at bat. Beals Becker has been playing right field for the Giants lately, but yesterday McGraw put in "Red" John Murray to get the benefit of his right-hand batting against a left-handed pitcher, and "Red" accumulated three hits to make up for his lost time.

Magee and Dooin Missed

The Phillies miss Sherwood Magee and Charley Dooin, there is no gain saying that. The Giants stole three bases on (Tom) Madden in the first inning, (Josh) Devore grabbing a pair, but thereafter they did not run so wild on the bases as might have been expected after such a start. Still, the absence of the Dooin pepper is very noticeable and the heavy bat of the pugnacious Sherwood would fit in well during this depressing season for the Forget crew.

McGraw introduced his latest volunteer player in the practice before the game. His name is Faust—Charley Faust—and he comes from Marion, Kansas. Charley is around 40, and is a pitcher and catcher, doing either with equal grace. He had a dream that he was to be a great baseball player, but the dream stipulated that he must play with the Giants and no other club, else the spell was crabbed. So Charley joined on with the Giants at St. Louis, and when McGraw pulled out of there and left him pat, he waited around until he acquired enough money to come on to New York. McGraw fell in a fit—presumably from joy—when the smiling features of Charley appeared in the clubhouse door yesterday, but Mac fitted him with a uniform and Charley practiced like a good fellow.

"No, I didn't come in a Pullman," he confided to an interviewer. "I can't sleep in the dumb things, anyway."

Ames Adds a Wonder to Hard Luck Record
(Aug. 13, 1911)
Phillies Get but Two Hits off Leon, but Giants' Error
Loses Games by 2 to 0 Count

"Red" (Leon) Ames, champion hard-luck pitcher of the world, lost a game to the Phillies yesterday afternoon that must stand out as a wonder even in his long record of misfortune in baseball.

The score was 2 to 0.

After holding the Phillies to one hit for six innings and two in seven when he was removed to permit (Red) Murray to bat for him, Ames encountered defeat through errors behind him, Fred Merkle starting the Phillies to victory in the eighth with a fumble. The other run was secured by the visitors off (Doc) Crandall, who took Ames' place. It was a homer in the rightfield bleachers.

(George) Chalmers, the young citizen of Gotham who opposed "Red" pitched great ball too, but it only emphasized Ames' hard luck. While he was holding the Phillies without a hit for the first five innings the Giants could not hit behind him. Outside of that inning they played good ball, but the moment Merkle wobbled it was curtains for Ames.

The blonde boy was never in better form and one of the two hits off him was a scratch.

Still Chambers must be give some credit for the great twirling which he did, and he was never very far behind "Red" at any stage of the pitching battle. Not a Giant got to third base.

The first Philly run was scored by Chambers himself, on a sacrifice fly after he had got around to third through the channel opened by Merkle's misplay. That one run would have been enough to win.

Mr. Faust Entertains

Prior to the opening of hostilities the big crowd was entertained by

"Hay Foot" Faust, McGraw's latest acquisition, under the personal humorous direction of McGraw himself. Faust is the Kansan who dreamed he was to become a great ballplayer with the Giants and who came all the way from the Sunflower State to attach himself to the club. Mr. Faust had already attained fame. It took the crowd about two minutes to get him in all his various angles. He pitched a little, caught a little and ran a few bases, assisted by members of both the Phillies and the Giants, while the crowd lay back and took in the show, with loud screams of admiration and delight.

Mr. Faust is a success as a provoker of laughter, if nothing more. Arlie Latham kept him warmed up in case of emergency.

Double Victory Over Reds Push Giants Back into Second Place (Aug. 18, 1911)

McGraw's Men Have Regular Picnic with Redlegs at Polo Grounds —

"Red" Ames Finally Shakes His Hoodoo — 25 Runs for Giants

"I don't know very much about this baseballing business," observed the slender young lady in the pink dress and ochre-tinted hat who had occupied a seat behind one of the steel pillars. "I don't know much about it, as I say, but I do think that was a splendid little entertainment they gave us between the games. That Harry Sparrow is just killing."

"That wasn't Harry Sparrow," denied her escort. "That was Charley Faust."

"Well, I don't care," said the lady. "They play a lot alike, and I thought it was the best part of the program. The rest was too serious."

You can't please everybody. There was one gentleman fan, for instance—a stout, heavy-bodied and weighty-minded man—who arose when Umpire (Cy) Rigler, worn out by his afternoon's exertions, called the second game in the eighth inning "on account of darkness" with the score 15 to 2 in favor of the Giants.

"I wish to voice my protest," said the fan. "It is still quite light in many parts of the field. The game should go forward."

Whereupon a rising vote elected him president of the Bug Club, without a dissenting note.

There were some present who alleged that the Reds were endeavoring to steal Charley Faust's stuff. Charley was the very life of the party, starring in a vaudeville sketch, which John J. McGraw arranged with considerable forethought for the intermission. It was well perhaps that he did so, because outside of that the bill was rather monotonous.

Mr. Faust a Dreamer

Mr. Faust, as may be remembered, is the first citizen of Marion, Kan.—a dream of dreams, and a player, after a fashion, of baseball. Moreover, he is the only warm-up entertainer in the world, discovered and copyrighted by John J. McGraw. Mr. Faust did a little batting yesterday; also a little base-running; ditto a little sliding, which Mr. Faust does entirely upon one, or the other of his ears. He was removed from the scene of the struggle by McGraw only because he was endangering the velvet surface of the sward.

"No Pie, No Mascot," Declares Giant Jinx
(Sept. 23, 1911)
Failing to Find Favorite Delicacy on Bill of Fare, C. Faust Desserts
and New York Loses to Cincinnati

CINCINNATI—These Monday morning tidings of defeat trace back to the breakfast hour this morning and to the gross carelessness of the proprietor of the hotel where the nearly-next champions of the National League are "beaming." This proprietor, a man with little regard for the epicure or idiosyncrasies of genius, ran out of apple pie during the regular Cincinnati rush upon that delicacy Saturday night, and caused the absence from the Giant bench today of Charles "Victory" Faust and the consequent defeat of Reuben Not-So-Victorious Marquard and the almost champions by a score of 6 to 5.

Without his apple pie for breakfast, the jinxing power of Charles "Victory" over the other fellow is wholly nil. He must have that Kansas matutinal bracer, else the charm is lost, and so when

Charles spread himself before a table this morning and learned the pieless news he was well nigh prostrated.

Couldn't Find His Pie

Armed with an appetite for pie, Charles went out upon the highways and byways of the city in quest thereof, but pie foundries are one institution that do not stay open in Cincinnati on Sundays, and before Charley could reconcile himself to "plain sinkers and draw one" and reach the ball yard, the Reds had started Reuben on the run.

It was most exasperating and painful, but it only goes to show that a private jinx must be attended to on Sundays as well as weekdays. This makes the second games the Giants have lost out of 14 played.

"On some Sundays," remarked Reuben Marquard ruefully, as he was taking his departure from the premises after the fifth inning this afternoon, while 20,000 Sundayized fans chanted a triumphant recessional in his noble ear. "On some Sundays, a fellow can't lay up a single game of ball."

And how true those words be.

Giants Home after Triumphant Western Sojourn; New National League Champions Are Here Today (Oct. 4, 1911)

Remaining Games of Season to Be Played at Polo Grounds and in Brooklyn—McGraw's Men Wear Off Rough Edges Against Quakers in Final Game Away from Metropolis—Crandall Pitches in Splendid Form

Lo-ho, the konkering hee-roes kum! (Ta-ra-zam!)

"My friends," said C. Victory Faust, the Official Jinx, on being interviewed at the Pennsylvania Railroad station last evening, shortly after the train bearing the pennant-winning Giants had slipped through the tube, "My friends, far be it from me to boost myself, but you can very plainly see what is what."

A 12 to 3 victory over Philadelphia, which included the scalp of Grover Cleveland Alexander, was among the spoils of war brought home by the big town boys when they landed on the shores of

Broadway at 7 o'clock last evening, and blinked their eyes at the familiar lights. This makes 17 victories out of 21 games played on the road—a clip that has brought another National League pennant to the Polo Grounds.

Not many people knew the exact hour of the arrival, and so the attendance at the train was limited to a few members of the players' families and taxicab drivers in search of prey. Those that recognized the Bertillons of the men raised a shout, but the baseballers ducked into vehicles and hastened to places of refuge.

Manager McGraw dodged interviewers at the station, but he gave out a brief statement on the train in which he said:

"We are ready for the World Series. I hope to have all my men in the best of condition, and if they are we will put up a good fight. This has been one of the most remarkable road trips made by a club during my experience in baseball, and I am naturally deeply gratified. I never make claims regarding the outcome of any fight, but I feel we will give a good accounting of ourselves against the Athletics. My pitchers are going great guns, and the balance of the club will be just as strong after a short rest."

The Giants open at Brooklyn this afternoon for a series of games. Mathewson will probably work today, and the big fellow is in grand form. Merkle's bad leg is practically recovered, and Wilson's split thumb is just about healed. This will give McGraw all his strength for the series.

"Nut" Faust Yields One Run in Inning
Against Rustlers (Oct. 9, 1911)
Official Jinx of Giants Pitches Nine Innings and Allows
Only One Hit; New Champions Lose

Charles "Victory" Faust of Marion, Kansas, official Jinx of the Giants, made his debut as a big-league pitcher at the Polo Grounds yesterday afternoon, working one inning, the ninth, against Boston. There were a few hundred half-frozen fans rewarded, getting a treat that money could not buy. When Umpire (Bill) Finneran bulletined, "Faust now pitching for New York," the crowd didn't believe it, but sure enough the famous "Nut" took the mound.

His record in words and figures follows:

(Bill) Rariden doubled over (Fred) Snodgrass's head. (Lefty) Tyler rolled to Faust, who threw the Boston pitcher out at first, Rariden taking third. This was some graceful fielding on the part of Faust. (Bill) Sweeney flied to (Red) Murray, and Rariden scored after the catch. (Mike) Donlin was tossed out by (Art) Fletcher.

The New York side was retired before Faust came to bat in his order, but Charley went in, anyway, and tapped to Tyler for an easy out, but he went around the bases anyway.

"Rube" Marquard was given a light World Series workout, holding his old enemies, the Rustlers, to a 2-2 tie in five innings. Then the southpaw king was taken out by McGraw and the lowly Beans won a frosty game of baseball while Louis Drucke was putting on a "comeback" stunt. The final score was 5 to 2.

Outside of that everything was perfectly lovely, Nobody seemed to care much how the game went. The lineups got all mixed up in the melee, and it was hard to tell who was at bat along about the eighth. McGraw used some of his colts, and (Boston manager Fred) Tenney used some not so coltish, including himself. It was the first game the Giants have been able to lose for some time, and one that they could afford to lose without distressing themselves.

It was a charitable loss at that, as Boston needs games as much as anybody in the league. The football weather held the attendance to the smallest Saturday afternoon crowd of the season. Heavy wraps were not to be despised. The field was wet and heavy.

Giants End Season Losing Two Games (Oct. 13, 1911)

Mascot Charley Faust Furnishes Comedy for Many Fans at Baseball Burial and Bill Dahlen Plays a Little Shortstop

"____ to have and to hold from this day forward, for better for worse, for richer for poorer, in sickness and in health ____"

It ain't? What says it haint?

Gentlemen in the rear of the house arises to deny that these are the last sad rites. Is probably single, but what's rites between old volunteer firemen? Nothing says you! Well, then, we buried the baseball season of 1911 yesterday aft. at the Polo Grounds in the presence of a large and assorted multitude of persons, most of whom were complaining in loud, querulous voices about that being one whatchucallit of a way to run a World Series ticket sale, and how they sent in their dough in to Bill by letter last Chuesday.

However, we buried the said season, as related, in the presence of the parties aforesaid, and Charles Marion Kansas "Victory" Faust, he helped.

The season is dead! Long live Johnny McGraw!

C. Marion K.V. Faust, he pitched an inning against Brooklyn, New York, and covered himself with glory and large patches of Mr. Groundkeeper Murphy's best bluegrass and things. This makes C.M. Kansas V. Faust's second inning in organized and when all hands have the long gray boys at the end of the chin.

The Giants, by the bike, lost two games to Brooklyn, the scores being 3 to 0 and 5 to 2, C.M.K. Victory Faust tallying one of the last two runs. Wicked William Dahlen, leader of the young men from the other end of the tunnel, played a bit o' shortstop for himself and friends in the second game, but after fanning desperately three times, hand-ringing William retired to the back of the grandstand and kicked himself in the same general vicinity.

Far be it from us to make any suggestions, but some people did say that Williams was trying to steal Charley Faust's stuff.

Ebbets Creates Columbus Day

In addition to it marking the close, s' help us, of the almost perennial National League season, the nearly comeback of Bill and the second appearance of Faust, it was otherwise quite a large, elegant afternoon. It was Christopher Columbus Day, so-called, which was invented by (Dodger owner) Charley Ebbets, of Brooklyn, especially for closing the N.L. season, although there are some people kind enough to say that they doubt if the Brooklyn philan-thropist would know him if he met him at the press gate.

Mr. Faust was not wholly content with the showing he made in the ninth inning, although he would have held the Dodgers hitless but for an error by Eugene Paulette, who is now viewed by suspi-cion with Chas. As it was, he hurled them back with a single smack (poetry) and stole two bases himself, not to mention the tally which he carried in himself by the nape of its neck. No, Mr. Faust was fretful, and aggravated. Seen under the shower bath at the club-house by your correspondent after the game Mr. Faust said, quote:

"When the wires wing the word to Marion K. tonight that Brooklyn was able to make a hit off the pride of the Jayhawker State, how will I look? Why—why—why! And, also, why! Words fail me at this juncture."

Faust Finally Butts In

Charley relieved Bert Maxwell, the Birmingham bear, who, in turn, has rousted Louis Drucke, of Waco, Texas, out of a job. Chas. wanted to go in prior to that time—some time prior, in fact. He would descend upon the pitching box every inning and announce to Cap. (Larry) Doyle that this was the time. The captain would send him out to the high grass in centerfield to warm up with Dick Hen-nessey, assuring the Kansas tornado that he needed more exercise.

A statistical shark has figured that the energy expended by Charles in warming up, running in from centerfield every inning, lifting his hat to (Giants' owner) John T. Brush and winding up after he got in the box, would transport the entire wheat crop of Kansas 600 miles of applied to wagon wheels.

Anyway, Charley finally finned in. Messr. Bill Brennan, the elegant ump, announced his name stammeringly, and the town of Marion was again on the baseball map. Grover Cleveland Hartley held mysterious consultation with Chas. before he started in on his celebrated windup and Charley nodded understandingly. Zach Wheat bunted a ball right at Faust's extensive feet, but the wily Charles fell upon it with one hook and heaved the fleet Dodger out at first.

Some may argue that Messr. (Bill) Klem overlooked a slight

space of daylight, amounting to less than four yards between Zach's arrival at the bag and the hurled ball, but be that as it may, Zach was out. (Jake) Daubert drove Fred Snodgrass over near the Harlem River after his fly, and then Paulette bobbled an easy toss on Daley's bounder, and Charley lost a no-hit game because (Dolly) Stark, the next man up, singled to left. (Bob) Higgins forced (Tom) Daley, (Charley "Buck") Herzog making the play without assistance.

Speed Marvel Faust Scores

Faust was the first man up for the Giants in their end of the ninth, and young Master Dent almost hit him on the wrist with a pitched ball, so Mssr. Brennan sent Charley to first. He stole second, and then stole third, busting into both bases standing up like a bombardier, The Dodgers saw him do it too. Then Charley Herzog laid down a bunt over toward first, and Faust came booming into the plate with a noise like a patent harvester.

And the crowd did some whooping—some whooping, indeed!

So the season is over, and the Giants failed to win 100 games (finishing 99-54), although they didn't try very hard at that. Vale, adios, and et cetera!

The Giants went on the loose the 1911 World Series in six games to the Philadelphia A's. Nothing more was ever heard from Charley Faust.

———

TY COBB

In Runyon's mind, the great Detroit Tigers superstar was right from central casting. Brilliant on the field and smart in business (Cobb was baseball's first millionaire, thanks to shrewd investing in Coca-Cola), he was dark, distrustful, and forever engaged in feuds. In playing the deadball game better than anyone, he earned Runyon's enduring admiration as the best player ever—Babe Ruth included.

In the long list of ugly incidents involving the fiery Ty Cobb
of the Detroit Tigers, the most notorious may have the afternoon
at Hilltop Park in New York, where he vaulted into the stands
to savagely beat up a heckler.

Ty Cobb Interrupts Game by Fist Fight (May 16, 1912)

Tyrus Cobb, the famous Georgia Jabber, leaped lightly into the grandstand back of the Detroit bench yesterday afternoon, speared for himself A. Fan, and hastily scrambled the features of the same.

But wait'll you hear!

Tyrus, the two-handed, did not know that a spectator to his fretfulness was Mr. Bancroft B. Johnson, president and everything, of the American League. This is the tip-off to Ty if he desires to escape into Canada before the blow falls: Mr. Johnson was sitting high up in the grand stand as large as life, which is truly large, and after he had seen what he had seen, he was observed to breathe heavily, and to issue words of speech.

Ty was engaged in his business of Cobbing for Hughie Jennings of Detroit, and that accounts for his presence in Frank Farrell's ball yard. A. Fan went there to see a good game of baseball, so the detectives have something to work on in the way of motive as far as he is concerned.

A. Fan sat right back of the visiting ball players' bench, and T. Cobb and the other Detroit players claim that he made offensive remarks to the Southern gem. A. Fan says—and he is supported by others—that he merely jested with the Georgian about a fumble of Cobb's in the second inning, and that Cobb replied with language that was scarcely fit to eat. A. Fan's version of the trouble appears to be as well supported as Cobb's.

Ty Hops Over Barrier

Anyway, Tyrus suddenly boiled over into the grandstand. In the fourth inning, when the Tigers were at bat, he hopped the low barrier between the seats and the field, and began shaking right and lefts out of his system full upon the upturned face of A. Fan.

Some confusion resulted. "Silk" O'Loughlin and (Fred) Westervelt, the umpires, hastened to the scene, remarking to one another upon what a busy place the Hill has become. All the ball players flocked to the spot in large quantities—the Detroit delegation being especially energetic in flocking. Those of the spectators who held ringside seats moved closer.

Meantime, Mr. Bancroft B. Johnson, of the American League, sat up yonder, and took notes on Ty's description for future reference. It was not a long mill, but a canvass of the audience gives the popular decision to Cobb by a plurality of 354. Ty managed to draw a little blood from A. Fan, but A. Fan was not injured.

Wanted Cobb Arrested

Also, A. Fan, who was Claude Lueker, secretary to the former Sheriff Thomas F. Foley, believed so strongly in the justice of his own cause, and the injustice of the assault, he wanted to have Cobb arrested. He left that particular portion of the stand with Tom Davis, secretary of the Yankees, and Tom O'Neil, of the special detective service, while Ty left the game at the earnest behalf of O'Loughlin and Westervelt, who love their peace.

And all this time Bancroft B. Johnson eyed Tyrus Cobb with a baleful glare, and made mental note of his name and address.

Several spectators went to A. Fan after the dust of battle had settled—on him—and offered to testify in court against Cobb, but the fiery Georgian finally left the field unmolested and was cheered by the crowd. Manager Jennings and other Detroit players claim they heard the man who was assaulted using offensive language to Cobb—and there you are.

But there is not Bancroft B. Johnson—not by any means.

"There's no justification for a ball player going into the grandstand to fight a spectator," Mr. Johnson is quoted as saying.

All of which leads to the belief that T. Cobb may hear further from the incident.

There Was Also a Game

Oh, yes! There was also a ball game! The Yanks were beaten by a score of 8 to 4. It does seem that they should be allowed to get their beatings in peace and quiet however.

Tyrus chose a most untimely moment to go digging into the stand—untimely for Detroit, that is, but extremely timely for New York. Just after he peeled off his decision, the Tigers got three men on bases, and Ty was due at bat. (Hank) Perry, the Providence slugger, hit in place of the pugnacious Georgian, and struck out.

However, the Tigers won without much trouble. They pelted Jack Warhop with freedom, and after the fourth inning the Yanks could do nothing with (Ed) Willetts. Young "Red" Hoff, who has pitched a number of games while warming up in right field lately, finally got into a regular contest yesterday, succeeding Warhop, but he was puzzling only briefly.

In the first inning, (Davy) Jones and (Sam) Crawford compiled a run with singles, and in the second Willett drove home two runs with a long smash, after (Jim) Delahanty had singled and (Baldy) Louden walked.

(Harry) Wolverton shook up his batting order yesterday, benching Earl Gardner, pulling (Roy) Hartzell into second and restoring (Harry) Wolter to right field. A walk to Wolter in the first inning, Hartzell's out and (Birdie) Cree's infield hit, followed by a fine double steal, netted the Yanks their first run. In the second, (Cozy) Dolan's single, which was followed by the tumultuous fumble of Cobb's, putting Cozy on second, and (George) Moriarty's error, gave the locals another. They got two in the fourth, when (Hack) Simmons started with a double, was sacrificed along by Dolan, and scored on Warhop's infield hit. Meantime, (Jack) Martin popped out and (Bob) Williams walked. (Donie) Bush fell over trying to get Warhop's bounder and Williams took second, scoring on (Guy) Zinn's single.

Tigers Pickle Contest

The Tigers pickled the game in the fifth. With one out, Delahanty was hit by a pitched ball and took second on a wild pitch. Moriarty's drive struck the first-base bag and rolled away for two bases,

Del scoring. Louden and (Oscar) Stanage pulled a double steal, and Louden scored on Willett's out.

Hoff got in some tight places thereafter, but managed to get out until the ninth, when the Tigers nailed him for two more runs.

So what would happen to Ty Cobb as a result of his actions? Most wanted him suspended, an action eventually taken by Ban Johnson, which the Tigers protested by striking en masse for a game.

❊ ❊ ❊

Eliminate Obnoxious "Rooters" (May 20, 1912)

Regardless of the merits of the Cobb controversy it will undoubtedly have one good effect, and that is the elimination of obnoxious "rooters" from the stands.

The man who finds pleasure in making a target for his tongue of ball players has long been a curious study in human nature. Men old enough to be the fathers of some of the young ballplayers will sit in the stand and hour after hour shower the most venomous abuse upon the lads who are doing their bets to furnish entertainment for them. If those same men heard someone abusing their sons in that fashion off the field there would be murder.

Many women have found baseball distasteful because of the so-called "rooting" which takes the form of obscene personal abuse. Men have had their afternoons spoiled by some loud-mouthed, leather-lunged fellow who delights in suggestive remarks to the players. Umpires are supposed to have authority, and instructions to suppress this sort of thing, but it has rarely been attempted in the past.

Sometimes the ballplayers are wholly blameless, but in nine cases out of ten they are only too glad to mind their own business if let alone. The abuse "bug" usually selects an individual player, and will keep after him throughout a game until that player is completely enraged.

Abuse New York Clubs

New York is not as bad in that respect as many other towns, but New York ball cubs probably get more abuse on the road than any others. The fact that they represent New York appears to be their unforgivable offense to the "bug."

A star ballplayer is always a particularly shining mark too, and even mild-mannered, gentlemanly fellows such as (Giants' Christy) Mathewson and (Chief) Meyers have come in for an astounding amount of vituperation, for no reason in the world except that they are ballplayers, and in a position where they are unable to resent the abuse.

Very frequently ballplayers are not above criticism in this respect. There are some players who rather enjoy arguments with the fans, and their responses are not always either guarded or temperate, but as a rule they avoid such discussions.

There is no comment on the Cobb case, one way or the other. Reputable witnesses have appeared on both sides and told stories that differ materially, and there is a prospect that these stories will be submitted in court.

The man Cobb assaulted says the player made a mistake and the Georgian has his version, but aside from this controversy it is a fact well known to all followers of baseball that the abuse "bug" has been in evidence wherever a game has been played.

"Strikers" Can Clean Up

Properly handled, a tour of the country by the striking Detroit players would probably make a big (financial) clean-up, and the advertising the club has received from the present fracas will not do it any harm as a drawing attraction when it resumes business on the American League circuit.

If the players went out through the country as strikers they would not be allowed to play in parks controlled by organized ball. They would have to play the independent yards, but there are enough of them to furnish good business for such a medium.

An astute business manager would very likely head due South with all possible speed.

Great Is Tyrus Cobb (May 25, 1915)

We venture the assertion that there are a number of men in the land who have as many natural gifts for baseball playing as Tyrus Raymond Cobb. We venture to say that there are many who are his equal, mentally and physically, in all departments of the game, and some who are his superior in a purely mechanical way.

But having said that, we desire to add in approximately the same breath that we will go broke on the proposition that no man in big league baseball has the ambition of the Gem of Georgia. There you have the reason why he stands head and shoulders above men who were born his equal in mental and physical skill; there you have the reason why — in our humble judgment — Tyrus Raymond Cobb is the greatest ball player in the organized game.

Baseball people call it Class. When Joe Jackson was breezing along at the top of the American League in batting one season, and it looked as if he would wind up the year there, a big league manager of our acquaintance — a National Leaguer, by the way, who had never seen either Cobb or Jackson play more than a few games — made a small wager that the Georgian would finish ahead of the belter from Brandon Mills (South Carolina).

It seemed to be a bad bet at the time it was made, but Cobb pushed out in front of Joe, and had something to spare at the finish. Wherefore we asked the manager why he made the wager; what premise he had for figuring Cobb best that year, and he replied:

"Well, I just thought the old class would tell in the long run."

And Class may be just as good a name for it as anything else, but, after all, it is ambition. It is an inordinate desire to be a little better than any one else, and Tyrus Raymond Cobb carries that desire around with him at all times, whether he is playing baseball or draw poker. Occasionally the desire is so strong that it borders on the selfish, but nevertheless it's what makes Tyrus the greatest of them all.

The Rivals of Cobb

There are a number of men in both leagues today who ought to be great ballplayers, but who are just a little above the average run because they lack ambition. Then, again, there are a number of players whose ability is nothing extra, but whose ambition they would be as great as Cobb, because it must be remembered that it is not ambition alone that makes the Jewel of Georgia great—it is ambition added to wonderful natural gifts for ball playing that makes him great and then greatest.

Eddie Collins is one of the number of men in baseball who probably possesses as many—if not more—natural gifts for the game as Cobb, but whose desire to excel falls a little short of the burning desire of the Georgian. We do not mean to say that Eddie lacks ambition, but he does not possess it in the same degree as Ty.

Tris Speaker is certainly a better outfielder than Cobb, and Nature gave the great Georgian no particular shade over the Texan in any other department of the game, yet most baseball people will unhesitatingly rate Tyrus the better all-around man, because Tris does not have that fiendish desire to overshadow his fellows. Tris may think he has it—but he hasn't.

Jackson, of Cleveland

The great natural gifts of Joe Jackson carry him along with the first flight of stars; his name is generally among the three outfielders selected by the experts for the so-called All-American teams, but no overweening Cobbesque ambition to be the very best is added to Joe's natural ability. Some may contend that Joe hasn't natural ability in the same proportion as Tyrus; that he isn't as fast, for instance, and that, therefore, he could not be as great as Cobb even if he desired, but we do not wholly agree with this view.

We hold that were Joe scorched by the same flame of ambition that sears of the soul of Cobb, he would be just as great a ball player—and maybe greater. Old-timers tell us that Mike Kelley did not have the natural advantages of some of his fellows; that he could not hit as well, and that he did not have the speed of many of them, yet the memory of Kelly stands out to this day—he was The King. He was best, because it was ever his ambition to be the best.

"Ty!" That Tells the Whole Story; Yankees Lose: Cobb 3, Yanks 0 (June 5, 1915)

Ty!

Having now told the complete story of the defeat of those Yanks by a score of 3 to 0 in a ballgame up at the Polo Grounds yesterday afternoon, we will just tack on a few details of the game itself to fill out this space, and go 'long.

The details of the game are as follows:

COBB, Tyrus R.—
Born Narrows, Banks County, Ga., Dec. 18, 1886; height, 6 feet; weight, 178 lbs.; bats left and throws right-handed; First professional engagement, Augusta, Ga., 1904; (First) Major-league engagement, Detroit, 1905.

He had some of the Detroit people with him yesterday at the Polo Grounds, did this Tyrus R. Cobb. He had Wahoo Sam Crawford and (Tigers' manager) Hughie Jennings, and several others along with him to keep him company, and to bear legal witness to him in the act of defeating the Yanks, but their participation on the pastime was purely incidental to the efforts of T.R. himself.

Listen to what he did:

He personally scored two of the Tigers runs and drove in the other. He got a triple and a single, and stole a brace of bases, including the well-known home plate. He's a regular Tycobb, that fellow, a regular Tycobb. When he came dusting home in the ninth, Mr. Jimes Johnston, the well-known fistic impresario, who has been hearing a lot about the quarrels at the P.G., and went up there in search of new talent for some of his shows, sighed heavily, and remarked:

"Say, I believe he'd draw well with Coffey."

Gets Aboard on Single

Tyrus R. got aboard first in that ninth per one single. Bobby Veach and Wahoo Sam were expunged on flies and then, with (Yankee catcher) Les Nunamaker holding the baseball in his hand, Tyrus pulled a delayed steal of second. Les took a shot at him and threw wild, and Tyrus stepped along to third as the ball filtered through Boone, on out into centerfield.

While Ray Caldwell was pitching to (Marty) Kavanagh, the Jewel of Georgia made a couple of dashes halfway down the third-base line to annoy the thin hurler. Finally, as Ray coiled his long frame into a windup, Tyrus tore out for home. Nunamaker got the ball in ample time to tag Cobb, but he failed to do so as Tyrus flung himself in the general direction of the plate. Neither did Tyrus hit the plate.

Leslie stood with the ball in his hand as Ty rose from the dust, and (umpire) "Silk" O'Loughlin, the cast-iron-throated thrush, waited patiently with both fingers cocked to see what he could see. Ty looked at Les, and Les looked at Ty. "Silk" glared at both. Suddenly, the light of understanding broke upon Tyrus Raymond Cobb, and he stepped lightly forward, brushing Leslie aside, and stamped his foot upon the oyster or home-dish. "Silk" promptly declared him safe.

Argument arose.

"What do you have to do to put a man out in this league?" demanded Leslie Nunamaker, querulously.

"You have to touch him," suggested (Yankee third baseman) Fritz Maisel, softly. Fritz had come up to hear the row.

Then Ray Got Angry

Ray Caldwell hurled his glove high in the air as a token of his disapproval of the decision, and "Silk" O'Loughlin had him out of that game of baseball quicker than you could say your Uncle Wilbert Robinson. Cyrus Piehrus came in to finish the pastime, but the pastime had really been quite finished before Cyrus Piehrus came aboard.

Then there was some question as what the pitch to Kavanagh that Cobb came in on should be entitled. Some thought it should be named a strike, others held that it was a ball. As a matter of fact,

Kavanagh struck at it. No matter what Charley Gebest tries to tell you about it, (Marty) Kavanagh took his Moriarity at that hurler. Honest, he did. We swear it. However, "Silk" finally let it go into the records without any particular name. Eventually Kavanagh got to first, but no farther.

In the opening inning, with one out, Oscar Vitt was passed by Caldwell, and then Tyrus Raymond Cobb belted a triple to right-center, scoring Vitt. Wahoo Sam Crawford followed with a single and Tyrus reported. This incident broke a record that Paul Armstrong had been carefully compiling.

"I've been coming to ball games for two or three years to see this Cobb play," said Paul, "and that's the first time I ever saw him do anything much. The very first time."

Caldwell began to do some real pitching right after it was a bit too late. Sam Crawford was left on base in that first frame, as Peck tossed out Veach, and Kavanagh fanned. Kavanagh is a Kearny (N.J.) lad, who is first-basing for Hughie Jennings in the absence of George Burns. It is said of Kav that he is the homeliest man in baseball, but have you ever seem Poll Perritt right up close?

For all of Ty Cobb's celebrated crankiness, especially toward opponents, he could be surprisingly gracious in mentoring promising young players, in this case, 25-year-old Yankee third baseman Fritz Maisel.

❧   ❧   ❧

Ty Cobb's Pupil (June 7, 1915)

"You're up there guessing at 'em again," yelled Tyrus Raymond Cobb to Fritz Maisel, the small third baseman of the Yanks, Saturday. "Why don't you look 'em over a little?"

Fritz is the favorite pupil of the Jewel of Georgia, who carries on a sort of school for youngsters all over the American League. Whenever Tyrus sees a lad who displays promise of future ability, he coaches the youngster along.

If the recruit has a batting weakness, Ty endeavors to teach him how to overcome it; if the young fellow has a lot of natural speed, the Georgian shows him how to run bases. It was Maisel's speed that attracted Ty's attention to Fritz some time ago, and the youngster has had the benefit of a lot of coaching from Cobb.

"Try to do things that the other base runners do not attempt," was one of Cobb's first suggestions to Maisel. "You are so very fast that you ought to be able to get away with almost anything. You ought to be the greatest base runner in the country. I only wish I had half your speed."

Then Tyrus took Fritz in hand and endeavored to teach him to hit, with the result that Maisel has greatly improved in that department. His failure to do anything against (Tigers' pitcher Hooks) Dauss prompted Ty's remark Saturday, but Fritz has his alibi for his showing.

"I don't remember that I ever did get a hit off that fellow Dauss," he explained naively. "He's one bird that seems to have my permanent address."

❊   ❊   ❊

Maisel has only once enjoyed whatever thrill there may be attached to an attempt to tag out Tyrus Cobb. The opportunities for plays on the Georgian at third base have been mighty rare, and just one time, up to Saturday night, had little Fritz got a stab at the flying frame of the Southern streak.

"I'd like to put the ball on him once in my life, anyway," says Maisel. Plaintively. "I'd like to do that once, just to see how it feels."

Cobb had good reason to keep his eye on Maisel. In 1914, with Cobb hobbled by injuries, one a broken thumb from a brawl in a butcher shop, the speedy Maisel led the American League in 1914 with 74 stolen bases. Back to form in 1915, Cobb stole 96 bases and again led the A.L. as he would for three years in a row. Maisel, nicknamed "Flash," continued to show promise, raising his batting average 42 percentage points to a respectable .281. But in '16 he broke his collarbone, and two years later, had played in his last big-league game.

See What You Can; It Means Something;
The Thrill of King Kelly: He Was a THINKER;
Tyrus Raymond Cobb (Apr. 11, 1923)

The writer holds that it is the duty of every man, every woman, to see the great human figures, the great events of the day, if the opportunity presents.

It is a duty to one's self, to one's children. It is a matter of education.

The man who says, boastingly, that he has never seen a game of baseball makes an admission that reflects upon his intelligence.

He SHOULD see a ball game, if only because it is an American institution, if only to understand something of what millions of Americans are deeply interested in.

❄   ❄   ❄

He may not like baseball. He may not care for football. He may think boxing brutal, golf a waste of time.

But the man who will not take notice of these very important phases of American life is in a class with the man who says, "I wouldn't go around the corner to look at President Harding."

Now, there may be nothing exciting in President Harding's appearance, none the less it is a considerable privilege for any man to gaze upon the chief of a great country. It is something to be able to say to the next generation, "I saw President Harding."

❄   ❄   ❄

It is something to be able to say to the next generation, "I saw John Barrymore play 'Hamlet,' or I once met Booth Tarkington," or, "I saw Christy Mathewson pitch against the Cubs."

The writer forever asking questions of old-timers about events, about characters of the past, sometimes runs into a man who lived in that day, who had the opportunity of beholding things with his own eyes, but who did not see.

The writer finds himself viewing such a man with pity.

❃   ❃   ❃

A blasé, disinterested attitude toward contemporaneous life is not a mark of superiority.

The man is foolish who would not seize the opportunity of seeing Charley Chaplin, Douglas Fairbanks, the Woolworth Building, Irwin S. Cobb, Vincent Astor, Niagara Falls, Arthur Brisbane, Man o' War, Percy Haughton, Tad Dorgan, Gene Sarazan, William H. Taft, Babe Ruth, Benny Leonard, a national (political) convention, the shrimp cannery at Brunswick, Ga., the Boston Common, Jimmy O'Connell, the $75,000 ballplayer.

The man is foolish who does not seize the opportunity of seeing every phase of our times that opportunity presents.

❃   ❃   ❃

The writer has often wished he might have seen Mike Kelly, called "The King," for the reason that whenever you mention ballplayers to old-timers they invariably present "The King" as the greatest they ever saw.

They have seen (Ty) Cobb, (Babe) Ruth, (George) Sisler, (Rogers) Hornsby, (Honus) Wagner, Eddie Collins—still "The King" stands out in their memories, their affections. He MUST have been a great ballplayer, when opinion is unanimous.

❃   ❃   ❃

Nowadays we go to see Babe Ruth hit home runs. That is the big thrill of baseball.

In the days when Kelly was King, men went to see him THINK.

Kelly was noted for his amazing active brain. He thought out, executed new plays before the eyes of the crowd everyday.

He was not a great hitter, not a home run hitter. But the nimble brain produced new plays so rapidly that it left the game behind it.

❉ ❉ ❉

Ruth produces his sensations by sheer physical force. Kelly's sensations were largely mental.

He demonstrated to the spectators what was going on in his mind by immediate action. Old-timers say be brought thinking to baseball.

Nowadays it is a rarity to see a play executed on the ballfield that is original, is without precedent. That is why the old-timers love the memory of Kelly—he always had something new.

❉ ❉ ❉

Tyrus Raymond Cobb, of Georgia, is said by old-timers to be the closest approach to Kelly MENTALLY in the modern game.

For twelve years—nine of them consecutively—Cobb was the batting leader of his league, best of the base runners until his legs gave out.

Take your young son to see Cobb if you have the opportunity. It will mean something for him to be able to say, "I saw Cobb," when he is older.

❉ ❉ ❉

Runyon reflects in a column written while covering the 1925 World Series.

Ty Cobb the Greatest, So Asserts Old-Timer.
No One Will Quarrel. Man o' War of Diamond.
He Has Been a Marvel (Oct. 8, 1925)

I gave the baseball old-timers their innings not long ago in this column, and you heard from them of the amazing prowess of the baseball players of a bygone period, of the mighty King Kelly and Buck Ewing, and Silver Flint and others whose names mean nothing to this generation of fans.

Now I have before me a letter from still another old-timer, who saw the stars of long ago, and who has lived to see the stars of today, and oddly enough, he declines to admit that ever a ball tosser wore shoe leather who could compare with a certain gentleman of the present era.

I say "oddly enough" because the average old-timer looking back down the baseball years sees rising out of the mists of memory only giants.

I do not think I ever met an old-timer until this one came along who would admit that there was ever a ballplayer like Mike Kelly called "The King." My correspondent, who signs himself only R.W.C.W., rates his certain gentleman of the present era about seven lengths ahead of all the players of all time.

❊   ❊   ❊

And his certain gentleman is, of course, the famous Jewel of Georgia, Tyrus Raymond Cobb. There could be none other.

My correspondent says he has seen all the great players since 1876, a matter of nearly 50 years ago, and that he puts in an average of four afternoons a week in the ball yards today. Thus he qualifies as something of an authority in the matter of comparing the players of the past and present.

"I saw some great players away back yonder when I saw Kelly, Long (Cap) Anson, (Tim) Keefe, (Silver) Flint, (Buck) Ewing, (John) McGraw and (Charlie) Bennett, and I saw some great players in a later day when I saw (Johnny) Kling, (Charlie) Gibson, (Nap) Lajoie, Wagner, (Christy) Mathewson, (Hal) Chase, (Frank) Chance, (Joe) Tinker, (Three-Finger) Brown, (Orval) Overall, and all the others of their period," he writes.

"But I defy anybody to name one great star who surpassed Ty Cobb. He has excelled them all in his amazing all-around work for 20 years, base running, hitting, fielding, and everything else. There is no department in which he has not shone. He is the real champion of the whole bunch, the Man o' War of the diamond for all time."

❖ ❖ ❖

I shall not quarrel with Mr. R.W.C.W.'s estimate of Tyrus Raymond Cobb. I do not expect to see another like him in my lifetime, and I have never seen a player that I thought even approached him in all-round ability.

I did not see Kelly, of course. He was years before my time. He must have been a wonderful player, peculiarly inventive, and resourceful, but he was not in the same class with Cobb as a hitter, according to the records.

The Jewel of Georgia is an old man now, as baseball age and service goes with over 20 years of baseball playing behind him, yet his is still a star player, as well as manager. Baseball posterity has something to shoot at.

❖ ❖ ❖

The thing that appeals to me about Cobb is that he is not ancient history. Every baseball fan of this era has seen him in action, and most of them have seen him at the zenith of his prowess.

It seems to be almost idle to speak of any of the other players of today in the same breath with Cobb, as Cobb was in the stretch of 10 years between 1908 and 1918. Then he had all his whirling speed, along with his hitting ability and mentality. He still retains all his baseball mentality, and much of his hitting ability, but the speed has gone.

Time and again the fans of today have seen Cobb win ball games almost single-handed. Time and again they have seen him upset the morale of an opposing club when got on the base paths. He was the most feared individual ballplayer of the past 20 years, that is certain.

❖ ❖ ❖

He figured in a World Series three times, 1907, 1908 and 1909, against the Cubs and the Pirates, and in two of them he was what is sometimes called "a bust."

In the first series, he got only four hits out of 20 times at bat for an average of .200, and he failed to steal a base. In the second series he did better, making seven hits out of 19 times up for an average of .368 and stealing two bases.

He played in five games in those two series. In 1909, against the Pirates, he played in seven games, getting only six hits out of 26 times at bat, and stealing two bases. On the seasons in 1907, '08 and '09, Cobb hit .350, .324 and .317, which shows you how even the greatest stars can fall down in the World Series.

❄   ❄   ❄

A great ballplayer, this fellow Cobb, and a shrewd fellow with it.

I think R.W.C.W. is quite right when he calls Ty Cobb the Man o' War of baseball.

———

BABE RUTH

The one, the only . . . the Babe.

Runyon was at the Polo Grounds the day Babe Ruth of the Red Sox socked the first of his 714 home runs, in the third inning off Jack Warhop of the Yankees. Ruth's performance that day was a clinic—at bat, he went three-for-five and scored a run, while on the mound, the 20-year-old lefthander gave up only two earned runs in 13 innings. But the game was bitter-sweet: Ruth, who Runyon calls by his first name of "George," was the losing pitcher, due in large part to four Boston errors and two unearned runs. He would finish the season 18–8 with four home runs, just four years away from breaking the all-time major-league home run record.

Yankees Tie in Ninth and Win in Thirteenth, 4 to 3 (May 17, 1915)

High's Single, Steal of Second and Cook's Hit Land Long Game from Boston Red Sox

There is not enough of Hughy High to make one good-sized hero for one story this morning, and so we add to him Luther Cook and thus compile a sufficient subject. Hughy and Luther bunched together, make something to talk about. They assisted the community in taking a notable decision over the municipality of Boston, Mass., yesterday afternoon.

The shades of the thirteenth inning were falling fast up at the Polo Grounds, and the Wild Yanks and the Boston Red Sox, champs presumptive of the Amurrick kun League, as Ban Johnson calls it, were clustered in a tie. The count was three all, with Will Evans, the gesticulator, eagerly searching the horizon for evidence of nightfall, when Hughy and Luther amalgamated and broke up the pastime, the final tally being 4 to 3 in favor of the grand-old Empire State.

In our own garrulous way, we shall now endeavor to tell you just how it happened, omitting only such details as we deem unfit for publication.

Hughy High, small but efficient, opened that thirteenth with a single to center. Walter Pipp struck out. Hughy High stole second. Luther Cook singled over Heinie Wagner's reach and mid the mad mumble of the multitude, Hughie High came tumbling in across the home plate with the winning run. How was that for High?

Having described the most important incident of the game, we now feel compelled to warn the compositors to clear away all obstructions below, and to either side so we can run right on down this column, and over into the next in telling about the goings on right to the moment mentioned, beginning with how in the ninth when we boys tied 'er up.

Luther Cook figured in that too. One was one in the ninth when George Ruth struck Luther with a pitched baseball. George pitched the baseball left-handed, and by giving it the body follow-through, he succeeded in raising a tumor on Luther's shoulder. Cap'n Roger

Peckinpaugh subsided without a struggle, while Luther tarried at first, mulling his wounded torso, and glaring at George Ruth. That made two out, and it looked as this story would have to open with sighs, when Luther Boone—but by all means a separate paragraph for Luther.

Luther Boone doubled to right, a solid, smacking, soulful double that knocked the bleacherites back on the Butt of their spines from the crunch that precedes the rush for the exits and which scored Luther Cook with the tying tally.

A moment later Luther Boone went on to third, when George Ruth made a bad throw trying to catch him off second, but Leslie Nunamaker could not bring him in, and the game passed on into extra innings and to the big punch in the story as outlined above.

Well, it was quite a pastime! Everybody said it was a great game to win. Everybody was so delighted that they almost forget about (umpire) Dominick Mullaney, who was cast for the character of the bad guy in this tale. Not that we intend to make Dominick out, because you know the size of Dominick. The day that we blacken the character of Dominick is the day after Dominick leaves town, and gets well beyond the confines of this newspaper's circulation.

Cook Again Enters Scene

In the seventh inning, with we 'uns needing a run to tie, Luther Cook singled. Peckinpaugh was duly expunged, and Boone hit the right-field wall with a blow which put Cook on third. The ball hopped back off the razor-backed sign in right into (Harry) Hooper's hands, and Hooper threw to first, instead of to second, as Boone anticipated.

Boone had taken "that old turn" after hitting first, in accordance with the advice of all coaches and was several feet off the bag when (Dick) Hoblitzel got the ball. Dominick said he was out, and the rally bogged down right there.

The crowd discussed Dominick in audible tones in account of that decision, and some thought it might be a good thing to assassinate him at once, but no action was taken in account of Dominick's size, and the presence of Ban Johnson.

We have been wondering ever since the season opened why

(Yankee manager) Wild Bill Donovan has been keeping little Jack Warhop warmed up down there in right field, and the reason developed yesterday. It was for the purpose of having Jack pitch this game, and Jack pitched very well indeed while he was pitching, proving the efficiency of warming up.

In the eighth inning, Charlie Mullen batted for Jack, but nothing came of it, as Mike McNally, the Sox's new third baser, and the noisiest man in the whole world, next to (Stan) Baumgartner, the Phil pitcher, made a smashing play on Charlie's drive. Fritz Maisel got an infield hit that inning, stole second, moved to third on (Bill) Carrigan's bad throw, and scored on (Roy) Hartzell's out.

Cyrus Pieh finished the game for the Yanks, and this story would be wholly incomplete without an eulogy of Cyrus. Tall, thin and very interesting, Cyrus would have a column all to himself did space permit. He compiled a masterly finish. Pieh had the trust, you might say, to use a slow curve on some of the sluggers of the Sox, and he made them appear mighty futile and inefficient.

In the eleventh, he gathered up (Everett) Scott's slow roller and made a two-base bad chuck to Pipp. Then he fanned McNally. (Olaf) Henriksen, who once broke up a World Series pastime (in 1912) on Chris Mathewson — long and long ago that seems — batted for Carrigan, who manages the Sox, and therefore has a right to refuse to hit against Cyrus Pieh any time he feels that way about it.

Henriksen singled and Scott took third, Henriksen moving to second on the throw in. Then Cyrus Pieh fanned Ruth and Hooper. How was that for Pieh?

Ruth Bangs Out Homer

Fanning this Ruth is not as easy as the name and occupation might indicate. In the third frame, Ruth knocked the snot out of one of Jack Warhop's underhanded subterfuges and put the baseball in the right-field stands for a home run.

Ruth was discovered by Jack Dunn in a Baltimore school a year ago when he had not yet attained his lefthanded majority, and was adopted, and adapted, by Jack for the uses of the Orioles. He is now quite a pitcher and a splendid hitter — when he connects.

In our boys' end of the eleventh, Pipp led off with a single, but Will Bill had Cook up there trying to sacrifice, and after failing in two attempts to bunt, Cook struck out whereupon he flung his bat and took on an expression of intense disgust. Evidently, the only way Luther likes to bunt is from his shoe cleats.

It was in that inning that Luther Boone was purposely passed for the first time in his brief career. In other days, pitchers would have passed the whole batting order to get at Luther, but yesterday Ruth let him go to fire at Nunamaker and Leslie did not betray Ruth's confidence. He lifted a fly to Hooper.

Baseball mythology suggests that when the Yankees bought Babe Ruth from the Boston Red Sox before the 1920 season, he was an unproven talent. But Ruth was already the game's greatest slugger—and he proved it in this game at the Polo Grounds where he set the all-time, single-season home run record. The previous record-holder, Ed Williamson, had hit 27 as a right-handed batter who had set the home run record as a member of the 1884 N.L. Chicago White Stockings, whose park had a 180-foot leftfield fence, the shortest such fence in big-league history; of Williamson's 27 homers, 25 had been at home. Less than two years removed as a pitcher, Ruth would finish the '19 season with 29 home runs, which he would break the following season, as a Yankee, by mid-July, making everyone quickly forget what he had accomplished in Boston.

❊   ❊   ❊

Ruth Sets Home-Run Mark; Drives Ball over Stand (Sept. 25, 1919)

That 35-year-old major-league home run record of Ed Williamson's was knocked plumb over the Polo Grounds' grandstand by Babe Ruth at 5:15 yesterday afternoon.

❊   ❊   ❊

It went along with a baseball that Bob Shawkey pitched at Babe in the ninth inning of the second game of a doubleheader between the Yanks and the Boston Red Sox at the P.G.

❋   ❋   ❋

Babe was the first man up in the Sox side of the ninth, Shawkey had the Sox 1 to 0. Babe had made seven previous trips to the plate without much result, although he had walked three times and once hit a triple that was cut down to a single because he pulled A. Merkle and failed to touch second.

❋   ❋   ❋

The first ball that Shawkey pitched at Ruth was low, and Babe let it go. The second was a slow curve.

❋   ❋   ❋

"Blooie!"

❋   ❋   ❋

Babe caught 'er on the end of his stick and the pill began traveling toward the rightfield stand, riding very high.

❋   ❋   ❋

It was a looping fly, and so tall it looked as if it were going to hit on foul territory, but it went between the fourth and fifth flagpoles well inside the "fair" mark, while the crowd went daffy for a moment.

❋   ❋   ❋

Ruth had 27 home runs when he went up to bat in the ninth. They dug up old Ed Williamson's record after Babe had beaten Buck

Freeman's (American League) mark of 25. Williamson's record was largely constructed in a yard with a very short fence, and not even the old-timers took it very seriously.

❀ ❀ ❀

This blow of Ruth's yesterday was his 48th homer since he has been in the league.

❀ ❀ ❀

It went on over into Manhattan Field, south of the stand. This makes it far and away the longest hit ever made on the Polo Grounds.

❀ ❀ ❀

Joe Jackson once hit a ball on top of the stand and that has been a record for some years. There were two boys on top of the stand yesterday and Ruth's lick passed right over their heads, so there is no argument as to where the ball landed.

❀ ❀ ❀

Incidentally, the hit was the tying run of the game, which went on into the 13th inning. It was won by (Wally) Pipp's triple and (Del) Pratt's sacrifice fly after (Waite) Hoyt had pitched nine hitless innings. Score, 2 to 1.

❀ ❀ ❀

The Sox won the first game by a score of 4 to 0.

❀ ❀ ❀

Ruth came up again in the 10th with two on and Shawkey walked him, Ruth starting for first before the fourth ball was pitched at him.

❊   ❊   ❊

Again, in the 12th, with (Bill) Lamar on first, Ruth drove (Chick) Fewster clear to the right-center wall after a terrific smash.

❊   ❊   ❊

(Red Sox owner) Harry Frazee and (Yankee co-owner) Colonel Til Huston, the Ruppertistas of the American League, sat together in a box and jointly thought horrible things about (A.L. president) Byron Bancroft Johnson.

❊   ❊   ❊

"He is just a behemoth," said Harry, quoting from the language of the legal brief.

❊   ❊   ❊

"Nothing but a cedar," said Colonel Huston.

❊   ❊   ❊

Ruth fanned twice in the first game against (Jack) Quinn, was passed over intentionally and hit a fly to center.

❊   ❊   ❊

(Reporter) Bill Hanna says the late Cy Seymour once hit a homer over into Manhattan Field years ago on the old grounds, but under no such conditions as the Babe's punch *(Seymour, who had played two stints with the Giants, had died just six days before)*.

❊   ❊   ❊

Frank Gleich, the Michigan Wolverine, batted for Quinn in the eighth and drew a pass. He was among the 14 Yanks left on the bases.

※ ※ ※

Deacon Sam Jones issued nine bases on balls, and still the Yanks couldn't do anything. Such is baseball in the waning days of old September.

※ ※ ※

(Boston's) Joe Wilhoit, who holds the world's record for consecutive clouting, appeared at the P.G. yesterday for the first time since he was a member of the Giants. Joe made his great record with the Wichita club of the Western League.

※ ※ ※

He drove in two runs with a smack in the fourth frame of the first game.

※ ※ ※

Quinn was a little wild. He filled the bases in the first by walking Ruth and (Wally) Schang after Wilhoit had hit safe, and (Stuffy) McInnis scored two with a single to right.

※ ※ ※

(Roger) Peck(inpaugh) singled in the ninth inning of the second game. (Red) Shannon snatched (Frank) Baker's liner close to the ground, making a great catch, and then threw the ball into the grandstand trying to double Peck off first. Peck had meantime departed from that station and was rounding second when they called him back to the initial sack, as it is called.

❀ ❀ ❀

It was a queer sort of play all around, and the Boston people thought they were entitled to a double after they had received the ball and tagged first before the return of Peck. The umps ruled that the ball was out of play when it went into the stand.

❀ ❀ ❀

Ollie Chill was the ump who made the decision, but Tommy Connolly, the ump-in-chief, said that as a matter of fact, Peck should have been sent back to second.

❀ ❀ ❀

Waite Hoyt, who is still the youngest 19-year-old ballplayer in the world, started against the Yanks in the second game, and was pretty lucky our boys did not score more than one tally in the first couple of frames. Then for eight frames not a Yank reached first.

❀ ❀ ❀

Shawkey intentionally walked Ruth in the fourth, with (Frank) Gillhooley on third and the crowd gave Bob the Gob the razz for his pains. They wanted to see Babe sock.

❀ ❀ ❀

Babe stole second, but was left along with Gillhooley.

❀ ❀ ❀

Ruth hit a ball over Fewster's head in right-center, which was good for three bases, but he failed to touch second base and the ball was relayed into Pratt and Peck for an out. However, Babe got credit for a (single).

❖   ❖   ❖

Ruth swings just two bats when he is awaiting his turn at the plate. (Tris) Speaker, (Ty) Cobb and (Frank) Baker twirl three.

The Life of "Babe" Ruth (Mar. 26, 1920)
Or What the Home Run King Hears as He Advances Nobly to the Plate, and Thereafter (Two on and Two out).

"Here he comes! That's him!"

"Here's Ruth! Here's the guy that cost all that money!"

"Oh, Babe!"

"Oh, you billion-dollar-baby!"

"Knock 'er a mile, Babe!"

"My, ain't he big? No wonder he can hit!"

"Hit 'er out, Babe!"

"Over the old fence, kid!"

"Look out, Mister Pitcher! Here's Babe!"

"Hey, you outfielders! Better git yourself horses!"

"Good boy, Babe!"

"Show us how, Babe!"

"Oh, Babe!"

THE UMPS—"STREE-IKE!"

"Oo-oo-oo!"

"Lookit that old boy swing!"

"Never mind that, Babe!"

"What a sock he took!"

"If he'd a-hit that ball, it'd a-been gong yet!"

"Lookit the size of that bat!"

"That's the way, Babe!"

"Knock the pitcher out from under his hat!"

"Come on, Babe!"

"Ain't he a bird!"

"He almost blew them fellers out of the yard with that swing!"

"Over the fence, Babe!"

THE UMPS—"STREE-IKE!"

"Missed it again!"

"Oh, what a swing!"

"Strike him out, pitcher!"

"Yeah, strike him out!"

"Strike him out!"

"Strike him out!"

"Make him whiff!"

"Right around his neck, now!"

"He can't hit you! Strike him out!"

"He missed it a foot!"

"He's a sucker for that slow one!"

"Strike him out!"

"Strike him out!"

"Strike him out!"

THE UMPS— "HEEZ ZOUT!"

"Well, you big bum!"

"Well, you big stiff!"

"Oh, you big tramp!"

"You billion dollars worth of cheese!"

"So you think you can hit, hey!"

"Cost a hundred bucks, hey!"

"Oh, you big crawfish!"

"How much are you worth now?"

"Go on and set down, you big sap!"

"How'd you get them home runs last year, you big chump?"

"Ought to be ashamed of yourself, you big simp!"

"Yah-yah-yah!"

"Boo-boo-boo!"

"S-s-s-s-s!"

"Sit down, sit down, you big ham!"

"Aw, go on and hide!"

"Who told you could hit?"

"Go back to pitching, you may get lucky again!"
"You big stew!"
"You big bum!"
"Yah-yah-yah-yah!"

In the wake of the Ray Chapman beaning, Runyon turned his attention to the possibility that a shot from Babe Ruth could very well injure somebody.

Hurler in Danger When Ruth Bats (Sept. 9, 1920)
Fear of Smashing Ball Back at Pitcher Causes Him to Swing High and to Right

Ballplayers say it is a blessing Babe Ruth does not commonly hit through the infield. He would kill or dangerously harm any men who in front of one of his powerful punches at short distances.

A ball thrown by Carl Mays had sufficient force to crack Ray Chapman's skull. Ruth drives a ball from his bat 10 times harder than the strongest man in baseball can throw.

Players who know the King of Swat say that he has always had a secret dread of smashing a ball back at a pitcher, or an infielder. It is probably that dread which causes him to pull his punches high, and to the right, clearing the infield.

No man has ever lived who hit a baseball as hard as Ruth. In the olden days, soldiers were equipped with slings and slew their enemies with missiles thrown from these slings, but it is doubtful if they got as much force behind them as Ruth puts back of a batted ball.

The weapon which was the nearest approach to Babe's deadly drive was the catapult.

❖   ❖   ❖

There are several little things about baseball that have always been matters of mystery to ballplayers, and spectators too. One is the psychics, or whatever you might call it, of the game, that protects pitchers from being hurt more often by balls batted back to them.

Thousands of balls are thrown by the average pitcher in the course of his career, and hit to either side of him by the batsmen. Yet few of them come close enough to the pitcher, even for him, to field them.

We have talked to numerous hurlers on the subject, and they all admit that they have frequently thought of the same thing themselves. In fact, two or three said that they always had a horror of that very thing occurring.

When a pitcher delivers the ball, he nearly always throws himself off balance. He would not have a chance to dodge if the ball was smashed directly back at him.

Only the other day at the Polo Grounds, Rube Benton of the Giants stuck his hand in front of a drive from the bat of (Frank) Withrow of the Phils, and the force of the drive split the hand so badly that Rube will be unable to work again for some days.

Rube might have ducked the ball, but his instinct told him to try to stop it. The same instinct prompts every ballplayer to make a stab for drives that he would perhaps let go by if he paused to consider the danger.

Some years ago Bert Maxwell, once a member of the Giants and then pitching for the Federal League, stuck his hand in front of a ball driven back at him and the ball hit the palm of the hand with terrific force. It drove the bones of his wrist back up toward the elbow and put Maxwell out of baseball for good.

❊　❊　❊

It is very rarely, indeed, that a pitcher gets a chance at one of Ruth's raps, and then generally the ball had hit the ground first and lost some of its force. Babe is always aiming for the rightfield wall, so much so that it is now a common joke in the American League for the third baseman, shortstop and second baseman to group themselves over back of second almost in short-right field.

Nevertheless, ballplayers say it is very fortunate, indeed, that Babe shoots high and far; otherwise, a heavy mortality list would follow his batting.

Ruth's first 50-homer season, in 1920, is now confined to a page or two in the biographies and baseball anthologies, since he would soon eclipse that mark with an even more impressive season. But it was big news at the time in part because the mark was so extraordinarily above the previous mark—the Babe's 29, set the year before. The mark also came the same month that that 1919 World Series fix by the White Sox was exposed, an incident that arguably could have wrecked the game if not for Ruth's heroics. The Babe's big feat then was all about timing—bringing excitement to the game and saving it in the nick of time.

❖ ❖ ❖

Homer No. 51 (a) Terrific Lick (Sept. 25, 1920)
Ruth Is Whole Show as Yankees and Griffmen Split a Doubleheader Before Big Crowd

Babe Ruth is the greatest showman of these times.

Nearly 30,000 people went out to the Polo Grounds yesterday hoping to see Ruth hit his 50th home run.

The King of Swat did it in the very first inning of the first game of a doubleheader between the Yankees and Clark Griffith's Washington club.

The crowd went quite mad for five minutes.

They had witnessed something no other people had ever seen before. Perhaps no one now living will ever see such a thing again.

Then in the first inning of the second game, Ruth hit another home run, increasing his record to 51. His homer in the first game was the only run scored by the Yanks in that game, which was won by Washington, 3 to 1.

His homer in the second game was the first of two runs scored by the Yankees in winning the game by a count of 2 to 1.

Ruth scored the second run in the ninth inning. He started the inning with a two-bagger to right field, making his fourth consecutive hit of Jim Shaw in that game.

When the Washington catcher made a throw to second in an effort to catch Ruth napping, the mighty slugger threw himself

back toward the bag, colliding with the Washington shortstop and
knocking him over.

Ruth Scores 154th Run of Season

Ruth scrambled to his feet and went on to third, while the ball
bounced out into centerfield.

Derrill Pratt immediately afterward banged a single to left-
center, and Ruth crossed the plate with what was not only the winning run, but his 154th run of the season.

This is another new record for the American League. Babe broke
Ty Cobb's record of 147 runs scored in a single season some days ago.

He almost scored another run in the sixth inning of the second
game. With the bases full, Ruth tried to steal home, but was tagged
out at the plate.

They built a sort of baseball street carnival around the doubleheader, and Ruth was the whole show. The boys' band from the
Baltimore institution (St. Mary's Orphanage) where Ruth got his
start in baseball, and in life itself for that matter, was stationed in
the grandstand back of third base.

This band made the last Western trip with the Yankees, on behalf
of a fund to raise money for new buildings to replace some destroyed
by fire. Ruth aided in the drive, which was very successful.

Yesterday, between the games, Nick Altrock, the comedian of
the Washington club, passed the hat and collected a good sum.

There were thousands of young boys in the crowd. They had
been taken by their fathers, who wanted them to see Babe Ruth.
When these boys are old men with white whiskers they will still be
telling how they saw Babe Ruth hit his 51st home run.

51st Homer Clears Fence in Right

It was a powerful smash into the rightfield bleachers over the
Piedmont sign. Davy Robertson, once of the Giants and now a
Chicago Cub, hit a ball in there several years ago. Ruth's first
homer yesterday landed in the far corner of the upper-right field
grandstand.

For a second it looked as if it would clear the stand. It was probably the blow that gave Ruth the greatest pleasure of any he ever struck. The tall fellow with the enormous big body and thin legs trotted around the bases with a smile, which showed all his teeth on his broad face.

George Burns, Slim Sallee and a number of the New York Giants were sitting in the press box. Ed Konetchy and a party of other members of the Brooklyn Dodgers were also present. Your Uncle Wilbert Robinson, manager of the Dodgers, sat in a grandstand box.

Bill Klem, a National League umpire, saw the game. The old Heinie Zimmerman Boosting and Bawling Out Bund from the Bronx, which used to get behind third base and root for Heinie, was on hand, shouting for Al Schacht, Washington pitcher.

Al is a Bronx boy. He did not work yesterday, but between games he gave a flower dance with Nick Altrock that had the crowd in an uproar. The Yanks couldn't hit Acosta, the little Cuban in the first game. Only Ruth hit Shaw with an effect in the second.

Rip Collins started to pitch the second game, but hurt his knee, and retired after a few innings. (Hank) Thormahlen, the left-hander, finished it for him.

✻ ✻ ✻

Here is Runyon on Ruth and Rogers Hornsby on the eve of the 1926 Yankee-Cardinal World Series.

Mr. Ruth and Hornsby: Two Greatest Hitters Are of Different Types but Get the Same Results (Oct. 1, 1926)
Mr. Ruth Is a Wonder

The World Series of 1926 is of unusual interest if only because it presents on the same bill the two greatest baseball headliners of these times.

They are Mr. George Herman Babe Ruth, sometimes called the Big Bam (Oh Mister Printer, PLEASE don't make that bum) and

Rogers Hornsby, the former Home Run King, and the latter probably the greatest right-handed hitter of all time.

Mr. George Herman Babe Ruth would seem to be entering the series with something of an advantage over his opponent in the matter of batting condition, Mr. Ruth being in the proverbial pink, while Rogers Hornsby has just closed one of the leanest seasons of his career because of illness. Mr. Ruth hit around .369 in the year, and nudged out some forty-seven home runs, so you can see he was feeling first rate all year.

Rogers Hornsby, on the other hand, got so far away from the .300 mark that he felt positively naked. He would up less than a score of points beyond .300, which is little more than infield batting practice to Rogers Hornsby. However, he may get going in the series and knock the boys bowlegged. You can't keep a squirrel on the ground.

❊　❊　❊

Mr. Ruth and Rogers Hornsby undoubtedly represent the greatest amount of pounding power that baseball has ever known. I mean to say they hit the ball harder than any batsmen that ever lived.

If you could combine their batting power into one punch it would probably be sufficient to drive a baseball from the Battery to the Bronx, which is quite a distance.

Of the two, I believe Rogers Hornsby hits the ball harder, and Mr. Ruth hits it farther. This seems contradictory, but I can explain it. Rogers Hornsby hits the ball on the beezer or nose, with a straightaway drive. It shoots from his bat like a rifle bullet, traveling in a straight line.

Mr. Ruth, as a rule, hits under the ball, lifting it when he connects as a golfer lifts a golf ball. Rogers Hornsby seems to always be trying to break the infielders' kneecaps, while Mr. Ruth seems to be firing at the landscapes beyond the walls. They both get the same general result, which are additions to their batting averages.

❊   ❊   ❊

Rogers Hornsby is perhaps not a great hitter in general than Tyrus Raymond Cobb, the Jewel of Georgia, at his best, but Tyrus Raymond Cobb is a left-handed batter. Moreover, Tyrus Raymond Cobb was one of the speediest men ever known to baseball, and he got many hits by outfooting short drives. He did not hit a ball as hard as Rogers Hornsby.

Before Rogers Hornsby's time there was a man named Ed Delahanty, one of a numerous baseball family, who was accounted the greatest right-handed hitter that ever lived. Then Rogers Hornsby came along, and the old-timers say that he is even greater than Delahanty.

Before Mr. Ruth, there were no hitters of his exact type worth mentioning in the same breath with Mr. Ruth. He is unique and peculiar in baseball. I doubt that we shall see his like again. He is certainly the most picturesque, colorful character the pastime has ever known. He is the only man I ever saw who can create a sensation by merely striking out, for Mr. Ruth strikes out with great regularity.

Rogers Hornsby does not strike out with majesty. In fact, he does not strike out at all. In the matter of cold precision, Rogers Hornsby has something on Mr. Ruth, but I never cared for precisionists myself. I like the wild abandon of Mr. Ruth.

As between the two in the matter of drawing power at the gate there is no comparison. Mr. Ruth could be hitting fifty points less than Rogers Hornsby and still outdraw the St. Louis man, because Rogers Hornsby, great hitter that he is, lacks Mr. Ruth's vivid personality and appeal to the populace.

However, Rogers Hornsby can do things that Mr. Ruth cannot do, one of them being to manage a big-league club to the pennant. I doubt that Mr. Ruth has the temperament to do that. Still, one of the last men in the world I would have selected to successfully manage a ball club is Monsieur Reeshard de Markee de Marquard, otherwise known as Rube Marquard, the old slab-sided left-hander of the Giants.

I would have said that Monsieur de Markee de Marquard lacked the proper temperament, though I esteem him most highly in many other ways. I still think he was the greatest left-handed pitcher I ever saw. And Monsieur de Markee de Marquard has just won a pennant as the manager of the Providence Cubs, more power to him!

Time may tame the temperament of Mr. Ruth and make of him a successful manager, too. It would be a pity if such a personality should pass from the big leagues when his playing days are over.

❈   ❈   ❈

In their meeting in the World Series, Mr. Ruth will have the inconsiderable advantage over Rogers Hornsby of absence of responsibility, other than that which pertains to playing the outfield and making home runs at stated intervals. Rogers Hornsby will be playing second base and managing his club at the same time. However, I seem to remember that the responsibilities thus involved did not keep the Washington club under Stanley Harris, from winning the World Series of 1924 from the Giants under the great John McGraw, whose only responsibility was sitting on the bench.

❈   ❈   ❈

Having just hit his 60th home run of the season, Babe Ruth on the eve of the 1927 Yankees-Pirates World Series becomes the greatest athlete of his era.

The Mighty Ruth (Oct. 4, 1927)

I expect the redoubtable George Herman Babe Ruth to clout out no fewer than three home runs in the series, and if George Herman Babe Ruth is inconsiderate enough to cross me up in this prediction, I shall deem him no gentleman.

There is a man to remember, my friends—George Herman Babe Ruth, the Battering Beezark from Baltimore. What a person he is, to be sure. Some years after the time the experts allotted to him in the large league, he hauls off and hangs up a new home-run record.

As far back as 1923 I heard the boys saying that George Herman Babe Ruth couldn't miss winding up in some kind of ward in a year or so. I thought, myself, at one time that he would fatten up until he wouldn't be fit for much of anything, except possibly the presidency of the American League.

But here he is, with those 60 homers behind him on the season, and the three more I have assigned to him in the World Series coming up. In which connection I am reminded of my old friend, Louie Sherwin, the reformed drama critic, wrote me not long ago demanding to know why any homers compiled by Ruth in a World Series shouldn't be included in his official record of homers on the season.

I never could see why, myself, but it seems that the baseball season is something apart from the World Series when it comes to setting down the figures, though for no intelligent reason.

(Ruth would hit only two home runs in the Yankees' four-game sweep of the Pirates, one each in games three and four. He would also hit .400.)

❊ ❊ ❊

Ruth Certain Hugmen Will Win Series (Oct. 5, 1927)

Pittsburgh — If you are asking me how the World Series of 1927 is coming out — and why not ask me? — I must reply that Colonel Jake Ruppert's New York Yankees will win it.

I make this answer partly on my own shrewd calculations and deductions, but more on the authority of Mr. George Herman Babe Ruth, the well-known Beezark of Kerblam, who drew me aside in the lobby of the Hotel Roosevelt this morning and breathed the above low-down in my sunburned ear.

The Roosevelt is Pittsburgh's newest hotel. It opened yesterday, and every room is equipped with the most modern contribution to

American hotel science, a bottle opener on the wall, so the clients will not annoy their fellow inmates of the hostelry by banging towel-wrapped bottle butts against the plastering. It is an excellent thought.

What "Babe" Revealed

But, returning to Mr. George Herman Babe Ruth, the Beezark of Kerblam, whose breath, I must hasten to add, disclosed no evidence of recent use of the bottle openers by Mr. Ruth. Whispered Mr. Ruth:

"The Yanks can't miss. You better mention it to your readers right away, so you'll have a scoop on the other boys."

Well, I have the utmost confidence in anything the Beezark of Kerblam says. He told me several years ago he would eventually break his own record of 59 home runs, and he has kept his word.

Mr. Ruth was out at the Pittsburgh baseball orchard with the rest of the Yankees today ostensibly engaged on light practice against the opening of the World Series tomorrow afternoon, but what he was really doing was taking measurement to see if his home runs would fit in that yard.

Consults with Lou

I judge from Mr. Ruth's statement to me that he was entirely satisfied with the result of his observations. He was seen in earnest consultation with Mr. Lou Gehrig, the Columbia (University) youth, who hit 47 homers in the season of 1927, and is presumed that they established their aiming points against the morrow's pastime.

Mr. Ruth and Mr. Gehrig are warm friends, despite the fact that Mr. Gehrig seemed to be infringing on Mr. Ruth's copyright during the greater part of the season. I am told, however, that the Columbia young man operated under written permission from Mr. Ruth, who felt that there were enough home runs in the American League pitching to be cut up several ways.

A Much-Sought Man

Mr. Ruth is what you might call a cynosure of all eyes as he moves about Pittsburgh, walking first on one foot and then on the other. The lobby of the Roosevelt was crowded all day by the Pittsburgh proletariat, eager to see what manner of man this is who can belt out 60 homers in a season.

There will be at least 40,000 citizens assembled in the baseball premises hard by the pleasant precincts of Schenley Park tomorrow when the Pirates and the Yankees take the field, and all these citizens will be torn between the desire to see the mighty mauler hit a homer and the hope that he doesn't.

Ray Kremer, of the Pirates, and Waite Hoyt, of the Yanks, will probably be the opposing hurlers, as we say. They are both right-handers.

Kremer Hero of 1925

Ray was one of the heroes of the 1925 series, when the Pirates beat the Washington club. It seems but yesterday that Waite Hoyt was the schoolboy wonder of baseball, but I hear him spoken of today as a veteran. Tempus fugit, and how it fugits.

In the meantime, the city of Pittsburgh is all steamed up over the series and the hotels are jammed and the betting is 7 to 5 on the series, with the Yanks the favorites. The folks are coming in from the thickly-populated territory contiguous to Pittsburgh, and from New York and other Eastern ports.

A number of wayfarers from the Pacific Coast, headed by Buster Keaton, the cinema comedian, have arrived to lend moral support to the Coast representatives in the series, especially the Waner boys (Paul and Lloyd, the Pirates' hitting twins who were actually from Oklahoma).

Mrs. Waner's Children

The Waner boys are Paul and Lloyd, of the Pirates, and Pittsburgh esteems them, and their contribution to baseball science, especially Paul. He is the top-notch hitter of the National League, and a baseball player from who-laid-the-chunk. No one will be surprised if Mrs. Waner's children stand out in the series.

The experts seem to think that the Pirates' curveball pitchers may stop the Yankee hitters, including the mighty Gehrig, and the mightier Ruth. As one of the expertist of the experts put it to me:

"The Yanks will hit 'em farthest, but the Pirates hit 'em oftenest."

———

MILLER HUGGINS

Runyon was quick to recognize the greatness of the much-maligned Yankee manager. Who could have predicted at the time that 5'4" Huggins would lead the Yankees to their first three world championships?

Huggins Signs to Manage Yankees for Two Seasons
(Oct. 26, 1917)

Leader of St. Louis Nationals for Five Years Transfers Allegiance to This City, Supplanting "Wild Bill" Donovan—Ruppert Makes Selection and Tenders Contract in Record Time

Peppery little Miller Huggins, for five years manager of the St. Louis Cardinals, of the National League, is now manager of the New York Yankees.

"Hug" yesterday signed a contract for two years with Colonel Jacob Ruppert, president of the Yanks, on shorter notice and with briefer negotiations than had marked the signing of a big-league manager in quite a spell.

It has been the baseball custom to introduce a lot of preliminary blather into those matters, prolonging the agony for weeks, but with characteristic abruptness Colonel Ruppert called Huggins to the Yankee office for the sporting writers, and the thing was over in a jiffy.

About the only concession to baseball custom was the photographing of the Colonel and Huggins in the act of committing the deed to paper. Quite a crowd witnessed the transaction.

The baseball vicissitudes which beset the Manhattan Island

American Leaguers under the management of "Wild Bill" Donovan made it apparent some time ago that a managerial change was inevitable.

Donovan Not to Blame

These vicissitudes were due to no fault of "Wild Bill's," but the baseball public, generally described as "fickle," rarely goes behind the returns to discover the reasons why a club is not winning. It looks only at the results. "Wild Bill" was not getting results.

The change had to come, and Colonel Ruppert has had a number of people in mind as Donovan's possible successor for some time. One of them was Huggins.

Colonel Ruppert admired Huggins' style of baseball and his constructive ability as shown by the gradual building of the Cardinals. However at the time the president of the Yanks first thought of him, Huggins was under contract with the owners of the Cards, and baseball ethics forbade negotiations.

Mr. Ruppert's Choice

However, Rickey seemed to take the view that the American League was trying to lure his manager away from him as a matter of "reprisal," because Rickey quit a job as business manager of the St. Louis Browns to accept the presidency of the Cards.

Furthermore, Rickey apparently tried to make it appear that Ban Johnson, president of the American League, was doing the dealing with Huggins. It was even announced that Johnson himself had signed "Hug," with the idea of placing him somewhere in his league, but Johnson denied this story.

The stout boss of the American circuit says he had no dealings whatever with Huggins, and Huggins says the same thing. He was selected by Colonel Ruppert on his own initiative. Whatever Rickey really thinks about the "reprisal" thing, it is likely that he is relieved that Huggins is gone. Huggins was the big man, metaphorically speaking, of the Cards, a state that Rickey himself greatly desires to occupy.

Brooks No Interference

Huggins was not the sort that would permit Rickey or anybody else to interfere with his conduct of a ball club, and for obvious reasons Rickey could not "fire" him. Branch is too sharp a baseball man to pull any such "boner" as that. All that the Cards did was attributed by the St. Louis public to Huggins.

It is said the little manager was not too happy in his proximity to Branch, though they seemed to be enjoying a harmonious success together, so take it all around, the change probably pleases all hands.

It will certainly please the New York fans. Huggins has always been very popular here. The Cardinals and his management were drawing well at the Polo Grounds. Local baseball followers were strong for Hug's aggressiveness.

They will welcome Huggins, but they will view the passing of "Wild Bill" Donovan with sincere regret. The old Detroit Tiger hurler leaves New York with a world of good wake. No other baseball man, not even excepting Christy Mathewson, had greater personal popularity here than Bill.

Misfortune Trails Bill

In the three years he handled the Yankees dating from the purchase by Colonel Ruppert and Captain T.L. Huston, now in France, he had a lot of bad luck, especially in injured players, but even so he did fairly well in his first two years.

At the beginning of this season it seemed as if he had a sure pennant winner, but misfortune again beset the Yankees, and at the time nearly all his players were down and out from injury. Because "Wild Bill" failed does not mean that he could not succeed elsewhere.

Huggins takes up a tough job; there is no doubt about that. He knows it is not as tough as the one he took when he accepted the managership of the Cards. It is said his successor there will be Ira Thomas, the old catcher of the Athletics, with Rickey taking the role of dictator, which he seems to like.

It is the impression of the baseball public that with his ball players Huggins is the "driver" type of manager, along the order of (George) Stallings and Pat Moran and (Hughie) Jennings and (Clark) Griffith and (John) McGraw.

Manager of Mack-Type

Those who know him, however, say he is of just the opposite school—that he inclines more to the "salve" of Connie Mack, or a Wilbert Robinson or a (Pants) Rowland.

In any event, he had done fairly well as a manager—especially last season, which, it is said, is the first season he has really had able cooperation from the club owners. This is by way of a compliment to Branch Rickey, who may not know a lot of things, but who is certainly an able baseball man.

Huggins ran third with his Cardinals in 1917, and wound up by licking the Browns in the post-season series. He was a good ball player himself in his ball-playing days. He was never a great hitter, but he was an exceptionally smart player. He was regarded by many as the best second baseman in the game when he was at the top of his career.

"Hug" was born in Cincinnati 37 years ago. He played semi-professional ball for Max Fleischmann's noted Catskill Mountain club in 1900, which had a lot of players who later became well known. His diamond career started in 1898 with Wapakoneta, Ohio, semi-pro-club, In 1899, he was with Mansfield, Ohio.

Enters Majors in 1904

In 1901, "Hug" went to the St. Paul club, and stayed there until 1903, when he was sold to the Cincinnati Reds. In 1904 he played second for the Reds, batting .263. In 1905 he hit for .273; in 1906 for .292; in 1907. .243; in 1908, .239, and in 1909, .213 in 46 games.

At the close of the season of 1900, "Hug" was traded to the Cardinals for Fred Beebe, a pitcher, and the unfortunate young Alan Storke. In 1910, and 1911–12, Huggins made the best record of his baseball career. He hit .265 in 151 games in 1910. In 1911, he hit .261 in 136 games, and in 1912 he rose to .304 in 120 games.

"Hug" succeeded Roger Bresnahan as manager of the Cardinals in 1913, and continued in active service up to a couple of years ago. He wears a uniform on the field, but no longer attempts to play.

"Hug" is a lawyer by profession. He is a very intelligent chap, with a good sense of humor, but he takes his baseball very seriously. He gained a reputation as a sort of David Harum of baseball when he first took hold of the Cards by giving Barney Dreyfuss (of the Pirates) a plastering in a trade.

Good Judge of Players
He seems to be a good judge of young ball players, and has developed quite a number of stars, and potential stars, including Rogers Hornsby, "Spectacles" Meadows, (Mike) Gonzales, (Walton) Cruise, "Mule" Watson and others.

In taking charge of the Yankees, he comes about ninth in a line of notables who were failures and semi-failures as leaders of the Manhattan Islanders. He is going up against one of the most formidable "jinxes" in baseball.

Clark Griffith ran second twice with the Yanks, once in 1904, and again in 1906, but only one other manager did as well in 15 years. In 1910, they landed second.

That was the year George Stallings was fired in mid-season, and Hal Chase took the job. Hal tried it alone the following year and was a "bust." The came luckless Harry Wolverton, who finished "ab—so—loot—ly," as the boys say, then the Cheerless Leader, (Frank) Chance, who tried it two years.

The job drive the Cheerless One right back to California, and Roger Peckinpaugh got the club home sixth that season—1914—about as well as Chance could have done.

Then Frank J. Farrell and his partners sold the club to Ruppert and Huston and Donovan came in. He finished fifth in 1915 and fourth in 1916. He was sixth this year.

Griffith managed the club for five full seasons and part of a sixth. Norman Elberfeld—the redoubtable "Kid"—spaced out 1908. The club wound up last that year.

❖   ❖   ❖

Here is Runyon after Miller Huggins brought home the Yan-
kees' first American League pennant. They would not win the
World Series for another two years, beating the Giants in 1923.

Sport Editorial: Huggins (Oct. 3, 1921)

Miller Huggins has brought the American League's first pennant
to Manhattan Island.

The feat speaks for itself.

The crafty (Clark) Griffith (the first Yankee manager, from
1903 to 1908), with a hand-picked club, failed to do it. (George)
Stallings (Yankee manager, '09 and '10), the "Miracle Man" of
1914 (as manager of the World Series–winning Boston Braves);
(Frank Chance) the "Peerless Leader" of the old Cubs; (Hal)
Chase, the ball-playing sensation of his time; (Kid) Elberfeld,
(Harry) Wolverton, ("Wild" Bill) Donovan, all fell ingloriously by
the wayside in pursuit of the same enterprise.

It has remained for the little flat-footed lawyer-ballplayer from
Cincinnati to finally fulfill that hope deferred for 19 long years to
the Yankee fans of this town.

We repeat, the feat speaks for itself.

❖   ❖   ❖

Huggins has won against tradition, against opposition and criticism such as few managers have ever encountered.

Assembling his ball club piece by piece, plodding along with
astounding patience, the small leader of the Yanks has scored one
of the greatest triumphs in baseball history, after one of the bit-
terest fights.

❖   ❖   ❖

We have heard carping critics say that Huggins ought to win
because he is backed by two liberal millionaire sportsmen, (Jacob)

Ruppert and (Til) Huston, willing to gratify his lightest whim in the way of baseball purchase. The same thing has been said of John J. McGraw with the rich Charley Stoneham behind the Giants.

This is the veriest nonsense.

The Fleischmann millions backed the Cincinnati club for years, and the Reds invariably finished in the ruck. The millions of Wrigley and Armour are behind the Chicago National Leaguers, and where is the club in the race?

The not inconsiderable fortune of (Charles) Comiskey is the financial bolster of the White Sox; the wealthy Shibes are interested in the Philadelphia Athletics; and every other club in both leagues has plenty of backing.

❈   ❈   ❈

You can buy the various parts of the finest automobile in the world, but what good are they unless you have a man who can properly assemble them? If you purchased all the greatest ballplayers in the two big leagues, they couldn't win a pennant without able direction.

Huggins has done well.

He is entitled to all the credit and the glory that goes with the leadership of a pennant-winning ball club.

He is entitled to an apology from those who have belittled his efforts.

It took the untimely death of 50-year-old Huggins from influenza to be fully recognized for his considerable talents as Yankee manager. Babe Ruth, who seldom got along with Huggins, broke down at his funeral, sobbing, "He was the only guy who could control me."

❈   ❈   ❈

Miller Huggins' Rise to Fame One of Highlights of Baseball History (Sept. 27, 1929)

Miller Huggins passes into baseball history as one of the great managers of all time. His name and fame rank with those of Harry

Wright, Frank Selee, Frank Chance, John J. McGraw, Connie Mack and all the great leaders, living and dead, of the game.

Too bad that he had to die in the full flush of his career. Too bad that, being dead, he can't read the encomiums now being passed upon by many of the same persons who once said of him that he would never do as a big-league manager, though happily he lived to hear most of them retract their judgment.

No man ever struggled harder for the laurels he earned as chief of a crew on the baseball grand circuit. No man was ever more patient under adversity and criticism. And no man ever more thoroughly put to flight his critics and vindicated the confidence his friends had in him. The results are in the records, and baseball judges its people on records.

There it stands—the Huggins score—and it is the measure of managerial greatness. Of baseball genius. A reticent, self-effacing little man, with none of the pomp and truculence attributed to some leaders. Huggins piloted a club, or rather a series of clubs, to all the triumphs that baseball has to offer, including a financial return to the owner beyond his wildest dream.

Huggins "Had" Something

Huggins always struck me as rather a pathetic figure in many ways early in his managerial career. He was inconspicuous in size and personality. He seemed to be a solitary chap, with few intimates. He wasn't much of a mixer. And for a long time there is no doubt that some of the high-priced giants that surrounded him viewed him with some contempt.

But the little man "had" something," no doubt of that. In time he came to win the respect of the haughtiest of his baseball players, and the admiration of the baseball fans, not only in New York City, the most critical baseball town in the land, but all around the big ring.

I don't need to say now that he knew his business. He proved that time and again in the only way you can prove it in baseball, which is by producing winners. True, he had a world of money at his command in building up his ball club, but it has been demonstrated over and over that mere money can't make a ball club. Money may buy the ballplayers, but it takes a manager to know what to do with them after they are bought.

Picked by Ruppert

I doubt that many persons know that Miller Huggins was made manager of the Yankees mainly on a personality that many people were never able to see until they knew him very well, but which appealed to one man in just one meeting.

That fan is Colonel Jacob Ruppert, owner of the Yankees. I happen to be familiar with the story, because I happened to be with Colonel Ruppert at the time he made the choice of Huggins. It was at a time when Colonel Tillinghast L. Huston was joint owner of the Yankee with Colonel Ruppert, and when Colonel Huston had gone to France with the engineers (during World War I), leaving Colonel Ruppert in complete charge of the club.

The Yankees were a pretty sad case at the time. They needed a manager, and they need ballplayers. They were occupying the Polo Grounds as tenants of the Giants, and they didn't have many followers. No one would then have ventured to predict that they would one day overshadow the National Leaguers in the baseball affections of the big town, and own their own mammoth baseball plant, and win pennants, and World Series, and play to as many as 80,000 clients.

Trip to Plattsburgh

Colonel Ruppert had taken a party of baseball writers on a trip by motor to Plattsburgh where the Yanks played an exhibition game for the soldiers there, the party including Sid Mercer, Bill Mac-Beth, Bill Farnsworth, and the writer, who rode in a car with the Colonel, while the others were in another car.

It was genuinely known that Colonel Ruppert was contemplating the selection of a new manager of the Yanks, and Bill Mac-Beth had received a cable from Colonel Huston in France only the day before the trip telling to urge upon Colonel Ruppert the merits of Wilbert Robinson, then managing the Brooklyn club. Colonel

Huston had also communicated his wishes to Colonel Ruppert of course, and in fact Colonel Ruppert had had some discussion with Wilbert Robinson on the subject.

But your Uncle Wilbert couldn't offer assurances that he was free to dicker with another organization, and in the meantime Miller Huggins had called on Colonel Ruppert, who had never met him before.

Huggins Gets Job

"There's something about the fellow I like," said Colonel Ruppert. "I like the business-like way he walked in on me, and the business-like way he talked to me. He's young—and he's business-like."

All the way to Plattsburgh he talked of Miller Huggins, not to me exactly, but more as if he were talking aloud to himself— as if he were arguing himself into favorable consideration of Huggins. It was a strange procedure. "I liked him," the Colonel kept saying, to which I could offer no comment, because I didn't know Huggins.

And when our party united at Ausable Chasm, Colonel Ruppert abruptly remarked to the others: "I'm going to make Miller Huggins manager of the Yankees. I like the fellow."

He had finally convinced himself with his arguments, it seemed. And he probably never regretted the decision, though it is said the selection of Huggins has something to do with the eventual split between Colonel Ruppert and Colonel Huston.

And all the days that Miller Huggins was manager of the Yankees, Colonel Ruppert upheld stoutly in everything that he did. The selection of Huggins was in a measure snap-judgment, but the Colonel never wavered from that judgment.

As far as Colonel Ruppert was concerned, Huggins could do no wrong, and the great plant beyond the Harlem, and the value of the Yanks' franchise today, and the Huggins' Yanks' place in baseball history proves that the dead man was a pretty fair choice, any way you take him.

—

JOHN McGRAW

The great John McGraw was a deadball legend and manager of the Giants for a generation. To Runyon, he became both a friend, and, as a member of the theatrical Lambs Club, an entré to the nightlife and Broadway scene that the young writer would later glorify.

❈　❈　❈

Here is Runyon on the eve of the 1923 World Series—the third straight Giants–Yankees' World Series.

The "Master Mind"—McGraw's Hard Task
(Oct. 9, 1923)

Our young friend, Mr. Arthur Robinson, enthusiastic authority in baseball, leans over and suggest that the World Series will be McGraw vs. Babe Ruth—the "Master Mind against Brute Force."

It is young Mr. Robinson's idea that if McGraw, sitting on the bench of the Giants, can transmit to his pitchers certain strategy in pitching to Ruth, the big slugger of the Yankees will be helpless, the Giants will win.

It is an interesting thought.

But McGraw himself cannot do the pitching to Ruth.

The baseball brain must be turned on Ruth SECOND HAND. That makes McGraw's task very difficult.

❈　❈　❈

Intelligence—a "master mind"—cannot offset brute force.

Put a gorilla in a stout cage, and an intelligent man standing

OUTSIDE the cage could easily devise a method of destroying the gorilla without harm to himself.

But if the man went inside the cage with the gorilla, all the intelligence in the world couldn't save the man.

Of course in this case the value of intelligence as opposed to brute force would be in the fact that intelligence would keep the man from going into the cage.

❖ ❖ ❖

McGraw, sitting on the bench of the Giants, with Ruth at bat, may see some method of outhitting the slugger.

But McGraw cannot personally execute the method.

He must explain it to his pitcher. If the pitcher doesn't also have a "master mind," what will happen?

That is on the knees of the baseball gods.

"(John) McGraw was without doubt the most picturesque figure in the past twenty-five years of baseball, bar nobody," Runyon write in a remembrance after the death of the longtime Giants' skipper. "More than any other man, he came to personify New York—the Big Town. When he marched onto alien territory at the head of his victorious men in the heyday of his career, the populace turned out to revile him, which was exactly what McGraw wanted."

❖ ❖ ❖

Record Books Give Truest Slant in McGraw
(Feb. 26, 1933)

As Player, "Mac" Revolutionized Mechanics of Third-Base Play

MIAMI—Baseball's record books furnish the truest estimate of the career of John J. McGraw.

"Figures do not lie," he used to say in a baseball argument. So in the tomes of the National League you find in figures, more enduring than brass, the history of his tremendous achievements on the diamond.

A great all-around individual player himself in the days when he was a scrawny kid with the famous Baltimore Orioles, and revolutionized the mechanics of third-base play, he became the mightiest leader of his time, winning pennant after pennant, for the New York Giants, and doing more than any one man to make baseball the big money proposition that it was down through the '20s.

Picturesque Figure

McGraw was without doubt the most picturesque figure in the past twenty-five years of baseball, bar nobody. More than any other man he came to personify New York—the Big Town. When he marched onto alien territory at the head of his victorious men in the heyday of his career, the populace turned out to revile him, which was exactly what McGraw wanted.

He loved to bait the enemy fans—to make them hate and fear the baseball prowess of his Giants. He was the center of every baseball tornado of his day, his hand against baseball executives and umpires, and everyone else that had the temerity to question the diamond dominance of the Big Town club.

A short, pudgy, cocky man, with a truculent manner, on and off the diamond, he reigned supreme as "The Little Napoleon" across the longest stretch of the tome that has yet to be allotted to a baseball leader. Only in the sere and yellow of his baseball days were they able to clip the wings of the stormy petrel.

And even then, he left behind him enough of a legacy in the New York Giants to convince the fans of Manhattan Island that something of his old-time cunning remained to him when he relinquished the leadership of the club.

Foundation Remains

There is still much of McGraw in the foundation of the world's champions of today.

I traveled with McGraw and his clubs over a period of nearly 10 years, and they were the clubs with which he rose to his greatest triumphs, especially his three-time winners of 1911, 1912 and 1913.

That was before the days of the lively ball, and the stand-still-and-swing type of baseball, and when McGraw was apostle of speed. I think he never became reconciled to the new ball, and the passing of base running, and baseball strategy.

He was a big-leaguer every way from the Jack. He thought big league, and he talked big league. His ball clubs traveled first cabin, stopping at the finest hotels. He encouraged his young men to wear good clothes. He impressed upon them the distinction of being a member of the New York Giants.

He asked no quarter and gave none to his enemies. On the other hand, he could be an extremely good friend.

He took his baseball as a personal and very serious matter. The winning of baseball games was his business and his passion. He disliked losing about as much as any man that ever lived, and yet in the big conflicts, like the World Series, he was a good loser. He was always first to congratulate his conqueror.

Ever Big Spender

From the time he first came into the big league McGraw was a big spender. Back in the days when his salary of $18,000 as manager of the Giants was considered terrific, and later when he came into real big money, he always had a gang around him and he was a star check-grabber.

He loved the good things of life. He loved to play the races, and few men would bet more on a horse than McGraw. That was about his only gambling, however, bar an occasional bet on a fight. He liked boxing, and was an excellent judge of a boxer.

In fact, there are few things in this life in the way of entertainment that McGraw did not like. He enjoyed the theatre, and probably had a larger personal acquaintance among theatrical people than any non-professional on Broadway. He lived life right up to the hilt, and he got his laughs as he went along in his younger days. Of late years, he had been much more sedate.

Good Sense of Humor

He had many a personal battle in his career, and for some reason was generally the loser. In fact at one time the roster of his defeats in street encounters was a standing joke on Broadway. But the point is he never ducked a fight. He was game as a pebble, whatever his physical shortcomings. He had a lot of fight on the baseball field, too, and usually came out second best.

I have known McGraw to afterwards laugh heartily at some of these encounters. He had a pretty good sense of humor, even when the joke was on himself. He had a marvelous memory, and was a great raconteur. I was with him on the trip around the word when the Giants would up playing the White Sox in the presence of the King in London. McGraw always considered a talk he had that day with the ruler of England one of his greatest experiences.

Of all the ballplayers with whom he was associated, he considered Christy Mathewson the greatest. Their friendship was very close. In the earlier years of his career as manager of the Giants he always had his old pal of his Oriole days, Wilbert Robinson, with him, Robbie afterwards going to the Brooklyn club.

(Wilbert) Robinson; Joe Kelly, the old outfielder; Sadie McMahon, pitcher; Steve Brodie, outfielder; Ned Hanlon, manager; and a few others of the Orioles still survive, but McGraw has gone to join Hughie Jennings and Arlie Pond, and all the other heroes of that glorious baseball day who have been called out by the Great Umpire.

They will be a long time turning up another John J. McGraw.

———

RUBE MARQUARD

In 1908, the Giants paid a then unheard-of price of $11,000 for minor-league left-hander Richard "Rube" Marquard. Compiling only nine wins in his first three years, the 6'3" stringbean was labeled "the $11,000 Lemon" before turning it around, and teaming with Christy Mathewson to lead to Giants to three straight pennants from 1911 to 1913, and winning 25, 27, and 24 in those seasons.

Marquard did so by combining a devastating curve with a Mathewson-taught screwball, and in 1912 earned wins in his first 19 decisions that remains a major-league record for consecutive-win record. In 1913 Marquard more than proved his mettle as a Runyon "guy" by marrying vaudeville star Blossom Seeley. It would take a while, but after 205 big-league wins, Cooperstown finally came calling, in 1971.

❖ ❖ ❖

Here, Runyon describes Marquard's 19th straight win. Marquard would go 26-11 in 1912, winning two more games that fall in the World Series against the Red Sox.

"Reuben" Is Rocketed to Victory in Nineteenth (July 4, 1912)

McGraw's Wonderful Southpaw Needs Horseshoes to Defeat "Nap" Rucker—Sixteen Straight for Giants

You can plainly see by the dawn's early light that the star-sprinkled Rube Marquard still proudly way-haves.

In fact, if the light is early enough it will catch him perched up yonder on the highest eminence, as we figure baseballic altitude, ever attained by a big-league pitcher; gasping a little from his recent exertions, perhaps, and slightly dazzled as he contemplates the resistance to the ground, but there—there with his legs dangling over.

Sheer good luck rocketed the wry-cheeked Reuben into his 19th straight victory yesterday afternoon when he beat Brooklyn by a score of 2 to 1, with the great Napoleon Rucker his opponent. Outpitched by the Georgia left-hander from start to finish, as proven by every angle of the figures on the game, and as was shown in the actual playing, the New York sensation managed to pull through and establish what is now conceded to be the greatest pitching record for consecutive victories by a pitcher in the history of baseball.

So many statements have been made regarding that consecutive victory record, and so many claims have been made for this and that hero of the past, that only a cockeyed man could keep track of the matter, but very recently eminent authorities on the game have gone down into the catacombs of history, carefully explored each nook and corner, and as carefully dusted and examined every scrap of evidence that came to light. The verdict, duly sworn and attested, is that the greatest number of consecutive wins by any pitchers back to Noah, and the days of the Arafat League, was 18.

This mark has been held jointly by Pat Luby, of Chicago, and Charley Radbourne. Some have claimed that Luby won 20 straight in 1890, but Eminent Authorities declare they are unable to locate any proof of the fact. They are willing to entertain any evidence that may have submitted, but unless Luby's lunge can be definitely established by figures, dates and things at over 18, Rube's run will stand as the greatest of all time — greatest by virtue of amazing luck yesterday afternoon.

Rucker Lacked Luck

Consider:

Rucker allowed but four hits against Marquard's nine; Rucker walked but one man, to Rube's four; Rucker struck out five to Rube's two.

Some people would like to be born lucky, as "Kin" Hubbard might put it, but others would Rube Marquard.

That same sort of luck was with the Giants, as a while throughout the afternoon, as they took both games of a doubleheader from (Dodger manager Bill) Dahlen's crowd, winning the second, and their 16th straight by a score of 10 to 9 in a rough-house sort of game, in which they were also out-hit by a wide margin. The Giants now have but one more to win to tie the Washington run of 17 consecutive victories — the best of the year in either league.

That the wonderful left-hander felt the strain of his attempt to break the best record hung up by the pitchers of all time, was manifest. He seemed nervous, and had little of the control, which had marked his good games. Neither did the ball break for him as usual, but it was probably all due to the fact that he considered this the great effort of his life, and was working at abnormal tension.

Rucker, with no more at stake than he would have in any other game, unless he placed some value upon the distinction of stopping the Rube's remarkable run, was cool and collected and pitched wonderful ball. Long regarded as one of the very greatest left-handers in the game, the Marietta marvel displayed his class yesterday, and the 18,000 people present applauded him time and again as he left the box.

The toughest break against him came in the fourth inning, when with the Dodgers a run ahead, "Red" Smith made a poor throw to (Jake) Daubert on (Jack "Red") Murray's grounder. That error gave McGraw a slight advantage, and he promptly seized it. He pulled an unexpected move on the Brooklynites when he sent Murray to steal second on the first ball Rucker pitched to Beals Beckers, Jack pulling up safely in a cloud of dist. Young Otto Miller, the Dodger catcher, had been holding the fleet Giants up fairly well throughout the game, too, but McGraw took the chance, and it contributed largely to Rube's victory.

Becker lifted an infield fly, which would have been easy for Daubert, (John) Hummel or Rucker himself—anybody but (shortstop Bert) Tooley or (third baseman Red) Smith. Tooley yelled that he would take it, however, and dashed through the box. He muffed the ball and then kicked it clear out of the diamond. Murray scored, tying the count and Becker took third. Miller reached clear into the left end of the press box and got (Buck) Herzog's foul, ending that inning.

Murray opened the seventh with a slashing drive to left center. Zach Wheat made a strong try for the ball, but it went for two bases. Becker bunted, and Rucker handled the ball with too much deliberation. He did not count on Beals' speed, and his throw to Daubert was a mere toss. Becker was safe and Murray took third. Herzog flied out to (Herbie) Moran, whose throw to the plate held Murray at third. Meyers smashed a long fly to Wheat, and

Murray crossed the plate with the winning run. Becker was out stealing.

❊   ❊   ❊

All streaks end eventually—and on July 8, 1912, Marquard dropped a 7-2 decision to the Cubs in Chicago after 19 straight wins. Runyon wasn't on the trip, but offered this analysis, triggered in part by the debate Marquard's streak touched off about the relative merits of present players versus the old-timers.

Old-Time Baseball Stars Entitled to Most Credit (July 9, 1912)

Modern Tendency to Discredit Work of Great Performers of Long Ago

Old-time fans seem to feel that there is a modern-day tendency to discredit the work of the baseball stars of the long ago. The arguments over Rube Marquard have probably been largely responsible for the development of this feeling. As a matter of fact, the old-timers of the game are entitled to much more credit for their accomplishments than their modern successors, just as the pioneers who blazed the path through the wilderness are entitled to more credit than the descendants who live in peace and quiet as a result of the achievements of their forebearers.

It would be idle to say that Marquard's record approaches that of Charley Radbourne, when it is considered that Radbourne made his run of 18 straight victories practically on consecutive days. The style of pitching, or the distance pitched, makes no particular difference—the physical and mental effort was there. It would be equally idle to contend that any modern-day ball club will match the record of the (Cincinnati) Red Stockings of '69 and '70. The base running of the (Arlie) Lathams and (Billy) Hamiltons and (Harry) Stoveys of the bygone time will probably never be touched by the modern-day players.

Certain it is, too, that not many of the catchers of today would stand the gaff that the old-timers took—catching day in and day out without gloves or protectors.

Sufficient Glory for All

Rube Marquard is a marvelous pitcher and has hung up a record that will probably stand for many years to come; he will probably be remembered for his work as long as they play baseball, but so, too, will the (John) Clarksons and the (Charles) Radbournes, and there is sufficient glory for all in the eras they represent.

But as for belittling the work of the old-time stars—NO, I wasn't there to see them, but I've been told, and I believe.

"Rube" Marquard Pitches First No-Hit, No-Run Contest of New Season (Apr. 16, 1915)

Giants Shut Out Dodgers; Score 2 to 0; McGraw's Sterling Southpaw Invincible in Duel with Nap Rucker, Star of the Brooklyns; Only Three Losers Reach First Base off Marquard

What is a dramatic moment in baseball? Well—

The ninth inning has come on up at the Polo Grounds and no Brooklyn player has ever made a safe hit off the pitching of Marquard—the lean, left-handed, wry-necked "Rube" Marquard. The score is 2–0 in favor of the Giants.

Two of the Brooklyn men have been retired in that ninth inning and Zack Wheat, dangerous long-distance hitter, is at bat. The voice of the rotund (umpire Cy) Rigler drones out his decisions—a strike—a ball—another strike—another ball—his arms rising and falling, first on one side and then on the other, like semaphores.

Two strikes and two balls is the count of the batsmen; then, with the next moment containing the possibility of one of the greatest of all pitching feats—or just a baseball game. And that's the moment that somehow appeals to our sense of the dramatic in baseball—or, at least, that's the way it appealed to us in that ninth inning up at the Polo Grounds yesterday afternoon.

The thin, leathery left arm of the skinny side-winder curls upward and back like a coiling whiplash, then suddenly snaps outward and downward. Hip-high the ball comes hopping in at Wheat. His long bat whirls like a bandmaster's baton, and—what's this?

Almost Becomes Nervous

Are these our feet that are shuffling nervously along the concrete floor of the press stand? Is this our blood that is crackling through arteries long since supposed to have been baseballically hardened in the heat of many a schedule of 154 games each? Is this excitement or just second childhood?

Well, well! The game is over. Rube Marquard goes rushing over toward first base, his long body bent like a figure 8 as his hands scoop up the easy roller from Wheat's bat, and he tosses the ball to Fred Merkle, then turns and flees toward the clubhouse, pursued by his fellow players who pound him on the back with enthusiastic fists.

Vaguely it occurred to us that someone should do a little pounding on the broad back of the sawed-off, hammered-down Hans Lobert, as his brief legs carried him swiftly across the greensward to the shower bath. Vaguely it occurred to us the back-pounded Marquard himself would be the proper person to pound the back of Lobert, for we still retained a picture of the Pennsylvania Dutchman as his marvelous stabs and more marvelous throws in the lee of the long Rube yesterday—but the game is over. The score remained as stated—2 to 0.

The game is over, and we remain seated in the press box, blushing over the memory of our inward stirrings at that moment when the "Rube's" no-hit game seemed so near and yet so far away. Withal, we do not feel ashamed.

Situation Causes Thrill

We are no hero-worshipper, mark you, we are oft-times bored from over-much baseball, and we have cultivated astigmatism from peering through that wire mesh; moreover, we have seen other and better no-hit games than that of yesterday, but we trust that we shall never become so blasé that we cannot feel that bit of a thrill that properly goes with such a situation as we have described.

You cannot feel it? Ah, well, then! We have failed to transmute our sensations into words, that's all. You would have felt it had you been there, being human and all that.

A no-hit game, if you don't know, is a baseball pitcher's card of admission to the gallery of baseball immortals. A no-hit game may not be much to look at; oft-times it is the dullest of all manner of baseball games from the spectator's standpoint; but a man may live a lifetime around baseball yards and never seen one performed.

The no-hit game pitched by "Rube" Marquard yesterday was not a perfect edition of the species, because three men reached first base on him; but it was sufficient to give him permanent place in the annals of the game along with some of the greatest stars of the past.

Few Real No-Hit Games

In all the years of baseball only seven men have pitched perfect no-hit games, where a runner failed to reach first. In all the years of baseball only 76 pitchers have turned in no-hit games of all descriptions. Yesterday was Marquard's first appearance this season and the Giants' second game.

Oddly enough, on April 15, 1909 in the opening game of the season against the Brooklyn cub, Leon ("Red") Ames, now with the Cincinnati Reds, held the Dodgers for nine innings without a hit or run, only to finally see the game lost by the Giants in the 13th inning.

The Rube was pitching yesterday against Napoleon Rucker, the famous old Brooklyn left-hander, who himself took a chair in the no-hit circle (in 1908), the very year that Marquard came into the National League as the highest-priced player known to the game.

If a rather tricky memory serves, it was against the crafty veteran from beyond the tubes that Marquard pitched the 19th and last game of his long run of consecutive victories in 1912: It was, in fact—relying in that capricious memory aforesaid—against Rucker that Rube began his run.

Wouldn't you know it? Later that season, Marquard, three times a 20-game winner for the Giants in the previous four years, would be sold to Brooklyn. He'd play nearly six years with the Robins, helping them to the pennant in 1916. Although Marquard would never match his previous glory with the Giants, he compiled 205 wins in the big leagues and, in 1971, was elected to the Hall of Fame.

—

TRIS SPEAKER

In his day, Tris Speaker was lionized as a great outfielder and leader; he managed the 1920 Cleveland Indians to the World Series title.

The Greatest Outfielder (May 18, 1915)

Not long ago we had a query from a feverish fan who wanted to know what outfielder we regarded as the greatest in the game, considering him just as an outfielder and without any reference to hitting.

We never had an opportunity of replying to the query, as we encountered that fan up at the Polo Grounds during the Yankee-Red Sox series and he announced:

"You needn't pay any attention to my question now. I know the answer myself."

He had been watching Tris Speaker, of Hubbard, Texas, in action.

Great Is Tris

Tris Speaker is assuredly the name we would have employed in answering the query. In our humble judgment no other outfielder in either league approaches the marvelous "Spoke" in the business of outfielding. No one who saw the Yank-Sox series here is likely to soon forget the exhibition of the great Texan.

They saw him run down and subdue a ground ball which was headed for a remote corner of the left centre field and which no other outfielder could have reached with a lasso; they saw him take the ball like an infielder, then turn and by a grand throw hold a fast runner to second. They saw him make one of the greatest catches of a fly ball ever seen at the Polo Grounds, cutting off what seemed a certain home run.

Shifting his position with every batsman to such a degree of nicety that he never once failed to call the turn, Tris showed that he studies the opposing hitters with remarkable care. Only one Yank had him guessing, and that was Walter Pipp, a free hitter, with a long-distance punch in his bat. Tris played Pipp dead center, trusting to his ability to go to either side after Walter's drives. A great artist, this Texas fellow, when it comes to playing his field, so great that he stands out almost all alone in that department.

One Grand Club

An old-timer spent a couple of afternoons watching the Lone Star Ranger patrol center and a large portion of right and left fields, and he remarked:

"If I had a ball club, consisting of just Speaker, poor old Rube Waddell, and a catcher, I could win the pennant in either league. The opposition couldn't ever hit Rube, and if they did they couldn't hit past Tris."

—

MIKE DONLIN

Mike Donlin didn't walk. He strutted, earning his nickname, "Turkey Mike." He could hit, too, and in 12 big-league seasons, most of them spent with the Giants, he compiled a .333 batting average, while charming everyone he met with his baritone voice, colorful stories and marriage to a movie star named Mabel Hite. "Turkey Mike" eventually opted for the movies as well, and after his baseball career ended in 1914, he spent many years in Hollywood.

Mike's Homer Was Like an Old-Timer (July 19, 1911)
Donlin Drives Ball into Bleachers for Circuit Clout, but Redlegs Take the Game

Viva la Mique Donlin, anyway!

Mique pecked a home run into the rightfield bleachers at the Polo Grounds yesterday afternoon, after (Clark) Griffith's Cuban Stouts had built up the foundation and superstructure of an 8 to 2 score, the said home run keeping it from being 8 to 1.

So viva la Mique!

The rest of the vivas must go to Cuba, and Germany and Cincinnati, and the other countries represented in Griff's cosmopolitan aggregation, which he prodded into sufficient life to lower the lilies of France, borne by our distinguished scion of Marseilles and Cleveland, Richard de Reuben de Marquis Marquard.

The Donlin thump flashed across a somber afternoon like a ray of gentle sunshine. The late Thespian struck for Reuben in the eighth and belted the ball, high and dry, into a niche in the center-tier of seats—as fine a blow as was ever dealt in a goodly cause. The cause happened to be all in at that writing but a run is a run any way you look at it.

And, runs being extremely scarce yesterday, and loud wails of anguish arose from the stands as they drew mental pictures of the terrible disaster brought upon our fair city by this defeat.

And yet, all is not lost.

There are various nice technical outs for the Giants, none of which can be called to mind right quick, suffice it to say, however, that they had a nice day for it, anyway, and being in third place is better than fourth.

Fates Were Against Marquard

Richard de Marquis lost a game. True, this has become such a rare occurrence that it is surprising, but it cannot be viewed in the light of a calamity while excuses hold out to burn. When all the nations of the globe are combined against a lone Frenchman, it stands to reason that Frenchie is in for a shade the worst of it, and it may be that after Richard took one flash at the Griffith bench he became alarmed.

Cuba, in the guise of one (Armando) Marsans, centerfielder, did right nobly throughout the afternoon, to the deep satisfaction of the editor of the *Havana Ed Mundo,* who is following the deviating course of the island players around the torrid ring, but it was not Cuba alone, which freed Cincinnati from the shackles of a slump, and preserved C. Griffith's situation from the hands of the infuriated rabble back home until nightfall.

Robert Keefe, the attenuated youth who used to be a Yankee, out on the Hilltop, and who has been to New York this season what Mathewson is to Cincinnati, pitched for the Redlegs, and did it so well that you can see it for yourself by the score. What few hits the Giants collected were far between, while the Redlegs had on their swatting make-ups and his Marquard with such fury and effect that they made six more runs than the Giants.

Errors back of the Reuben assisted them to some extent, and after the Reds had taken a long jump the Giants seemed to slump a bit in both offense and defense.

"Turkey Mike" Drops In. Back to His Old Town. Started with St. Louis. Is Now in the Movies. A Rare Old Character. (Oct. 11, 1926)

I think of all the old-timers who bobbed up in St. Louis for the World's Series, the one who had the best time was Mike Donlin—"Turkey Mike"—who began his baseball career years ago in the very city where he was pounded almost out of shape a few days ago by the back-slapping of old friends.

It has been a long time since "Turkey Mike" appeared in baseball circles. He had been out on the Pacific Coast working in the movies, and he recently gained renewed fame by the statement of a caring director to whom he had applied for a part in a baseball picture that "he wasn't the type for a ballplayer." It seems the director didn't know "Turkey Mike."

The years have thinned him down to some extent, and put a few streaks of gray in his hair. He was always a wiry, dapper fellow. The dapperness came in the later years of his baseball career, however. Before that, he was a rough-and-tumble, devil-may-care sort, a rootin,' tootin,' cuttin,' shootin' son-of-a-gun from Butte, you might say.

Only he didn't come from Butte. He came from California and he was recommended to the St. Louis Nationals of nearly 30 years back as a left-handed pitcher. He was said to have been the wildest left-hander the world has ever seen.

❊   ❊   ❊

"I'm not a pitcher; I'm a hitsmith," proclaimed Mike, and as a "hit-smith" he achieved his fame. He was one of the greatest hitters the game has ever known. He would be one of those $200,000 ballplayers today.

In St. Louis "Turkey Mike" met the man responsible for him coming to the big league, John B. Sheridan, the famous old-time baseball writer, who wore a flaming red necktie in honor of the Cardinals, and who was being affectionately greeted by all the veterans.

It seems that a man who was in jail wrote to Sheridan about "Turkey Mike," and Sheridan passed the news on to the management of the St. Louis club. Mike cost about $500, which was no inconsiderable sum for those days. In St. Louis, at Cincinnati, at Baltimore, with the Orioles, and finally with the New York Giants, "Turkey Mike" Donlin made his name in baseball history.

He was afterwards with the Braves and Pittsburgh, but that was when his baseball glory had faded. He could hit to the last. In fact, "Turkey Mike" coyly claims that he can still hit. He narrates playing with an Old-Timers' team out on the Coast not long ago and getting a two-bagger. Then he got caught napping off second because his legs wouldn't function under him.

More than most of the old-timers has "Turkey Mike's" fame been preserved even unto the present generation. The young baseball writers in the grillroom of the Hotel Jefferson, where Sam Breadon, the St. Louis magnate, had established headquarters, were greeting him as effusively as the old-timers.

❊   ❊   ❊

"Turkey Mike" was the most picturesque, colorful baseball player I ever saw. He had more color than that mighty man, George Herman Babe Ruth. It is a sure thing that Mike had the greatest personal acquaintance and following of any player the game has ever known.

He was at his best as a member of the Giants, because Mike somehow belonged to the big town. He loved the theatrical profession, married into it, and was an actor of no small ability himself. He played in the famous "Turn to the Right" before he went into pictures, and had considerable vaudeville experience.

Mike was always a cosmopolitan, a good dresser, a glib talker and a great mixer. In these times he would be drawing one of the biggest salaries in baseball, because he always knew what he was worth. He got big money for a ballplayer in the days when it was the exception instead of the rule, as at present.

"Turkey Mike" came East to play a part in a new baseball movie and is returning to the Pacific Coast at once. He had not even seen a big-league baseball game for years, and his eyes at once lighted on one of the Cardinals as his favorite type of a ballplayer—Jim Bottomley, the first baseman.

It may have been no more than a coincidence, but a lot of people have been remarking that Jim Bottomley somehow reminds them of some old-timer by his walk and manner, and I can now tell them the name of the old-timer they are trying to recall.

It is "Turkey Mike" Donlin.

Runyon called Turkey Mike Donlin hands-down the most colorful of all the thousands of ballplayers he covered. That's high praise from a man who glorified the colorful and eccentric.

❖   ❖   ❖

A Streak of Bad Luck for "Turkey Mike" (May 12, 1927)

"Turkey Mike" Donlin, one of the greatest baseball players that ever wore a cleated shoe and one of the most picturesque characters ever produced by the old game, has come upon a streak of bad luck.

He is ill at his home in Hollywood and, as only too often happens, when a fellow encounters illness, the exchequer is a trifle short. One of the proudest men you ever saw and sensitive, Mike kept his troubles to himself until one of his friends recently became apprised of the true state of affairs.

Now a testimonial has been launched out in Los Angeles, the objective being to send Mike up to the Mayos in Rochester, Minn., to ascertain the exact nature and extent of his illness, and a coterie of gentlemen, the likes of which probably never before banded together for a cause of this nature, is in charge of the matter.

John Barrymore, the actor, is chairman of a committee that has charge of the testimonial, which will be held at the Philharmonic Auditorium in Los Angeles, June 9. He is one of "Turkey Mike's" oldest friends and admirers.

"Macks" Rally to Call for Help

In the meantime, world of Mike's situation has reached New York, and his old manager, John J. McGraw, and Willard Mack, the playwright, and other friends were preparing to start something here when they heard of the Los Angeles enterprise. Now they are lending their efforts to making that a complete success.

It would not only have been necessary for Mike to hint at his troubles any time to start immediate action among his old friends in the East, but that wouldn't be Mike. He never asked the world for anything but an even break in his life. He was always helping someone else in his heyday, but he never intimated he might need help himself.

On the committee with John Barrymore are Otis Harlan, Winnie Sheehan, John Considine, Jr., Mark Kelly, Jim Young, B.L. Frank, Jack Gardner, Lewis B. Garvey, Tom Mix, Felix Adler, Dr. H.W. Martin, Paul Nicholson, David H. Thompson, Victor Schertzinger, Ben Harris, Patrick J. Cooney and George O'Brien of Los Angeles.

J.M. Dodge of San Diego; Dan Flannery of San Jose; Eddie Graney of San Francisco; Bill Hanlon of Sacramento; Jimmy Callahan of Chicago; Otto Floto of Denver; Joe Humphries of New York; and Lou Houseman and Harry Bailey are also members.

Callahan, Another Old Pal, on Job

It is a line-up of familiar names, mainly motion-picture and sporting people. Not many baseballers among them aside from Mike's old pal, Jimmy Callahan, of Chicago. They played together, lived together and fought together for years when they were young fellows.

But the call will get many a response form the eastern baseball world, where "Turkey Mike" was admired and loved beyond any man that ever played baseball in the big town, with the possible exception of Christy Mathewson.

I have never seen another ballplayer of Mike's color and personality. Babe Ruth may be able to hit more home runs, but Babe never had quite the appeal to me as a showman that Mike did. No one who ever saw him will forget that walk of Mike's moving to the plate.

He could hit—few better. He always smacked that old apple right on the nose, hard and far. No ballplayer of my experience had any more natural batting grace than Mike. He was a bold and truculent fellow in his baseball prime, always in jams with the umpires, desperate in his efforts to win baseball games.

Broke in as Crazy Southpaw Twirler

But no umpire ever harbored any hard feeling against Mike after the pastiming was over. He lived and loved baseball from the time he broke in as a crazy southpaw pitcher from a California town until the day, many years later, he pulled off his big-league shoes for the last time.

He was one of the best-known figures on Broadway in his time. He fitted naturally into the big-town picture. He loved the theatre. He followed the races, and no greater fistic fan ever lived.

He was of the era of the old Metropole, of Rector's, and Shanley's, and of Hammerstein's theatre. Young and spirited and always nattily dressed and twirling a light bamboo stick, "Turkey Mike" was one of the big white line as much as he was of the baseball diamond.

I never knew a man who had more friends. When his baseball

days were over and he went out to Hollywood and the pictures, he took with him all his old personality, as is evidenced by the members of that committee that is now working to help a pal in distress.

———

WILBERT ROBINSON

Make that "Your Uncle" Wilbert Robinson, the onetime Baltimore Oriole great turned Brooklyn Dodger manager, whose kindly ways and portly stature make him seem to Runyon, like, well, your uncle.

Vance Is Speediest. So Says Uncle Wilbert.
No Man Was Ever Faster. Mathewson Stood Alone.
He Had Pitching Brains. (Oct. 6, 1928)

Your Uncle Wilbert Robinson, president and field manager of the Brooklyn Dodgers, of the National League, has been around in baseball for quite some semesters. He is rising 60-odd, and over 40 years of his life have been devoted to the national pastime.

You would not think your Uncle Wilbert lugs so many years to see him at this ease—a portly, comfortable well-fed man, bulging with life and buoyance, and talking of his dogs and hunting with youthful enthusiasm. A great old boy is Your Uncle Wilbert, who has lived young, and will die young.

He was calling on his friend Joe Heintzman of Cincinnati in the Hotel Belmont in New York the other evening, and with him was bosom pal, Colonel Tillinghast L'Hommedieu Huston, formerly one of the owners of the Yankees who sold his half-interest in the club to his partner, Colonel Jake Ruppert, and retired to a life of more of less leisure.

Colonel Tillinghast L'Hommedieu Huston bought a yacht and spends his winters with Your Uncle Wilbert cruising the southern waters. They generally wind up at Dover Hall, hard by Brunswick, Georgia, a hunting preserve long the haunt of the baseball folk.

❖　❖　❖

The passing from baseball of Colonel Tillinghast L'Hommedieu Huston was something of a calamity, I believe. He was not a baseball man in the beginning; he was a civil engineer, but he brought a lot of horse sense to the game that he has done it much good ever since. He is one of the men largely responsible for the salvation of baseball in the dark days of the Black Sox scandals.

There have been many rumors that Colonel Tillinghast L'Hommedieu Huston might again return to baseball, but these, I think, are groundless. He is a rich man. He served his country in two wars and he is taking a long rest. He is one of the few men I know who has learned how to live.

But that is not what I started to out to talk about. I started out to give you Your Uncle Wilbert Robinson's idea of the speediest right-handed pitcher he ever saw. And to show you how young Your Uncle Wilbert thinks, it is not some old dodo of other days that he has in mind, but a pitcher of the present, Dazzy Vance of the Dodgers.

Dazzy Vance got away to a bad start this year after a sensational season in 1925. Toward the close of the present season, however, he was going great guns and wound up by striking out 15 opponents.

❖　❖　❖

"I put him beyond any right-handed pitcher I've ever seen in my experience in baseball," said Your Uncle Wilbert Robinson. "And I've seen them all. Yes, it is a sure thing he has more speed."

"More than Walter Johnson?" I asked.

"More than what I've seen of Johnson," replied Your Uncle Wilbert.

"More than Amos Rusie?" I queried, rather vaguely, going back to a right-hander that the old-timers have always told me was "tops" in the matter of speed.

"Yes, more than Rusie," said Your Uncle Wilbert firmly. Of

course, Rusie was more of a curveball pitcher than Dazzy, who is strictly a fastballer.

"More than old Cy Young?" I persisted, going back to still another marvel of other days.

"Far more," said Your Uncle Wilbert.

"I am not saying he is the smartest pitcher I've ever seen," Your Uncle Wilbert continued. "If he had Christy Mathewson's head out there on the mound he would be an absolute marvel, but Dazzy isn't quite that type. But when it comes to burning 'em over, he is in a class by himself, and you can go back to the earliest days of the game and not find his superior."

❀   ❀   ❀

Your Uncle Wilbert undoubtedly made Dazzy Vance a great pitcher. "The Dazzler" had been with the Yankees and other clubs before Your Uncle Wilbert got hold of him and was not accounted a sensation. He always had the "stuff," but he didn't know what to do with it until Your Uncle Wilbert showed him.

As a coach of pitchers, the old president-manager of the Dodgers stands out. He knows how to get the most out of a pitcher's style and "stuff." He has made good pitchers out of bad pitchers. He had a weak-hitting team this past season, but the absence of Vance early in the year is probably all that accounted for the Dodgers ending up in the second division.

Uncle Wilbert said: "I always thought one of the best right-handed curveball pitchers I ever saw was "Red" Leon Ames of the Giants some years back. Ames had a world of stuff, but was always bothered by one bad fault: He let the ball get away from him too soon. He mastered that fault after some years, and few men could pitch better when he was right.

"Mathewson?" Uncle Wilbert asked. "There was only one Mathewson. I doubt that any other pitcher ever lived who was in his class for sheer pitching brains. He knew how. He may not have had more stuff than a lot of other pitchers, but he could make it seem like twice as much. He was a wonder. I wouldn't mind having a couple of Mathewsons for my club next season. I could use a pennant in 1927."

———

ARNOLD ROTHSTEIN

How odd that Runyon didn't put together a piece on the notorious gambler and alleged mastermind of the 1919 World Series fix Arnold Rothstein until November 7—three days after the mobster had been gunned down outside the Park Central Hotel. Not only was Runyon with Rothstein some hours before he was shot, but the story came after days of headlines in the papers that outlined every aspect of the incident. Even more curious, he filed the story from Baltimore.

Runyon's piece remains a marvel—informative and surprisingly critical, considering how he is noted for glorifying the gamblers and con men of Broadway. Although Runyon had long given up drinking by this time, he was still a gambler himself. Rothstein was shot after a poker game gone bad. His killer was never found.

Life Not Worth White Chip, Yet Rothstein Had No Fear (Nov. 7, 1928)

BALTIMORE—Life, for the average man who is active in his own affairs, is about even money.

That is to say, when he walks out of his door in the morning it is 50–50 that he will return safe and sound.

A gentleman was arguing to the contrary with me last night. He holds that everything is 6–5 against, no matter what the proposition.

I recall that the late Mr. Dion O'Bannon, the Chicago Robin Hood, remarked to me on occasion that it was 4–1 at any season of the year that the snow wouldn't fly on his back.

But in those days, Mr. O'Bannion seemed a little pessimistic. And in any event it was a price.

Odds Against Him

Arnold Rothstein is the only man I ever encountered who was "NO PRICE." When he stepped beyond his threshold he was "out" in the betting.

It was regarded as a sure thing that he would be "scragged" sooner or later, that a gambler wouldn't lay you a quarter on him, especially in late years. A Chicago "whiz bang" was a better risk.

"Rothstein can't miss," was the brief comment of his associates. Meaning that he couldn't miss getting killed. And no one could tell you exactly why. They called him "jocularly," "the master mind" and the "Brain" because his name came to be mentioned in every piece of skull-duggery that happened in the underworld or in sport.

Ninety-nine percent of the mention was wrong.

Rothstein was too smart to permit himself to become connected up with criminal transactions. He may have bankrolled bootleggers, or other mobsters, but you can bet he had no part of the play.

That he engineered many a tremendous gambling coup there is no doubt. Gambling may be illegal, but it doesn't seem to be regarded as criminal. Some called him, not so jocularly, "the wolf," because of his depredations against the lambs of the gambling game.

Cordially Hated

He shunned quarrels. He had no few physical encounters in his life, generally due to gambling disputes, but he managed to avoid open hostilities as a rule by his ability to "con" his way out of a ticklish situation. He was a master hand with the "salve."

He had a few friends, and many enemies. Some of the latter were of years standing. But they were not enemies calculated to do a foe bodily harm. They took it out in hating him and execrating his name.

So, then, as I say, no one could tell him exactly why the impression prevailed that he "had to go," as the boys say. It was just a vague feeling. The cards lay that way, so to speak. I think perhaps Rothstein had the feeling himself of late. Certainly he knew that he was in dire jeopardy when he refused to settle his $285,000 losses in the now-famous stud game.

But I doubt that he felt he was "no price." He had faced other desperate-looking situations before when he was told that his life wasn't worth a white chip, and brazened them out. Rothstein had plenty of physical courage, make no error there.

Also he had enormous vanity. His bump of ego was the size of a watermelon. He liked to talk about himself. You got a thousand "I's" in the course of a couple hours conversation with Rothstein.

"I'm a 100 percent right," was his favorite expression.

He was one of the strangest men who ever stepped in shoe leather.

He was rich beyond dreams of avarice. He had a lovely wife, a magnificent home. He had Rolls-Royces, every form of luxury. He had his health, and he was in his thirties when he got hold of his first big money. He could go anywhere, do anything.

But he never went anywhere. He rarely took a pleasure trip. He seemed to have no pleasures. He used to like racing, baseball, boxing. Of late years his interest in all these things waned.

He could have associated with fine people, visited nice homes, been a man of consequence, for all his gambling career. Other men have risen above such things.

But Rothstein chose, instead, to hang out with the fellow gamblers of high and low degree, to remain a citizen of the underworld. You could catch him at all hours of the morning at Lindy's or nearby.

On many a sweltering Summer dawning I have seen him walking up and down Broadway in front of Lindy's, which is near 50th Street, his coat swung wide open, his hat in his hand, talking with some gambler. He would get up early, and go to his insurance office, or visit the Fairfield Hotel on 72nd Street, which he owned, but along toward 1 o'clock he would show up in Lindy's.

Clung to Old Life

He couldn't get away from his old life. He went through the pleasant fiction of retiring from gambling some years ago, and the story was printed as large news on the front page of a New York paper. And while Rothstein did abate gambling houses he owned in the 40s, he kept up a house at Long Beach.

And he gambled constantly himself. He won and lost huge sums of money in crap games. Men gamble, as a rule, to get out of gambling, to get into something more respectable. Rothstein had all the money one man ought to have, but he couldn't stop gambling. It was an absolute disease with him. I believe that is the true explanation—a disguise.

If he saw a couple of newsboys shooting craps in the street and they had only about two dollars between them, I think Rothstein would have joined them. I think Rothstein would have joined them, running the risk of losing thousands of dollars to win these two. Not that he wanted the two. Just for the excitement of play.

He was accounted a hard man with his money, yet he would often display an astonishing liberality. If he liked a chap, he would go a long ways for him. True, he didn't like many.

It was his pretense that he regarded gambling strictly as a business, and nothing else. I have heard him say there is no such thing as luck, but all gamblers say there is, then talk about getting their "rushes" or streaks of luck.

While Rothstein was undoubtedly one of the most successful gamblers this country has ever known, he wasn't the most spectacular. With all his vanity, he knew when to say "No." He didn't often play another man's game until comparatively recently. He liked to let the other fellow play his game—one he owned, or bankrolled. In other words, he liked to have the house percentage running for him.

Million in Day!

He won his biggest bet that hot July day at Aqueduct, when his horse, Sidereal, backed down from 30–1, beat some of the most powerful stables in the country. Sidereal was by Star Shoot out of Milky Way, and the name means "of or pertaining to the stars." Rothstein won in the neighborhood of $1 million that day, and there was plenty of talk about the race.

They didn't care much for Arnold Rothstein around the racetracks thereafter, and he sold his stable. He always denied that he was requested to take air. He liked to tell you what he said to August Belmont, then the head of the jockey club. Rothstein was fond of telling what he said to Belmont, or Ban Johnson, when Ban was president of the American League, and the Black Sox of 1919 developed.

Rothstein was accused of fixing that series with the assistance of Abe Attel, former featherweight champion of the world. That charge is the one thing that always seemed to weigh on Arnold's mind. Time and time again he brought it up in conversation with me, and others, to declare his innocence.

Switched to Reds

Somehow I always thought that Rothstein may have taken advantage of certain information that came to him in the form of a proposition that he didn't actually have any part on the transaction. He was a great hand for taking advantage of information that came to him that way. He had bet on the White Sox, but he switched to the Reds when he heard the plot, and among others, beat the late E.E. Smathers for quite a wager.

Rothstein was very fond of baseball for many years. He always bet on the games and he told me that he never had the faintest idea there was any crooked work in the pastime until a St. Louis American League pitcher came to him years ago and "propositioned" him to throw a game.

Rothstein was a charming conversationalist. He had at least a working education. He kept up with the affairs of the day. He had a ready flow of languages and a fund of stories.

He was getting a bit corpulent of late years, but was always well-dressed and looked the man of affairs. When he was younger he was a dapper, nimble fellow, good-looking, quick-witted and rather genteel. Well-bred, he always showed his breeding.

Disappearing Act

A lot of phony tradition grew up around him of late years. It was said he would never sit with his back to a door, which was the bunk.

He paid no attention to where he sat. But he could move very rapidly. He was sitting in a booth in Lindy's one night, surrounded by a lot of cronies, when the lights suddenly went out accidentally.

When they were turned on again, Rothstein was in a booth across the room. Houdini couldn't have gotten out of that corner with greater expedition. He would get up a score of times in an hour to answer telephone calls on some mysterious business, probably pertaining to the gambling operations about town. It is inconceivable that associates on the insurance business would call him on business at the weird hours he got his calls in Lindy's.

He started hanging out in Jack's Restaurant when it was the heart of the nightlife of the big town. That was nearly 20 years ago. Thereafter he always had a hangout. From Jack's he began moving uptown, jumping from place to place, generally an all-night restaurant.

He halted at a restaurant at 59th Street and Columbus Circle during the war. Rothstein's following always moved with him. Then he moved on up beyond 72nd Street to a delicatessen and restaurant. His crowd went with him, but the proprietor requested him to stop hanging out there.

Personally, he was anything but a bad fellow. He was nearly always good-natured, and liked practical jokes. He was a great "kidder." He had about one companion at a time, and for a spell they would seem to be real pals. Then he would pick up with somebody else. He wasn't popular with his associates by a long shot.

Was Not Secretive

I have read that he was secretive about his personal affairs, such as the domestic discord that came into his life for a time. As a matter of fact, Rothstein was quite gabby on subjects the average man shrinks from discussing. He would tell his troubles to Tom, Dick and Harry.

I have read too, that he was too old-fashioned to keep up with these modern-day mobsters, yet, Rothstein seems to have been trying to keep step with the times when he developed a bodyguard. That was something absolutely new for him.

He had the utmost contempt for mobsters. It was often said that some of his hangers-on were his bodyguards when they couldn't even guard themselves, let alone taking on customers to guard. Rothstein liked to play a lone hand too much to employ body-guards—besides, he didn't need 'em until lately.

Then, it seems, he picked up a fellow who was supposed to pro-tect him against certain force, which would indicate that Rothstein was a bit uneasy in his own mind. The rumors that Rothstein's "mob" is rallying to wreak vengeance upon his killers is poppycock.

He had no "mob." The lone wolf seeks no companions.

Like Cabarets

Rothstein often visited cabarets. He liked to sit around with a crowd buying wine. He drank very little. He never smoked. He could use bad language on occasions, but he didn't make a practice of it. He was very restless, and wouldn't stand or sit on one place very long. He was cordial to a chance acquaintance.

He had bright, snappy brown eyes, loaded with expression. That old poker mask stuff you read about didn't apply to Roth-stein. His face was lively with expression at all times. He was any-thing but the typical gambler in appearance, or anything else.

He was certainly no John Oakhurst or Jack Hamlin, as I understand those characters of Bret Harte's fiction, because those gentlemen were pictured as sporting gamblers. I wouldn't call Rothstein that. He didn't mind a shade the best of it when he could get it. Gambling was a business, as well as a mania, with him.

When he lost, he often kept people waiting for their money, and he didn't give them a "scratch" or "I.O.U." for it, either. He always paid in the end of course, but that stage wait seemed part of his system. He usually knew those he kept waiting. Sometimes, he would say he could not raise the money immediately, which is what he was telling his creditors in the big stud game for a time.

Pleaded Poverty

He often pleaded poverty. No one knows why. He must have had a fortune for years. Some of the gamblers who did not like him say he held the winners off as long as possible in the hope that he would get them in a game again and beat them for their winnings before they had a chance to spend or invest the money.

He gambled with the highest—with the oil millionaires who played chemin de fer around the hoity-toity hotels a few years back—for enormous sums, and with the lowest, with the rag-tag of humanity who infest crap games.

I never regarded Rothstein as picturesque. I always thought of him as pathetic. For all his money he seemed to get little material enjoyment out of life. Yet it was his own fault. He rarely went home to take advantage of the company and comforts there. He liked to attend first nights, an opening of cafes and all other Broadway events, but did not like to stray too far from Broadway.

He was a keen judge of a ballplayer or a fighter. Fifty percent of the takes of his winnings and losings on fights were his bunk. Certainly his money did not show in the process and money must show there. He won a good bet on the first (Jack) Dempsey-(Gene) Tunney fight. He lost a chunk on Jack Sharkey to beat Dempsey—about $47,000.

He put up $11,000 for Harry Pollok to take Freddy Welsh to England to win the lightweight title. This was as a matter of friendship to Pollok. He would lend his money on security and sometimes on notes, and he wanted it right back on the nail. He hated to admit that he was ever wrong.

"You owe me a month's rent," he said to "Good Time Charley" Freedman one night. Freedman occupies an apartment in a house in the Fifties owned by Rothstein.

"No, I paid you and I've got the cancelled check to prove it," replied Freedman.

Why He "Welshed"

"I'll bet you $500 to $25 you're wrong," said Rothstein. "I never made a mistake on my books in my life."

"That's a bet," replied Freedman. He came around the next day with a cancelled check for the exact amount of the rent.

"That's a check I cashed for you—I gave you the money,"

argued Rothstein, but the exact amount was a bit of a poser. He didn't speak to Freedman for a couple of weeks, then credited him with $500 on the recent.

His vanity undoubtedly brought about his death. He could have paid off the $285,000 markers like breaking sticks, and he would have done so regardless of whether he thought he had been clipped or not, if they hadn't attempted to bring him what the boys call "strength: on him. Rothstein felt that if he settled under pressure after being speared, he would be the laughing stock of the company.

His gambler associates at once dismissed his suggestions, that he had been cheated as idle. They argued that even if he was, he ought to be paid off, It is the code. One of his creditors in discussing a settlement with Rothstein kept using the word "welsh," the most odious word in all the gambling lexicon. He repeated it purposely over and over.

"Well, if you're going to welsh," they would say.

"My God, will you stop using that word," finally roared Rothstein.

It got on his nerves. For all the mysterious sinister figure that the dime novel stories of Rothstein would make him, I thought him singularly transparent and open, easy to read. He generally expressed his thoughts, anyway.

Loyal to Friends

The general guess at his finish for the past 10 years has been that he would be killed in a backroom crap game, or by some "nut" along Broadway with a fancied grievance. If Rothstein took a liking to a chap, you couldn't shake his judgment of that chap. He liked to back his selections among humanity the same as he liked to back certain horses.

One fellow that Rothstein was very fond of betrayed his confidence time and again, but Rothstein did not quit on him until comparatively recently and it must have cost him a lot of money.

Another young man, this one apparently a real good bet, got Rothstein to invest a fortune in real estate, but Rothstein was confidently awaiting the day when the young man's manipulation of this real estate would return him tenfold.

2 Memorable Moments

Yankee Stadium, opening day 1923

At his core, Damon Runyon was a great reporter, a writer who could make otherwise dull opening-day ceremonies interesting and deliver sharp-edged or sentimental commentary. In covering the catastrophic fire of the Polo Grounds of 1911, Runyon reaches for something different in baseball coverage: nostalgia. Seven years later, while in France to cover the late stages of American involvement in World War I, Runyon re-creates the last moments of ex-Giant "Harvard Eddie" Grant in a memorable piece.

Runyon's coverage of his first regular season big-league game — the 1911 Giants' opener at the Polo Grounds — is a marvelous mix of game coverage with his soon-to-be-patented descriptions of what people were wearing, how the weather was, and just about anything else that happened that day at the ballpark.

GIANTS LOSE TO PHILLIES, 2 TO 0 IN BIG REGULAR SEASON GAME (APR. 13, 1911)

Over Thirty Thousand See "Opening Day" Jinx Pursue McGraw's Men
"Red" Ames Appears on Mound at Polo Grounds in Familiar Role
of "Traditional Hoodoo"

Over thirty thousand people saw the unveiling of the Giants' well-known opening day Jinx at the Polo Grounds yesterday after-noon, when with "Red" Leon Ames in his familiar role as custodian of the Hoodoo, they lost the first game of the 1911 season to Philadelphia, 2 to 0.

Silver sunshine, a record-breaking first-day crowd, a band, the Mayor, and other pomp and circumstance, attended the great occasion, but old Tradition, whose other name is Tough Luck, was also present, and McGraw's men got away to a minus standing.

It is so customary for the Giants to drop that initial game that no one was greatly surprised, but the sympathetic thirty-some-odd-thousand had nothing but expressions of deep commiseration for "Red" Ames, who pitched as hard luck an opener as he ever lost. And that is saying a great deal.

The Phillies had a rabbit's foot or some other lucky symbol tied around big Earl Moore's neck in the first place; in the second place, they had a two-base hit concealed on the stalwart Mr. (Fred) Luderus, formerly of Chicago, which no one suspected at all, and he pulled it in the ninth inning, with two out and two on base, after one little quirk of Fate had put the Giants in a hole. Prior to unburdening himself of the two-bagger Luderus stepped right up and fanned right out twice in succession, so it was natural that he should be regarded as harmless when showed up the last time.

Ames in Rare Form

Ames pitched magnificent ball. He only allowed four hits, but two of them got into that distressing ninth. He fanned eight men, and was as steady as a boarder, but he couldn't beat both tradition and Earl Moore's swastiko, or whatever it was the Philly heaver had. Moore was only hit safely twice, but he walked seven men, and was constantly in holes so deep that Charley Dooin had to jeopardize his personal safety leaning over the edge of them to rescue that vacillating Earl.

Prior to losing that game we had events, of course. The crowd started arriving early, there being a line outside the gates soon after noon, and they poured into the well of seats until the moment the game was started. A band was stationed near the Giants' bench, and poured sweet musical nothings into the unresponsive ears of the multitude, which was more diverted by throwing balls of papers at the late-comers.

Ladies, with the latest in Spring bonnets, were special targets, and they had to run the paper-wad gauntlet if they wanted their seats. Blushing escorts were also bombarded freely. A fight or two in the far recesses of the stand afforded some entertainment.

It was none too warm in the shade, of course, but no one noticed the chill of the air until after the ninth inning.

Giants in New Uniforms

The Giants appeared for the first time in their new Summer scenery, which is done in a black and white that sets off their physical pulchritude in a manner beautiful to behold. Especially their legs. The Phillies also had new attire, with delicate touches of pale mauve here and there. The ensemble is somewhat startling, but outside of that it is all right.

Mayor Gaynor's appearance was almost dramatic. At exactly five minutes to four as the band said, "Tee-tum-m-m" a gate back of rightfield flew open, nearly knocking a policeman and Jack Murray over, and Bill Gray showed in the distance. With him was an officer of the law in plain clothes. Then the Mayor. Then some other people.

All hands moved up stage, and the Mayor shook hands with Jack Murray and wished him well. A bevy of photographers fluttered before Mr. Gaynor over the sward as he moved forward beneath a tall plug hat. Next the Mayor shook the hand that muffed a ball in an inning or so later on. The hand belonged to Cap'n Larry Doyle of the Giants.

After this the Mayor and those that camp with him, got into a front box in the upper tier back of third base and the photographers still pursued 'em. At 4:07 the Mayor arose from where he sat, and chucked a baseball at Umpire Johnstone, while the band played "The Star Spangled Banner," the crowd stood with bared heads, and the business of playing baseball went forward.

Looked Rosy for the Giants

For eight innings it was a ding-dong affair, with the Giants always having a little edge, apparently because they were getting men on bases constantly. Then came that little turn of fate in the first of the ninth, which started the Phillies upon their way to two runs and a victory. Hans Lobert—he of the serious face and mild demeanor—got one of those very few hits that were taken from Ames during the game. Sherwood Magee, premier smacksman of the National League, who had fanned on two previous appearances, hit a grounder to Ames, and "Red" threw a bit wild to Merkle. Magee was safe.

Lobert went on to third while this play was going on. Magee stole second. (Dode) Paskert hit to Ames, who threw to Catcher Meyers to stop Lobert at the plate. Meantime Magee had run down to third himself, and stayed there while Meyers chased Lobert back to that station. Magee was called out, and Lobert was adjudged the tenant of the bag.

Then along came the innocent-looking Luderus with a record of two strikeouts pasted against his name, and he snagged a curve right at the break and drove it far over John Devore's head in left. Lobert and Paskert scored. Tradition was as safe as a church.

It was one of those replete games, at that, being filled with stirring incidents and also numerous chances for the Giants to score. Even in the ninth, after custom had been served and the game was in the Dooin locker, Merkle walked, but successive fly-outs left him gazing blankly at the fence.

Ames Begins with a Pass

Ames started by walking (John) Titus, the first man up, and he moseyed around the third on (Otto) Knabe's sacrifice, and Lobert's out, but Merkle was playing very deep for Magee on his first trip up, and nicked his heavy grounder.

In the Giants' end of the same inning Doyle singled, and that was the first and last hit that Moore let go of for quite a spell. The Giants' first offensive play of the season was pulled off by Joshua Devore. He bunted to Moore, and was a distressingly easy out.

In that first inning, however, the Giants had two men on through Doyle's single and Knabe's error on (Fred) Snodgrass's drive, but they stayed there. In the second inning, "Red" Ames fanned Paskert, Luderus and (Mickey) Doolan in succession.

Doolan made a wonderful one-handed stop of Merkle's drive in the second, which cut off an average of no little danger. "Red" Charley Dooin was at least thirty-three and a third of the Phillies' club back of that pan. He cut down the fast-flying Giants when they got on the base with comparative ease, although a couple got by him very nicely.

The Giants had the bases cluttered in the fifth, with two out. In the eighth, with Josh Devore at second, Snodgrass and Murray fanned one after the other. The Giants simply could not get that run across, and Moore hobbled along in Dooin's shoulder through the whole session, and won his game.

Today is another day.

—

The 1911 season had barely kicked off before the spectacular Polo Grounds fire of April 14, 1911, sent flames shooting from the all-wooden ballpark into the Manhattan night, and Runyon reaching for something new in column-writing: a play at nostalgia. The Giants would play the next several months at Hilltop Park, home of the Yankees, before moving back June 30 into the Polo Grounds, rebuilt with concrete double-deck from the leftfield corner, around home plate and back out to right-centerfield. It became the first concrete-era stadium in New York.

HOME OF THE GIANTS A CRESCENT OF ASHES

One woe doth tread upon another's heels so fast they look like a parade, as the poet shrieked when his rent fell due, coincident with the dealer plucking his last chip. Fire, flood and defeat are a parlay of circumstances, which would put the books to Optimism in any man's town.

All day yesterday a crowd gathered on the bluffs above the Polo Grounds, gazing mournfully down into that temporarily extinct crater of baseball activity. Sorrowing small boys and long-faced men poked aimlessly about the debris. Only a blackened crescent, with here and there a gaunt girder still standing upright, marks the site of the beautiful double-decked stand.

The home of the Giants is in complete ruin.

Few incidents of the last decade in the sporting world caused so much excitement as the destruction of the famous ball park, not only in New York, but elsewhere throughout the United States—wherever red-blooded men keep track of the game. In this city there was little else talked about yesterday. Daylight found the heights above the grounds speckled with sightseers, and the number increased as the morning wore on.

Wreckage Unbelievable Until Seen

Then the rain came and soaked the dismal pile of ashes and drove the curious to cover. But they had seen what they had felt to be utterly preposterous—the Polo Grounds in wreckage. The Metropolitan tower might suddenly sink from sight; the Brooklyn Bridge might collapse, but the destruction of the Polo Grounds was something not to be believed until seen.

In Base Ball Land—and that means the big cities of the East, of the West, of the North, and of the South, where they follow their uniformed clubs and leagues and associations; it means the hamlets where the infielders of the town "nine" wear mustaches; it means those wide places in the road where the storekeepers suspend business to play "work-up" with the village loafers; it means the tiniest spots in all these United States wherever the crack of the bat has been heard—in Base Ball Land, generally, the name "Polo Grounds" has been known and revered for a score of years.

Ask some little towheaded shaver down in Rubeville, Arkansaw, as he tosses his yarn ball against the side of the old weather-beaten barn, where the Athletics play. Maybe he'll have a hazy notion that it is Philadelphia, but it's a two-ace bet that he doesn't know whether Shibe Park is the name of a cigar or something good to eat.

Name Revered in All Baseball Land

Ask him where the Giants play and watch his eyes light up!

"The Polo Grounds!"

You bet! He knows that!

Ask that hobbledehoy studying the score board in the busy

street of some far Western city, with his noisy hand-me-down habiliments and his hat stuck to the back of his hair, where the Pirates, or the Tigers, or the Cubs play. Likely he'll tell you Pittsburg, Detroit or Chicago, because he reads the sporting pages, but he cannot say the name of their parks to save his life. Inquire the home hive of the Giants—not New York, understand, but the Giants. Never betray your ignorance when away from New York by referring to them in any other fashion. Just ask him where the Giants play and see his look of pity for your innocence.

"The Polo Grounds!"

Aye, the Polo Grounds! Why, the name has become almost synonymous with the very game itself. Why, the Polo Grounds is where Christy Mathewson pitches! Why, the Polo Grounds is where you can see John McGraw, and Big Chief Myers, and "Hooks" Wiltsie, and "Bugs" Raymond and "Rube" Marquard! Why, the Polo Grounds is where Amos Rusie and John Montgomery Ward and all those fellows used to play, you know! Why, the Polo Grounds is where all the famous actors, and actresses, and politicians, and sporting men, and people like that, whose pictures get into the papers, can be seen on pleasant afternoons!

That's how much they know of the Polo Grounds in places where you can't find a man, woman or child who ever heard the name of the Mayor of the Greater City or who don't even suspect the general locality of the State of Maine!

All Knew the Home of the Giants

Away down in the Sticks, where the flowers of tomorrow's baseball glory are ever blooming, and those of the yesterday are ever fading, the name stands as the acme of all things desirable in baseball. To play on the Polo Grounds is the everlasting dream of the coming major leaguer; to have played there once is a memory that will never fade from the minds of those who will not be back.

The Polo Grounds! It means the Big Town; it means the Big

City club; it is all the lights of Broadway and the lure of Gotham summed up in two words. To those who analyze it is, perhaps just a baseball park of some beauty, as baseball parks go, which, on baseball days becomes a bowl of howling humanity in rather grimly setting beneath Coogan's euphoniously named bluffs; to the rest of us it is the home of excitement; of some romance, and much baseball glory and achievement; it is a place of surpassing magnificence, sparkling beneath the silver sun like a great green jewel, and, best of all, it is the abiding place of the Giants!

Now, of course, the ground upon which the players play has not been mopped up; the diamond and its appurtenances have not vanished completely, and the destruction of the Polo Grounds applies only to that portion of the plant represented by the grandstand, and some of the bleachers, but it might as well have been the whole thing—home plate, foul lines and green turf—so far as the feelings of the fans are concerned.

That beautiful sod diamond is smudged with cinders and mud, but it can be gotten into shape for playing immediately.

———

Dispatched to France to cover the late stages of American involvement in World War I, Runyon re-creates the last moments of ex-Giant Eddie Grant, the first big-leaguer to be killed in action there. Grant, a 10-year big-league journeyman infielder with four teams, had retired in 1915 with a .249 batting average, but stood out in other ways: He was a Harvard College & Law School graduate who had retired from baseball in 1915 to work in a New York law firm. Stirred by fellow Ivy League idealist President Woodrow Wilson's crusade to make the world "safe for democracy," Grant, by then a widower, joined the Army in 1917—going to France in an infantry battalion commanded by his former law school classmate Major Charles Whittlesey.

EDDIE GRANT DIED LEADING HIS BATTALION (OCT. 23, 1918)

Major Had Passed over Command to Ex-Giant a Few Minutes Before the Latter Was Killed

WITH THE AMERICAN FIRST ARMY, OCT. 22—Harvard's Eddie Grant, the old Giant third baseman, sleeps in the Forest of Argonne, only a few yards from where he fell.

His grave is marked by some stones and a rude little cross tenderly reared by his men.

Eddie died leading his battalion in a desperate fight to relieve Whittlesey's beleaguered men some two weeks ago. He was commanding a company of the 307th Infantry from Camp Upton, when the battle began.

Game to the Last

For four days and four nights his company was part of the command, which was trying to get to Whittlesey. On the morning of the day that relief was effected, Eddie was so worn out he could scarcely move. Some of his brother officers noticed him sitting on a stump, with a cup of coffee in front of him.

Two or three times, they say, he tried to lift the cup, but was so weak he couldn't do it. Finally, with a terrible effort, he gulped down the coffee when the command came to move.

He stepped off at the head of his company as briskly as ever. On the way through the forest, fighting at every step, Grant came upon stretcher-bearers carrying back the major commanding the battalion, who had been wounded. The major called to Grant:

"Take command of the battalion."

Eddie Grant was then one of the few officers left. The major had hardly spoken when a shell came through the trees, dropping two lieutenants in Grant's company. Eddie shouted:

"Everybody down!"

Without hunting cover for himself, he called for more stretcher-bearers for the two lieutenants. He was calling and waving his hands when a shell struck him. It was a direct hit.

115

Fought Without Sleep

Officers and men say Eddie's conduct during the fight was marvelous. He never slept while the drive for Whittlesey's position was on.

The writer yesterday saw Christy Mathewson, Grant's old teammate and his roommate while Eddie was with the Giants. "Matty" was greatly saddened by the news. He is a captain the gas corps.

One of the men who saw Eddie Grant was a former policeman at the Polo Grounds. This man said today:

"Eddie Grant was dog-tired, but he stepped off at the head of his outfit with no more concern than if he were walking to his old place at third base after his side had finished its turn at the bat.

"Like many others, he was worn down almost to a shadow. He staggered from weakness when he first started off, but pretty soon he was marching briskly with his head up."

Grant is the first big-league ballplayer to be killed in the war. His chum, Harry McCormick, was shell-shocked some time ago and is back in the States. They went to (officers' training camp in) Plattsburgh (N.Y.) together.

Joe Jenkins, former White Sox catcher, was discovered yesterday scraping the mud off himself in a wayside billet. He had just come out of the line with his outfit. He has seen quite a lot of service.

Some of the men of the 77th are now at a "de-lousing" station. This is just what the name implies. There's no use making bones about it. "C'est la Guerre," as the Frenchman says and the "cootie" is part of it.

The men are marched there direct from the lines. They strip themselves and each man's clothing is tied up in a bundle with his name on. The bundles then are passed through a steaming process, which destroys what the soldiers call "seam squirrels." This process takes about 40 minutes. In the meantime, the men wait ground with nothing on but their raincoats, sometimes not even them.

"Jerry" Leaves Cooties

After being rid of their unwelcome roommates, they got rest.

The Germans are great hands at building elaborate dugouts and other shelter in their trenches. Our men move into these habitations as fast as they can chase the Germans out.

They always discover that "Jerry" has left many of his pet cooties behind. When a man gets the German breed mixed up with his good old-fashioned, home-like Uncle Sam gray back, much unrest develops.

The fighting has passed beyond the Argonne, but every day scores of new stories come floating out of the forest of startling incidents of the great campaign. A whole book could be written about the battle in the woods.

One division was under command of General Alexander Bluff, a thickset old warrior. He made the division bop like a new saddle from the moment he took hold. One of his brigades was under General Wittemeyer, who started the division at Upton.

He helped form and develop the outfit and saw through its baptism of blood on the Vesle, as well as through its great trial by fire in the tangled grove of eastern France that will forever be hallowed to Americans.

Wittemeyer is a grizzled-foot soldier who has followed the flag all over the world. He was with the Ninth Infantry in the Boxer Campaign (in China). Hand-to-hand scraps were frequent.

Last night, we had the first clear moonlight in the region close to the front in many weeks. "Jerry" Fokkers promptly took the air.

Fokkers Sightseeing

They went out sightseeing. In one little town, which was once the scene of much bombing during different periods of the war, a major or commandant walked into an officers' club where a big crowd was dining. He announced casually that an "alert" had been sounded and that it might be a good idea for folks to go to the abris or shelter.

Then he sat down calmly and began eating his own meal. No bombing was reported.

"Gentlemen, it's my birthday, and I am bringing some of my

friends over to take dinner with you" was the naïve announcement of the German officer in surrendering to Lieutenant Rerdon of New York's 77th Division.

He spoke perfect English. His face was wreathed in smiles. He waved his hands toward the woods behind him. Out popped 30 German soldiers. They also were smiling. They had been surrounded by a detachment of the 77th for some time. After making a brisk fight, they decided to give it up. It seems that it really was the German officer's birthday. He and "his friends" got their dinner with the Americans all right.

Eddie Grant had actually fallen October 6, but fighting was so fierce that the news didn't reach the United States for more than two weeks. U.S. troops fighting in the Argonne Forest in the fall of 1918 suffered devastating losses; in six weeks, more than 26,000 men were killed, with nearly 96,000 wounded. Runyon's dispatch helped make Eddie Grant more famous in death than life; in 1921, a plaque in deepest centerfield at the Polo Grounds was dedicated to Grant, and in the years that followed, Commissioner Landis championed his name for the Hall of Fame. Grant was never elected, and sadly, his plaque disappeared after the Giants' final game at the Polo Grounds in 1957 when fans tore apart the field. Major Whittlesey, meanwhile, earned the Medal of Honor for leading what became know as his "Lost Battalion."

———

After a war-shortened season in 1918, Runyon welcomes back baseball and a degree of normalcy and festivity on opening day of 1919. Note the names of the two Red Sox stars of the game — the 24-year-old Red Sox slugger, Babe Ruth, who homered in the first inning, and the pitcher, Carl Mays, both of whom would be Yankees within the year. In only his first season as a full-time batter — Ruth had been a Red Sox pitcher for five-plus seasons — the Babe would set the all-time big-league, single-season home-run record of 29. In 1920, Ruth would hit 54 home runs and Mays would win 26 games, both for the Yankees; later that year, even Sox manager Ed Barrow would join the Yanks as general manager.

30,000 WATCH YANKEES LOSE OPENING GAME (APR. 24, 1919)

Record Crowd Acclaims Return of National Pastime Here—Red Sox Win by Score of 10 to 0; Ruth's Home Run in First Inning Decides the Issue; Notables in Civic and Military Life Present

It all came back yesterday afternoon like the fulfillment of a precious dream—the good old game of baseball!

Not the half-dead-and-half-alive baseball of the dark wartime period; not the pallid wrath of the pastime that stalked ghostly across the dreary days of Summer for the past few years, but the old game itself, full-lunged, and red, red-blooded.

It came back, as it should come, to the sound of the sweetest music in all the world—the great booming of human pipes pouring out the enthusiasm of the soul.

Thirty-thousand voices were in under the gigantic chorus that lifted out the bowl they call the Polo Grounds, yesterday afternoon, to go rolling in a crashing volume up over Coogan's scraggly cliffs.

It produced a sort of seismic shock out on 8th Avenue, where long lines of belated fans were fairly chomping their teeth in impatience as the appointed hour for the start of the game between the New York Yankees of the American League, and the world's champion Red Sox, of Boston, befell and the gates were still clogged.

Ruth Hits His Homer

"Dammitall" said one fan, whose sensitive organism responded immediately to the shock, "I s'pose that Ruth has just hit a home run or something like that? Dammitall!"

Well, it was indeed something like that, dammitall!

A first-inning homer by the giant slugger of the Sox was an incident of the 10 to 0 beating administered to the Yankees by the Boston champs.

It was a sad enough baseball game from the home-town stand-point, perhaps, but that didn't spoil the return to Manhattan Island of the best-loved of all American sports.

Sunshine poured into the old bowl up on the Harlem River in a silvery flood. A delicate breeze rippled the banners on the many-peaked stadium and rippled the shoals of bunting along the façade. The air warmed the cockles of the heart.

And from noon on, the folks were moving toward the Polo Grounds; packing the wobbly "L" trains to the doors, clinging to the straps of the 8th Avenue surface-cars, and coming in battalions from the subway and bus stations on Washington Heights.

Bleacherite Mere Memory

They quickly filled the lower stand, and soon obliterated the black spaces in the upper tier. The right- and center-field bleachers were well loaded, but the old-time bleacherite seems to be becoming a memory, for the very simple reason that he has acquired money enough to affect the higher-priced seats.

But "Bodieville," the homelike leftfield bleacher (named for Yankee outfielder Ping Bodie), was not forsaken. It has too strong a hold on the affections of its inhabitants ever to be abandoned for bleakly unfamiliar seating in the lordly stands. Out yonder they put in the time before the game, as always, in spoofing everybody in reach of their long-ranged voices.

In the grandstand back of third base where of late years jocose souls have been gathering, there were goings-on. (The comedian) Johnny Cook, whose daily performances over yonder have become familiar to Giant followers, transferred his show to the Yanks for the occasion and assisted Frank's hand in diverting the audience before the game.

Colonel Jacob Ruppert, president of the Yankees, held forth in a box near the press cage, a wide smile on his countenance, which hastened until the end of the first inning. He got a roll of telegrams congratulating him on the opening and wishing his club success, including one from Louis Mann, which he promptly submitted to

Harry Frazee, president of the world champions, who was in another box.

Colonel Feels Jubilant

The Colonel had a right to feel jubilant. It was the biggest crowd that ever witnessed a Yankee opener, or any other Yankee game in New York, for that matter. It was the culmination of a long struggle by the rank management to give the American League a real representation in point of patronage in Manhattan Island.

Colonel T.L. Huston, vice-president of the club, entertained a big crowd of members of the 16th Engineers of which was the lieutenant-colonel in France and which got back yesterday. There were thousands of soldiers and sailors scattered through the stands—men who have been through "hell and high water," and who were forgetting it all in the enjoyment of the sunshine and the old game.

Many of the players on the field were only recently discharged from the service, yet war seemed very far away indeed in the presence of that scene yesterday afternoon.

Down in the press box, it was like Old Home Week. There, too, were many men who have just picked up their pencils and readjusted their typewriting fingers after months in uniform. Captain Frank P. Adams dropped in and was welcomed as an old-time inmate. Captain Bill McGeehan of the *Tribune* was there; so was Captain Denis Brown, formerly of the *Sun*. Weed Dickinson of the *Telegraph* was back.

The Old Familiar Faces

There were many other familiar faces that were good to see. Maximilian Foster, the novelist, called in. "Wild" Bill Donovan, formerly manager of the Yanks, now running the Jersey City club, sat with Johnny Lavan, the little short-fielder once of the St. Louis Browns, who was in a naval uniform.

Grantland Rice was back. (Cartoonist) "Tad" (Dorgan), the incurable Yankee rooter, chaperoned Joe Smolien, "The Candy

Kid," from Bayside, just home from driving an ambulance with the French. Eddie Leonard, the actor, occupied his old seat by the water cooler. "Eppy," the scorecard merchant, and Harry Safir, the demon announcer, were on view.

And, of course, (concessionaire) Harry M. Stevens was there. Of course.

The Lord only knows how many baseball openings (Stevens) the good Duke of Niles has seen since the world began. Sixteen of the American League starts here—that's certain. There have been just that many on Manhattan Island.

Harry patrolled the press cage and adjacent boxes, shook hands with everybody he knew, and absent-mindedly, with a lot he didn't know, sustained nervous prostration over the result of the game, and generally had a typically Harry M. Stevens-time of it.

A baseball opening in New York without Harry would be like that much mooted performance of Haig & Haig without any heather in it.

All Notables Present

Al Munro Elias, the "Figger Filhart" (and stat king of Elias Sports Bureau fame,) leaped from crag to crag uttering strange cries. Once, in his passage, he dropped the information that "Trolley Wire" Everett Scott of the Red Sox was playing his 337th game without a miss. That is, without missing a game.

Harry Sparrow, business manager of the Yankees, was on guard at the outer portals with his assistants, Mark Roth and Tommy McManus, and the rotund Harry's famous blood pressure attained a high visibility under the excitement of the afternoon.

Tammany Young, movie actor and dramatic pinch hitter, appeared in the press box just as Ned Hill of the *Sun*, putting forward the theory that Tam would never get there, and that the opening therefore would be quite illegal.

There was a Broadway fringe along all the boxes. Many noble and notable actors were present, with others of the theatrical profession not necessarily actors. Jack Welch answered to his name when the roll was called. George M. Cohan, a Yank fan to the expulsion of all other clubs, said "Here!"

First Straw Hat Appears

It was a bubbly sort of the crowd. It fairly leaked enthusiasm from every core. The inevitable first straw hat showed up, and got the inevitable smashing. This is a sort of religious rite at Polo Grounds' openings.

Tommy Connolly, gray, and imperturbable, serving his 20th years as an umpire in the American League, appeared with his mask and chest protector, and the crowd gave him a hand. Tommy has reached that stage of umpirical existence where he is a member of the family, and is applauded or derided by the crowd, according to circumstances. An umpire has to live a long time to reach that stage in New York.

Dick Nallin was Tommy's assistant. He worked out on the base lines. The afternoon passed without incident for the umpires, because there be little umpirical incident in a game where the score is 10 to 0. Occasionally, the Boston players fretted at Tommy, but the gray gesticulator from old Natick pooh-poohed them paternally.

Major-General Thomas Barry, commander of the Department of the East, and Rear-Admiral Harry McP. Huse, of the Atlantic battle fleet, were guests of Colonel Ruppert and Colonel Huston and occupied boxes behind the bench of the home players. They were accompanied by their staffs.

Robert Moran, president of the Board of Aldermen, performed the time-honored function of throwing out the first ball, ever a pleasing little ceremony, but which was executed with more grace by Mr. Moran than is usual. In fact, the president of the Board of Aldermen is as good a first ball thrower as has ever been seen at the Polo Grounds.

"Babe" Ruth's homer on the first inning had something to do with the defeat the Yanks, but the pitching of Carl Mays was chiefly responsible. They got but four hits off him, and he fanned eight. A club cannot win if it doesn't get any run at all—that's certain.

All the great hitters of the big-town club were helpless before Mays. Only (Wally) Pipp, "The Pickler," got more than one hit. (Frank) "Home Run" Baker, called "The Maryland Mauler," popped 'em good and high, but not far. Duffy Lewis, old (Red Sox) teammate to Mays, was equally helpless.

Underhand Ball Effective

Carl is that pitcher who starts the ball going down around his shoelaces. He is the (Iron) Joe McGinnity of this baseball era. Erskine Mayer of the Pittsburgh Pirates is another of those underhand hurlers, but he is scarcely as effective as Mays. Besides having that queer delivery, Mays is a shrewd fellow on the mound and mixes 'em up on the opposition.

"Black Jack" Barry, one of the stars of Connie Mack's old $100,000 infield, and just as much a star since going to the Red Sox, was back at second base, although it had been rumored that he was through. On first was his Philadelphia teammate, Stuffy McInnis, with Amos Strunk in the outfield, Joe Bush coaching at first base and Walter Schang behind the bat.

Schang got four hits in five times up—three doubles and a single—which perhaps answered the inquiries of the Yank fans as to why the ex-Yank, Al Walters, was not catching. At third base, the Sox had Oscar Vitt, once with the Detroit Tigers, a great fielding third baseman, though not much of a hitter.

(Harry) Hooper, hero of many a World Series—one of the greatest "money" players of all-time—guarded rightfield for Ed Barrow, the stout, good-natured leader of the Sox, who watches his club from the bench.

Little Work for Huggins

Miller Huggins, dour of countenance, barked at his Yanks from the coaching line. He had scant chance to attempt any managerial strategy. The Sox were too securely ensconced behind Mays's queer quirks.

Roger Peckinpaugh, usually "Old Reliability" itself, had a bad day at short. Everything was hit at him, and nothing bounded right for him. Sam Vick, young and probably very nervous in the presence of the biggest crowd he has even seen, had some tough luck in rightfield.

"Ping" Bodie was half-sick and couldn't hit a lick. And in addition to all this, George Mogridge's old-time magic wasn't working. Not since September 4, 1917, had the Sox been able to beat the thin lefthander. He had licked them six times in a row.

But yesterday, Harry Hooper, the first man to face him, singled to right on the second pitched ball. Barry followed with a sacrifice bunt to Mogridge, who threw to Peckinpaugh at second, getting Hooper. Amos Strunk lifted a pop to Peckinpaugh. A wild pitch by Mogridge advanced Barry to second, and this brought forward Ruth, nicknamed "Tarzan of the Apes."

"Babe" Can Slug 'Em

The crowd let go a long cheer as the huge Marylander came straddling to the plate, whipping the air with a bat as if it were a switch. The crowd knows Ruth can slug 'em, and the crowd ever loves the slugger. As Ruth reared his huge bulk alongside the plate, Mogridge ripped a curve at him, and Ruth slammed the ball to right-center.

Under ordinary circumstances, it would have been just a single, but the ball took a queer bound, skipped over Duffy Lewis's shoulder and rolled to the fence. Barry raced home, with Ruth thundering in behind him.

What happened after that made no particular difference as long as the Yanks could not score. In the ninth, a fumble by Peckinpaugh put Scott aboard the bases, and Schang doubled to left, lifting "Trolley Wire" to third. He scored on Mays's sacrifice fly to Vick. Schang took third after the catch. Hooper bounced a single off Peckinpaugh's foot, scoring Schang. Hooper stole second, and went to third when Barry singled past Peck.

Strunk grounded to Pratt and Hooper beat the throw to the

plate. Ruth singled to right and the ball got away from Vick, Barry and Strunk scoring, and Ruth reaching third. McInnis flied to Lewis. Peck fumbled Vitt's roller, and Ruth scored. Scott bunted safely, Vitt taking second, but Schang struck out.

Pratt Hits for Two

(Del) Pratt opened the Yanks' side of the second for a double to the rightfield wall, but Lewis and Bodie struck out, while (Truck) Hannah was an easy infield victim.

Peck started the sixth with a single, but nothing exciting happened after that. The Yanks simply cold not hit Mays with any effect, and the fast-fielding Sox behind him gave him excellent support.

Peck walked in the eighth, only be to caught off first, Pipp following with a single that would have helped. It wasn't the Yanks' day so far as baseball playing was concerned, but it was an American League day, and the old American game day otherwise.

As the fellow says: "You can't have everything."

———

Beanings are a baseball fact of life. Every few years, it seems, a player is hit by a pitched ball seriously enough in the head that their career is marred; Hall of Famer Frank Chance was seriously beaned, as were 1960s-era players like Tony Conigliaro and Bobby Wine. But only one major leaguer ever died as a direct result of being beaned: It was Cleveland shortstop Ray Chapman, whose skull was fractured August 16, 1920, at the Polo Grounds by a pitch from Carl Mays. The tragedy came in the middle of a furious three-team American League pennant race among the Indians, Yankees, and White Sox that Cleveland would eventually win, taking the World Series that fall as well. Here is Runyon's game report, with a sidebar on the Chapman injury.

S. O'NEILL, HE BINGLES A FEW (AUG. 17, 1920)

Backstop of the Cleveland Club Is Quite a Factor in Beating the Yanks

There was much sound and fury in the ninth inning up under Coogan's enchanted mesa yesterday afternoon.

When the tumult and the shouting died, however, and Cap'ns (Roger) Peckinpaugh and (Tris) Speaker, and Kings Jake Ruppert and Til Huston had departed, the score still seemed to be 4 to 3 in favor of Cleveland, Ohio.

Everything seems to be in favor of Ohio nowadays.

It was in the first presentation on the home premises by the Yanks since their ramblings and rumblings around through the West. The answer is S. O'Neill, of the "two L" family.

S. O'Neill is a backstopper of parts at all times, and something of a hitter sometimes. Yesterday afternoon was one of those times. S. O'Neill was 50 percent of the Cleveland show. He scored two runs, one of them a homer, and was generally nefarious.

The game was marred by the accident to Ray Chapman, the Cleveland shortstop. Carl Mays accidentally hit Chapman on the head with a pitched ball, at the beginning of the fifth frame.

O'Neill's Single in Fifth Scores Run

The Yankees beat the Clevelanders four straight games in Cleveland not long ago, and Speaker's club was mighty down-hearted about the matter. It looked as if M. Huggins's men had their addresses.

Yesterday, outside of that final stab, it looked as if Tris' boys had swiped our folk' little red books, and were calling up all the numbers themselves. The run that proved to be the winning run was put over in the same inning in which Chapman was hurt.

The shortstop was the first man up in the fifth. After he had been carried from the field, (Harry) Lunte ran for Chapman, but was forced at second by Speaker, (Elmer) Smith struck out. Larry Gardner singled, putting Speaker on third, and Steve O'Neill singled to right, scoring his manager.

Going into the ninth inning, the Yankees were four runs to the rear. Babe Ruth led off with a single, which was about his most important feat of the day, barring a swell fielding play on Jamieson's tough fly in the preceding inning.

(Del) Pratt walked. Duffy Lewis pushed Jamieson up against the leftfield wall for his drive, and (Wally) Pipp grounded out to Doc Johnston. Then Ping Bodie doubled, and (Babe) Ruth and Pratt checked in. (Muddy) Ruel singled to left, scoring Bodie. The fans, who had sat through part of the game in a rainstorm, were raving as Frank O'Doul, the fleet Californian, came up batting in place of Lefty (Herb) Thormahlen.

Ruel Muff at Plate Helps Indians to Run

(Lefty) O'Doul rolled to (Bill) Wambsganss, forcing Ruel at second, and ending the game. It was in the nature of a big relief to Stanley Coveleskie, who felt himself slipping just as plain.

In the fourth, Mays passed Gardner after one was out. S. O'Neill belted a single to center, putting Gardner on third. Muddy Ruel then muffed a throw to the plate from (Roger) Peckinpaugh on (Doc) Johnston's grounder (and) Gardner scored. (Aaron) Ward fumbled Wambganss's grounder, and (Stan) Covesleski's sacrifice fly scored O'Neill.

O'Neill's homer into the leftfield bleachers in the second gave Cleveland its other run. Steve was certainly a valuable man for Tris Speaker yesterday.

———

PITCHED BALL IN YANKEE GAME FRACTURES CHAPMAN'S SKULL (AUG. 17, 1920, SIDEBAR)

Tragedy stalked the field at the Polo Grounds yesterday afternoon.

Twenty thousand people saw a man go drifting into the valley of the shadow of death.

Ray Chapman, the grand short fielder of the Cleveland club, was hit by a pitched ball from the hand of Carl Mays in the first game of the Yankees' new home engagement.

His skull was fractured. He is in a very serious condition at the St. Lawrence Hospital. His recovery is still a matter of grave doubt.

Chapman was the first man up at the start of Cleveland's side of the fifth. Mays's first pitched ball cracked against Chapman's temple and the shortstop dropped to the ground as if he had been slugged with a blackjack.

It was purely an accident. Chapman is a good hitter, and Mays was working on him with care. The ball broke so sharply that Chapman did not have time to duck his head and it hit him with all the force of Mays's right arm behind it.

The Cleveland players rushed to the assistance of their comrade. He was unconscious and bleeding from both ears. A doctor was summoned from the stand and partially revived Chapman, but he collapsed again when the Cleveland players lifted him to his feet.

Carried Him from Field

He was carried off the field to the clubhouse, and an ambulance took him to the hospital.

An X-ray examination of Chapman disclosed that he was suffering from a depressed fracture on the left side of the skull and a fracture of the right side. Immediately after the exact nature of the injuries became known, Dr. M.J. Moran, head operating physician at the St. Lawrence Hospital, and Dr. T.D. Merrigan held a consultation with Dr. D.J. Donovan of the Police Department; Tris Speaker; Walter McNichols, secretary of the Cleveland club; and Charlie McManus, business manager of the New York club, and an immediate operation was decided upon.

This accident, witnessed by 20,000 horror-stricken people, means much more than the above paragraphs might signify. Besides the life of a human being, which is worth more than treasure, it may cost the Cleveland club the American League pennant.

This is secondary in the thoughts of the Cleveland players in their concern for their comrade, but it may have to be written into baseball history. Chapman is one of the most valuable ballplayers in the country and has done much to keep Cleveland in the race.

Late last night, it was stated that his condition is extremely critical.

Recalls Fewster Accident

The accident recalls the narrow escape of Chick Fewster of the Yankees, at Jacksonville, during the spring training session this year. Big Jeff Pfeffer of the Brooklyn club hit Fewster in an exhibition game, and for weeks Fewster was in a serious condition. He has been unable to play regularly since.

Some years ago, Russell Ford hit Roy Corhan of the White Sox with a pitched ball at the old Hilltop grounds of the Yankees, and Corhan lay for days in a hospital unconscious. The blow put him out of big-league baseball although he still plays on the Pacific Coast.

—

Runyon was there when Yankee Stadium opened as the greatest sports palace of all time.

RUTH'S HOMER WINS IT FOR YANKS, 4–1 (APR. 19, 1923)

74,000 Jam New Park; Shawkey Humbles Ehmke
With Stage All Set, and Two on Bases, Master Mauler Hits Circuit Clout as Stands and Bleachers Shriek with Joy

"Wouldn't it be simply immense if Ol' Babe should bust one right now," remarked a gentleman of high dramatic instinct as he gazed out over the acres covered by 74,000 folk at the Yankees' new field yesterday afternoon. "Wouldn't it be just"—

Well, whatever it would be, it WAS.

Blooie—that same old blooie—and the King of Swat has supplied the big "punch" to the scenario for the opening of the American League season of 1923, a scenario that couldn't have been better if the members of the Baseball Writers' Association of America had mapped it out in advance with a view to making the event "good copy."

Blooie—and a vocal blast that seemed to rock the Bronx— that certainly shook up some of the rocks of the Bronx, rolled out of the towering stands, and boiled up from the broad bleachers, as the thing happened that everybody had come to see happen.

That's a great sound, that blooie, especially when there are two runners on the bases, as was the case when Babe Ruth stepped to the plate in the third inning yesterday, and the Boston Red Sox, the Yankees' playmates in this opening game, began spreading their lines of defense.

Aaron Ward had opened the Yankees' side of the third with a single to left—this is all arranging the stage for Ruth's appearance, you understand.

Stage Is All Set

Everett Scott bunted to Burns, the Red Sox first baseman, and McMillan crossed in behind Burns and took the put out at first. "Red Sleeves" Bob Shawkey hit to Ehmke, the Boston pitcher, who threw to Fewster at second. Fewster tossed to Shanks, who got Ward at third after a brief run-up. Shawkey rested on second.

Witt walked, and Dugan singled to center, scoring Shawkey and sending Witt to third. Now then, there's your stage, all dressed, Ruth lumbering up out of dugout with a bat at his heels, and 74,000 of the big town citizenry teetering with excitement.

Here it was that the Yankees won the game by a score of 4 to 1, a fact which should have been made public earlier in this story, but which has been suppressed up to now for no ulterior motive.

Ehmke, the Red Sox pitcher, who deems it a point of pitching honor to pitch to Ruth, rather than pass him off with no more consideration than four wide ones, "laid 'er in there" for the King of Clout, who brooded over each pitch.

Into the Bleachers

Two balls and two strikes was the count, when the King uncoiled himself in his mighty lunge which always produces a "blooie," or nothing. The ball flew out over right field, traversing territory hitherto unchartered by the Babe's "blooies" and landed among a dense collection of Bronxonians gathered in the rightfield bleachers to make this opening a most auspicious occasion.

The two runners already present on the bases, and Ruth himself, moving with kingly dignity, trotted around the bases to the tune of three tallies, and the crowd cut itself loose, and erupted exclamations into the bright, but somewhat chilly air.

Ballgames, and blooies will be common occurrences at the Yankees' new field the next few months, but grand openings and 74,000 persons, the largest paid attendance at a ballgame in the history of the sport, may not be so common.

Compared with Coliseum

The writer, groping for a comparison to indicate to the reader the size of the Yankees' new stadium, where all this business went on, thinks of the Coliseum of Rome. Or, at least, what we had read of that famous structure. It must have been pretty big.

We have never met anyone that saw the Coliseum in its palmy days, but history tells us that it accommodated 350,000 men, women, and children. On that basis even the most loyal inmate of the Bronx, which claims the Yankee stadium as its very own, would have to admit that it outsized the Ruppert-Huston effort.

However, the Bronxonians can claim for the Yankee stadium that it has the advantage over the Roman structure of hot and cold running water in every room, and a magnificent view from one side of the rival Polo Grounds across the gleaming Harlem.

Judge in the Picture

It was a grand day, with the sunlight spilling into the big oval, and tinting the gray hair of the good Judge Kenesaw Mountain Landis, the big boss of baseball, as he stood out on the field flanked by the beaming features of the Colonels, Jacob Ruppert and Tillinghast l'Hommedieu Huston, and had his picture taken.

The photographers used on the Judge the very last of their films. The rest had gone taking pictures of Babe Ruth, Miller Huggins, Frank Chance, the dour manager of the Red Sox, and all the other celebrities of the moment.

The folks began rushing the ball yard along toward noon and by 3 o'clock most of them had finally solved the puzzle of the entrances, although some kept walking round and round the outer walls in great bewilderment until the gates were slapped in their faces.

Gates Are Shut Early

They locked the place up shortly after 3 o'clock. There were no more chairs. Meantime a steady stream of taxis and motor cars wound across the Harlem River bridge and pedestrians kicked up the dust of the newly-made road approaching the towering walls.

However, at 3:30 o'clock, which was the game time, everybody was comfortably seated, wondering how they were going to find their way out again, and saying to their neighbor, "Gee whiz, this is a big joint."

The two colonels responsible for this comment held open house in the offices on what is called the mezzanine floor, to make it sound Biltmorish, and assisted by the Messrs. Stevens, Harry M. and Frank, dispensed ham sandwiches, hot coffee, and Ruppert's one-half-of-one-percent to all comers.

Mr. Egbert Barrow, the business manager of the Yankees; Mr. Joe Kelley and Mr. Bob Connery, the Yankee scouts, and all the other Yankee attaches stood in the ballground with expressions of pride on their serried countenances.

Sparrow's Spirit There

Somewhere about the premises beaming with the material souls was undoubtedly hovering the rotund spirit of the late Harry Sparrow, the first business manager of the Yankees under the Ruppert-Huston regime, to whom three thousand persons was a great and gladsome crowd. Harry used to dream his little dream of the Yankees in a home of their own, but alas, he did not live to see it materialize.

The Seventh Regiment band marched in at 3:15, all dolled up in uniforms that made them look like the guardsmen of Napoleon's day, long gray coats, shakoes, white trousers, white belts.

Presently a familiar figure in a dark blue military uniform stepped briskly across the field, and the crowd gave a whoop of recognition, as John Philip Sousa took command of the musicians.

The Yankees, in gray sweaters over their white uniforms, fell in behind the band, then the Red Sox emerged from their dungeon in flaming scarlet sweaters over their gray toggery, and the parade moved, with everybody out of step, after the time-honored custom of baseballers.

Managers Hoist Flag

Mr. Sousa led the boys around the yard to center field, where there is a flagpole almost as tall as the new apartment hotel that is rearing its roof not far beyond the center field wall.

Miller Huggins and Frank Chance planted themselves under the flagpole, and as the band played "The Star Spangled Banner" they gripped a rope in their calloused palms and hauled a huge copy of Old Glory to the peak. The crowd stood, heads bared.

Then Huggins and Chance took hold of some more ropes, Huggins' face assuming a very tired expression at this juncture, and hauled up a flag which said something about the Yankees being the American League champions of 1922. This was in case anyone might have forgotten it.

The crowd cheered as the flag went up. One man in the grandstand let out a terrific "boo." He must have been a traitorous Giant partisan.

Governor Smith in Parade

The band came back across the field, now headed by Governor Al Smith, Judge Landis and a number of military gentlemen in olive drab, generals, colonels, majors, and the like. They had been waiting over in center field for the flag ceremonies.

The crowd gave the Governor a big cheer as the parade disbanded in front of the stands. Under cover of the general excitement Harry Frazee surreptitiously crossed the field and joined his club. Not a funeral note was heard as he glided stealthily to the dugout.

Tribute to Huggins

A number of strong men came out lugging a floral horseshoe of roses, only slightly smaller than the playing field, which seemed to be intended for Miller Huggins. The present surprised Mr. Huggins, who has heretofore been the recipient of wreaths of raspberry bushes rather than roses.

Now came that imposing ceremony known as "throwing out the first ball." A baseball opening wouldn't be complete without that. It is believed that in the first game ever played in the world somebody threw out the first ball.

Wally Schang got himself all done up in his catching regalia, and went over in front of Governor Smith's box, hard by the Yankee bench. Wally squatted in stereotyped catching posture. The Governor got up, took off his hat, and flung a new baseball into Wally's outstretched dukes.

There's really nothing much to the ceremony, but it is considered highly necessary. Colonel Jake Ruppert, with a red rose from Huggins's horseshoe in his lapel, and his derby hat in his hand, stood by and watched the Governor do his throwing.

Takes Lot of Detail

Wally trotted to the Governor's box with the ball, presented it to the Governor, shook the gubernatorial fist, then the game got to moving. It takes a lot of detail to get one of these first games of the season started.

"Red Sleeves" Bob Shawkey with his flannel underwear partly exposed, who had been warming up so long he was already tired, shambled to the pitching mound, and fixed a piercing eye upon "Chick" Fewster, the Red Sox second baseman, who used to be a Yankee.

While Bob's first pitch to Chick was no more important than a thousand pitches he will make during the season, it may be related here that it was pronounced a ball by Umpire Tommy Connolly. Tommy was assisted in the umpirical labors by two other gesticulators, the Messrs. William Evans and "Ducky" Holmes, who took things easy out on the pillows, as we call the bases in the slang of the day.

Shawkey fiddled around with Fewster until Chick finally knocked the baseball down to Everett Scott, the Yankee short fielder, who passed it over to Walter Pipp ahead of the galloping Fewster.

First Hit by Burns

George Burns, not the Giants' George Burns, but the Detroit and Cleveland George Burns, got the first hit of the occasion, a single to center in the Red Sox side of the second inning. Then George Burns got reckless and tried to steal second. Schang had the ball in Ward's hands a yard ahead of George Burns.

We almost forgot to mention Babe Ruth's "first." It was a fly to right. One of these seasons the Babe's "firsts" will be no more important than any other pastimer's "first," if the Babe doesn't get to slapping 'em regularly.

The crowd was a great spectacle. The heads were packed in so close that Al Goullet, the six-day rider, could have ridden his bicycle around the oval on a track of hats. It is a mile around the stands and the bleachers and practically every inch of seating space was chinked in.

Quite a Fall

The upper tier of the stand juts out over the field like a hanging cliff, with a sharp downward shoot. Only a veteran dweller of tenth and eleventh floors of apartment houses can sit up there without feeling a bit squeamish. It would be a long fall from the top seat to the ground. A man would have time to think over a lot of things.

Under this tier, but well back, as if it had suddenly shrunk from alignment, is the so-called mezzanine floor, below this the seats of the lower stand. The place looks most imposing when it is all filled up, but it will seem mighty empty when it is empty.

Colonel Jacob Ruppert, president of the Yankees, still wearing the red rose from Huggins's horseshoe, watched the game from the press box, and wagered the writer a suit of clothes that there were over 71,000 persons on the premises.

It began to cloud up in the fifth inning, but by that time the crowd had experienced a little bit of everything. Long Bob Meusel busted a two-bagger in the fourth and was expunged at third on Schang's push to the box. Ward doubled to right, an Schang was put out at the plate after a desperate gallop.

Ruth's First Muff

Ruth and several other well-known Yankees pursued a fly off Harris's hickory in the fifth, and Ruth, arriving under it ahead of the others, scored his first muff of the season. Harris pulled up at second, but nothing else happened.

"Whitey" Witt, so-called because of his cotton-colored hair, singled in the Yankee phase of the fifth, and Ruth got a base on balls amid some booing of the peering Ehmke, although Ehmke was pitching quite earnestly at Bambino. After a man gets slugged for a home run he is bound to be careful.

Two were out when all this transpired, and Pipp, the old-time "pickler," popped futilely to McMillan, while the band played "Mr. Gallagher and Mr. Shean."

The crowd in the centerfield bleachers began filing out, perhaps taking the cue from Governor Smith. With the disappearance of the sun, the air grew chilled. The folks thought of home and mother. Even the band tore out.

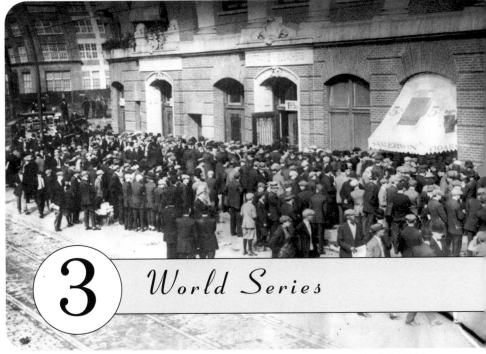

3 *World Series*

1911 World Series, Shibe Park (Philadelphia)

Few events put Runyon's reportorial gifts on display more than the World Series. For a quarter century, he seldom missed a single Series game even long after he'd left the full-time baseball beat. Runyon would arrive early and begin writing—producing prodigiously long, batter-by-batter summaries of the game that would usually begin on page 1 of the paper and rattle on inside for columns. Just as entertaining was Runyon's coverage on travel days that covered the gamut from what the gamblers were saying to the softness of the beds on the Pullmans and just about anywhere else his creative mind roamed.

With the Philadelphia A's leading the Giants two games to one in the 1911 World Series, Runyon journeys to Philadelphia for game three, and picks up the banter on an off-day. Although the Series had been eventful already, particularly with Frank Baker's two home runs in the A's 3–2 win in game three, Runyon writes little here about baseball, choosing to focus on the conversation of gamblers on the train, and the modern convenience in Philadelphia houses of mirrors over the front door to announce a visitor. "The wonder is that it has not spread over the land like a reeking pestilence instead of being confined to Philadelphia," Runyon writes of the mirror contraption. Chances are no other writer ever has used the term, "reeking pestilence" in a baseball column.

RUNYON SAYS GIANTS ARE STILL CONFIDENT (OCT. 19, 1911)

Philadelphia, Oct. 18—Let us, at this time, thrust a ghoulish hand into that Potter's Field of pleasantry where all poor old gags lie buried, trying to die; haul there from a feeble fable and stand it upon its tottering pins for the purposes of this rainy day relation:

A crowd of men were conversing in the smoker of a dilatory Pennsylvania train this morning as it splashed juicily over the Jersey paddy fields en route to Philadelphia.

"I," said a stout, garish-looking man, apropos of nothing but the excuse for this lead, "I can invariably tell what town a man is from by his looks."

"I'll make a little bet with you on that," said another member of the party. "I'll bet you a satchel of wine you can't."

The wager was laid. Together they started on a tour of the train to make the test of the stout man's observational powers.

They came upon a man in the chair-car, who was slumped far down in his seat; a pallid, dejected-looking man, whose eyes were expressive of deep woe.

"Ah," said the stout man, triumphantly. "Ah—here is a New Yorker!"

"No sir!" he denied. "Not me. I'm from Dadeville, Alabama. I've been sick—that's what makes me look this way."

A crime, it is true, but when beaten baseball players immure themselves in recesses of silence, and rain falls heavily outside, and there is no game of World Series ball, one must have copy, even if one must despoil the dead.

Goes to Philadelphia Unwillingly

Who goes to Philadelphia on a rainy Wednesday from New York goes unwillingly. The strength of twice 10,000-horse and all the string-halt locomotives that puff asthmatically hitherward could not drag the average holder of a pew along Gotham's big, bright aisle to this patient town at this particular time were it not for that fourth game of the big mill, because Quakerdom is on a strut and speaking stridently.

In front of the houses in Philadelphia, especially in the residence sections, they have an untoward arrangement which hangs near the windows on the second story, just over the front stoop; an arrangement of mirrors, into which, when the doorbell rings, the householder may peer from the privacy of the second floor and see who it is at the door, without himself being seen.

It is a secretive device of amazing value when one contemplates the coming of the bill collector; the wonder is that it has not spread over the land like a reeking pestilence instead of being confined to Philadelphia. Thus today the jubilant Quakers could sit at their elegant ease indoors, their ears set for the noise of car-locks in the street outside; they could take note of each passerby, and if happened, as was frequently the case, to a funereal-looking New Yorker, the Philadelphians could pop their heads from their windows and shout the strange jargon of their kind.

New York Has Nothing to Say

New York says nothing, largely because New York has nothing to say.

It is the day of damp—oh, Mr. Printer, beware that "p"—Philadelphia's triumph, and they are making it a full-case deal.

Some time between the hour of sunrise—or, that is to say the hour at which the sun would have risen had it been so disposed—and noon, the National Commission officially declared the game off. Then it resumed the official contemplation of all that dough it will get out of the series. You who have never seen a National Commissioner's supper tab cannot be expected to appreciate the pleasure of this contemplation.

Meantime some thousands of New Yorkers had rowed or swam across the channel intervening between here and there, and Philadelphia gave another cheer, because New Yorkers have to eat when they are cast away in Philadelphia just the same as when they are home. However, the local joy over this necessity was short-lived, as most of the crowd returned home rather than take a chance.

———

Rain in Philadelphia, causing another day's postponement of game four of the World Series—leading Runyon to manufacture another rainy-day column full of weather-contemplation and series-related ruminations of whether Fred Snodgrass of the Giants intentionally spiked Home Run Baker of the A's in game three, as the Philadelphians claimed.

GIANTS' PROPHETS WITH A LOT OF "IF," STILL SEE VICTORY (OCT. 20, 1911)

They Expect McGraw's Men to Win Today's Game, Provided It Is Played

PHILADELPHIA, OCT. 19—Having deposited the sealed verdict in the hands of Judge Pluvius, the jury of fates disbanded again today, and our Ruzzielambs won't know whether they are to get any dough in that breaches of promise case against old Lady Fortune until tomorrow afternoon.

You will note the dateline.

Philadelphia.

Do you realize why anyone with a lacerated heart remains in Philadelphia, with the World Series standing two games to one in favor of their boys?

The answer is rain. Rain, no less, Philadelphia rain.

They postponed the fourth game of the string for the second time this morning because of wet grounds, setting the morrow as the time for play, and meantime the Giants' prospects gorge and wax more corpulent upon a diet of delay.

No Riot of Protest

There was no riot of protest around their camp when the postponement was announced.

There is no paucity of news. A rumor ran around the town this morning that Fred Snodgrass, the Giant outfielder, had been shot, or something, by an infuriated Philadelphia fan over the Baker incident. This was a mistake. It is against the law to shoot persons in Philadelphia. It is especially against the law to shoot any member of Oxnard Parlor, No. 2. Native Sons of the Golden West, of which Mr. Snodgrass is such.

The only man shot in Philadelphia today was an inoffensive resident of the Bronx, and they did it to him in the arm for resuscitatory purposes when he heard that Philadelphia was planning to demonstrate against Snodgrass tomorrow afternoon. The idea of a demonstration in these parts was too much for the Bronxite.

It would appear that Philadelphia is growing a large oak from a small acorn. Snodgrass has denied that he intended to spike Baker, and everybody else has denied saying that Snodgrass intended to. That ought to be enough. The shooting rumor was deemed of sufficient importance for the Associated Press to take cognizance of, however.

Can't Find Any Bullet Holes

When interviewed at his hotel concerning the matter. Mr. Snodgrass felt himself over very carefully before replying, and then said:

"I am unable to detect any bullet holes."

John J. McGraw, manager of the Giants, was reproved by the National Commission today for not being more secretive in his opinions concerning Tommy Connolly in the game at the Polo Grounds. The reproach extended $100 worth to Fred Merkle, the Giants' first baseman, who also spoke to Mr. Connolly. Both were threatened with disbarment from future World Series games.

The National Commission, be it understood, is a large body, surrounded by much authority. A bird's-eye view of the National Commission reproving anybody is an impressive orgy, and an expensive one as well, as Merkle can testify.

Under ordinary circumstances Fred Merkle wouldn't give two cents to talk to Connolly, and here he has to dig up one entire century of the winner's end.

Time for a Lighter View

When they commence to circulate rumors about a ballplayer being shot for something that happened in a game, it does not look like it is about time to settle back and take a little lighter view of things generally. As for the reproaches of the National Commission, while they may not be viewed lightly under pain of further reproaching, it would seem that in this instance that august body took a more ponderous view of the case than circumstances justified in view of Merkle's previous splendid record.

Somebody had Arthur Wilson, the popular catcher of the Giants, rumored into the sneezer too. It was something about tickets. Now, of course, Arthur was never pinched in his life, and probably never pinched in his life, and probably never will be, and the story was particularly laughable, because it centered about one of the most gentlemanly young fellows in the business.

So, all in all, the Giants are getting a shade the worst of all that is doing in the rumor line, but they will probably manage to survive, and will be out there playing ball tomorrow.

———

The rain finally stopped—and the World Series ended with an A's' rout in game six.

ATHLETICS WIN WORLD SERIES, BEATING GIANTS 13 TO 2 (OCT. 27, 1911)

Connie Mack's Quakers Slaughter McGraw's Band, Virtually Batting Three Pitchers out of the Box; Championship is Retained by Hard Slugging
Philadelphia, October 26—A little of that soft, slow, slobby music, professor! All right—let 'er go:

> The tumult and the shouting dies,
> The players, with the dough depart;
> The dope, to our intense surprise,
> Was wrong—be still, oh aching heart!
>   (Piano.)
> There are some dollars that we bet—
>   (Extremely pianissimo.)
> Let us FORget—let us forget!

Thirteen members of the Athletic Baseball Club touched the home plate at Shibe Park this afternoon, and Umper Bill Klem admits it: wherefore, the World Series of 1911 passes into history with the Philadelphia American League club still champion of the world, and environs, because while this unlucky number of runners, trotters and pedestrians were passing in review before the astounded eyes of 20-some-odd-thousand people, the Giants' footprints tracked the plate but twice.

In all the bright lexicon of N. Webster, there is no such word as adequately describes the sixth and last game of the post-season meeting of the clubs that were best in their respective leagues.

"Massacre" Too Sedate

A searching finger slides past "massacre" and "slaughter" as too sedate and conservative to fit the cases. If anybody had suggested that there were so many runs in all the world as were made by the Athletics in the seventh inning alone, the suggestion would have been rejected as the vagary of a distorted brain.

Thirteen to two!

Well, well—so passes the bog series along with its scandals and dissensions and spikings and untouched home plates; so pass the actor-author-athletes, who have been in or of the battle, and now that it is all over, who shall say that the best team did not win?

Not Connie Mack, at all events.

"Big Chief" Bender pitched this afternoon after a brief rest, and Leon ("Red") Ames, George ("Hooks") Wiltse and Rube Marquard were the Giant twirlers who were squashed in the final charge of the White Elephant.

The score is close to a record for a World Series; it represents the worst whipping Johnny McGraw's Giants have taken from any club this season.

Ingloriously Routed

Broken and beaten and on the run from the fourth inning, the Giants grew worse instead of better against the onslaught of the Athletic sluggers. Had the series ended Wednesday with the Giants beaten four straight it still would have been considered a notable battle by the big-town boys, and there would have been no regrets, but they won Wednesday by a wonderful stand at the eleventh hour and gave their admirers so much hope that several thousand New Yorkers

moved upon Philadelphia today, only to see the black-robed Polo
Grounders routed ingloriously.

They got away well, and were out in front up to the third inning.
In the fourth, "Red" Ames, the unlucky Ohioan, who was pitching
for the Giants, made a bad throw, which threw the McGraw crew
clear out of their stride. In the seventh inning, the Athletics fell
upon "Hooks" Wiltse, the veteran left-hander, with fury, and
whaled his shoots to all corners of the lot, herding in a whole flock
of runs.

There was no fight left in the Giants after that, Marquard was
sent in and scored two runs by immediately unleashing a wild
pitch over (Chief) Meyers' shoulder. The crowd began leaving
when the seventh closed.

Unluckiest Good Pitcher

On April 12, 1911, the National League season was officially
opened at the Polo Grounds by the unveiling of "Red" Ames; justly
notorious Jinx—the blond Ohioan boy being the tender of the
most savage Jinx in the big league.

A small concourse of Philadelphians were present on that occasion, representing the National League club of that city. It was fitting, perhaps, that "Red" should close the baseball festivities and
funerals of the year by again displaying his renowned charge
before another crowd of Philadelphians.

Ames is called the unluckiest good pitcher in the upper circles
of baseball. He proved it this afternoon. In the Wednesday game
(five at New York, won by the Giants, 4 to 3), Ames relieved Marquard and pitched superb ball. He looked like a good bet on a
coolish day such as today, and he stepped out bravely.

The Giants slipped him a one-run lead in the first inning, and
Ames cherished it up to the third. It looked as if he was keeping the
Jinx under cover too, but in the fourth he gave the crowd a peak.

The score at that time was 1–1. J. Franklin Baker of Trappe,
Md., who is making a collection of base hits to touch up the gloom
of the parlor back home, singled to right center.

On a hit-and-run play, Danny Murphy, who was resting under suspicion of owning a solid beam in his dome, because of that catch at the Polo Grounds Wednesday, skipped a single to left center, and Baker shoved along to third. Thereafter, hitting the ball was the best thing Danny did, too.

What Happened to Doyle

(Red) Murray finally let (Harry) Davis' foul fly drop to the ground, and then Davis cracked a bounder to (Larry) Doyle, who made a pretty play getting the ball. Then, Larry hesitated, and the old copy books tell us that he who hesitates is lost, which is what happened to Larry and the game. He took a look around.

There seemed to be time for Doyle to make a play at the plate on Baker, who was scudding for home, or on Davis and Murphy. Finally, Doyle shot the ball to Meyers, but Baker was in by that time. Davis was sale at first, and Murphy had whipped it on to second.

At the interesting juncture, "Red" Ames unveiled his jinx. He got hold of "(Jack) Barry's bunt and threw it toward first to get the shortstop. The balk cracked Barry on the head and bounced past Merkle into right field. Murray picked it up out there and fired it wild to (Art) Fletcher, at second base, to head off Barry, who was legging it in that direction, Davis and Murray, meantime, bustling in over the plate. The ball bounced out into left field, where Josh Devore got it fir the purpose of examination. Josh also fumbled, so Baker went on himself.

That was all.

There went to the world's championship title, and something like $1,200 from each and every Giant player—that amount representing the difference between the winner's and the loser's end.

Charles Victory Faust Is Glad

"I am glad," said Charles Victory Faust, of Marion, Kan., the Giant Jinx dispenser, who has been off his feed during the series, and who looks very much like a man without a situation at this writing.

"I am glad that the championship remains in America. . . . Yours truly, John L. Sullivan."

The seven runs the Athletics snared in the seventh made no particular difference. That was merely rubbing salt in the Giants' wounds, G. "Hooks" Wiltse was out there on the mound with nothing much but a bare left arm, and the youthful disciples of the serious McGillicuddy, stepped blithely to the bat, one by one, and passed the ball to the outskirts of Philadelphia.

The Giants had a band with them—the gray-clad boys of the Catholic Protectory—who played them into action Wednesday, and the musical youngsters did their best to instill tuneful courage into the hearts of the Giants, but they were past the soothing charm of even melody.

When the Gotham crew were getting the hooks in the seventh, Philadelphia laid back and guffawed. It was the first hearty laugh they have had over there at New York's expense since 1905 (when the Giants beat the A's in five games with Christy Mathewson winning three).

They had their usual demonical instruments for disturbance, and they made a noise like a Chinese New Year's celebration throughout the stampede.

Sitting on the New York bench, gray as a badger from his season's worry, and marked with lines about the eyes that were not there a year ago, Johnny McGraw, the pudgy leader of the big-town boys—the man who "ran a shoestring into a pennant"—watched the rout.

What his feelings were no man knows.

What baseball wonders he has worked in winning the National League pennant with the material he had any baseball follower can tell; what a near-miracle he accomplished by holding the sensational Athletics the way he has in this series will be told in the years to come.

Hard fights, close scores—a peek at the very championship itself—so much had he wrought, and how he sat there on the Giant bench and watched the devastation of his hopes and kept his thoughts to himself.

Tommy Connolly, the American League umpire, who came in

for much criticism during this series, worked behind the plate today. Big Bill Brennan of the National League was on the bases; (Bill) Klem, the Columbus of the untouched home plate, was out in left field, and Bill Dinneen was in right.

Crowd Smallest of Series

The stands and bleachers were comfortably filled and there was an overflow in the fields, but the crowd was the smallest of the series. It grew less as the game went on.

Many a prophet of the stands declared when Bender (who had gone the distance two days before in game four, winning 4–2) appeared that the Chippewa would never be able to repeat after such a short rest, and he got away so wobbly as to make their predictions look good. Once he got on even terms with the Giants, however, he buckled up and was invincible.

Of the Giants who have played in this series, the man who stands head and shoulders above all the rest is John J. (Chief) Meyers, the Mission Indian, who has done the bulk of the catching for McGraw this year. His work was so far superior to the others that there is no comparison.

Close followers of the game are now ranking him with the best catchers of the big leagues, if not the very best. It was predicted in some quarters the Indian would lose his head and go to pieces. He was the coolest, headiest player in McGraw's collection. His work was almost flawless, and his heart was in every game.

Next to him stands Charley Herzog, the former Bostonian (Braves), gamest of the game, who came to the Giants in mid-season, and lightened the infield into a pennant winner. Fred Merkle played a marvelous fielding game, although he did no hitting; Larry Doyle started hitting late, and fell off in his fielding as he did so, just as he fielded faultlessly and failed to hit during the first games.

———

That the Giants would lose their second series in two seasons — they would lose again to the A's in 1913—highlighted what many believed was a major flaw in John McGraw's teams: "his strong preference for players who fit his system" writes Don Jensen in Deadball Stars of the National League. *The Giants were generally considered less talented than other teams; Johnny Evers called them a second-class club with a first-class manager. And as Jensen points out, McGraw's teams also seemed to make mental errors in big games, "as though as they didn't know what to do or were paralyzed at the thought of how the Old Man might react if they lost."*

Of Fred Snodgrass's drop of an easy fly ball that many believed cost the Giants the 1912 World Series, Runyon was sympathetic to the 23-year-old Californian arguing that the dropping of Tris Speaker's foul pop a few moments before was perhaps the real blow that sealed the Giants' fate. Poor Snodgrass, who'd be traded to the Braves in 1915 and leave the majors just two years later to enter the appliance business in California, was forever haunted by the muff. "Hardly a day in my life, hardly an hour, that in some manner or the other the dropping of that fly doesn't come up," he'd say in 1940. "On the street, in my store, at my house . . . it's all the same. . . . They always ask." Even death didn't spare him—his 1974 obituary in the New York Times *was headlined, "Fred Snodgrass, 86, Dead, Ball Player Muffed 1912 Fly."*

ERRORS OF OMISSION AND COMMISSION PROVE FATAL (OCT. 17, 1912)

World's Championship Twice within Grasp of Great Matty, but Ragged Fielding Flicks Away Hard-Earned Advantage

BOSTON, OCT. 16—Twice this afternoon, Christy Mathewson held the championship of the world in his grasp, only to see it flicked away by errors of commission and omission by the men behind him, and tonight the Boston Red Sox are the holders of the coveted title, which means supremacy in baseball.

The end came in the 10th inning of the eighth game of the hardest-fought series in the history of the game, when the gallant

Sox rushed in through the gaps in the fielding defense of the great pitcher and won by a score of 3 to 2.

Outpitching two young, fresh opponents—Hugh Bedient and Joe Wood—the wonderful veteran, who had already fought two bitter engagements in the battle for the championship, carried his team along to what seemed certain victory for six innings. Then began a series of breaks behind him that finally lost the New York Giants the greatest prize in the world of sport.

It is detracting in no way from the victory of the Sox to say that no pitcher ever lost a game involving such a stake under such unfortunate circumstances. Baseball men are talking tonight not so much of the winning of the championship by the Boston team as of the greatness of the old star.

There is no excuse for the Giants. There can be only individual absolution of the sins of error. The sympathy is all for Mathewson, who emerges from the long series without having won a single game, but with all the laurels.

Story of How the Giants Lost

Curiously enough, the story of today is not the story of how the Red Sox won the championship, but the story of how the Giants lost it. Some in seeking to place the blame single out Fred Snodgrass, the black-haired centerfielder, who made a bad muff of a fly ball in the 10th inning and started the Sox to two runs and the title. But while that happened to be the most conspicuous error of commission, it was not the play which turned the Giants down the lane of defeat.

Two errors of omission figured as prominently in the downfall of the big-town boys as that muff by the luckless Snodgrass, who seemed to have been picked out by an evil fate this afternoon as a shining mark and who feels more keenly than anyone else the stings of the shafts of misfortune.

It might be remembered, too, that whatever else he has done, the Giants might not have been playing that game this afternoon but for the California boy, whose catch at the Polo Grounds last

Monday kept them in the series. Anyway, when it is considered that the Giants, headed by one of the greatest of baseball leaders (John McGraw), have been able to outgeneral the Sox through eight games, have outhit them and made a show of them on the bases, but still could not win because of mechanical fielding deficiencies, it becomes apparent that no one man should be picked out for blame.

How the good, game Sox came on from behind and tied the score on Mathewson in the seventh is the story of one of the grave errors of omission of how young Olaf Henriksen, a 23-year-old outfielder, grasped one of those opportunities for fame which comes on rare occasions during a World Series to a youngster on a big-league bench.

Red Sox Tie Score

Mathewson had been toiling along on a scant margin of one run. Harry Gardner was the first man up in the Sox side of the seventh and he raised an easy fly to Snodgrass.

Jack Stahl, leader of the Sox, raised a high fly pretty well back of the short field, over toward center, which might possibly have been caught by (Red) Murray, Snodgrass, or (Art) Fletcher, although it would have been a hard chance for any one of them. Fletcher went back peddling rapidly into the field, with Snodgrass and Murray closing in on either side of him. It seemed that it would have been easier for Snodgrass than any of the others to make the catch. That is mere conjecture, as the ball was being carried by the wind as the trio came in, one of those misunderstandings as to which man should make the play arose, and the ball fell safe between them. Stahl had easy sailing.

Heinie Wagner drew a walk from Mathewson, who was more liberal with passes today than ever before in an important game. (Hick) Cady hit the first ball pitched to him for an easy pop to Fletcher, and "Big Six" seemed to believe easy sailing.

Stahl called for young Henriksen, and sent him up to bat in place of Hugh Bedient, the young pitcher who took a decision over

Mathewson in one game of the series last week, and who was again giving the Giants a strong argument. (The 24-year-old) Henriksen had never faced Mathewson before, and is not considered a desperately hard hitter under ordinary circumstances. A youngster facing the Old Master for the first time is generally regarded as handicapped to some extent, especially if Mathewson is fully extended, as he was today.

Matty quickly got two strikes in the Wareham (Mass.) lad, then put two balls across. He figured that if Henriksen hit the next one at all, he would hit it to left and give Murray a chance to throw Stahl out at the plate, but as Henriksen rapped the ball, a puff of dust arose from the third-base bag as the drive ticked the canvas, and then the ball sped away down the leftfield foul line to the only place where Murray could not get it.

Matty's Work Goes for Naught

Stahl scored and Wagner took third. (Harry) Hooper hit the first ball offered him for a fly to Snodgrass, and the inning was over. All of Mathewson's magnificent work through the earlier innings now counted for nothing.

"Smoky Joe" Wood, who had been kept warmed up by Stahl for just this contingency, entered the box as the Giants opened the eighth, and the boy who was battered so hard in the first inning by the Giants the day before, seemed to have some of his famous "stuff."

In the Giants' end of the 10th, after Wood had tossed out Snodgrass, Murray smashed a line drive into the leftfield bleachers for two bases. Fred Merkle followed him with a double to center, giving the Giants another one-run lead, and apparently, the game.

Stahl played his last card as the Sox went into the 10th, withdrawing Joe Wood and sending up Clyde Engle, the former Yankee, as a pinch-hitter. Engle lifted a high fly in deep left-center. Snodgrass ran over, got under the ball and stood waiting for it to fall. It seemed an easy chance—but they all look easy from the stands. The centerfielder had the ball in his hands, then dropped it, and Engle pulled up safe at second.

Immediately afterward Snodgrass made a fine running catch of Hooper's dangerous-looking fly. (Steve) Yerkes walked, and this brought Tris Speaker, the slugging Texan, to bat. Speaker raised a short foul pop back of the first-base line and over about midway between first base and the plate. (Chief) Meyers took off his mask and started after the ball, which would have been easy for Merkle, and Matty hurried across from the box. Merkle seemed to make a late start, and the general result was that no one got the foul.

Engle Scores Tying Run

Speaker then singled to right, scoring Engle, Yerkes taking third and Speaker reaching second on (Josh) Devore's throw to the plate. (Duffy) Lewis walked, filling the bases, and Mathewson seemed very tired. He gave Duffy four balls in succession. Matty motioned to his outfield to move over toward right for Larry Gardner and pitched a couple of called balls to him. On the next ball, Gardner raised a long fly to Devore and Yerkes scored with ease after the catch. The game was over.

Perhaps no team ever won a world's championship at such cost as the Boston Red Sox, or, rather, the Boston Red Sox management. The smallest crowd of the series (only 17,034 showed up at Fenway Park that day . . . imagine that!) saw the game today, there being great splotches of vacancy in the bleachers and the stands. The treatment of the "Royal Rooters" by the local management, which failed to reserve seats yesterday for the body of fans who have been following the Sox throughout the fight, caused a general boycott on the game and lost the management most of the fat gate it had anticipated.

The failure of Stahl to start Joe Wood last Monday in New York, and make a desperate effort to finish the series then and there, has done inestimable damage to the game here. For in addition to jeopardizing the championship, it has given rise to much criticism of the cupidity of the management.

So soon as Yerkes scored the winning run today, McGraw trotted over to Stahl and extended his congratulations.

The Giants left for New York early this evening, and most of them will leave New York immediately for their homes. All were bewailing their hard luck, but the least cast-down was Mathewson, veteran of 13 years, and good, bad and indifferent luck on the diamond. "Big Six" is now eagerly anticipating a hunting trip as soon as he gets back to New York.

———

Runyon's post-mortem on the 1912 World Series was an intriguing mix of what went wrong for the Giants, with an intimate look at some of the team's players and what they'd be doing for the winter. Few sports reporters had ever written much about the personal lives of the game's players of the deadball era; note the references to baseball's close connection in those days to vaudeville, which was a lucrative way to cash in during the off-season. Marquard, for instance, appeared on stage that winter, meeting in the process his future wife, the dancer Blossom Seeley. Enterprising agents soon booked them to appear at the Palace Theater and on stages across America, where they joked, bantered and performed their hit song, "The Marquard Glide."

VANQUISHED GIANTS OFF TO WINTER HABITATIONS (OCT. 18, 1912)
Several Contemplate Dash into Vaudeville; Others to Go to Bermuda with All-Star Team

Having been assured that there is no possibility, under the rules of the National Commission, of any more ballgames being played this season in the World Series of 1912, Chris Mathewson, the author [His book *Pitching in a Pinch: Baseball from the Inside,* written with John Wheeler, had just been published.], has left this island extremely flat and gone on a hunting expedition.

His publisher has his address in case it is decided to resume the series as a winter attraction in Boston, but the consensus of public opinion hereabouts is that the ballplayers should let the matter

drop for the time being and devote their attention to their vaudeville engagements.

It is said that Chris finds it very difficult to reconcile himself to
the changed condition of affairs, which makes it unnecessary for
him to stand around with a baseball in his hand. Also he misses the
story of the game on the front pages of the newspapers as he par-
takes of his morning mush, and so he has gone on a hunting orgy,
denying with grave emphasis that he intends potting any center-
fielders or first basemen out of season.

A few columns of alibis may have been omitted here and there
in the papers through inadvertence and a desire to vary the
monotony of the printed pages, but otherwise the series seems to
be "all in," and so are the fans.

Richard de Marquis de Marquard, the noted Thespian, is out with
his vaudeville announcement, in which he states that he is going to
play Hamlet left-handed. He will receive real money for appearing on
the stage; but not from us, oh, gentle reader, not from us!

McGraw to Go into Vaudeville

It is said that Manager John J. McGraw is also going to take a
whirl in vaudeville with a monologue, and if the manager of the
Giants agrees to tell us all he knows about umpires and things, as
well as something of what he thinks, he ought to knock 'em out of
their seats.

Speaking of umpires, which we do as inoffensively as possible,
Bill Klem, the National League motion man, was wandering up
and down Broadway yesterday afternoon with $1,000 in his pos-
session and a glad grin on his frontispiece.

It seems that the National Commission intended paying Klem.
"Silk" O'Loughlin, Bill Rigler and Billy Evans $750 each for their
work in the World Series, but after duly considering the fact every
one of the famous gladiators escaped from Boston and the Polo
Grounds without once being taxed with larceny, arson or murder by
the players or fans, the commission tacked $250 to each man's salary.
The commission will never miss the money out of their bit from the

series, and the umpires can display it to their grandchildren as proof that once upon a time the world treated them with kindness.

McGraw Not an Umpire Baiter

The umpires are singing the praises of John McGraw, who was so busy recently trying to win a world's championship without the consent of some of his players, that he wholly overlooked the presence of the platoon of arbitrators. The American League representatives must have expected him to bite his initials in them, judging from their intense surprise, not knowing that McGraw long ago gave all umpires up as hopeless.

"He's the greatest loser I ever saw," said one of the American Leaguers yesterday. "There's no one in his class in that respect."

The Giants will soon disperse to their various homes. Josh Devore, who left Boston announcing that he intended leaping off the Brooklyn Bridge as soon as possible, changed his mind on reaching New York and will wait until he spends his $2,500. Josh will probably go to Terre Haute or some other remote western place, out among the buffalo and the Indians.

Herzog to Study at Cornell

Charley Herzog, who shares with Mathewson the honors of the series, so far as the Giants are concerned, will take a course in agriculture up at Cornell. Charles is interested in perfecting a rindless cantaloupe for his farm in Ridgeley, Md. Leon Ames is going to Warren, Ohio, where $2,500 is considered some means, but he will return later to go to Cuba with an all-star baseball team being organized by Bill Rigler, the umpire, who is the official groundskeeper of the baseball yard in Havana.

Several other Giants may take this trip, including Charles M. (Jeff) Tesreau, the bear collector, although Charles is first going home to Perryville, Mo., to show the homefolks some of that yellow-backed city money, which he has picked up around here.

Otis Crandall will, of course, go to Wadina, Ind., for a Winter in Wadina without Otis would be a dreary social season, indeed.

Fred Snodgrass and Arthur Shafer will probably go to their homes in Los Angeles. Grover Cleveland Hartley will just naturally knock 'em dead in Osgood, Ind., when he shows up with his Broadway apparel; while Fred Merkle will resume bowling and legal pursuits around Toledo, Ohio. Bowling is Fred's winter dish. Arthur Devlin hibernates in Collinsville, Ill., and Arthur Wilson gives Bloomington, Ill., a strong play.

Doyle to Remain Here

Chief Meyers is tearing for Riverside, Cal., where he is investing in a grove of orange trees. Larry Doyle expects to remain right here in New York, where he can buy better gasoline for his new auto than he could in Breese, Ill. Jack ("Red") Murray has already vanished; Jack loses himself in the winter somewhere around Elmira.

It is the judgment of baseball men that Fred Snodgrass's muff in the 10th inning of the last game at Boston, while very costly, is being greatly magnified, and that, as a matter of downright fact, the Giants have only themselves, as a team, to blame for not winning the series without having to play eight games at all.

The figures on that series need no comment. The big-town boys lost because of rickety defense of superb pitching, even while they were outhitting and outplaying the Sox generally, and when McGraw was making Stahl look foolish in the managerial end of the game.

Anyway, as even Mathewson has pointed out, it was not Snodgrass's muff that beat the Giants as much as the failure of someone to get Jake Stahl's pop fly back of the infield, which fell safe with Snodgrass, Fletcher and Murray in pursuit. What came after that was unnatural and unnecessary, including Merkle's failure to get the pop foul from (Tris) Speaker's bat in the 10th.

Poor Snodgrass's error merely happened to be peculiarly glaring, but it was no more damaging than other plays of other games in the series, which were largely responsible for prolonging the battle.

Those who have been suggesting that Snodgrass's error may drive him off the Giants evidently don't know McGraw, and forget his attitude in a similar case of long ago. The Giants lost that series not on the individual boots of any one man, but on a combined team deficiency in caring for easy chances—and they are offering no excuses.

———

Boston's "Miracle Braves" of 1914 was among the great sports sagas of the era. Fifth the year before and in last place at the end of July, the Braves mounted a sensational second-half drive, to storm past the fading Giants, clinch the N.L. pennant—and then steamroll past the defending champion and heavily favored Philadelphia A's in the first four-game sweep in series history. Led by George Stallings, their driven, foul-mouthed manager with a taste for Shakespeare, the Braves combined the strong starting pitching of Dick Rudolph, Lefty Tyler and "Seattle" Bill James with the inspiring play of Johnny Evers, their captain and second baseman late of the Cubs, and shortstop Rabbit Maranville. Only one regular, leftfielder Joe Connolly, hit .300. The Braves won the pennant in their last year at the South Ends ballpark, but played the Series in Fenway Park, the more spacious quarters of the Red Sox home. It was the Braves' first and last World Series triumph in their 76 years in Boston.

BRAVES WIN WORLD'S TITLE IN 4 STRAIGHT (OCT. 14, 1914)

Rudolph Again Humbles Athletics in Final Game, 3 to 1—
Boston National Establish Record by Clean Sweep in World's Series

BOSTON—This thing today, when the Boston Braves won the championship of the baseball world, was like watching an old, old play, with familiarity precluding the possibility of surprise, and with no prospect of variety save in the manner in which the actors handled their respective roles.

The result always seemed a foregone conclusion. The score of 3 to 1 would indicate a close game, but it did not seem close. It did not feel close. It was as if every act but led up a well-remembered climax, and when that climax finally came the thrills therein were only perfunctory. The plot seemed too old.

The mad demonstration of the Boston baseball fanatics about the bench of the triumphant Braves at the finish, the parade of the "Royal Rooters" with the band shrilling "Tessie" and "Sweet Adeline," the cheers and the speeches and all the rest of the moil and turmoil, and finally, the silent, sober file of the defeated Philadelphia Athletics picking their way through the crush, somehow seemed anticipated. They somehow seemed but carefully rehearsed scenes in an ancient show.

Win in Four Straight

It was rather a curious culmination of the greatest feat in the history of baseball. The Boston Braves have won the championship in four straight games. No other club has done that since the World Series was inaugurated between rival National and American Leagues. Once the Tigers, of Detroit, failed to win a game from the Chicago Cubs, but one game was tied, and the series had to go to five games.

It might therefore be expected that the finishing touches to such a record as the Braves have established would be attended by manifestations of enthusiasm surpassing any of the wildest outbreaks that have occurred during the astounding rush of the Boston boys, but it was not so at Fenway Park this afternoon.

The nervous tension seemed to have relaxed. The crowd seemed to know what was going to happen long before it happened. They sat during those closing innings that saw the complete reading of one of the greatest baseball machines ever assembled, as a crowd might sit at an opera.

When the last man was retired, the "Royal Rooters," in the temporary stand in left field, and the bleacherites from right field, rose up and billowed across the field in a gigantic wave, but long before that thousands of the grandstand spectators had started digging their way toward the exits, and they viewed the antics of their brethren on the diamond below impassively. No one seemed surprised.

Athletics Finally "Quit"

As the Athletics' batting end of the ninth came on, the former World Champions could be seen slipping on their blue mackinaws and gathering up their gloves and other paraphernalia on the bench. Then the most of them stood up in an expectant line watching Eddie Collins at bat. They were ready for a hasty departure from the field.

Their attitude told plainly that they had "quit."

In the old days of triumph they used to march up to the plate in a line, swinging their bats menacingly, whether the club was in front or behind.

A somber figure in a ministerial black remained seated on the bench. The ignominy of the worst defeat ever administered to a championship club sat heavily upon the shoulders of Connie Mack, but he did not quit. He was the last to leave the bench; and as he stalked thinly across the field in the wake of his beaten flock, he still had a dry little smile left for expressions of sympathy.

When (Johnny) Evers tossed out (Frank) Baker in an easy roller for the second out in the final inning, the exuberance of the Braves manifested itself. Charley Schmidt, the Baltimore butcher, playfully threw the ball at (Pat) Moran out in right field, and Moran let the ball through him to the farthest corner of his district.

Indulge in "Horse Play"

Instantly, a dozen fans, poised for the dash to the exits, leaped out on the field and fell on the ball in a scrambling heap. A policeman rushed up and joined the struggle, and the Braves laughed loudly when the officer finally rescued the ball and returned it to Moran.

The Athletics looked on dumbly. They had little interest in horse play. They reminded one of a heavy loser in a poker game along toward the early hours of the morning, with all the winners ready to quit, and no chance for the losers to get even.

When (Stuffy) McInnis had been retired, for the last out, the Athletics tramped to the exits, some of them hastily snatching the hand of one of their conquerors, as the Braves dashed for the shelter of the coop to avoid the crowd. The leftfield contingent of fans came marching in bearing Leslie Mann on their shoulders, and he kicked and squirmed vainly in an effort to get away.

Most of the "bugs" were seeking Dick Rudolph, the Bronx boy, who won his second victory of the series, but Dick never had much heart for this sort of thing, and he had disappeared.

"Lank Hank" Gowdy, hitting hero of the series, came in with his hat off, and he was belabored about the head with newspapers in the hands of fans hanging over the railing of the grandstand back of the home team bench, until he was glad to hide. (Braves' manager) George Stallings disappeared early, and hurried to his hotel to avoid demonstration.

Wants Word with Ban

It has been said that the swarthy chief of the Braves is planning a small demonstration of his own. It has been said that he has vowed if he won this series to hunt up Ban Johnson, president of the American League, in the most public place, and tell him a few things that have been resting heavy upon the Stallings memory for some years.

It is a matter dating back to (George) Stallings's days as manager of the Detroit Tigers, and his enmity toward the fat president of the American League has never cooled. But in this hour of triumph it is doubtless that sober second thought will deter Stallings from carrying out his plan.

Mayor James Curley and ex-mayor Fitzgerald, of Boston, who have been having a terrible struggle as to which would gain the most prominence out of this series, both made speeches from the rampart above the Boston bench at the close of the game, while the fans jammed close together on the field cheered them impartially. The redoubtable "Honey Fitz" has outshone his rival in the publicity campaign to some extent, being backed by the "Royal Rooters" and their band.

The Athletics played this afternoon just as they played throughout the series, with the exception of yesterday. They had little spirit. They have acted all along as if they were carrying the championship in a gallon bucket and were afraid of spilling it. Only on one or two occasions have they displayed the fighting heart expected of champions.

On the other hand, the Braves were even cockier and more confident and more impertinent today than they have been at any time before. The luck that has clung to them throughout the championship struggle was with them today. Baseball men will be telling through the years to come that this is the luckiest club in the history of the game, even granting it the highest possible credit for ability.

Fortune Favors Braves

The "boner" by Johnny Evers yesterday that would have placarded him in headlines from one end of the country to the other had it not been lost in a maze of subsequent events; the base-running "bull" of Charlie Deal when he was caught napping over in Philadelphia, only to have Wally Schang commit a greater error of judgment that turned Deal's mistake into a Brave victory and gave that young man great glory—these are samples of the fortune that has followed the Boston club.

Nothing goes wrong for the Braves—but then nothing ever goes wrong for the winner in baseball, and the Stallings youngsters must today be given full credit for what they are —*the gamest crowd in baseball.*

It was Johnny Evers who broke up the game on the Athletics in the fifth inning today, and there was even then more or less of what baseball people call luck, although to the average observer it seemed another manifestation of the spirit of the Braves.

(Rabbit) Maranville, now pronounced the greatest short-fielder the game has ever known, was an easy infield out at the opening of the Braves' end of the fifth. Deal was also quickly retired, but then Dick Rudolph, who is an unusually good hitter for a pitcher, singled to center. Up to that time Bob Shawkey, one of Mack's young righthanders, had been pitching along very steadily.

Herb Moran followed Rudolph with a hit that went for two bases. "Rube" Oldring made a flying lunge at Moran's blow, and Rudolph raced around to third as the big outfielder missed his leap. Shawkey pitched with great care to Evers, and finally had the count, three balls and two strikes on the lantern-jawed captain of the Braves. Then Johnny smacked a single across second, and Rudolph and Moran tallied, with one more run necessary to win the game. A moment later Shawkey made a quick throw to McInnis and caught Evers flat-footed off first for the third out.

"Lord" Byron, the National League umpire who worked behind the bat this afternoon, and who is one of the newest of the big-league arbiters, was the first umpire to silence the babble from the bench of the Braves. Throughout the series the Bostonians have been "riding" the Athletics with verbal whip and spur.

When Frank Baker was at the bat in the fourth inning, the young Bostonians got aboard the Maryland slugger — and mentioned his name with scant respect.

"I'll have no more of that!" yelled Byron, removing his mask and glaring at the bench, and there was silence for a moment at least.

Speculators "Stung"

It was a clear day, but the coolish wind was whipping in off the sea, and great fur coats were numerous in the grandstand. A few empty seats told of financial disaster to some speculators. After the game, the speculators were massed at the entrance, eager to buy (home) third-game tickets at a discount, because the Boston and Philadelphia clubs must redeem these tickets at their full face value.

The fact that the series went to but four games is a terrific blow to the management of both clubs, as the players get the greater part of the receipts. Had the umpires called the game yesterday in the eleventh inning on account of darkness, as they might have done without arousing criticism, it would have meant something like $60,000 more to the managements.

While there was a tremendous demonstration when Evers broke up the game, it was nothing compared to an outburst that followed a smashing play by little Maranville on Eddie Collins in the sixth. "The Rabbit" made an almost impossible stop and throw, cutting off a sure hit, and Schmidt followed it with a marvelous catch at first.

Throughout the series both Maranville and Schmidt have starred in their positions, and the big first baseman's first work rather disproves the theory that Stallings has only three pitchers, a catcher, and a second baseman and shortstop.

Break Up Rally

With one out in the fourth, Baker got a hit on a hopper to Schmidt that the butcher could not handle, and in the play, Schmidt got the breath knocked out of him, so that the game had to stop until he recovered himself. Stuffy McInnis singled to left, and Baker tore around to third. McInnis tried to move up to second, but a fast relay by (Joe) Connolly and Deal, and then from Deal to Evers, put the ball on McInnis in spite of a great headfirst slide. (Jimmy) Walsh ended the inning by striking out.

That was about as good a chance as the Athletics had at any stage of the game. They got their one run in the fifth when (Jack) Barry hit safely over Deal's head, and took second on Schang's infield out, Evers to Schmidt. Shawkey, after hitting at as poor a ball as was ever thrown at a batter, doubled to center, scoring "Black Jack."

Shawkey reached third on Murphy's out, but Oldring fanned. Oldring got his first hit of the series today, and also got to first for the second time. He was out trying to steal second.

In the fourth inning Evers drew a walk from Shawkey and took second when Collins threw out Connolly. Collins them fumbled Whitted's bounder over near first and Evers took third. The official scorer gives this as a hit, but in the opinion of many old baseball men who sat in the press box, it was an error. In any event, it was rather a hard chance for Collins, who seemed to have injured himself in going after the ball. The Athletics' trainer dashed out from the bench and examined Eddie, and then the game went on.

Schmidt hit a short roller past the box, Barry getting the ball and tossing out Schmidt, while Evers scoffed, and the band played, "When Johnny Comes Marching Home." There was no chance for Barry to make a play at the plate. Shawkey tossed out Gowdy and closed the inning.

Young (Herb) Pennock, a left-hander, took Shawkey's place in the sixth, as the Braves went to bat, and Stallings promptly removed Connolly and put Mann, a right-handed hitter, in leftfield. He did not remove Moran and substitute (Ted) Cather as usual, however.

Mann hit for Connolly and was out on a fly to (Jimmy) Walsh, and (Possum) Whitted then got a single down the third-base line that was fair by about an inch. Schmidt hit a grounder that squirted up off Collins's show for a hit and Whitted took third.

"Lank Hank" Gowdy was called out on strikes and he viewed Byron with the solemn glare of a slugger betrayed. "Lank Hank" has grown mighty confident of himself up there at bat the past week or so. A double steal was started by (Butch) Schmidt and Whitted, but Collins intercepted the throw from Schang in behind the pitcher's box and the heavy-footed Schmidt was run down between first and second before Whitted could score.

—

An analysis of how the Braves, a fifth-place National League team a year before, rose to become the team forever celebrated as the "Miracle Braves."

STRUGGLE OF BRAVES MARKS BASEBALL EPOCH (OCT. 15, 1914)

Manager Stallings the Real Hero of Wonderful Conquest—His Steady Faith Triumphed—Maranville Greatest of Infielders

One way and another, it is pretty soft for the posterity of our national pastime.

Posterity will be able to open baseball history at the chapter dealing with the interesting period of 1914 and see that the Boston National B.B. Club of that era could play baseball.

Posterity can gather this information in a few minutes by no more effort than is required to turn over a printed page, whereas it has taken the present generation some months, and Heaven alone knows how many words, to collect the same news.

Posterity will read that the Boston National League club of 1914, and perhaps for several ensuing years was regarded as one of the greatest and gamest ball clubs of all time, but posterity will probably never hear by what devious labor, and reluctance, that verdict was produced. It is pretty soft for posterity.

Gamest Club of All

We repeat the words: One of the greatest and gamest ball clubs of all time. There can be no question as to the status of the Braves now. They go into history linking with the memory of the Baltimore Orioles, the (Frank) Selee Bostonians, the Cubs, the Athletics and all the other great clubs that have risen to high power over the baseball world.

George Stallings, always regarded as a great constructive manager who never had a real chance, has finally come into his own. His is today the big commanding figure of the diamond, overshadowing all rivals with his record of four straight games in a World Series and the defeat of one of the most remarkable baseball machines ever assembled.

Make no mistake—it is to George Stallings that credit must first be given. It was his unquestionably dominating personality that lashed the Braves on to victory, that swept them to the National League pennant and on into the world's championship.

He had faith on his future and the future of his club when baseball people only felt sorry for him as they listened to him; he had faith when his owner wanted to sell the club out, and he finally converted even the owner to his faith.

Stallings the Real Hero

Johnny Evers, (Rabbit) Maranville, Hank Gowdy, Dick Rudolph, the "Young Marster," and "Big Bill" James are ranked as the heroes of the series, and so they were, but without Stallings there would have been no series, and no heroes.

The showing of Evers against the Athletics merely added more luster to the prestige of a man already secure in his niche in baseball history as one of the greatest players in the game, but Maranville came out of the battle classed as the greatest short-fielder of all time, while Gowdy, Rudolph and James have risen to rank among the big fellows of the pastime.

The writer of this screed has taken occasion several times during the past season to mention that the showing of the Braves was the tip-off of the strength of the National League, and that statement seems to call for a retraction.

The Braves proved that the National League had a lot of class to even hold such an aggregation fairly close.

One chap who seems to have escaped general attention but who, in our opinion, should be classed close to the top of that list of heroes is Charley Schmidt, the Baltimore butcher, who hit .294 in the series and handled 56 chances without a bobble.

Without Schmidt on first the showing of Maranville and Evers might not have been so dazzling. His work was nothing short of marvelous, and Schmidt more than any other man confounds the critics.

The only regrettable incident of the series was the quarrel between Connie Mack and George Stallings over in Philadelphia, when Stallings claims that Mack refused to let the Braves have the use of Shibe Field for practice before the first game. Mack says that he was willing to let the Bostonians use his yard at any time except between the hours of 2 and 4, when he had ordered the Athletics to work out.

Not every one—not even many of Stallings' best friends—agree with him in his stand that Mack's was unsportsmanlike. Rather they regard Stallings's request as surprising because he could have used the Philadelphia National League club.

The contention that the Athletics were familiar with Fenway Field, where the Braves play, is true enough, but the Braves are on Fenway Field by courtesy of the American League, and without that courtesy, the Braves would have been in sad shape this series.

A Big Manager

A word here for Connie Mack: He has been ignominiously beaten, and the world seems to rejoice, but he has been a great character in baseball, and he is still a great character in the game. He has always been a baseball man: He rose from the ranks, and he has given his life to baseball.

New York fans have no reason to love him, but they have always respected him and the Mack teams. He has fought many a hard battle with McGraw, but there is no harder or more aggressive fighter than McGraw, but whether conquer or conquered, they always quit with a hearty handshake of mutual respect.

Every dollar that Connie Mack has made out of baseball, and every dollar he owns—and those dollars are not as numerous as some people think—is invested in it. As a magnate he is no carpetbagger of baseball, with an eye to any little side issues. He is in baseball, and of baseball, and the money he has taken from, and out back, in the game is clean money, without taint. It would be a good thing for baseball if all the stockholders of all big-league clubs could say as much.

Connie has always been a good winner and always a good loser. It is a great thing to be a good loser, but it is a greater thing to be a good winner.

—

Among the Giants, Yankees, Brooklyn Dodgers and Mets, New York teams have faced one another 14 times in the World Series. This Giants-Yankees matchup was the first of the intracity matchups that became known as the "Subway Series." Here are Runyon's thoughts on the eve of the '21 series, which pokes fun

*both at New Yorkers' lather of excitement and blustery predic-
tion of victory from Giants' manager John McGraw, looking for
his first world championship since 1905.*

HE IS IN A SWEAT (OCT. 3, 1921)

Well, sir, here I am in a terrible sweat about the World Series
between the Yankees and the Giants, and which outfit will win is
something I do not know.

Furthermore, if I do know, it is no cinch I will tell anybody in
the way I look at it; such information will be very useful to me in
my bets.

I am reading with much interest in the papers yesterday what
(John) McGraw has to say about the proposition, and I see where
he says the Giants will win, but that is what John says every time
the Giants are in one of these World Series, and from the way things
turn out, I am commencing to think John is sometimes mistaken.

I also read that Miller Huggins says, and Miller claims the Yankees will win, but the way I figure it, Miller is never in a World
Series with the Yankees before, so how in what-you-call-it does he
know what is going to happen?

Anyway, even if it happens, whatever it is, Huggins will get a
panic because it happens to him, or does not happen in a different
way, so what is the use of listening to him?

Reading the Experts

I am reading what all the experts have to say every day until I am
almost cockeyed trying to keep up with them, and I judge from
what I see that the Giants are a sure thing if they can hit the
Yankee pitching and the Yankees cannot hit the Giant pitchers,
and vice versa, and so on.

I see where the Giants are the tightest club, and naturally that
makes them very tight indeed, although a waiter at the Aldine over
in Philadelphia, where both the Giants and the Yanks hang out in
that town, and wishes to bet one and all in such a proposition, and
furthermore that will he lay a nice price.

The Yankees have the best hitters if they can hit, and the Giants have (Art) Nehf, one great lefthander with a wonderful curve, but what good is a curve if Babe Ruth gets hold of it and knocks the ball so far out of the yard they cannot play with it anymore?

The answer to this proposition is, it is not worth a whoop.

About Babe Ruth

I see where Babe Ruth says he is going to bust up these ball games all day on the boys, if they do not look out, and I wish to say I do not put such a thing past him, at that.

If I am John McGraw running the Giants in the World Series, I would certainly be very careful about Babe. I wish to say if I am John McGraw, I will not trust this fellow around one of my pitchers a minute.

I see where some of the Giants say their pitchers will pitch to him, but if I am John McGraw, I will tell them to be very careful when they pitch to him. I will tell them not to pitch to him in the Polo Grounds anyway, and that any time they feel even as much as a need to pitch to him coming on, to go on out of the yard.

Of course, Babe may not hit a lick in the World Series if they pitch to him, but then again he may, which is talk like an expert. What is true is, he is no guy to trust around a pitcher, because he is certainly true with that old apple knocker.

Town All Smoked Up

Everybody in town is much steamed up about this series, with many arguments going on here and there.

McGraw has many friends, except in the Lambs Club, who hope he will win, and Huggins has many friends in St. Louis and Cincinnati, who hope the same thing.

The owners of the ball clubs have no friends whatsoever when they start giving out the duckets for the series, but they are not bad guys who do not get the coveted (tickets).

When it comes to the owners, it looks as if the Yanks have the edge because they (Jacob Ruppert and Til Huston) out-colonel (Giants' owner) Charley Stoneham two-to-one.

I am getting a ridge on the back of my neck from nodding at guys who say the Giants will win and to guys who say the Yanks will win, but personally I do not care a whoop which wins. The way I look at it, when the boys get together and start cutting up the old do-rei-me-fa-so, I will not be declared in anywhere along the line, so what's the sense of getting excited?

The only prediction I wish to make—and I do study all the odds this way and that, and backwards and forwards—is that the world's championship will be won by New York, and if it is not, I am a liar.

———

Backed by flawless fielding, Giants' pitcher Art Nehf blanked the Yankees 1-0 in game eight of the 1921 World Series—giving John McGraw his first world championship in 15 years, five games to three over the Yankees. Runyon offers some final thoughts on the Series:

WELL, THAT'S OVER! (OCT. 15, 1921)

Up at the Hotel Commodore Thursday night, the (Yankee owners) Messrs. Colonel Jake Ruppert and Til Huston made impassioned speeches in the following order:

(1) Colonel Jake,
(2) Colonel Til,
(3) Colonel Jake and Til, together, and in concert.

Down at the Waldorf, in the magnificent suite that was once the home of the late George Boldt, Messrs. Charley Stoneham and John McGraw (of the Giants) also made speeches, in much the same order as above.

The Commodore is too far from the Waldorf for the Colonels to hear what Charley and John were saying, and the Waldorf is much too distant from the Commodore for Charley and John to get all that the Colonels were uttering, although all hands spoke loudly.

A happy solution was finally at:

The Colonels went down to the Waldorf, and then they all made speeches together.
The Colonels, as one gathered from their addresses, were sorry to lose the World Series, but glad Charley and John won.
Charley and John were glad to win, but sorry the Colonels had to lose.
Everything promptly went to even money.

Judge Had the Right Idea

Judge Frank McQuade, treasurer of the Giants, had the right idea.

The judge waited until he caught the speechmakers on a semicolon and then he rushed into the conversational fray with this proposition:

"Three cheers for New York!" said the Judge.

This suited everybody, and the cheers were given with a jolly old tiger at the end.

Nobody was mad at nobody.

"It's been the greatest series in the history of baseball," said McGraw, when he finally discovered an oratorical oasis where he could exercise his voice without being crowded. It has been clean and sportsmanlike all the way through.

"I certainly appreciate the visit of Colonel Ruppert and Colonel Huston here tonight to congratulate us, and I only hope the same clubs meet again next year.

"As for myself, of course, I'm happy. I admit I was mighty nervous the last two days for the first time in all the years I've been directing ball clubs. I'm glad it's over and I'm glad we won, but I cannot say too much for our opponents and for the gentlemen who own the Yankees."

It Was Fair Enough

All of which seemed fair enough.

The Colonels returned to their headquarters at the Commodore, and resumed their speechmaking there, to the answering cheers of many admirers.

Charley and John, and the Judge remained at the Waldorf, and all evening a procession of fans and baseball notables passed through the gilded halls offering their congratulations.

"Cozy" Dolan, the Giant coach, and Jack McKeon acted as a reception committee. Jim Tierney, the new secretary of the Giants, offered one of the gladdest hands that has ever been seen in baseball. Eddie Brannick, Jim's assistant, was giving everybody the old "how-d'-y-do," and dreaming of the furniture he is going to buy with the thousand bucks he got out of the series.

Mason Peters, Brandon Tynan, Frank Belcher, Gene Baker, and scores of others were tastefully draped about the ornate chairs. All the New York baseball writers drifted in at some time or other during the evening to say "hilo."

It was quite an occasion.

Meantime, hundreds of friends of the Colonels called on them, and offered condolences, but the bereaved losers declined to look, or feel that way.

They said "cheerio" to one and all, and muttered ominously about next year.

Bill Was Sunk

Only one member of the Yankee entourage seemed to be really sunk. That was (minority owner) Billy Fleischmann, but as showing the spirit of the day, even Bill managed to lift his chin off the second button on his weskit and get down to the Waldorf to congratulate the winners.

Last night, the Colonels entertained the members of the Yankees at a dinner at the Hotel Commodore, the invitations including the families of the ballplayers. The Giants went to a theater party at the Winter Garden.

Throughout the series, the best of feeling has prevailed between the owners, even when the pastimers were growing a bit fretful toward each other on the field. Ruppert and Huston frequently called at the Giant headquarters, and Stoneham and McGraw returned the visits.

It was all quite lovely, indeed.

McGraw is planning to leave for Texas in a few days to look over some oil interests there, and will then probably spend most of the winter in Cuba.

Stoneham is also planning a long trip, and Colonel Huston is going down to Dover Hall in Georgia, for a rest. The toil of counting up the series money had almost exhausted the magnates.

Most of the players on the Giants and the Yankees live far from here, and they will be dispersing to their various homes one by one during the next few days.

By Way of Farewell

Now for a little sweeping out and dusting up.

Down through the baseball ages, there will be much parleyvoo about certain incidents in the series:

The Yanks will probably always believe that if Chill had called the ball a strike on (Ross) Youngs in the first frame of the last game, the Giants wouldn't have scored on (Waite) Hoyt.

The Giants, in turn, will ever revert to a decision at first in the game when (Babe) Ruth beat out a bunt and turned the result to the American Leaguers, the Giants holding that the throw beat Ruth for first.

These and many other little things will enter into the discussion, but when all is said and done even Bill Fleischmann, fiercest of the Yankee rooters, admits that the better baseball machine won.

And the beauty of the thing is that it ends without any ill feeling and that all hands can get together and make speeches about each other.

It has undoubtedly been the speechmakingest series in the history of the world.

———

Some comments on the eve of the third Giants-Yankee World Series in three years:

WORLD SERIES SHOULD BE EVEN MONEY — MCGRAW AND RUTH (OCT. 8, 1923)

The Giants and the Yankees should be "even money and take your pick."

There is not sufficient difference in the strength of these clubs to make one favorite over the other.

The writer is of the opinion if there is any advantage it is with the Giants. It is the advantage of having beaten the Yankees twice.

This advantage is purely psychological. If you believe in psychology in baseball, you must pick the Giants to win.

❋   ❋   ❋

It has been said that as Ruth goes so go the Yankees.

A pleasant compliment to the great slugger of the American League club, to be sure, but not entirely true.

Ruth in the big series that opens Wednesday may fail as completely as he did in 1922. Some obscure, unconsidered member of the club may bob up as a "demon" at hitting—may win the Series for the Yankees.

That is baseball.

❋   ❋   ❋

McGraw uses a species of psychology on Ruth in these games.

McGraw knows Ruth feels the weight of responsibility on his shoulders. McGraw knows that Ruth, realizing what the public expects of him, is wildly eager to live up to expectations, to his great reputation, is apt to be strained, nervous, over-anxious when he steps to the plate.

McGraw has his pitchers pitching to Ruth as if he were an ordinary hitter, pitching calmly, fearlessly, giving him pitching that he MUST hit at.

Perhaps the fact that the pitchers show no great respect for his slugging reputation is highly disconcerting to Ruth. Any man is apt to be somewhat take back when he finds a low valuation placed upon his ability.

———

In one of Runyon's most famous articles, he helped turn "old" Casey Stengel's inside-the-park home run to win game one of the 1923 World Series for the Giants against the Yankees into a legendary dash around the Yankee Stadium bases. At 33, Stengel was a tad long in the tooth for a ballplayer, but not that "old," as Runyon writes. For the record, this slow-footed journeyman outfielder with a reputation for fun, would have a mammoth Series, hitting another homer in game three, and batting .417 in the Series, despite the Giants' loss in six games to the Yankees. The numbers didn't help him; he was soon traded to the Braves, where he'd play two seasons and retire in 1925. It wasn't until much later, as a manager, that Stengel would find his true calling, leading the Yankees to many of their greatest seasons. His run would last all the way to 1965, when, after four years managing the Mets—enough to make anyone feel their age—Stengel would retire, at 75.

STENGEL'S HOMER WINS IT FOR GIANTS, 5–4 (OCT. 11, 1923)
60,000 Frantic Fans Screech as Casey Beats Ball to Plate

This is the way old "Casey" Stengel ran yesterday afternoon, running his home run home.

This is the way old "Casey" Stengel ran running his home run home to a Giant victory by a score of 5 to 4 in the first game of the World Series of 1923.

This is the way old "Casey" Stengel ran, running his home run home, when two were out in the ninth inning and the score was tied and the ball was still bounding inside the Yankee yard.

This is the way—

His mouth wide open.

His warped old legs bending beneath him at every stride.

His arms flying back and forth like those of a man swimming with a crawl stroke.

His flanks heaving, his breath whistling, his head far back.

Urges Himself On

Yankee infielders, passed by old "Casey" Stengel as he was running his home run home, say "Casey" was muttering to himself, adjuring himself to greater speed as a jockey mutters to his horse in a race that he was saying, "Go on, Casey! Go on."

People generally laugh when they see old "Casey" Stengel run, but they were not laughing while he was running his home run home yesterday afternoon. People—60,000 of 'em, men and women—were standing in the Yankee stands and bleachers up there in the Bronx roaring sympathetically, whether they were for or against the Giants.

"Come on, Casey!"

The warped old legs twisted and bent by many a year of baseball campaigning, just barely held out under "Casey" Stengel until he reached the plate, running his home run home.

Then they collapsed.

"Casey" Slides

They gave out just as old "Casey" slid over the plate in his awkward fashion with Wally Schang futilely reaching for him with the ball. "Billy" Evans, the American League umpire, poised over him in a set pose, arms spread to indicate that old "Casey" was safe.

Half a dozen Giants rushed forward to help "Casey" to his feet, to hammer him on the back, to bawl congratulations in his ears as he limped unsteadily, still panting furiously, to the bench where John J. McGraw, chief of the Giants, relaxed his stern features in a smile for the man who had won the game.

"Casey" Stengel's warped old legs, one of them broken not so long ago, wouldn't carry him out for the last half of the inning, when the Yankees made a dying effort to undo the damage done by "Casey." His place in centerfield was taken by young "Bill" Cunningham, whose legs are still unwarped, and "Casey" sat on the bench with John J. McGraw.

No one expected much of "Casey" Stengel when he appeared at the plate in the Giants' side of the ninth inning, the score a tie at 4 to 4.

Ross Youngs and "Irish" Meusel, dependable hitters, had been quickly disposed of by the superb pitching of "Bullet Joe" Bush.

No one expected Stengel to accomplish anything where they had failed. Bush, pitching as only Bush can pitch in an emergency, soon had two strikes and three balls on "Casey."

Fans Start Fidgeting

He was at the plate so long that many of the fans were fidgeting nervously, wondering why he didn't hurry up and get put out, so the game could go on. "Casey" Stengel is not an imposing figure at bat, not an imposing figure under any circumstances. Those warped old legs have something to do with it. A man with warped legs cannot look very imposing.

People like to laugh at "Casey"—"Casey" likes to make people laugh.

A wayfarer of the big leagues—Brooklyn, Pittsburgh, Philadelphia, and finally New York—he has always been regarded by the fans as a great comedian, a funny fellow, a sort of clown.

The baseball land teems with tales of the strange didoes cut by "Casey" Stengel, whose parents started him out as Charles, with his sayings.

Maybe Bush Lapsed

Who knows but that "Bullet Joe" may have been thinking of "Casey" Stengel more as a comedian than as a dangerous hitter when he delivered that final pitch yesterday afternoon? Pitchers sometimes let their wits go wool-gathering.

"Bap"—Stengel's bat connected surely, solidly. The ball sailed out over left field, moving high, moving far.

"Long Bob" Meusel ("Irish" Bob's Yankee brother) and "Whitey" Witt, the Yankee outfielders, raced toward each other as they marked the probable point of the ball would alight, and in the meantime, "Casey" Stengel was well advanced on his journey, running his home run home.

As the ball landed between Meusel and Witt, it bounded as if possessed toward the left center field fence. Everybody could see it would be a home run inside the yard, if "Casey" Stengel's warped old legs could carry him around the bases.

Race to the Plate

Witt got the ball about the time Stengel hit third, and about that time Stengel was laboring, "all out." Witt threw the ball in to Bob Meusel, who had dropped back and let Witt go on. Meusel wheeled and fired for the plate, putting all the strength behind the throw. Few men have ever lived who can throw a baseball as well as Bob Meusel.

Stengel was almost home when Meusel's throw was launched, and sensing the throw "Casey" called on all that was left in those warped old legs, called no doubt on all the baseball gods to help him—and they helped.

It is something to win a World Series with a home run, and home run inside the yard.

John J. McGraw perhaps feels that his judgment in taking Stengel on at a time when "Casey" was a general big-league outcast has been vindicated.

Comes from Old K.C.

If you are curious to know the origin of the nickname "Casey," it might be explained that Stengel's home-town is Kansas City.

The nickname comes from "K.C." One of these many little coincidences that are always popping out in baseball is the fact that "Casey" and "Bullet Joe" Bush are great pals. They made the baseball tour last Winter as roommates.

Stengel is around 33, if you are seeking more information about the first hero of the World Series of 1923. They call that "old" in baseball. He has been with the Giants since 1921, from the Philadelphia club. He is all right, "Casey" Stengel is, and you can prove it by John J. McGraw.

—

Arguably, the great Walter Johnson was the hardest-throwing pitcher of all-time. The great Johnson debuted in 1907, and won 413 games over a 21-year career, all of it spent with the mostly lackluster Washington Senators. But in 1924, the Senators under 27-year-old rookie player-manager Bucky Harris, won its first American League pennant, going to the World Series against John McGraw's New York Giants. So Johnson was 36 and coming off a 23-7 season before he made it to the Series. A lot of people were rooting for Johnson, not only one of the game's great strikeouts, but a well-liked, humble man, affectionately known as the "Big Train" and "Big Barney." But the Giants beat Johnson in games one and five; Curley Ogden started game seven for the Senators, but Johnson was ready if needed. He was — in the ninth inning — and the end of the game was Johnson's triumph — and Washington's only Series title in history.

SENATORS CHAMPIONS; GIANTS BEATEN IN 12TH INNING 4–3 (OCT. 11, 1924)

Johnson Saves the Day; Veteran Pitcher Rushes to Pitching Mound in Ninth with Count Even at 3 to 3 and Wins the Credit for Victory

WASHINGTON, D.C., OCT. 10 — Hooray! Hooray! HOOROPE!

That's the voice of Washington, as well as type can express it, screaming to the nation that she and Walter Johnson have come into their baseball own.

They've just won the World Series of 1924 here—Washington and Walter Johnson—and don't forget Stanley ("Bucky") Harris, (centerfielder) Earl McNeely and (catcher) "Muddy" Ruel and the rest of the boys, and they're still trying to split the eardrums of the U.S. by yelling over it.

They whipped the mighty New York Giants by the score of 4 to 3 after 12 terrific innings in the seventh and deciding game of the series late this afternoon, with "Big Barney" pitching them on to glorious victory.

That's why the blood pressure of the citizens of Washington is at this moment, without doubt, the highest ever registered by medical science among the peoples of any race. Apoplexy is almost epidemic. Heart trouble is a common complaint.

Seven women fainted simultaneously as young Earl McNeely, the Washington center fielder, brought "Muddy" Ruel home with the winning run in the 12th after one was out.

Ruel, the little catcher, who hadn't gotten but one hit since the series started, and that was a dinky little infield thing earlier in the game, had doubled. Walter Johnson, who had come into the game in the 8th inning, relieving the troubled Fred Marberry, was also on the base paths at the time, placed there by an error by Travis Jackson.

Winning Blow Bounces Over Lindstrom's Head

McNeely's hit bounded over the head of 18-year-old Freddy Lindstrom at third, and on into left field. Strangely enough, a drive by Stanley Harris, the Washington manager, earlier in the game, had taken just such a bounce and brought in the runs that tied the score for the home club.

As Ross Youngs retrieved the hit by McNeely in deep left and came walking in with it in his hand because it was useless to attempt to cut down the speedy Ruel, most of the 35,000 fans in the stands and bleachers were boiling out on the field.

The Washington players had to flee for their very lives. They sensed the riot of joy rolling across the field and turned and rushed to their tunnel, like men seeking the safety of a cyclone cellar.

The President of the United States (Calvin Coolidge) watched their hasty retreat for a moment from his box near the Washington bench. He had been standing up most of the time during the last inning, as excited as any small boy in the distant bleachers. He, too, just escaped the tornado of gladness that went sweeping over the players.

Johnson just barely escaped. Frantic fingers were grabbling at his sweater as he went through the tunnel. Stanley Harris, the 27-year-old manager of the new world champions, was fairly hurled through the little opening by the rush.

Old Nick Altrock, the famous baseball clown of Washington, and some of the other players, had dashed out on the field to be the first to welcome Ruel. They were leaping high in the air and yelling. Then they had to fight their way back through the mob in front of the Washington bench. Hats, cushions, and torn newspapers rained on the field. Dignified-looking men were tearing one another's clothes in the jam; every face was screaming, and every throat was pouring out a screech.

The beaten Giants made a concerted rush for the Washington bench and the tunnel and they were soon being tossed around like bits of driftwood in a running stream.

The crowd remained on the field, gathered about the Washington bench for over an hour after the game, a coterie of self-appointed cheer leaders standing on the roof of the bench and suggested cheers for everything and everybody connected with the Washington club from Clark Griffith, the old "Silver Fox," who is president of the club, down to the bat boy.

"Big Barney" Pitches with Great Cunning

At intervals, they would get a new cheer out of the crowd for "Barney" Johnson, who waited 18 years to get into a World Series, then was beaten in two games, and finally came into this big decisive game late in the day and got credit for the victory. No one will say that Johnson shouldn't get this credit. He pitched with great cunning, if not with all his old-time power.

Twice he intentionally passed Ross Youngs when a hit would have scored a New York run, and twice he followed this by striking out George Kelly, From start to finish, his game was a battle of baseball wits between the gray (John) McGraw and young Harris.

The New Yorkers will probably always say that the unexpected bounds the ball took over the head of Lindstrom were "bad breaks" for them. Perhaps they were, but the "breaks" one way or the other always decide these games. The score today was the same, only the result was reversed, as in the opening game of the series (won by the Giants 4-3).

Stanley Harris's home run and his single accounted for all of Washington's runs until McNeely's winning punch. McNeely was brought from Sacramento of the Pacific Coast League for a big price by Washington. Baseball men will agree that in many ways this has been the greatest series ever played. It was between two teams, neither one of which may ever be rated as great, as baseball rates greatness, but which proved themselves unusually courageous.

❊   ❊   ❊

Bluege Lets Kelly's Rap Sift through for Error

(In the New York sixth with Giants leading 3–1) Johnson was warming up down in right field. (Virgil) Barnes hit a long fly to (Sam) Rice for the second out. With Jackson on third and (Hank) Gowdy on first, (Firpo) Marberry struck out Lindstrom on three pitched balls, Lindstrom taking the last swing.

Kelly was back on first, (Hack) Wilson in center and (Irish) Meusel in left when Washington went to bat in their side of the sixth. Lindstrom threw out Ruel, who was up his 16th time at bat in the series without a hit.

Lindstrom also threw out Marberry. Youngs got McNeely's high fly.

Ruel made a great catch of Frisch's high foul over near the

screen in the Giants' seventh. Youngs walked, with the count of three balls and two strikes. Kelly rolled to Taylor, who made a great play throwing him out. Youngs took second. Meusel bounced to Marberry, who tagged him out running down the first-base line.

Single by "the Goose" Follows Double Play

Harris was first up in Washington's batting side of the seventh. He hit a slow roller to Jackson for an infield hit. The crowd awoke and began cheering for a rally. Rice hit the first ball pitched at him, bouncing it to Kelly, who stepped on first and then whipped the ball on to Jackson at second for a double play. The crowd subsided. (Goose) Goslin singled to right. It was the third hit off Barnes. (Joe) Judge hit the first ball for a fly to Wilson.

In the Giants' eighth, Wilson fanned, Jackson was safe on (shortstop Ossie) Bluege's fumble, Gowdy raised a fly to Goslin and Barnes fanned.

Bluege started Washington's batting side of the eighth by fouling out to Gowdy. Nemo Leibold, batting in place of (third baseman Tommy) Taylor, doubled to deep left. Muddy Ruel hit a slow infield roller between first and second. Kelly tried hard for the ball, but Ruel beat it out and Leibold went to third. (Bennie) Tate was sent up to bat for Marberry and walked. The bases were filled.

The crowd had been fairly boiling since Leibold made his hit. The din was now terrific. (Mule) Shirley was sent to first to run for Tate. Barnes's first pitch to McNeely was a ball. The crowd broke out with renewed fury, the noise halting suddenly as McNeely hit the second pitch on (a) fly to Meusel. Gowdy went over to the Giants' bench, apparently for instructions from McGraw, as Harris walked to the plate.

Harris took two steps forward in the batter's box as Barnes lifted his arm and pitched. Harris swung, hit bat just meeting the ball and driving it toward third. It looked an easy chance for young Lindstrom, who set himself to take the ball on the bounce as it hit the ground.

Harris's Freakish Hit Scores Two, Ties Count

In nine cases out of 10, the bounce would have been directly into Lindstrom's hands. This was the 10th case, and the ball bounced over his head into left field for a hit. Leibold and Ruel, both in motion as Harris swung, scored (to tie the score at 3–3) while Meusel was chasing the ball. Shirley stopped at second.

These Washington crowds have put on many demonstrations in this series, but never one to equal this. The President of the United States was on his feet pounding his hands together and all his fellow citizens were also on their feet screeching.

From the bench of the Giants, McGraw signed for Barnes to step aside, and little (Art) Nehf, the pitcher of the previous day (he went 7 innings in the 2–1 loss) came marching up from the warm-up station. He has been the only Giant pitcher of any real effectiveness in this series.

Meantime, the tumult continued. In fact, it grew. Bells were ringing, whistles blowing all over the stand. The Washington fans had evidently come prepared for a demonstration. The cheering was even taken up by the crowd waiting outside the gates.

Rice smashed a bounder at Kelly, who took the ball back of first and jumped on the bag for the third out.

The crowd kept right on roaring as Walter Johnson shuffled his way toward the mound (to start the ninth). Oddly enough, Johnson and Nehf were the pitchers who started the series. Ralph Miller was back on third base and he got Lindstrom's pop fly.

Frisch Hits a Triple, but Fails to Register

A strike and a ball were called on (Frank) Frisch when he swished his bat with little apparent force and caught the ball on the very tip of his stick, knocking it to deep center, between the racing Rice and McNeely, for a triple.

Youngs was next at the plate and he was intentionally passed, Johnson pitching four wide balls. Johnson seems to have had some sort of fear of the Texan every time he faced him in this series.

Now he swished three consecutive strikes over on the crouching Kelly, who swung every time "like a gate," as they say in baseball. Meusel fouled off the first pitch for a strike. Harris rushed in from second and said something to Ruel. The guess was that he told Ruel not to attempt to throw to second if Youngs stole. On the next pitch, Young stole and Ruel didn't throw. (Umpire Big Bill) Dinneen called the pitch a ball.

Meusel hit to (third baseman Ralph) Miller and was thrown out although the throw almost pulled Judge off the bag.

Goslin, first up in Washington's ninth, hit a fast hopper to (second baseman) Frisch, who fell as he got the ball, but managed to get it to Kelly ahead of "the Goose." Judge slashed at the first ball pitched by Nehf and singled across second. Bluege hit the ball directly to Kelly, who dashed off first to take it.

Jackson's Muff Spoils Possible Dual Killing

Kelly promptly wheeled and threw the ball to second to force Judge and start a double play. Jackson leaped over from the short field and muffed the ball. Judge went on to third and Bluege remained at first.

Nehf left the box and Hugh McQuillan took his place. Anything would win the game. The anything didn't happen. Ralph Miller was the batter, and he hit to Jackson and this time, Jackson didn't miss. He jerked the ball to Frisch at second ahead of Bluege and Frisch sent it on to Kelly ahead of Miller for a double play.

Johnson got only one strike over on Wilson in passing him (to start the 10th). He struck out Jackson however, pitching only four balls. Gowdy hit to Johnson who turned and threw the ball to Bluege at second, starting a double play on Wilson and Gowdy.

Ruel hit to Frisch in Washington's 10th, Frisch getting the ball at the far edge of the grass and tossing out Muddy. Johnson was wildly applauded as he walked to the plate, but McQuillan whipped two strikes on him in a jiffy. The next was a ball, then "Big Barney" put his shoulders out behind a heavy swing and drove a long fly to Wilson. McNeely struck out.

Crippled Groh Makes a Single in a Pinch

Heinie Groh, the crippled veteran third baseman of the Giants, made his first appearance in the series batting for McQuillan in the Giants' eleventh. He singled to rignt, and Billy Southworth went to first to run for him.

Lindstrom sacrificed, Judge tossing to Harris, who covered the bag. Southworth went to second. Frisch struck out. Again Johnson purposely passed Young.

Johnson's first pitch to Kelly was called a strike. Long George was bent almost double over the plate. He fouled off the next. The next was high and was called a ball. Johnson put everything he had behind the next, which was a curve, and Kelly swung out.

The crowd stood in a fever of excitement as Washington went to bat for the eleventh. Jack Bentley, the left-hander, was the Giants' pitcher. Harris was the hitter. The crowd looked for great things from him, but he lifted a fly to Young. Wilson got Rice's long fly. Goslin dropped a fly in right center, Frisch racing back and Wilson and Youngs racing in for the ball. None of them had a chance to get it, and Goslin pulled up at second.

McGraw now adopted Harris's strategy. He ordered Bentley to pass the dangerous Judge, which was done on four widely pitched balls. It was unusual strategy, because Judge is a left-handed batter, Bluege a right-hander. Then McGraw moved Youngs to left field and put Meusel in right.

Two Big Breaks Give Senators Victory Run

This was done to guard against a hit to left, which might require a throw to the plate. Youngs has a powerful arm and Meusel's is weak. If Bluege hit at all it was probable it would be to left. As it turned out he did hit it in that direction, but Jackson got the rap, a roller, and tossed to Frisch for a close play on Judge at second.

Meusel opened the Giants' twelfth with a single to right. Johnson then fanned Wilson. Jackson hit the first ball to Bluege who threw to second, getting Meusel. Jackson beat Harris's relay to first. Goslin got Gowdy's high fly.

(In the Washington twelfth) Hank Gowdy threw off his mask as Ruel lifted a high foul over the plate and the mask got tangled up with Hank's feet, causing him to drop the ball. Two strikes were called on Ruel, then a ball, then he slugged a drive past Lindstrom far down the left field foul line for a double.

Johnson hit the first ball to Jackson, who fumbled it. Ruel had started off second but turned back when he thought Jackson had an easy out. A Washington player rushed out from the bench and helped Johnson on with his gray sweater.

McNeely fouled off Bentley's first pitch. On Bentley's next pitch McNeely swung, slashing the ball toward Lindstrom at third. It hit the ground in front of the slim young third baseman and took the same identical hop over his head that Harris's drive had taken earlier in the game to score the tying runs.

Ruel was in motion, so was Johnson, the latter doing a dignified trot, the former racing for his very life as the ball spun down the foul line. Youngs retrieved the ball but didn't even attempt a throw. Ruel was too far on his journey to the plate, and the World Series of 1924 was over.

—

Fate Favored Harris' Players; Everybody Glad Washington Won. It Made Something of Victory. Harris Was the Hero of Series (Oct. 13, 1924)

Do you believe in Fate in sport?

Consider the result of the World Series of 1924 and the manner of that result.

A ball took a peculiar bound over (Fred) Lindstrom's head, enabling Washington to tie the score. You would have wagered that such a bound wouldn't occur again in a baseball game in years.

In the twelfth inning another ball bounded over Lindstrom's head in almost identically the same manner as the first, giving Washington the victory.

What caused these bounds?

A bit of hard ground near third base, perhaps. It may have been no larger than a 25-cent piece. No ball struck there during the season or the Washington groundkeeper would have meticulously removed it.

Do you believe that Fate, seeking a way of giving Washington the victory, twice directed the ball to that bit of hard ground?

❊   ❊   ❊

The New Giants no doubt feel deeply aggrieved at Fate.

Those two peculiar bounds cost each member of the Giants about $1,500.

They perhaps forgot they once won a World Series by a similar bound, which brought distress to the members of the New York Yankees.

A ball hit at Aaron Ward in 1922 struck a hard piece of ground in front of him and bounded over his head in much the same manner as the balls bounded over Lindstrom's head, giving the Giants the victory that year.

That was baseball Fate working in favor of the Giants and against the Yankees.

❊   ❊   ❊

No one who saw the demonstration in Washington Friday night could feel sorry the Giants lost.

The Washington victory was a tremendous thing for baseball.

Had New York won, the victory would have been discussed a few minutes, then forgotten. The big town has become blasé to those things.

Washington made something of it. Washington appreciated its new honor.

The writer has seen many demonstrations, many riots of joy. He saw Paris celebrating the armistice. He has been in Boston time and again the night of a Harvard football victory; has seen New Haven feverish with a Yale triumph.

He has watched New Orleans rollicking through its Mardi Gras; has seen any number of political celebrations, of public rejoicings over notable events. None of them approached Washington's celebration of its baseball victory.

❀   ❀   ❀

The thing went on all night. Joy never let down for a moment until the physical bodies were completely exhausted.

The people tramped the streets hour after hour, laughing and shouting and tooting horns. They cheered and cheered until one marveled at the vitality of the human voice.

Clark Griffith, president of the Washington club, the old "Silver Fox" of baseball, stood on the steps of the Hotel Willard and ladies kissed him jovially. The victorious players were pulled and hauled wherever they appeared.

The President of the United States (Calvin Coolidge) went home from the game rejoicing and issued a long public statement about it, more in the spirit of a citizen of Washington than as chief of the nation.

❀   ❀   ❀

It was wonderful. The writer is glad he lived to see it.

Umpire Bill Dinneen, the burly American League official who worked in the series, enjoyed himself hugely wandering about town and inquiring naively of excited citizens:

"Who won the ball game?"

Some were so utterly appalled at this ignorance they were disposed to call the police and have him taken to a sanitarium for observation. Others seemed to feel a man in his benighted condition should immediately be put out of his misery.

There was no real disorder. New York couldn't have been on

this celebration, sudden extemporaneous, without quarrels, fighting. Washington simply wallowed in its own joy and the sourest pro-Giant couldn't have helped feeling joyful with it.

❈   ❈   ❈

Who was the real hero of the series?

The writer is inclined to assign the honor to Stanley Harris, manager of the Washington club.

His reason is this:

Harris not only played great ball in the field and at bat, but also he was managing the club. Thus he was constantly "carrying weight," a real test of horse and human.

Harris realized at all times the tremendous responsibility placed on him. He knew he would be blamed for any mistakes. He did make some mistakes, to be sure, but Fate was kind to him and invariably gave him the opportunity to offset these mistakes.

Harris may not be the greatest individual player in the game, but the writer thinks he easily carried off the laurels of the series.

———

Nothing got Runyon's creative juices like a rainout, particularly in a World Series with so much rich material floating about nearby. Here are his ruminations on the eve of game seven of the Pirates–Senators' World Series of 1925.

BERTH MYSTERY SOLVED (OCT. 15, 1925)

PITTSBURGH, OCT. 14—In my nervousness over catching trains between Washington and Pittsburgh, and vice versa, and struggling with my fellow citizens for the lower births, I fear I have shamefully neglected the many clients of this agency with reference to reports on the activities of my celebrated operative, T-44.

I wish to state that T-44 has been extremely busy since the World Series of 1925 started. A great many mysteries have developed during the series, and the services of T-44 have been constantly in demand.

Only yesterday representatives of the great traveling baseball public called on me and requested that I assign T-44 to an investigation into the matter of why the bunks on the B & O Pullman sleepers are so hard. I have his report, with expense account attached, at hand, and I gather that this is one of the simplest cases in T-44's long career, though it defied the average mind.

He states that the traveling baseball public would find the bunks on the B & O sleepers as soft and downy as so many feather beds if they would have the forethought to remove the flasks from their hip pockets on retiring.

I have forwarded copies of T-44's report on this investigation to the Chambers of Commerce of Pittsburgh and Washington, and all way stations, and to President Jim Gould of the Baseball Writers' Association of America.

A Mystery That Mystifies

One of the very first cases that came to me was what I might call the mystery of the Pittsburgh infield.

Oddly enough, this seems to be the one mystery that the infallible T-44 has as yet been unable to clear up, although he offers some interesting facts and deductions.

This mystery developed in the second game of the World Series. When, with the bases loaded, the Pirates two runs ahead, none out, and Mr. Robert Veach, serving in the sinister role as pinch-hitter for Washington, someone pulled the Pittsburgh infield close to Mr. Veach.

The matter was referred to me by a large delegation of veteran baseball managers and players as a crime against baseball nature. They held that it violated all the laws and ethics, and the technique of baseball, which demands that the infield, under the conditions, be pulled back.

They desired to ascertain the identity of the person responsible for this felony, and to report back to them that he might be brought before the bar of baseball justice or any other bar that might be available for punishment.

It was obvious that some member of the Pittsburgh baseball club must be the guilty party, although T-44 states in one report that for some hours his suspicion fell upon the groundkeeper of Forbes Field, his first deduction being that no member of a well-regulated baseball club in these times could possibly commit such a faux pas.

He informs me that he interrogated a number of the members of the Pittsburgh club, after the groundkeeper had established an alibi, as the responsibility for the play, and in every case they replied to him as follows:

"Oh, go to such-and-such a place, will you?"

My personal operative, T-44, remarks, in passing, that he will not. He adds that he is forced to the conclusion from these replies that the members of the Pittsburgh baseball club are shielding someone higher up.

———

PITTSBURGH CAPTURES WORLD TITLE IN RAIN (OCT. 16, 1925)

Senators Lose in Finish of Wettest and Wildest Sort; Johnson Puts up
Game Fight but Is Hard Hit and Loser; Final Game of Series, 9 to 7

FORBES FIELD, PITTSBURGH, OCT. 15—In the wildest and certainly the wettest World Series, the Pittsburgh Pirates struggled to victory and the baseball championship over the Washington Senators by a score of 9 to 7 late this afternoon.

These pallid lines cannot hope to inform the reader of the scene that befell when young Hazen (Kiki) Cuyler, outfielder of the Pirates, came up in the eighth inning with the score tied, two out, and the bases full, and slugged one of old Walter Johnson's fast shoots down the first-base line, driving home the winning runs.

It was equaled only by a scene produced a moment before when Carson Bigbee, a utility outfielder of the Pirates, batting for Ray Kremer, pitcher, knocked in the tying run with a two-bagger.

"Hot Time" Indeed!

Both scenes were presented to the 40,000 spectators, most of them exposed to a driving rain.

As the game ended, at least 20,000 of these well-soaked spectators poured out into the muddy field and surrounded the red-coated bandsmen, who shook water out of their instruments and blared "They'll Be a Hot Time in the Old Town Tonight," which there undoubtedly is.

The crowd chased the Pittsburgh Pirates off the field, trying to capture some member of the valiant baseball crew that has brought a world's championship to this city. The fans desired to make someone an object of boisterous adulation, and they didn't much care who it might be.

They would have preferred Hazen Cuyler, or Carson Bigbee, or "Oil" Smith, the Arkansas man, and the talkiest citizen the game of baseball has ever known, whose two-bagger in the eighth, after two were out, started the Pirates to victory.

They would have been satisfied with even "Red" Oldham, the lefthander whose pitching in the final inning held the Senators helpless, or Max Carey, captain of the Pirates, who was a powerful figure in the general assault.

How That Band Played

All the Pirates escaped to their clubhouse, however, and the crowd marched behind the band to the Washington bench, and stood, with the rain sprinkling their bare heads, while the band played "The Star-Spangled Banner."

Then they all marched over to the Pittsburgh bench and the anthem was repeated with a woman singing the words in a high soprano.

It was an hour after the game before the crowd finally leaked out of the ball yard, many of them jamming the streets outside for a peek at the triumphant Pirates, as they emerged from their clubhouse in street apparel.

Tonight the hotels and cafes of the downtown district resound of the joy of Pittsburgh.

It was the seventh and deciding game of the series, with each club having won three games. Before it was over the spectators could scarcely see the ball through that curtain of misty rain, and the outfielders were outlines, vague and shadowy.

Towels Badly Needed

Time and time again the game was halted, while the ball and bats were wiped dry with towels, and twice Walter Johnson asked for a delay that he might get sawdust to scatter around the pitching mound, to give his sliding feet a firmer hold.

The base lines were channels of mud. The base runners had to keep kicking their cleats and clinging earth. Meantime the spectators were gradually sopping up rain water, as they sat in the exposed seats of Forbes Field.

The Washington club got off to a four-run lead in the first inning, which seemed to put the Pirates at a hopeless disadvantage, especially against the pitching of the mighty Johnson, who had them as helpless as so many manikins in the other games.

But it is a fighting crew that (Pirates' manager) Bill McKechnie has assembled here in Pittsburgh, and they kept on fighting until a foreign hope carried through.

Oddly enough, it seemed to me that at no time did the spectators seem to regard the cause as lost.

Even when Roger Peckinpaugh broke up a 6 to 6 tie in the first of the eighth inning by knocking a home run over the leftfield wall, and with but two innings left to the Pirates, the crowd kept bawling encouragement to the home club.

Poor Peckinpaugh's eighth error of the series, which is a new World Series record, contributed no little to the last-minute shove by the Pirates.

His bad toss in the melee of the eighth inning filled the bases. Had the toss been accurate it would have been the third out of the inning and would have left the score tied. Let me briefly sum up that Pirates' eighth, leaving out the cheers, and jeers, and the nerve-racking tumult from the stands:

With two out, Smith doubled. Emil Yde ran for him. Bigbee,

batting for (Ray) Kremer, doubled to left, scoring Yde with the tying run. (Eddie) Moore walked. (Max) Carey hit to Peckinpaugh, whose toss to S.(am) Harros to get Moore at second was high, and nobody was put out. Cuyler doubled to right, scoring Bigbee and Moore. (Clyde) Barnhart popped out.

There you have it all in a few words.

Plaything of Fate

Fortune set her face sternly against Roger Peckinpaugh. The baseball writers, dripping in the press section, were thinking of the drama of the situation when Peckinpaugh broke up the tie in the eighth, because Peckinpaugh had contributed to Washington's distress by muffing an easy fly in the seventh, permitting the Pirates to tie to tally.

His homer glossed over a lot of things for Roger Peckinpaugh in the eighth. It looked as if he was to finally emerge from the series in one of the most important roles.

The entire Washington bench turned out in the rain to give old Roger a cheer as he trotted in from his trip around the bases after that blow.

But baseball is mighty fickle. A few moments later Roger Peckinpaugh had slipped back into a more dismal pose. It seems strange that one of the greatest infielders that ever lived should wind up with more errors in a series of games than any other player has ever made.

Bothered by Wet Ball

The wet ball seemed to trouble the mighty Johnson more than it did Ray Kremer, Johnny Morrison, or Oldham, but not as much as it troubled Vic Aldridge, the Hoosier state right-hander, who was dismissed from the game in the first inning.

Aldridge, like Johnson, had won two games of the series. He could not control the ball, which was then not as wet and slippery as it became later.

Here again you have an illustration of the fickleness of baseball fortune, for Aldridge seemed almost certain to make a good showing on the strength of his past performances.

I believe that a great club has won this series of 1925—a real championship club. It has some great individual players, and it has tremendous fighting spirit. It proved that by winning three consecutive games and the championship after the Senators had them three to one in the series.

I am inclined to think that this may eventually prove one of the greatest clubs of many years in baseball, ranking with the old Athletics, and the Cubs, the Red Sox and the Giants of other years.

Band Invited Rain

Everything seemed all right in the ball yard until the band played "Let It Rain." The elements seemed to regard this as an invitation and down came the rain in a thin drizzle about 1:30 P.M.

At this time the yard was well filled and the streets outside the walls were packed with the incoming crowd.

The bleacherites had their improvised shelters of newspapers and the field-box occupants had come provided with umbrellas. It was a strange setting for a baseball game, with the umbrellas raised and the spectators bundled up in raincoats and heavy wraps.

The skinned surface of the field near the players' benches had been covered with sawdust, which stood out against the dark and soggy turf like fresh yellow paint.

The tarpaulins were peeled from the infield about 1 P.M. and the Senators and the Pirates began practice. Fresh lime had been distributed along the base lines and the bags marking the bases had been whitened anew, but the grass of the outfield looked as wet and miry as a swamp.

Two Stars to Pitch

Walter Johnson warmed up near the Senators' bench and Vic Aldridge went through the same performance over near the Pirates' coop, so there was no doubt as to the pitching selections.

The four umpires in their somber garb filed out just before 2 P.M. and stood at the plate, conferring. Judge Kenesaw Mountain

Landis, the Commissioner of Baseball, was in his box adjoining the Senators' bench, observing the weather with a critical eye.

At 2 P.M., the red-coated band marched to the flagpole in centerfield and played "The Star-Spangled Banner," while the crowd stood. A soprano singer lifted her voice in the words, but the air was so heavy that only the last few notes carried to the grandstand.

Then the one-armed announcer bawled the batteries through his megaphone, and the Pirates trotted to their stations.

The air was so soggy with water that the flags, well soaked the day before, were wrapped limply around the poles, feebly stirring at intervals in a light breeze. The smoke from the chimneys on the buildings in Schenley Park beyond the leftfield fence lifted lazily and banked white and steamy in the murky atmosphere.

Revenge for Jeers

Sam Rice got the well-known Bronx cheer as he walked to the plate to start the game. The Pittsburgh fans have been picking on Sam ever since the return from Washington, because of his catch off "Oil" Smith.

Rice singled through the box by way of reply. Bucky Harris hit a fly to Barnhart, and in two pitches (Vic) Aldridge failed to get the ball over the plate.

Then he tried a very slow ball. It was so slow it hit the ground in front of the plate and bounded away from "Oil" Smith. Rice took second on this wild pitch.

(Goose) Goslin got his base on balls, Aldridge getting just one strike over on him. Old Joe Harris let the first two slings pass for called balls, and on the next, Aldridge cut loose another wild pitch, the ball again hitting the ground in front of the plate and skidding past Smith.

Both runners advanced. On the next pitch he walked Joe Harris, filling the bases with only one out.

Just Walked Home

The first pitch to Joe Judge was a ball. The next was low and outside, but was called a strike. The next was high. Ball two. Ball three.

(Pirates' first baseman) Stuffy McInnis walked up to Aldridge and spoke to him. The Hoosier hurler got the next pitch over the plate, making the count three balls and two strikes, with the bases filled.

Judge fouled off two, Stuffy McInnis making a desperate try for a twister into the boxes back of first. Judge next hit a long foul to right, then the ball seemed to slip out of Aldridge's hand as he pitched, and flew so high that "Oil" Smith had to jump up to get it. Judge walked and forced in Rice.

(Ossie) Bluege took a strike, a ball, then swung and missed for another strike. Then he drove a fly into the haze of left field, which Barnhart apparently lost in the mist. It dropped behind him for a hit, Goslin scoring. Barnhart got the ball on the first bounce and made a fast return to the infield.

McKechnie beckoned Aldridge from the box and Johnny Morrison, the right-handed curveball pitcher, came in to face Peckinpaugh with the bases still packed. His first pitch was a dropping curve that was called a ball by (umpire) Barry McCormick.

On the next pitch "Oil" Smith touched Peck's bat as Peck swung, knocking the ball to (Glenn) Wright. Peck immediately turned to McCormick and complained, and McCormick began waving his hands as Wright was throwing to first and Joe Harris was crossing the plate.

McCormick had seen "Oil" Smith's act, and sent Peck to first, and allowed Joe Harris's run to score. The Pirates, led by Mc Kechnie, gathered around McCormick. Protesting, but the interference had been apparent even to the spectators, and McCormick waved the protesters away.

"Muddy" Ruel hit to Eddie Moore, who fumbled the ball, and Judge scored, bringing up Johnson. The Jayhawker Cyclone knocked a slow roller down the first-base line and Johnny Morrison chased it without touching the ball, gambling on it rolling foul. It did. Johnson then struck out.

Did He Recite Poem?

Moriarity, the poet umpire, halted the game and talked to Stuffy McInnis as if admonishing him.

Sam Rice, up for the second time in the inning, with the bases still loaded, had two strikes and two balls when he lined to Barnhart, ending the inning. Four runs is not much scoring for all the things that happened in that inning.

Little Nemo Leibold stood at the plate warming up Johnson while the Pirates were making ready to bat. It was an ideal setting for Johnson's speed—a dark day and a weaving background of humanity for the batters.

The Pirates had evidently decided to take advantage of Johnson's bad knee and make the big fellow move around as much as possible.

Moore, the first man up. Bunted, and Johnson, moving rather stiffly, got the ball and threw the runner out at first.

Max Carey showed a disposition to bunt until Johnson slipped two strikes over on him. Then Carey waited until the count was three and two and doubled to right center.

Crowd Happier

The crowd, which had been greatly depressed by the incidents of the Senators' side of the inning, woke up and began cheering.

Johnson poured speed at Cuyler and struck him out on three pitched balls. Then he struck out Barnhart. Even the Pittsburgh fans applauded Johnson as he walked back to his bench.

Johnny Morrison got his curve to working in the second inning, and reduced the Senators in order.

The rain had ceased as play commenced, but now an occasional drop spattered down. Glenn Wright singled sharply across second in the Pirates' second, after (Pie) Traynor had been thrown out. The ball was a line shot past Johnson, who tried to stop it with his gloved hand. McInnis singled in identically the same manner, Johnson again missing a grab for the ball as it flew past him. Wright stopped at second.

"Oil" Smith rolled to Buck Harris, who tagged McInnis coming down the baseline, and then threw to first, doubling up Smith.

Error on Fine Catch

Joe Judge singled to right center in the Senators' third, and after

Bluege had gone out, Cuyler made a great catch on Peckinpaugh's fly in short rightfield. Cuyler slipped on the wet grass as he got the ball, rolled over, and came up with the ball.

Judge had started for second and Cuyler fired to first to catch him, making a bad throw to McInnis as Judge returned to the bag. Judge then went on to second. Thus Cuyler got an error after a brilliant catch. Carey made a good catch of Ruel's long fly to deep center.

When (Johnny) Morrison was at bat in the Pirates' end of the same inning, Eddie Moore was waiting with four huge bats on his shoulder. He finally discarded three of them as Morrison singled to center.

Ty Cobb set a record by swinging three bats as a preliminary to taking his place at the plate, but four is a new mark.

The exercise must have done Eddie Moore some good, as he slugged a terrific drive to left-center between Goslin and Rice.

Johnny No "Mud Horse"

Big Johnny Morrison legged it around the bases from second, making a mighty effort of the job of running, with the crowd in an uproar.

Peckinpaugh went out into the outfield to take the relay from Rice, which was none too accurate, and Morrison thundered across the plate, Moore taking second.

Carey singled, scoring Moore from second, and Carey took second on Cuyler's infield out. The crowd was roaring madly as these incidents transpired. The rain was lightly spattering on the hats of the exposed citizens, but nobody paid any attention to it.

Carey stole third on Johnson, and now the crowd shrieked and shrilled. Johnson squatted on the ground, toying with a handful of earth, as if in deep thought.

Barnhart took a strike and three balls, then jolted a little fly into right for a single, Carey scoring.

The spectators were commencing to get a little hoarse. Most of them were standing shaking their fists in mad jubilation.

The great Johnson was undeniably in retreat. He walked around and around in the box stooping and picking up bits of dirt before pitching to big "Pie" Traynor. From the coop of the Pirates came hoarse staccato shouts.

With a strike and two balls called on Traynor, Johnson split the plate with a pitch and Traynor rolled to Peckinpaugh, who tossed to second for the force play on Barnhart. Bucky Harris's throw to first to double up Traynor pulled Judge off the bag and Traynor was safe. Wright popped to Moore and the crowd settled back exhausted.

The crowd booed Rice with great spirit as he came up in the Senators' fourth after Johnson had lifted a fly to center. It was getting dark over the field. Matches lighted in the distant bleachers flared up like torches out of a black night.

Sam Rice hit his twelfth of the series, a single, and even the most spirited boosters had to admit that this was considerable hitting.

Bucky's Bat Useless

Bucky Harris, the Senators' manager, who has had little luck this series, struck out. The crowd jeered on. The Pittsburgh fans were now certainly wide awake and going full blast.

The haze increased until the roofs of the buildings in Schenley Park showed in mere outline.

Goslin singled to left, and Rice tore around second base by some daring base running, Barnhart throwing the ball in to Traynor, who tossed it to Moore at second for a close decision on the flying "Goose."

Joe Harris got his 11th hit of the series, a double to right-center, which scored Rice and Goslin.

The tumult in the stands died down suddenly. Only a few chirped as Cuyler grabbed Joe Judge's long drive out of the air, but the folks cheered up as McInnis opened the Pirates' side of the fourth with a rousing single to left. Rice got "Oil" Smith's fly after a hard run and a scooping catch.

McKechnie now sent (George) Grantham up to bat in place of

Johnny Morrison. He hit a long fly to Joe Harris. Moore flied to Goslin, ending the inning, and Ray Kremer went in to pitch for the Pirates.

Traynor made a sensational play on Bluege's high bounder, and Glenn Wright made a grand stop of a free traveling roller from Peckinpaugh's bat in the Senators' side of the fifth. Carey made a great running catch on Ruel's fly.

Ruel got Traynor's foul off the first ball pitched by Johnson. Ruel was talking spiritedly to Johnson between pitches. With the count on him two strikes and three balls, and Cuyler in motion from second, Wright popped to Stanley Harris.

The magnates probably heaved a sigh of relief. The game was officially "in," no matter what might happen thereafter. Kremer quickly disposed of Johnson on a fly, Rice on a roller to Wright and Bucky Harris by a strikeout in the Senators' sixth.

———

No question that the 1925 World Series was a rousing affair. But Runyon offered a few ideas on how to make it better.

SERIES IS TOO DRY. NEEDS A SHOWMAN. OLD BOSTON KNEW HOW. THE GREAT ROYAL ROOTERS, BRUSH AND THE GIANTS. (OCT. 17, 1925)

I wish Flo Ziegfeld, or Sam Harris, or George White, or some other enterprising and resourceful showmen would get into baseball and make the World Series something more than a perfunctory playing of a number of games to determine the ownership of the major share of the gate receipts, and a large, cheap banner, usually not unfurled until the following Summer.

I mean to say I would like to see the World Series trimmed up and staged, and properly produced, and made into a real spectacle, something on the order of the Army and the Navy football game. In fact, I would be satisfied if they would just restore some of the color and festivity that used to surround the series.

It seems to me that most of this color and festivity has quite vanished. A few flags here and there and a band are the modern magnate's contribution to the adornment of the series that brings him anywhere from the $15,000 of 1905 to the $300,000 or more of this year.

＊　＊　＊

I hold that the magnate owes it to his baseball public, when he wins a pennant, to present something beyond a mere baseball game.

The price of admission is advanced. The series is supposed to be an unusual event in every way, and the big event of the baseball season. I assert that the magnate should dress it up in a manner befitting its importance.

You might think that after 16 years of waiting for a pennant, Barney Dreyfuss, owner of the Pittsburgh club, for instance, would have made the affair something pretentious, as he might easily have done by the exercise of a little imagination.

But Barney's imagination did not progress much beyond having the uniforms of his player freshly laundered. (Senators' owner) Clark Griffith, in Washington, with the President of the United States as a central figure around which he might have built a vast spectacle, did little better than Dreyfuss this year.

＊　＊　＊

This surprised me, too. Griffith is a dour man, but I always suspected him of being at heart a showman from the fact that even in times of great vicissitude he carried with his club the famous baseball clowns, Nick Altrock and Al Schacht.

They are very funny men, pantomimes of some talent and inventiveness. They provided the crowd in Washington and Pittsburgh with amusement before the games, but I regard them as part of Griffith's regular performance, and I rather expected him to add new acts of an unusual and startling nature when he first got into the World Series.

I do not know just what these acts might have been. I am not a showman. I did not look for any trained elephants or trapeze performers, but I thought Griffith would surely dig up something new and novel.

❀   ❀   ❀

The parades of the ballplayers from the home plate to the flag-raising ceremony in centerfield and the perfunctory handling over of flowers and other gifts to local and visiting favorites are regular features of the World Series program from year to year, old now and hackneyed.

It seems to me that a real showman would think of something else. When John Brush, dead these dozen years or more, owned the New York Giants, and they won a pennant for him in 1911, he garbed them in new uniforms of solid black, with white trimmings, and when the crowd was all assembled on the field he had them make a most dramatic and effective entrance.

❀   ❀   ❀

They were collected under the stand in centerfield, and at a signal a gate was opened, and out they came on the run, while their opponents, the Philadelphia Athletics, in dully dusty-looking gray uniforms, stood over their bench fairly dumbfounded.

John J. McGraw always claimed that this theatrical entrance had a pronounced psychological effect on the Athletics, and enabled the Giants to win that first game, though they did not win the series.

❀   ❀   ❀

But perhaps the lack of color and atmosphere to a series nowadays is not so much the fault of the magnates as it is the cities. Boston always made more of a World Series than any other city in the big leagues.

No baseball fan who saw the Boston Braves and Red Sox in a World Series will ever forget the Royal Rooters from Boston, with their band playing "Tessie" interminably, or "Honey Fitz," the musical Mayor singing "Sweet Adeline."

You can never make me believe that this rooting support did not help the Boston clubs, and it certainly added to the Boston prestige. The Royal Rooters were a lesson in civic loyalty wherever they went.

The Boston merchants always decorated their windows as profusely for a World Series as they do for a Harvard-Yale game. The city went in for baseball to a man—aye, and to a woman. It made other cities fairly ashamed of themselves when the Royal Rooters would come marching into the stands behind their blaring band playing "Tessie"—always "Tessie."

That was the popular tune when the Boston Red Sox played the Pittsburgh Pirates 22 years ago (in the first World Series, in 1903). No tune has since taken its place in Boston baseball. "Tammany" was generally identified with New York in the Giants' World Series, but no Royal Rooters marched behind the Giants or the Yankees.

❊ ❊ ❊

Washington cut loose with a night of celebration last year after the Senators won their first World Series, and it was such a night as no other city has produced for any occasion other than the armistice in many years.

But it was an extemporaneous affair, without any previous attempt at organization. Perhaps it was all the more memorable for that very reason. I hope to live to see St. Louis win a pennant in one league or the other.

Somehow I think St. Louis would make something of that incident.

—

Three home runs in a single World Series game! The Babe's heroics are the wonder of the era.

Ruth's 3 Homers Set Mark; Yanks Seize Game, 10 to 5, Babe Proving Whole Circus (Oct. 7, 1926)

St. Louis Fans Gasp Over New Idea of "Progressive Punch"
As Drives Go Longer, Longer

Sportsman's Park, St. Louis, Oct. 6—That mighty man, George Herman Babe Ruth, went to Sportsman's Park today for the fourth game of the World Series of 1926 burbling like a camel over a brilliant idea that had come to him during the night.

"The boys ain't hittin'," reflected that mighty man, as he sat by his hotel window last evening, peering out into the darkness made hideous by the noise of the agitated St. Louisians celebrating yesterday's (game three) victory over the New York Yankees.

"The boys ain't hittin', and that's fact, and if we don't look out, we'll lose all that dough."

Ah! The Way Out!

The thought appalled that mighty man, G.H.B.R. He said to himself:

"I know what I'll do, I'll do hittin' myself."

An inspiration, you may well say.

Under the influence thereof, that mighty man, George Herman Babe Ruth, burst into the baseball orchard this afternoon, and in the presence of 38,825 astounded customers, he ran what you might call a very considerable muck.

He belted out three glowing home runs, one for each of his official times at bat. He was up five times, and walked twice.

Even Stephen Again

He personally carried in four runs and drove in a fifth, or 50 percent of the Yankees' total score of 10 to the Cardinals' 5.

He was largely responsible for the Yanks moving up to even terms with the St. Louis club in the series, with two games each, at a time when they seemed to be on the run.

That mighty man, George Herman Babe Ruth, hug up a new home run record for one game of a World Series, equaling in that single game the home run record for an entire series, held by himself, (and) Goose Goslin and Joe Harris of the Washington club.

He hit two of his homers today into the rightfield pavilion and the third smack-dab into the centerfield bleachers, leaving the hometown rooters simply speechless with astonishment.

It shows you what can come of a man devoting a few minutes of an evening to quiet reflection.

Inspiration to All

Under the inspiration of that mighty man's mauling the rest of the Yankees chirked up and did some auxiliary pounding against an assortment of pitchers of one kind and another produced by Rogers Hornsby.

They got 14 hits, all told. So did the Cardinals. And I might add, it was just that kind of a baseball game.

It dragged across 2 hours and 39 minutes. Waite Hoyt, that old-time schoolboy, staggered through the entire game for the Yanks, although there were many times when the dull thud of a baseball against a catcher's "pud" reached his ears from the station where the relief pitchers warm up.

Urban Shocker pitched almost a full game down in the old "bullpen" against a call to the succor of Waite Hoyt. About all the veteran schoolboy seemed to have was plenty of nerve.

Rogers Hornsby had some pitcher getting ready throughout the pastime. The series was just about due one of those games.

"Just an Accident"

The crowd thought the first home run by that mighty man, George Herman Babe Ruth, was an accident. The ball was just inside the foul line in rightfield. They laughed it off with scorn.

They felt that the second one, flush, plump into the rightfield pavilion was intentional, all right, but they continued to laugh not too heartily however.

They decided that the third homer, which traveled farther than most folk could carry a baseball in a basket, was rubbing it in, and based entirely on malice.

They stopped laughing and began scowling at that mighty man, George Herman Babe Ruth, who suddenly became the soul of affability. Up to today, that mighty man had been so morose that his friends were a little troubled. They did not suspect he was thinking.

After his third blow, that mighty man smiled all over the place, and also all over his face. He chatted gaily with the boys in the left-field bleachers in front of which he disports. He was the soul of good humor.

Future Golden

Occasionally, he would think of his employer, Colonel Jake Ruppert, sitting back there in a box, with whom that mighty man will presently be discussing the terms of a new contract.

And then George Herman Babe Ruth will rattle off a guffaw.

It was a great day for that mighty man, G.H.B. Ruth. Perhaps he will devote another evening to reflection before the series is over, and who knows what may happen then?

The game today was a hodgepodge affair, with loose fielding, looser pitching, and fluent hitting. Taylor Douthit and Chick Hafey, the brilliant young California outfielders of the Cardinals, came together while pursuing a fly ball, and knocked each other bowlegged for a moment, but were able to continue playing.

The series now travels back to New York City after the game tomorrow. There is no chance that it will be ended here, which is a sad blow to the hopes of the Cardinals' rooters. They thought Rogers Hornsby's men were going to make it four in a row, over the Yanks.

They failed to take into consideration that mighty man, George Herman Babe Ruth.

Fever a Trifle Less

It was sunny, and windy, and cool today, and the fever of the St. Louisians had abated to some extent, following a wild night of celebrating the victory of the Cardinals and the strange festivities of the Veiled Prophet.

Their temperature was still several points above normal, however, as they packed into Sportsman's Park, a little sleepy-eyed and footsore from marching up and down the streets half the night. Their voices were hoarse, too. The vocal chords will stand just so much.

A devoted little flock of early birds again roosted at the bleacher gates all night long, but the chattering of their teeth kept them awake. The jolly old autumn time is creeping down from the upper reaches of the Mississippi.

The bleachers loaded up soon after the gates were opened, and the boys and girls out there took catnaps in the soothing sun until they had thawed out.

No Beds, No Sleep

The city of St. Louis was hard-pressed to take care of all the visitors last night. The combination of the World Series and the ceremonies of the Veiled Prophet overtaxed the bed slats of the community. Some of the strangers were laid out on cots in hotel hallways; others found refuge in private homes. Then there were a great many who saw no sense in going to bed at all.

They remained out in the streets and assisted in the hollering and beating of tin pans that went on until the small hours of the morning.

It was fairly noisy in St. Louis the night before, but last night old George Pandemonium himself, in the person, broke loose, and burbled all over the joint.

The parade of the Veiled Prophet was followed by other extemporaneous parades throughout the night. A barrage of backfire thundered over the city. Ladies and gents, eventually somewhat dishelved, straggled along the streets.

It is rumored that some persons were seen violating the Volstead Act (or Prohibition, which outlawed drinking), but it is believed that they were New Yorkers who had been driven to drinking hair tonic after watching the Yankees trying to hit.

Yanks in Bad Humor

The streets were ankle-deep in torn papers this morning, and echoes were still weakly giving back the last remnants of the rebel yell. It was certainly a hot time in the old time last night, and it is by no means cool here tonight.

There was a presentation scene before the game today. A bald-headed man appeared on the field with a basket from which he passed out little packages to the assembled Cardinals, while the movie men took shots of the ensemble.

The bald-headed Santa Claus seemed to be somebody of vast local importance.

The Yanks came out on the field looking very grouchy and discontented. That mighty man, George Herman Babe Ruth, was scowling sourly at the world.

The Yankee cheering section, composed of Colonel Jacob Ruppert, president of the club, and his secretary, Al Brennan, seemed none too happy. They were unable to produce any concerted cheering for the dear old Bronx Stadium before the game. They just sat and thought, and sometimes they just sat.

Flier Again Alarms

The crazy aviator who frightened the spectators silly yesterday again appeared over the field, although everyone had been hoping that he had been jailed for his wanton carelessness.

He was flying an old parasol that he must have found in some ashcan, and he was advertising a theatrical attraction. The crowd sat cold with terror as he hung over the field.

The noble little band bravely squirted music from a position back of third base, the musicians occasionally scuttling away as a foul ball came in their direction. There was the same display of Cardinal red hats by the girls in the grandstand as on the first day, and many of the gents wore red ties.

Will Klem, one of the noblest Romans of 'em all, the bowlegged, autocratic umpire of the National League, appeared for the first time in the series as the gesticulator-in-chief. Burly Bill Dinneen of the American League was on first, (Hank) O'Day the iron umpire on second, and (George) Hildebrand on third.

Sensitive Soul, Bill

Will Klem has quite a manner when it comes to umpiring. Also, it came out that he has a very bald head when he doffed his cap as the band played "The Star-Spangled Banner."

It would ill behoove any ballplayer to mention the matter of the bald head of Will Klem in the heat of contest, however. Will is very sensitive about some things. Ballplayers have been known to be cast into outer darkness by Will Klem just for suggesting that his mouth reminds them of that noble animal, the catfish.

Will Klem called a third strike on Earle Combs, the first man to face Flint Rhem, the young pitcher whose name sounds like a patent medicine, and Earl gazed reproachfully at Will.

Nice Golf Shot

His reproach was not nearly as poignant as that of Mark Koenig, who swung out with great rapidity, although of course Will has no control over a man swinging out.

Flint Rhem was getting very chesty over his success, and he pitched to that mighty man, George Herman Babe Ruth, as if he was nobody at all.

George Herman Babe reached for that first pitch and sarcastically golfed it into the rightfield pavilion for a home run. The drive followed the foul line so faithfully that it looked as if it was in there by a couple of inches more or less.

As George Herman Babe Ruth trotted about the bases, the crowd gave him quite a hand and Flint Rhem did not seem quite so chesty.

Bob Meusel got his base on balls, and (Lou) Gehrig singled through (Jim) Bottomley's legs. Bob got around to third, o.k., and when he saw that (Billy) Southworth had chucked the ball into (Rogers) Hornsby at second as Gehrig moved for that point, Robert started homeward.

Hornsby whipped the pill in to (catcher Bob) O'Farrell at the plate, and although Robert took a long, long slide, Will Klem pronounced him quite out. Robert arose and mumbled at Will, but nothing came of that at all. A ballplayer wastes his time mumbling at Will Klem.

Hoyt in Trouble

Things did not look so rosy for Waite Hoyt . . . as he pitched to Taylor Douthit. The young man singled to deep short, beating Koenig's throw by a Grecian nose. On a hit-and-run play, Southworth singled over second, putting Douthit on third. Waite Hoyt looked very, very troubled, and so did Miller Huggins.

Waite got a ball and a pair of strikes on Hornsby, when Hornsby singled to right, scoring Douthit and putting Southworth on second.

Lou Gehrig trotted over from first and spoke in Waite Hoyt's ear, while Urban Shocker bustled down to the bullpen and started warming up.

Bottomley raised a fly to Ruth, and runners held fast. (Les) Bell hit a fly to Combs, and Southworth moved to third after the catch, Hornsby sticking to first.

Hornsby stole second as the count reached three and two on Hafey, (Hank) Severeid dropping the ball as Rogers broke out running; then Waite Hoyt fanned Hafey on the next pitch, ending the inning.

Tony Too Eager

Tony Lazzeri, the young Yankee second baseman, tossed away a run in the Yanks' second. He drove the ball to deep left for a nice, comfortable two-bagger, but tried to make it a triple, and was squelched at third.

Severeid followed with a single to center after (Joe) Dugan had gone out, and Lazzeri might easily have scored. Hoyt popped to Hornsby.

Douthit and (Tommy) Thevenow coupled up a brace of beautiful throws in getting the ball to Bell ahead of Lazzeri. However, that was no excuse for "Poosh-up Tony."

O'Farrell, Thevenow and Rhem were quickly effaced in the Cards' second, the latter on strikes.

(Art) Reinhart, a left-hander, began warming up in left-center as the Yanks went to bat in the third. Combs and Koenig were promptly extinguished, then up came that mighty man, George Herman Ruth, again.

Still Longer Drive

He hauled off and banged the first ball pitched to him by Flint Rhem into the rightfield bleachers, almost on a line. This time he drove it into the very heart of fair territory, so there might be no argument.

The crowd whooped. Even the most delirious St. Louisians could appreciate the artistry of such an effort. That mighty man George Herman Babe, lifted his cap from his noble bean in response to the kind applause as he trotted around the paths.

Two homers in two times up is some hitting in any vicinity. Flint Rhem threw out Meusel.

After Koenig had tossed out Douthit in the Cardinals' third, Billy Southworth dropped what they call a Texas Leaguer in back of second, a lazy little looper that no one could get. Waite Hoyt steamed up and fanned Hornsby, and Lazzeri tossed out Bottomley.

Columbia Lou Gehrig opened the Yanks' batting side of the fourth with a college strikeout, a college strikeout being more artistic than an ordinary whiff. Lazzeri got his base on balls.

Then Jumping Joe Dugan hit a short fly to left-center, and Douthit and Hafey went after the ball. They apparently did not see each other and both reached for it at the same time.

The impact of their bodies knocked them both cold on the grass and the ball skittered away.

Lazzeri kept running from first as the ballplayers lay stretched on the greensward. Thevenow chased the ball and threw to the home plate, but Lazzeri scored ahead of the throw by a long slide. Dugan pulled up at second.

Then time was called and the entire Cardinal bench hurried to their fallen brethren. Douthit was the more winded of the two,

Hafey's right arm having hit him in the chest. They both finally scrambled to their feet and play was resumed.

Severeid singled to center and Dugan tried to score from second. Douthit made a nice throw to the plate and Jumping Joe was waved out by Will Klem.

Just Running Wild

The Yankees seemed to be running daffy on the bases.

Hoyt was called out on strikes. The crowd gave Douthit a big hand as he came in from the field.

Koenig made a remarkable catch of a twisting fly from Bell's bat in the Cards' fourth, going away back into leftfield after the ball.

Hafey singled over second. Suddenly, Long Bob Meusel came in from rightfield and asked for a cessation of hostilities while a segment of St. Louis, in the form of gravel, was removed from one of his eyes.

This operation seemed to require the attendance of the entire Yankee team and Al Woods, the agile trainer of the club.

When play was resumed, Koenig booted O'Farrell's grounder, Hafey taking second. Thevenow pumped a drive across first base along the foul line for two bases, scoring Hafey and putting O'Farrell on third.

(Specs) Toporcer, batting for Rhem, hit a fly to Combs in short center and O'Farrell scored the tying run after the catch, beating a throw that was none too accurate.

Nipped at Plate

The crowd had an attack of hysteria.

Combs really ought to have had his man.

Douthit hit a long drive in between Ruth and Combs, up against the right-center wall for two bases, scoring Thevenow. Southworth singled to left but the Yanks finally got a real throw from their outfield, Ruth shooting the ball to Severeid in time to peg out Douthit at the plate, ending the inning.

Reinhart, the southpaw, succeeded Rhem on what the boys call the rubber.

Reinhart started out by passing Combs. Koenig lifted a high fly over short rightfield and Hornsby, Bottomley and Southworth all had the thought of going after it, but they failed to elect one of their number to the task in time to prevent the ball from falling safe.

Combs ran all the way home, tying the score again.

Ruth got his base on balls.

Meusel had a count of three and two and walked, filling the bases with no one out. Reinhart was having no luck, and Herman Bell, a righthander, began warming up in leftfield.

Downfall Begins

Gehrig had a count of three and two and walked, forcing in Combs. That ended Reinhart and Bell came in.

Lazzeri lifted a long high fly to Southworth over against the rightfield wall, and Ruth scored after the catch, Meusel moving to third. Gehrig remained on first.

Dugan hit a high bouncer in front of the plate and O'Farrell ran out, got the ball and threw to first, getting Dugan. Meusel had a very long lead off third, however, and scored behind O'Farrell. Gehrig took second and Herman Bell committed a balk that advanced Columbia Lou to third.

Severeid was intentionally passed by Herman Bell on four wide pitches. It was good judgment, as Hoyt tapped weakly to Hornsby, forcing Severeid at second.

Hoyt gave his first base on balls to Bottomley in the Cardinals' fifth, but no damage resulted to the Yanks.

Combs walked to start the Yanks' sixth, and Koenig struck out. When George Herman (Babe) Ruth shambled to the dish, Hornsby had a consultation with Herman Bell. He probably told the pitcher to be careful with the Babe.

He was—for a time. He had three balls and two strikes on Babe, the strikes being represented by fouls.

Then Herman Bell put over a high fastball and Babe clouted it into the centerfield bleachers.

It was a terrific smash. Douthit backed up rapidly, then stood gazing blankly at the startled crowd in the bleachers.

The spectators just gasped "Whoo-ee!" and fell back in their seats.

They had never seen anything like this before in all their born days. A few revived sufficiently to applaud George Herman Babe Ruth and he plowed around the bases, Combs traveling ahead of him.

Meusel singled to right, but was thrown out trying to make it a two-bagger. The incident passed almost unnoticed. The crowd was still babbling about George Herman Babe.

Gehrig doubled to the leftfield wall. Lazzeri popped to Thevenow.

The hometowners were a little bit sunk after Ruth's last exploit. The boys in the leftfield bleachers gave Babe a big hand, however, as he walked to his position and Babe could be seen pointing toward centerfield as if to indicate to his neighbors in leftfield just where he put the ball.

(Ruth repeated a three-homer game in the 1928 World Series, again against the Cardinals in game four of a Yankee sweep. Reggie Jackson of the Yankees is the only other ballplayer to have a three-homer game in the World Series, against the Dodgers in 1977.)

———

Complete game coverage of the day that Grover Cleveland Alexander left a barstool and "ambled" onto the Yankee Stadium mound to fan Tony Lazzeri and deliver the 1926 World Series title to the Cardinals.

BASES LOADED, LAZZERI FANS; RUTH TAGGED (OCT. 11, 1926)
Babe's Fourth Home Homer Breaks Record, and When Passed in Ninth He Makes Great Try
Old Grover Cleveland Alexander, Hurled into Fray, Brings St. Louis Out on Top of 3 to 2 Score

Old Grover Cleveland Alexander with his cap perched high above his ear, shambled in out of a fog into the seventh game of the World Series of 1926 up at the Yankee Stadium yesterday just in time to fan Poosh 'Em Up Tony Lazzeri with the bases full, and to hold a one-run lead that made the St. Louis Cardinals champions of all the baseball world.

They beat the New York Yankees 3 to 2, which was the situation when Old Grover Cleveland Alexander appeared on the scene, bowed by the weight of his 39 years and nursing a crick in his venerable back.

Jesse Joseph Haines, the corn-fed man from Phillipsburg, Ohio, had been pitching for the Cardinals and doing fairly well, when he sustained a split finger just as the Yankees packed the satchels up in the seventh on a single by Earle Combs, a sacrifice by Marcus Aurelius Koenig, a pass to Mr. George Herman Babe Ruth and a pass to Columbia Lou Gehrig, after Long Bob Meusel had gone out on an infield roller.

That sacrifice by Marcus Aurelius Koenig caused some subsequent chatter among the hometown folks. It was ordered by Mr. Miller Huggins, the sawed-off manager of the Yankees.

Fond of Tavern

Of course Mr. Huggins's many volunteer assistants in the grandstand said it was punk baseball.

Anyway, it is fortunate for the Cardinals that they located Old Grover Cleveland Alexander at the moment that Jesse Joseph Haines's finger began to pain him. Some say Grover had been heating himself up under the bleachers.

Others claim that he was found in his favorite chair down at the Tavern, discoursing over his previous two victories in the series with Mine Host Will LaHiffe and that the Cardinals chipped in towards a taxi to send for Grover.

They sent word by the taxi jockey that his presence was urgently requested at the baseball orchard and that it might be worth $2,000 to him to make the trip, the difference between the individual winners' and losers' end of the series.

Old Grover sighed and accompanied the taxi back to the Yankee Stadium, but is said he insisted that Mr. LaHiffe go with him.

He did not care to take such a long ride without somebody to talk to. I do not vouch for this report, you understand.

All I know is that Grover Cleveland Alexander may usually be found in the Tavern when he is in New York and that he appeared out of the fog that hung over the Yankee yard in the seventh inning.

Short Wait Sure

Mr. LaHiffe waited for him in the taxicab outside the yard. He knew Grover would not be long. Meantime, poor Antonio Lazzeri, known as Poosh 'Em Up Tony, the pride of San Francisco, was waiting at the plate.

It was a long wait for a very young man and Tony's mind was doubtless filled with foreboding as he watched Grover Cleveland Alexander shambling in out of the fog, walking first on one foot and then on the other.

Grover fanned Tony on exactly four pitched balls, then the pastime moved on to a conclusion rather somber for the New Yorkers.

It ended with Mr. George Herman Babe Ruth being squashed on an attempt to steal second, a magnificent effort at that.

Everything Mr. Ruth does is magnificent. His home run in the third, breaking the World Series record for homers, was magnificent. A galloping catch performed by him was magnificent.

Glorious in Defeat

Even the four bases on balls extended to him during the game was more or less magnificent.

Old Grover Cleveland Alexander does not get credit for this game in the official archives, but he gets it in the minds of the clients who viewed the pastime.

The official rating belongs to Jesse Joseph Haines, which gives him two victories in the series.

Waite Hoyt, the veteran schoolboy, draws the defeat, although Herbert Pennock, the fox farmer, was in there bending 'em over before the finish.

The Cardinals won the game in the fourth on errors by Marcus Aurelius Koenig and Long Bob Meusel, the former booting one and the latter muffing a fly, these incidents rattling Waite Hoyt's pitching equilibrium.

Tommy at It Again

Then Thomas Thevenow, the Cardinal short fielder, knocked in a couple of runs with a single.

This Thevenow was a most disturbing element to the Yanks all afternoon. He performed stunts at short that would get him a job with John Ringling, once climbing up into the fog and pulling down a smack that would have meant a run for the Yanks as sure as you're born.

Waite Hoyt pitched O.K. but the boots behind him would have made anyone tired. Still, they at least served the purpose of producing more drama in one game than all the games that had gone before put together, assuming that baseball in any form can come under the head of drama.

Now, Then! All March?

The Yanks won the first game in New York and lost the second. The Yanks won two out of three in St. Louis and the Cardinals won two here. They can resume the parading in St. Louis that ended rather abruptly there last week.

I would say that the outstanding figure of the series is the somewhat warped figure of Old Grover Cleveland Alexander, wanted by no one except Rogers Hornsby when the Chicago Cubs asked for waivers on him last Summer, and was sold down the river for the now incredibly cheap price of $4,000, which is what they call the waiver price in the big leagues.

There is room for doubt that Jesse Joseph Haines could have carried on to a successful conclusion yesterday, and it is a sure thing that no other pitcher on the St. Louis club could have made such an artistic finish as Old Grover Cleveland Alexander.

Predictions Wrong

Most of the inmates of the greater city responded to their alarm clocks yesterday morning, peered out into the fog and said to themselves, said they:

"Heigh-ho, there will be no game today."

Then they fell back upon their pillows to plow the deep once more, sighing contentedly over the surcease from baseball.

They forget that it was World's Series tome. They were thinking of midseason when a big-league baseball club will postpone a game if someone stumbles over the groundskeeper's sprinkling pot and upsets it.

Some of the more optimistic bugs went out to the baseball arbor from force of habit, and discovered the Yankees and Cardinals engaged in batting practice with a large crowd consisting of Mr. Harry Moseley Stevens's peanut dispensers looking on. The cash clients were rather painfully absent.

An occasional drizzle fell while the Yankees and the Cardinals were engaged in batting practice. A ball batted off into the fog was held to be out of bounds.

Just as the game started, Herbert Pennock, the fox farmer from old Pennsylvania, was seen slipping unostentatiously out toward the center field bleachers, attended by a catcher.

He was apparently going under the bleachers to heat himself up, which showed that Mr. Miller Huggins had none too much confidence in Waite Hoyt.

However, Waite abated Holm and Southworth without much difficulty. Rogers Hornsby singled across second, but Sunny Jeems Bottomley hoisted a high fly to Gehrig. The fog was masking Waite's speed very neatly.

Young Mr. Holm came out of the haze in center field to make a surprising catch of Earle Combe's extremely well-meant smack, which started the Yanks off in the first. Earle Combs had borrowed Mr. Red Sleeves Bob Shawkey's red flannel underwear for the occasion.

The crowd enjoyed a good boo at Mr. Haines's expense when he hurled 'em wide to Mr. Ruth after Marcus Aurelius Koenig had been effaced. Mr. Ruth walked.

Long Robert Meusel singled across second after Jesse Joseph Haines had pitched to him with great care, to the extent of two balls and two strikes, and Ruth struggled to third, galloping the last furlong with great fury.

Great Catch by the Babe

Columbia Lou Gehrig banged a red-hut bounder at Rogers Hornsby and Rogers juggled it as if it singed his fingers. He recovered the potato in time to get Columbia Lou at first.

Lester Bell whacked the first ball tossed at him by Hoyt in the second to Jumping Joseph Dugan. Chick Hafey tried to bunt, then breezed, whiffed or fanned.

Hankus Severeid thundered back to the stand trying to grab a high foul from O'Farrell's bat and Mr. (George) Hildebrand (the umpire) thundered right with him for the exercise.

Then O'Farrell slugged a long fly to deep right center and Mr. Ruth plunged far out of his right field character to invade Earle Combs' domain, making a gloved hand snatch of the ball that brought the clients up squeaking shrilly. It was a tremendous catch.

Both sides were taking the old toe hold on the right-handed delivery of Hoyt and Haines and hitting the ball hard and far.

Hit Proved Useless

After Poosh 'Em Up Tony Lazzeri had pooshed up a lot of fog trying to hit Jesse Joseph's sidearm curve, Jumping Joseph Dugan singled, but was erased trying to steal second.

Jumping Joseph squawked a bit over the decision, but Mr. (Big Bill) Dinneen (the umpire) at second merely peered at him reproachfully and Jumping Joseph walked away.

Hankus Severeid singled briskly with a count of three and two. Waite Hoyt hit to Haines for an easy out.

Thevenow opened the Cardinals' third with a single to left, and Haines craftily advanced him to second with a bunt to Hoyt. Severeid removed his cap and mask and caught Holm's foul over by the Cardinals' bench. Long Bob Meusel collected Southworth's fly.

Earle Combs spent some time picking out a hickory switch and came up lugging three at once in the Yankees' third, but was permitted to use only one in grounding out to Sunny Jeems Bottomley. Hafey crossed over into center and grabbed Koenig's fly.

And Away It Went!

Haines heaved a very slow ball at Mr. Ruth and the old boy barely nicked it with his bat. The next pitch was called a ball by Mr. Hildebrand; then Haines tried another slow one.

Mr. Ruth leaned against this one with all his poundage and the next heard of the ball three men were fighting hand-to-hand for it in the rightfield bleachers, while Mr. Southworth and Mr. Holm were standing outside looking in on the fray and saying to each other:

"Jesse hadn't oughter pitched that a-way to him."

It was Mr. Ruth's fourth home run of the series and a new record for homers in one series. The record stood at three and was held by Mr. Ruth, Goose Goslin and Joe Harris. Mr. Ruth established the record for homers in one game with three at St. Louis.

Meusel Muff Costly

As he returned from his tour of the bases, with the plaudits of the clients ringing in his ears, Mr. Ruth lifted his cap, disclosing the shape of his head. Long Bob Meusel closed the inning with a fly to Hafey.

Hoyt tossed out Rogers Hornsby, then Sunny Jeems Bottomley singled to left. Marcus Koenig booted Lester Bell's grounder and nobody was put out.

Chick Hafey hit a fly into his own favorite wind over short left, knowing by experience the trickery thereof. Koenig back peddled after the ball and Meusel came up fast, but the ball fell safe, behind Koenig's clutch, for a single, filling the bases.

Long Bob Meusel crossed over into Combs's district after O'Farrell's high hoist. Long Bob was probably thinking of the throw to the plate to head off a run and the ball plumped out of his fingers.

He was throwing it before he had it, so to speak

Tommy Dazed Them

Sunny Jeems Bottomley scored and the bases remained loaded.

Thevenow, the most dangerous pinch hitter of the Cardinals, singled to right, scoring Bell and Hafey. The clients moaned.

Haines fanned in an unostentatious manner, with O'Farrell on second and Thevenow on first. Young Mr. Holm chucked his bat away, missing a second strike. Then he rolled to Koenig, who stepped on second, forcing Thevenow.

Columbia Lou Gehrig got his base on balls to give the Yanks a jolly start in their side of that same disastrous session, but Poosh 'Em Up Tony pooshed one up to Holm.

Haines tossed out Dugan. Severeid smacked a line drive at Thevenow that was ticketed for a single and Columbia Lou was aboard it, riding home, when Thevenow leaped high in the air and nailed the ball with his gloved hand. The clients gasped, then burst right out crying.

"It was like Tunney to win."

So remarked a boxing expert in the press stand.

Southworth popped to Gehrig in the Cards' fifth and Rogers Hornsby raised a fly to Combs. Earle waved Long Bob Meusel back when Bob showed a disposition to come over and help him out on the fly. Earl wanted no more of Long Robert's assistance. Lazzeri tossed out Bottomley.

Afraid of Bambino

Thevenow threw out Hoyt to start the Yanks' fifth, and Earle Combs hit a sharp single across second that made Mr. Dinneen run for his life. At that the shot just missed Mr. Dinneen's coat tails and it roused him from a deep reverie.

Marcus Aurelius Koenig hit a fly to Hafey and the clients mumbled as Mr. Ruth shuffled to the plate.

Haines was not to be made a sucker of again. He rolled four very slow, very wide pills at Mr. Ruth and Mr. Ruth hurled his stick from him in great indignation, and took a walk for himself. Then Jesse Joseph personally tossed out Long Bob Meusel on a weak poke to the box.

Bell lifted a fly to Meusel in the Cards' sixth, and Dugan gave

Hafey a life at first on a wide throw of a hot grounder. O'Farrell popped to Koenig and Hafey was out stealing, Severeid to Koenig.

Thevenow made another astounding throw on Gehrig in the Yanks' sixth. Lazzeri struck out and Dugan singled to center.

Needed Kind Words

Jesse Joseph got a little wild pitching to Hankus Severeid and O'Farrell went out and soothed him after he had pitched three consecutive balls, Then Jesse Joseph struck over two strikes.

On the next pitch, Hankus singled to left.

Hafey made a foolish play trying to snatch the ball with one hand instead of playing it safe and it bounced away from him, Dugan scoring and Severeid taking second.

Jumping Joe Dugan made a wild slide over the plate though there was no throw on him.

Ben Paschal batted in place of Hoyt, and Spencer Adams ran for Severeid. Jesse Joseph stuck a strike over on Paschal, which was called by Mr. Hildebrand in a loud voice. Ben swung at the next and missed. The Mr. Hildebrand in a loud voice announced a ball.

Foxy Herb Stepped In

Herb Pennock, the fox farmer, arrived from under the bleachers, where he had been pitching quite a game, and Pat Collins went behind the plate as the seventh opened.

Thevenow was the first man to look Herbert in the eye, and he retired him on a roller to Dugan. Haines, who has become a great, desperate hitter in this series, singled to left and was forced at second by Holm, who outfooted a double play.

Pennock pitched three successive balls to Southworth before he put over a strike. Then he had Southworth three and two when William hit the ball back at him, Pennock deflecting the ball to Koenig for an out at first.

Earle Combs banged a single over Thevenow's head to start the Yanks' seventh, Thomas making a wild jump for the ball and just touching it. The clients began to mutter loudly.

Koenig sacrificed, Lester Bell throwing him out on a slow bunt down the third base line. Mr. Huggins, as usual, was playing for a tie—the old army game, as the boys call it.

Still Afraid!

Haines and O'Farrell conferred on Mr. Ruth's case, then passed him on four wide pitches, the clients moaning dismally over this procedure. Long Bob Meusel hit to Bell, who tossed to Hornsby, forcing Mr. Ruth out at second, Combs taking third.

Mr. Hildebrand called a strike on Columbia Lou Gehrig, then he fouled one for another strike. Jesse Joseph pitched the next two outside, then tried to curve one over the far corner of the dish for a third ball. With the count three and two, Jesse Joseph peered all around at his support, then passed Gehrig, filling the bases.

Poosh 'Em Up Tony Lazzeri advanced to the plate and the entire Cardinal infield went into huddle formation around Jesse Joseph, asking him how he felt and all that sort of thing.

Jesse said he didn't feel so good.

Mr. Hildebrand tried to poke his nose into the huddle, but the boys moved out of earshot of him and then suddenly all turned their backs to the crowd and stood looking off into the distance like anxious mariners on a desert isle and seeking a sail.

Alex to Rescue

Out of the fog over left field came shambling the ungainly figure of Old Grover Cleveland Alexander, with his cap perched high above his ears and his old red sweater dangling about his shoulders.

He was in no hurry. He advanced with reluctant step and the clients gave him a cheery hello. It seems that Old Grover had been steaming up under the bleachers.

He tried a couple of pitches to O'Farrell, then pitched what Mr. Hildebrand called a ball to Lazzeri. The next Mr. Hildebrand said was a strike. Then Tony fouled one into the stand that caused the clients to jump. It was the second strike.

On the next pitch Poosh 'Em Up Tony shattered the air with the force of his blow and everybody got right up and yelled for Old Grover.

It was announced that Jesse Joseph had been taken out on account of a split finger, which shows that even the fates seemed to be favoring the Cardinals at that moment.

Hornsby Hit It

Rogers Hornsby singled to center to open the Cards' batting end of the eighth, and Bottomley sent him on to second with a sacrifice push. Bell hoisted to Combs. Hafey beat out a very warm punch to Jumping Joe Dugan, Hornsby taking third. O'Farrell forced Hafey at second on a punch to Koenig.

Thevenow threw out Dugan in the Yanks' eighth. Collins fouled to Bottomley. Pennock popped to Hornsby.

Thevenow hit a fly to Mr. Ruth in the ninth and Old Grover Cleveland shambled to the bat, getting lots of applause from the clients. Koenig threw Grover out on a slow roller, after fumbling the ball. Fortunately Koenig had plenty of time, as Grover merely jogged to first.

The clients rattled around noisily as the top of the Yanks' batting order came on in the ninth, with Earle Combs the first man up. Old Alex got two strikes on him, then bent over and peered at O'Farrell, trying to see the signs through the gathering dusk.

Two Gone!

Combs rolled to Lester Bell, who threw him out at first. Marcus Aurelius Koenig was next, with Mr. Ruth rattling at his chains in the background.

The first to Koenig was a ball, then he fouled off one for a strike. He fouled off another for strike two, then hit to Bell an was thrown out at first.

This produced Mr. Ruth and the crowd was all a-buzz. Grover Cleveland gazed at Mr. Ruth rather quizzily and tossed him a strike. The next was outside for a ball. Mr. Ruth fouled the next one into O'Farrell's face for strike two.

Old Grover was pitching to him—and how! They gave Alex a new baseball and he pitched it over to the outside for ball two.

Another in the same place was ball three. The crowd booed, thinking Alex was trying to pass Mr. Ruth, but Grover hung the next one over the plate.

Mr. Hildebrand said it was a ball, passing Mr. Ruth, and old Alex stood with his hands on his hips, gazing reproachfully at Mr. Hildebrand. He thought it was a strike.

Grover had two strikes on Long Bob Meusel and Mr. Ruth tried to steal second. He was rushing forward quite briskly when O'Farrell got the ball and chucked it down to Thevenow as Mr. Ruth hurled himself onto the bag.

Mr. Dinneen waved his hand.

Mr. Ruth was quite out.

So did Alexander really descend from a barstool and head to Yankee Stadium that day? Most definately not, argues his biographer Jack Kavanagh. "Everyone who has bought into the story in the years that follow accepted it," Kavanagh writes in his 1996 book Ol' Pete: The Grover Cleveland Alexander Story, *"not because it was witnessed but because its easy assumption made a good story." Alexander himself swore that after the previous night's celebration of his complete-game 10-2 win in game six, he went back to the hotel that night and stayed sober, "although there were plenty of other nights when I wasn't." Not helping matters was Hornsby, who, in the jubilation of the winning clubhouse, blurted out, "Alex can pitch better drunk than any other pitcher sober."*

———

Here is Runyon on the eve of the 1927 World Series sweep of the Yankees over the Pirates. Led by Babe Ruth's 60 home runs, Lou Gehrig's 47, and three 20-game winners, the '27 Yankees won 120 games and are generally considered among the greatest teams of all time.

SOME MORE EXPERTING (OCT. 4, 1927)

The noble experts are now massed on the borders of baseball, prepared to move, horse foot and portable typewriters, into

Pittsburgh Wednesday to brave the terrors of Pittsburgh taxi-cabbing, and incidentally do a little off-hand experting on the World Series of 1927.

I do not look for the very best results from the experting in Pittsburgh, however, because of the terrors of the Pittsburgh taxi-cabbing aforesaid. After the most evenly balanced expert in the world has journeyed from the railroad station to a hotel in a Pitts-burgh taxicab, he is in no condition to give his best efforts to experting. He is apt to be too badly frightened.

The preponderance of gray hair among the baseball experts of this period is by no means due to age, as you might suspect. It is the direct result of experting the Pittsburgh-Washington series of a couple of years back. Young men with hair as black as coal voy-aged to Pittsburgh and wound up at their hotels with silvery threads among the coal after the briefest experiences in a Pitts-burgh taxi.

Thus a lot of the experting was thrown plumb out of kilter. You cannot expect a badly frightened expert to produce good exper-ting. Many of them proved that Washington would win the series, whereas they would formally have shown that Pittsburgh would finish on top.

That Long, Long Hill

The experts who resided in the downtown hotels during the last World Series in Pittsburgh did not suffer as much as those who went to the hostelries hard by the baseball orchard.

There is a long, long hill that leads up from the railroad station to the neighborhood of the Schenley Park district where Forbes Field is located, and the Pittsburgh taxi jockeys take this hill, up or down, on the buzz. Quite a number of the baseball experts who went to the last series in Pittsburgh are still in that city, inmates of sanitariums for the relief of mental disorders.

They are mainly those who rode down the hill. Those who rode up the hill in the Pittsburgh taxi-cheaters escaped with their minds intact, but some of them will never be the same again. So I say we should not expect too much of the experting in Pittsburgh on the World Series.

———

Arguably, the anticipation of the 1927 World Series was greater than the games, starting with Yankee batting practice before game one at Forbes Field, when Ruth and Gehrig deposited home run after home run into the rightfield stands. The Waners hit— Lloyd .400 and Paul .333—but so did the Yankees, particularly Ruth, who batted .400, but only managed two home runs, not three, much to Runyon's disappointment.

YANKEES WIN IN NINTH; SWEEP SERIES (OCT. 9, 1927)

Miljus' Wild Pitch, with 3 on, Sends in Deciding Run

In the midst of chills and fevers of baseball drama up at the Yankee Stadium yesterday afternoon there suddenly came a sort of "plop," and the World Series of 1927 ended in what you might call an anticlimax with the New York Yankees the victors of four straight games over the Pittsburgh Pirates.

It was like getting all lathered up over a tense, nerve-wiggling dramatic scene, and then having the low comedian step out and whack somebody over the noggin with a bladder, for, with the score tied at three all in the last half of the ninth, the bases loaded with Yanks and two out, John Miljus, of Pittsburgh, tore off a wild pitch that scored Earle Combs from third, giving the Yanks the fourth and last game by a score of 4 to 3.

Second Time in History

It is the second time in modern baseball history that a club has won four consecutive games in a World Series. The Boston Braves, under George Stallings, did it in 1914 against the Philadelphia Athletics. The Giants won four games from the Yanks in the series of 1921 but a fifth was tied. Its exploits against the National

League champions undoubtedly establishes Miller Huggins' 1927 club as one of the greatest of all time.

It was an almost ludicrous windup in view of the events of the ninth inning. The Yanks had the bases packed with no outs when John Miljus, who had relieved the bespectacled Carmen Hill as the Pittsburgh pitcher, struck out the slugging Lou Gehrig and Long Bob Meusel. The Pittsburgh rooters in the crowd of 60,000 were fervently imploring him to do the same to "Poosh 'Em Up" Tony Lazzeri when Miljus banged away with a pitch that eluded John Gooch's clutch.

The Pirate catcher just touched it with his gloved hand and the ball bounded over toward the Pirate bench, out of which poured the Pittsburgh utility men as Combs came tearing in from third with the other two Yankee runners, (Mark) Koenig and the mighty Ruth, in motion.

The crowd from the boxes and the lower stands immediately swept over the field, cheering wildly and John Miljus worked his way through the mob, swinging his pitching glove dejectedly. Over by the Yankee bench, the New York players were fighting their way out of the crowd while the fans reached eager hands for them.

Ruth Cause of It All

The fans seemed particularly anxious to grab the large mitt of Mr. George Herman Babe Ruth, whose second home run of the series, a drive into the rightfield bleachers in the fifth, apparently stowed the game away right then and there. The Bambino's smash scored Koenig ahead of him, giving the Yanks a lead of 3 to 1. It was Ruth who drove in the first run, too, a tally which tied an early score by the Pirates.

And for that matter, the shadow of the mighty Babe fell athwart the Pittsburghers throughout the game today, for it was John Miljus' anxiety in pitching to him in the ninth that put Combs on third. At the time Ruth came up, Combs was off second and Koenig on first, with no one out. Miljus could not pass Ruth under the circumstances.

He tried to put too much on the ball in pitching to him. Thus his first toss became a wild pitch and the runners advanced. Then Ruth was purposely walked and Miljus set the stage for his own defeat.

Wiley Moore finally got credit for a victory in the series. You know Waite Hoyt got the official brackets for the game that Farmer Moore finished up for him in Pittsburgh. Of the 47 games in which Farmer Moore figured during the season of 1927, he started but few. Today he pitched all the way though the Pirates clouted him rather freely.

"Butter Fingers," as the kids used to call 'em, kept the Pirates in the game until the last of the ninth. Old Wiley Moore himself and "Poosh 'Em Up" Tony Lazzeri fumbled the ball about in the seventh, letting the Pirates up to a tie, and for the moment annulling that mighty swat by the Bambino in the fifth. But perhaps it was just as well, because it produced the finish that gave the lie to that tradition that there's nothing new in baseball. This was brand new for a World Series, anyway.

Under the grandstand, Mr. Egg-Bert Barrow, the genial business manager of the Yanks, joined his tears with those of (concessionaire) Mr. Harry M. Stevens, after the game, the former weeping for the $217,000 that he must turn back to the clients because there will be no Sunday game, and the latter brooding over the lost hot dog traffic of today. For a couple of innings it looked as if the fumbles of Wiley Moore and Lazzeri would be worth about $108,500 apiece to the Yanks.

Five Pennants for Hug

Miller Huggins has won five pennants for New York in the American League since taking up the management of the Yanks. His years are 1921, 1922, 1923, 1926 and 1927. The record proves him a great manager.

By way of settling any arguments on the point, John Miljus is not charged with an error for letting a man score on the wild pitch.

I would say that the old Bambino and Mark Koenig stood out

in the series for the Yanks, with much to be said for Wiley Moore and Herbert Pennock. Koenig was in all the big rallies and played a great fielding game. The star of the Pirates was perhaps Lloyd Waner, the youngest of the Waner children, though (Pie) Traynor and (Glenn) Wright did well on defense. Paul Waner started off with a big burst of hitting speed but died away.

Umpire Has Bad Start

The game got going at 1:33 after the Seventh Regiment Band had played "The Star-Spangled Banner," and the first thing that happened to annoy the home-town customers was Lloyd Waner's out-footing of a blow to Koenig. At least, Ernie Quigley, the National League umpire, who was posted off first base, said Lloyd had licked the throw, although some of the folks complained about the decision.

Waner took second on (Clyde) Barnhart's infield out, Koenig making the throw. (Joe) Dugan threw out Paul Waner and Glenn Wright singled to right, scoring the youngest of the Waner children from second. The Pirates had taken a pretty good peg at every ball tossed by Wiley Moore so far.

Traynor hit to Dugan, who tagged Wright galloping down the baseline.

The aisles were fairly throbbing with the inrushing clients during the first inning and the belated crowd was not entirely seated by the third. The scattering of Pittsburgh fans in the stands, game to the last ditch, cheered when Lloyd Waner scored, and Egg-Bert Barrow, the business manager of the Yanks, commenced to feel that life might be worth living. You know Egg-Bert had the joint sold out for Sunday's game and the idea of returning all that dough was most depressing to him.

Carmen Hill, another of those bespectacled pitchers who seems to thrive in Pittsburgh, peered carefully at Earle Combs before letting fly with a pitch in the Yanks' first. Combs singled through Grantham, who was back playing second for the Pirates. Mark Koenig, one of the star hitters of the series, followed with a single to right, putting Combs on second.

Ruth Ties It Up

Mr. George Herman Babe Ruth came up in this situation, and shortened up one of his usual home runs to a single to right, scoring Combs and putting Koenig on third. Then to the great astonishment of the customers, Mr. Ruth stole second on "Oil" Smith, the garrulous backstopper of the Pirates. The folks cheered no little over this exploit.

Now Carmen Hill, peering thoughtfully through his specs, began doing some real pitching. He struck out Lou Gehrig, (Bob) Meusel and Lazzeri, the first taking his Moriarity, or swing, the other two being called out by "Red" Ormsby, the American League umper, and a hero of Argonne Forest. The boys disregarded Red's service to his country and glared at him most vindictively as he pronounced sentence on them.

Hill Gets a Hand

Three hits and three strikeouts in the same inning constitute one for the book, I would say. Carmen Hill got quite a hand when he took his turn at the Pirates' second, which was after Grantham was thrown out by Dugan, and (Joe) Harris had out-galloped a roller to Koenig. In between "Oil" Smith raised a fly to Ruth.

Carmen Hill fixed glittering glims on Farmer Wiley Moore to such effect that the old sodbuster from Oklahoma gave him a base on balls. The farmer tried to snatch up a little bunt from Lloyd Waner's bat and fell right on his plow handles in the grass near first base. From a squatting posture Wiley chucked the ball to Gehrig but the youngest Waner child was already on the bag by that time thinking of what he would do next.

Wiley Comes Through

This filled the satchels with two down, as we say at the club. Farmer Moore looked somewhat perturbed. He consulted with Pudgy Pat Collins, the pitched to Barnhart, who rolled the ball down to Lazzeri. The hero of Telegraph Hill was so close to second at the moment that all he had to do to force Lloyd was to reach out with one apprehensible toe, and touch the sack.

Wright made a snappy play getting Dugan's deep dab and his throw to first nipped "Jumping" Joseph by a nose. "Oil" Smith put his hands on his hips and glared through his mask at "Red" Ormsby, of Argonne fame, when "Red" called a ball on "Pudgy" Patrick Collins that "Oil" thought was a strike. "Red" gave him glare for glare.

Then Collins doubled briskly to left as the sky overhead got darker and darker. Wright threw out Wiley Moore, holding Collins to second. Wright also threw out Combs. Wright was doing plenty of short fielding.

Mayor Jimmy Walker arrived on the premises right on time, which was half an hour late, and the crowd was so busy applauding Hissoner as he marched to Colonel Jake Ruppert's box that it didn't see Paul Waner single to left in the Pirates' third. Wright tapped to Lazzeri, who tagged Paul Waner and threw to Gehrig, doubling up Wright. Traynor hit a fly to Meusel.

Mark Koenig almost got his eighth hit in the Yanks' side of the same inning, but Grantham robbed him by a great stop back of first base. Ruth rolled to Harris for an easy out. Grantham threw out Gehrig.

After Grantham had grounded out to Gehrig in the Pirates' fourth, Harris singled to right. "Oil" Smith rolled to Koenig, who tossed to Lazzeri, getting Harris. It was a good stop by Koenig. Lazzeri tried to double up "Oil" at first, and Gehrig had to stretch himself to clutch a wide throw. Collins got Hill's high bounder in front of the plate and hustled the throw to beat Carmen at first.

Traynor threw out both Meusel and Lazzeri in the Yanks' side of the fourth. Dugan slugged to left center and Lloyd Waner fumbled the ball long enough to let Dugan go to third. Wiley Moore struck out. Old Wiley is no great shucks as a hitter anyway. He got his first blow this series after playing 30 games of baseball.

Lloyd Waner led off the Pirates' fifth with a single to left, but Barnhart hit into a fast double play that passed from Dugan to Lazzeri to Gehrig, Koenig threw out Paul Waner.

Babe Breaks It Up

Combs singled to center in the Yanks' end of the fifth. Hill and "Oil" Smith conferred earnestly over the case of Mark Koenig, and then Hill struck him out. It was rare pitching, if anybody asks you.

This produced Mr. Ruth. He took a ball, fouled one, then belted the next pitch into the rightfield bleachers, off toward center. It was a towering hoist, the ball rising so high Paul Waner had time to run right back to the bleacher barrier where he stood watching the dropping pill.

The crowd blew off steam over this one. The folks had been sitting quietly, waiting for the break of the game, one way or another, and as Combs and the Old Bambino trotted around the bases, the leaden air throbbed to the vocal outburst. Wright threw out both Gehrig and Meusel.

As Ruth marched to his position in right, the bleacherites broke out that strange welcome, which they have been giving him since late in the season when he neared the home-run record. They rose, waving handkerchiefs and folded newspapers like a college cheering section, and as Babe approached them, he doffed his cap.

With two out in the Pirates' sixth, Grantham beat out a throw to Gehrig, but Combs got Harris's long fly.

Lazzeri struck out and Dugan fouled out to Traynor in the Yanks' side of the same inning. Collins walked, Moore smacked a single to right center, putting Collins on third, an exploit so unexpected the fans laughed loudly. This brought up the top of Yanks' batting order, but Combs hit an easy fly to Barnhart in left.

Bucs Pull Up Even

"Oil" Smith rolled a grounder to Gehrig back of first in the Pirates' seventh and Wiley Moore lumbered over to take the throw. The ball squirted out of Moore's hands, and "Oil" was quite safe. Now some of the crowd set up the old whoop for Hazen (Kiki) Cuyler, the benched Pirate outfielder, but Donie Bush sent (Fred) Brickell to bat in place of Carmen Hill, while Emil Yde, the side-winder, ran for "Oil." It seems that "Oil" isn't as fast as Yde, which is pronounced "Edy."

Lazzeri fumbled Brickell's grounder and Yde was safe at second. Lloyd Waner bunted, Gehrig running in and picking up the ball, while Lazzeri took the throw at first.

The runners moved up. Barnhart took a ball, then singled across second, scoring Yde, while Brickell took third. Paul Waner hit a fly to Combs and Brickell scored after the catch with the tying run. Wright tapped the ball to Moore for an easy out.

The game now took on renewed interest as the Yanks went to bat in their end of the seventh. John Miljus went to the mound for the Pirates, with John Gooch behind the plate. Miljus did some great hurling as a relief pitcher in one of the Pittsburgh games.

Koenig took a ball and a strike, then belted his eighth hit of the series across second, Grantham making a good stop back of the bag. Ruth rolled weakly to Traynor, as the crowd babbled in anticipation. Traynor threw to Wright getting Koenig, and Wright relayed the ball to Harris, doubling up the heavy-footed Bambino. Gehrig hit a high fly to Barnhart, ending the inning.

Miljus Misses Chance

Dugan threw out Traynor in the Pirates' eighth, cutting across the short field to get the ball. With two strikes and two balls called on him, Grantham singled to right. Lazzeri threw out Harris, Grantham taking second. Lazzeri fumbled the ball an instant but quickly recovered.

John Gooch was purposely passed by Moore, filling the bases, the crowd murmuring discontentedly at this strategy. It would have been a great spot for Hazen Cuyler to do a "Frank Merriwell," but Bush let Miljus hit for himself. Moore whipped over two strikes, the next two were called balls. Miljus fouled off one, then got another ball, making the count three and two. He swung at the next pitch.

Traynor tossed out Meusel in the Yanks' eighth. Long Bob hasn't had much hitting luck in this series. Lazzeri walked on five pitched balls, only one being called a strike. On a hit-and-run play, Dugan tried to hit behind the runner and fouled one off. Dugan is the best hit-and-run-man on the Yanks. Miljus tossed a couple to Harris to hold Lazzeri to the bag. Dugan popped the next pitch to Harris.

And So Does Moore

The stout Collins pelted a hot drive to second, Lazzeri taking third. Lloyd Waner juggled the ball for an instant and Lazzeri thought some of going on home, but Art Fletcher halted him. Wiley Moore took a futile swing at Miljus' first pitch. He got a ball, fouled one into the rightfield stand for strike two, then swung out.

Lloyd Waner was the first Pirate up in the first half of the ninth. He rolled lightly to Lazzeri for an easy out at first. Meusel got Barnhart's fly after Moore had worked on the batter for some time. Paul Waner fouled the first one over near the leftfield stand, Dugan making a futile chase after the ball. The next pitch was called a strike by Mr. Ormsby, the hero of the Argonne, then Paul almost knocked his fellow Oklahoman off his feet with a ball that Moore knocked down to first.

Combs was the first Yank up in the last of the ninth. Miljus pitched three consecutive balls and called for a new ball.

"In the old days," remarked Tommy Connolly on occasion, "when a pitcher went bad, they took him out. Now they take out the ball."

Combs walked on the fourth toss. Miljus' first pith to Koenig was high, then Koenig bunted. The ball dropped to the right of the plate as Traynor moved in fast for it. He got it on the bounce, fumbled it and was unable to attempt a throw. It went for a hit. This set the game for Ruth.

It was a tough spot for Donie Bush. He could not order Miljus to walk Ruth with two men on and no one out. Miljus cut loose a wild pitch that bounced away from Gooch and let the runners move up. Combs started home from third, slipped, fell down, and scrambled back to the bag while Gooch was retrieving the ball. The damage having been done, Bush now ordered Ruth walked, Miljus throwing three more wild balls to Gooch, filling the bases.

Gehrig Strikes Out

Gehrig swung at a curve for strike one. The next one was low and wide, and a ball. Columbia Lou missed a slow heave for strike two. He got another ball. Then he missed on a fierce swing at a pitch inside, and retired somewhat discomforted. It was a great piece of pitching by Miljus.

A strike was called on "Long" Bob Meusel on Miljus' first pitch. Then came a ball. Missed swing for the second strike. Gooch went out to the box, lifted his mask and mumbled something to Miljus. Another ball. Gooch again spoke to Miljus, and Wright and Traynor came up on either side of the pitcher and spoke to him. A foul down the third-base line. Another missed swing and back to the bench went "Long" Bob.

Tony Lazzeri cracked the first ball pitched to him into the far-away left bleachers for a foul. On the next pitch, high and wide, the ball flew out of Gooch's fingers, bounding away toward the Yankees' bench—and the World Series of 1927 ended, as Combs raced home from third.

—

Runyon's coverage of the famous game three of the 1932 World Series will do little to solve the debates about whether Babe Ruth "called" his third-inning home run off Cub pitcher Charlie Root. While Runyon certainly captures the raucous atmosphere that day at Wrigley Field, he seems more focused on the appearance of New York governor Franklin Roosevelt, just a month away from being elected president, but dances around the subject of the "shot." "He makes gestures with his hands, in case his voice is not heard" is the closest he'd come. So "called shot" or not? It's still hard to tell.

BABE AND LOU HIT TWO EACH AS YANKS WIN THIRD, 7 TO 5 (OCT. 2, 1932)

Governor Roosevelt Sees Battle That Leaves New York Team Close to World Title; Root Knocked Out, Cubs Using 4 Pitchers, While Pipgras Goes Route 'Til Ninth

Wrigley Field, Chicago—Governor Franklin D. Roosevelt, of New York, manages to mask his New Yorkishness behind a polite perfunctory smile when Ol' Babe Ruth belts out his first homer this afternoon.

This is the first inning of the third game of the World Series, and starts the New York Yankees off with a three-run lead over the Cubs as two runners are on in the bases when the Babe blasts.

Governor Roosevelt, always the soul of courtesy, is the guest of the city of Chicago at the baseball game. Thus it is only fair that he remain neutral especially as the stout "Tony" Cermak, Mayor of Chicago, and a lot of other good democratic voters of Illinois are hard by, all looking somewhat flabbergasted as the first returns on the scoreboard show the Yankee plurality.

Forced to Roar

But in the first inning, when the score is a tie, and Babe Ruth busts his second homer, one of the longest drives ever seen in these parts, Governor Franklin Delano Roosevelt, of New York, forgets himself. He roars:

"Haw—haw—haw!"

"I beg your pardon!"

So says Mayor "Tony" Cermak, gazing stiffly at Governor Franklin Delano Roosevelt.

The Governor, recovering swiftly, and dropping back to neutral pose, remarks:

"Oh—er—on—a nice bunt."

But shrewd observers of the political situation say the damage has been done, and if Governor Roosevelt doesn't get as many votes as he expects from this precinct he can attribute it to permitting the New York in him to pop out at a most unpropitious moment.

Mayor Cermak quit the Chicago baseball premises late this afternoon in company with 50,000 fellow Democrats, and perhaps some Republicans, at the end of a 7 to 5 drubbing administered the Cubs by the Yankees, all these citizens looking as if they never care to hear of anything from New York again.

How They Hate Him

They are especially sore at Ol' Babe. They have been sore at him all day. Lemons whistle about the devoted ears of the aging king of swat all afternoon—yellow pellets of local disfavor.

These lemons are buzzed at him when he is at the plate. They bounce on the green grass around him when he is playing leftfield. One hits him on the head and ricochets back into the bleachers. The Babe has a hard knob.

Through the bombardment, he goes on about his business of getting two home runs, and a base on balls, besides hoisting a mild fly and hitting into a double play. He engages in brisk repartee with the Cubs, and the fans. He makes gestures with his hands, in case his voice is not heard. He breaks his own record of 13 home runs in World Series games, running it up to 15.

Forced to Admire

He spreads the amazing personality that has been the breath of life in baseball for 15 years or more over the 50,000 spectators to such an extent they are having a hard time hating him as the game breaks up with the Yanks holding the Cubs 3 to nothing in the World Series, with the likelihood that they will end it tomorrow in four straight.

The New York club has now won 11 consecutive World Series games, counting the clean sweep over Pittsburgh in 1927, and the mop-up of the Cardinals in 1928.

"Columbia" Lou Gehrig hits a homer in the third, and follows Ruth in the fifth with another homer, both into the open pavilion in right field, which are the winning runs of the game if you wish to figure it that way. Gehrig now has made three homers in the series.

The Yankees batter the delivery of Charlie Root, who announces before the game that he will sidearm them to a whisper. They hammer Big Pat Malone, and Jakie May, the southpaw, and (Bud) Tinning, a recruit, is pitching against them at the finish.

Pennock Gets Chance

George Pipgras, the tall right-hander of Joe McCarthy's club, who establishes a new World Series record by personally striking out five times, holds the Cubs well in hand until the ninth, when "Gabby" Hartnett hits the sixth homer of the game, and Bill Jurges singles right behind him.

Bad Error to Star

Root's first pitch to (Earle) Combs as the game opens is called a ball by (Umpire Roy) Van Graflan. Another ball, and then Van Graflan announces a strike. Combs fouls off one for his second strike, the raps to Jurges for what seems to be an easy out.

Jurges heaves the ball over (Cubs' manager and first baseman Charlie) Grimm's head into the Yankee dugout, and Combs takes second. The crowd groans derisively.

Governor Roosevelt is obviously trying to watch the ball game, but he seems to be pestered by introductions to visitors to his box. He is leaning forward, his arms folded across his chest, his eyes following every move on the field.

(Joe) Sewell gets a base on balls. The crowd boos Ruth as he steps to the plate, and (second baseman Billy) Herman and Grimm rush to the box and confer with Root. Someone chucks a lemon at Ruth, which lands near the plate.

Root's first pitch is a low ball. So is the next. Root is nervous. He lifts his right arm slowly and drops a ball in where Ruth likes it.

Bobble Proves Costly

The Babe connects. The ball rises high, and then higher, and sails away over the space between (Kiki) Cuyler and (Johnny) Moore to drop into the crowd in the open pavilion for a home run. Combs and Sewell trot around the bases ahead of Ruth.

The sail of the ball is perhaps helped by a wind that is blowing the flags in right and center fields out straight across the rightfield wall. Gov. Roosevelt half rises from his chair at the mighty smash; and the crowd roars, particularly in admiration but more in dismay.

The Cub infielders gather about Root and Herman slaps him on the back, as if to say:

"Don't worry about that, old boy."

Gehrig is out on an easy grounder to Herman. (Tony) Lazzeri, with a count of two and two, lifts an easy foul that (Woody) English muffs, then is called out on strikes.

(Bill) Dickey singles past Grimm, (Ben) Chapman singles to left, Dickey taking second, but (Frankie) Crosetti ends the inning with a long fly to (Riggs) Stephenson.

Plenty of Errors

Ruth is applauded by the leftfield bleachers as he moves to his position, then feeling that they have done their duty the bleacherites start "razzing" Babe, who turns and talks back to them. An occasional lemon drops at his feet. The Chicagoans must have devastated the local lemon market for this occasion.

Pipgras passes Herman, the first batsman for the Cubs, getting over only a single strike. He pitches three balls to English before he gets a strike across, then Van Graflan calls another strike as English jumps around in the batter's box, shaking his bat at Pipgras, trying to disconcert the pitcher. English finally hits a long drive to right field that just clears Chapman's outstretched fingers as he leaps for the ball. It is a two-bagger, and Herman scores from second. The crowd wakes up, and lets out a tremendous bellow.

Ready for Change

Stephenson rolls to Crosetti for an easy out at first. Cuyler sticks to second, Johnny Moore walks. The crowd fairly babbles, Wiley Moore is sent to the warm-up station in right field by Joe McCarthy with Cy Perkins. Moore begins warming up fast.

Manager Grimm rolls to Crosetti for an easy out at first, ending the inning.

Pipgras swings out on strikes in the Yanks' second. Combs hits a fly to Moore, who makes such a job of catching the ball that it is apparent the wind is very bad for the fielders. Sewell walks.

Another lemon whizzes past Ruth's skull as he arrives at the plate. Root's first pitch is declared a strike by Van Graflan, the next a ball, also the next. Another wide pitch gives Babe a count of three and one, so Root has to lay one in there. Ruth promptly hits a line foul into the rightfield stands.

Nearly Gets Another

He connects with the next pitch, and sends Cuyler up against the wire fence in front of the rightfield pavilion to get it. It's a narrow squeak from another homer.

Crosetti throws out Hartnett to start the Cubs' half. Jurges singles sharply through the left side of the infield. Root is called out on a half-swing at the ball, and Charley O'Leary and "Red" Corriden, the Cubs' coaches, rush up to Van Graflan and squawk loudly, claiming Root didn't really strike at the ball. Charley Grimm joins the protest, but Van Graflan shoos them all away.

Jurges steals second, Dickey holding the ball a shade too long, then throwing high to Lazzeri. Ruth gets Herman's hoist after a brisk trot.

Lou Turns Trick

Gehrig, first man up in the Yanks' side of the third, hits the first ball thrown at him by Root for a homer into the rightfield pavilion. There is no fuss and feathers about it. "Columbia" Lou just hauls off and hits. His mother is somewhere in the stand watching her boy.

Jurges makes a nice throw from deep short on Lazzeri's roller to get his man at first. The wind gives Moore trouble on Dickey's high one, but he gathers it in. Chapman walks. He tries to steal second and Hartnett nips him with a throw to Jurges.

Crosetti chucks out English starting the Cubs' third. Cuyler bangs a homer into the rightfield bleacher, which gives the citizenry something to yell about. It is the third home run in less than three innings, all hit into the same pavilion, which shows you what a joke that stand is.

❊   ❊   ❊

We now have the score tied (at 4) going into the fifth.

Jurges throws out Sewell on a close play at first. The crowd boos Ruth as he steps up. He gestures at the Cub bench.

Two strikes and two balls are called when Ruth reaches out with his bat for a low pitch and sort o' golfs the ball into the remote corner of the open pavilion in right, just where it meets the green scoreboard in centerfield.

It is one of the longest home runs ever hit in Wrigley Field. Moore starts going back at the crack of the bat and bumps up against the scoreboard before he realizes that the ball is going beyond his reach.

Wait! More Coming!

The crowd simply has to roar at his punch and big Babe trots around the bases shaking his clasped hands in derision at the Chicago bench. Gov. Roosevelt laughs openly and his eyes follow Babe to the bench.

Immediately thereafter, Gehrig hits his second homer into the upper section of the rightfield pavilion, just inside the foul line—so narrowly inside that the Cubs are inclined to argue the ball is foul.

Van Graflan says it is safe, however.

This ends Root's career for the day and Pat Malone, another speedball pitcher, takes his place. It is a tough position for any pitcher.

—

Dodging angry bottle- and fruit-throwing Detroit fans, the Cardinals rout the Tigers to win the 1934 World Series.

FANS RIOT AS CARDS WIN WORLD SERIES (OCT. 10, 1934)

Dean Pitches 11-0 Game Amid Riot; Landis Ousts Medwick When Bottle and Fruit Shower Halts Game 20 Minutes

NAVIN FIELD, DETROIT, OCT. 9—On a prodigious batting spree, the St. Louis Cardinals came roaring into the baseball championship this afternoon.

The vital statistics:

Seventh and last game of the World Series of 1934;

St. Louis 11 Detroit 0;

St. Louis 4 games, Detroit 3 games.

Tigers Massacred

The Cards massacre five Detroit pitchers—Eldon Auker, Lyn-wood ("Schoolboy") Rowe, Elon Hogsett, Tommy Bridges and Fred ("Firpo") Marberry, rolling up 17 hits for their 11 tallies. Meanwhile, the picturesque Jerome "Dizzy" Dean is shutting out their American Leaguers with six scattered hits, the only shutout of the series.

A sixth Detroit pitcher, Alvin Crowder, is on the mound before the finish, the only one to escape the general bludgeoning.

So the Cardinals take their first world championship to St. Louis in nine years and win the third title for the National League out of the last four World Series.

Fans in Uproar

Judge Kenesaw Mountain Landis, the snowy-haired pooh-bah of baseball, had to rise in his box during the slaughter of the Tigers today, lending voice and gesture to quelling a sort of long-distance riot among the Detroit fans packing the leftfield bleachers.

There are about 17,000 of these fans, out of the total of 40,902 that see the game today. They become incensed at Joe Medwick, the Cardinal leftfielder, and bombard him with enough pop bottles, apples, oranges and other fruit to fill several big sacks of buckets when the groundkeeper and his crew start gathering up the debris.

Medwick slides into Marvin Owen, the Tigers' third baseman, during the Cardinals' batting end of the sixth, his spiked feet stuck out straight in front of him as he slides. Owen apparently takes a little kick at Medwick as the runner comes in and then, while on his back, Medwick seems to kick back. They scuffle about a bit on the ground before they finally get untangled.

Shower of Fruit

When Medwick walks back to his position in left after the Cards'
end of the inning, the bleacher fans greet him with all the loose
fruit they can get their hands in and they suddenly discover an
amazing amount.

The game is held up more than 20 minutes, during which there
are umpirical threats to forfeit the game to the Cardinals by the forfeit score of 9 to 0, which is exactly the official score at that moment.
After two or three innings to get things going again with the
bleacher fans resuming their pelting every time Medwick comes
near them and even disregarding a plea by Manager Mickey
Cochrane, of the Tigers, Judge Landis finally takes a hand.

He calls (Frankie) Frisch, manager of the Cardinals, and
Cochrane, Owen and Medwick to his box and asks Medwick:

"Did you kick him?"

"Yes," Medwick replies, disputing the ocular testimony of many
observers, who did not see Medwick's kicks connecting. Landis
retorts:

"Then you're out of the game."

In this inning, the Cards get seven hits and seven runs, "Dizzy"
Dean, himself, starting the onslaught and coming up again a
second time in the inning. The Cards bat once around and two
over before they are headed off, slugging Auker off the mound and
keeping up the mad tattoo on "Schoolboy" Row and Elon Hogsett.

Tommy Bridges stops it for the time being, though Tommy is to
get his later on. The Cardinals make it four runs after two are out
in this inning. They get three bases on balls—one from Auker, one
from Rowe and one from Hogsett.

. . . (In the Cardinal third with the game scoreless, Leo)
Durocher . . . hits a fly to (Jo-Jo) White. Dean slaps one down to
left field and gallops past first and slides around (Charlie)
Gehringer on (Goose) Goslin throw to make it a two-bagger.

(Pepper) Martin rolls to (Hank) Greenberg, who has time to
beat Pepper to the bag, but elects to toss to the rushing Auker, who
is a step slower than Martin, so the latter gets a hit, and Dean goes

to third. Martin immediately steals second, Gehringer dropping Cochrane's throw. (Jack) Rothrock walks on four consecutive pitches, filling the bases.

Frisch fouls one for a strike, then a ball is called, and he fouls the next for another strike.

Auker seems to be getting plenty of raise on his "subway" delivery. Frisch hits a long foul to right that makes the fans moan as the ball starts traveling. He hits another to left.

Frisch drives to right. (Pete) Fox misses a stab at the ball, and all three runners tally. Frisch gets a two-bagger. The count is three and two when he hits.

This ends Auker, and Lynwood Rowe comes in. The depressed Detroit fans cheer his advent. Rowe is supposed to have a sore right hand. He has Joe Medwick as his first opponent, with one out and Frisch on second.

After a few preliminary pitches to Cochrane, Rowe fires a slow one at Medwick, who knocks the ball to (Billy) Rogell for an easy out at first, Frisch taking third.

(Ripper) Collins singles on the first pitch to left, scoring Frisch. From the Cardinal bench comes the yell at Rowe:

"Hey, hey, how am I doin'?" It seems the "Schoolboy" made this query of his sweetheart when he was doing all right, and the ballplayers have good memories.

(Bill) DeLancey smashes a long two-bagger to right, scoring Collins from first, and the Tigers cluster around Rowe. The "Schoolboy" is through, and Elon Hogsett, the southpaw, comes to the mound.

"How am I doin'?"

Hogsett starts out by passing (Ernie) Orsatti. Durocher, up for the second time in the inning, singles to right, filling the bases again. It is the first time in the series a club has batted around in one inning.

"Dizzy" Dean, up again the second time, beats out an infield hit to Owen, DeLancey scoring. The ball travels so slowly, Owen cannot make the play.

Dean, at first, dons a red sweater. Auker and Rowe have come and gone since he first appeared at first in this inning. The bases are still loaded. Hogsett throws four balls to walk Martin, forcing in Orsatti.

This finishes Hogsett, and after a long wait, Tommy Bridges comes in, the saddened crowd cheering feebly. Bridges, a winner in St. Louis, confronts Rothrock with three on and two out, Rothrock bangs the ball through Bridges to Gehringer, who tosses to Rogell, forcing Martin at second and ending the inning as the fans cheer derisively.

In the Tigers' third, Fox lines to Orsatti, Bridges grounds out to Frisch, and White hits a fly to Orsatti.

Collins Gets Third Out

Gehringer throws out Frisch in the Cards' fourth, and Medwick drives a long fly to Fox. Collins gets his third hit, a single to right. Goslin raises a fly to Medwick and Rogell forces Gehringer at second in a roller to Frisch.

Orsatti starts the Cards' fifth with a fly to Goslin. The "Goose" also gets Durocher's hoist. Dean is heartily applauded as he steps to the plate. He swings out on three pitches.

Greenberg gets the Tigers' second hit off Dean, starting the Detroit fifth with a single to right center. Owen drives a long fly to Rothrock. Fox, with two strikes and a ball counted on him, doubles to left center, putting Greenberg on third. It is the Tigers' third safe blow.

The apathetic crowd wakes up a bit. Bridges is called out on strikes. Dean is blazing 'em through just now. He is trying for a shutout. Durocher makes a nice play, going over to second base and grabbing White's fast grounder to get his man at first.

"Pepper" Martin stretches a single into two bases in the Cards' sixth, Goslin getting an error for a slight fumble on the ball. Goslin gets Rothrock's fly and White collects Frisch's hoist. Medwick triples to the centerfield pavilion, scoring Martin.

As Medwick slides into third, Owen squats on him and Medwick makes a kick for the third baseman. Immediately, there is a small mob scene at third, the Tiger infielders clustering about Medwick, and Owen and (umpires Bill) Klem, (Harry) Geisel and Brick Owen joining in. No blows are exchanged. The crowd boos Medwick.

Medwick Tallies

Collins singles across second, his fourth hit. It is a clean single to center and Medwick scores. White fumbles and Collins moves up to second. DeLancey fans, Cochrane dropping the third strike and throwing DeLancey out at first.

The leftfield fans give Medwick an extra loud boo as he walks to his position. They throw lemons, oranges, apples and an occasional pop bottle at Medwick until the field is littered with the junk. The groundskeeper's crew goes out and gathers up the debris.

Medwick picks up an apple and nonchalantly juggles it in his hands. The uproar continues and the game comes to a halt. Medwick stands with his hands on his hips facing the fans as the shower continues. A groundskeeper's assistant takes a gunny sack out and starts filling it with the missiles.

The Cardinal ballplayers and the umpires stand in leftfield debating the situation. A trainer takes Dean's sweater. The photographers add to the throng on the field, taking pictures. The announcer gives it out that the umpires will be compelled to forfeit the game to the St. Louis Browns unless there is order.

The groundskeeper's men rush out once more to gather the sheaves. It is strange not a member of the Detroit club goes out to warn the fans that the game may be forfeited. After a long delay, an attempt is made to resume the game, but the bombardment of Medwick continues with renewed fury. Finally Cochrane, the Detroit manager, goes out and waves pleadingly, at the fans.

Now the Cardinals and the umpires all march in together headed for Judge Landis's box. Klem, Frisch. Cochrane and Owen gather in front of the Judge's box and talk to him. Medwick joins the group.

The Judge orates with many gestures, then decides that Medwick go to the bench, a surprising compromise by Landis. The thing to do is to forfeit the game, as the writer sees it, because Owen is as much a fault as Medwick in apparently squatting on the runner in the play that starts all the trouble.

The game is held up at least 20 minutes. (Chick) Fullis goes to leftfield and the fans applaud him. They have gained a wonderful "victory" over Medwick. Frisch consents to Medwick's removal.

Cochrane hits a long fly to Rothrock in right.

Durocher makes a great play, throwing out Gehringer at first on a fast bounder. Collins gets Goslin's foul.

Medwick is removed from the Cardinal bench at this moment, with six cops following him as a guard.

Orsatti, first up in the Cardinal seventh, hits a fly to White. Durocher triples to the center-field pavilion. Owen throws out Dean, holding Durocher to third. Gehringer fumbles Martin's easy roller and Durocher scores. Martin steals second, his second theft of the game, Cochrane's throw bouncing off Gehringer's glove. It is a low throw. Rothrock doubles to left-center, scoring Martin. Fox gets Frisch's long fly to right.

Rogell popped to Durocher to start the Tigers' seventh. Greenberg strikes out. Frisch throws out Owen.

Fred Marberry goes in to get a little exercise pitching for the Tigers. Fullis singles past Rogell to start the Cardinals' eighth. Fox gets Collins' long fly. Gehringer throws out DeLancey, Fullis taking second. Orsatti walks but is forced by Durocher on a hit to Rogell.

Fox opens the Tigers' eighth with a double to left. Gerald Walker bats in place of Marberry. He hits the first ball pitched to him on a fly to Fullis. The Cards' bench gives Walker a verbal "ride" as he passes it. Dean is trying to protect his shutout, and pitches carefully to White. He has him two and two, and White swings out. Rothrock gets Cochrane's hoist, which drops in foul territory in right.

Alvin Crowder, called "General," goes in to pitch for Detroit, with (Ray) Hayworth behind the bat. It is the first change in catchers by either club in the series.

Goslin gets Dean's fly to start the Cardinals' ninth. Greenberg gets Martin's foul near first. Rothrock swings out.

As the Tigers take their final turn at bat, Dean turns on all his pitching magic to Gehringer. With a count of two balls and a strike, Gehringer singles to left, Goslin forces Gehringer at second on a roller to Collins, the latter trying to double up Goslin at first without success.

Rogell singles across second, putting Goslin on second. Greenberg swings out. Owen misses one swing, a second strike is called by Geisel, then a ball, and Owen drives to Durocher for a force of Rogell at second to end the series.

The Tigers would get the best revenge — taking six games to beat the Cubs in the 1935 World Series.

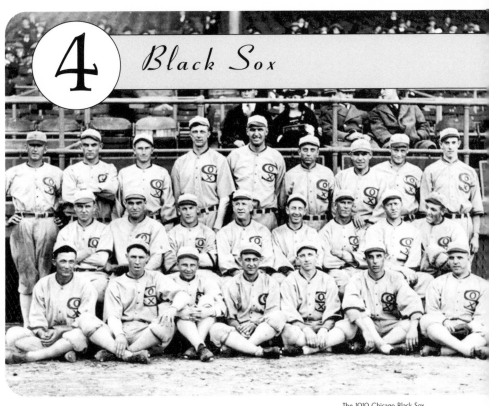

4

Black Sox

The 1919 Chicago Black Sox

The 1919 World Series fix by members of the heavily favored Chicago White Sox shook baseball to its core, and deeply affected Runyon's faith in the game. Although many had heard the rumors that there was some dishonesty associated with the Series, he and others were later stunned at the enormity of the scandal. Reading through his coverage makes for fascinating reading in light of what we now know about the fix.

Here are the preseries and game one wrap-ups in their entirety—Runyon covered details of the scoring in a sidebar—which captures the excitement of the start of the Series in its detail of the pregame festivities, followed by abbreviated dispatches from other games. In hindsight, it seems hard to believe that Runyon didn't suspect that the series was crooked, given his friendship with Arnold Rothstein, the financial power behind the fix.

CICOTTE TO FACE RUETHER; WHITE SOX 7 TO 5 FAVORITES (OCT. 1, 1919)

Cincinnati Crowded with Every Vintage of Baseball Fans on Eve of Big Series

CINCINNATI, SEPT. 30—Fans looking for tickets. Fans looking for rooms. Fans looking for drinks. Fans who have found drinks.

❊   ❊   ❊

Yes, indeed, this is Cincinnati. And just before the battle.

❊   ❊   ❊

Fans from Cleveland, Ohio. Fans from Toledo, Ohio. Fans from Youngstown, Ohio. Fans from Niles, Ohio. Fans from towns in Ohio that Ohio never knew before were in Ohio. Young fans. Vintage fans. Fans with whiskers which began growing the last year that Cincinnati had a championship ball club.

❖ ❖ ❖

Much jabber. Much walking up and down. Much walking back and forth. Many sore feet. More excitement than the time old John Morgan, the rebel son-of-a-gun, came riding up into Ohio on that raid. Remember? Ohio sat startled through all those summer days. For strange wild men were galloping over her broad highways.

❖ ❖ ❖

Or words to that effect. Well, anyway, Morgan's men had nothing in point of strangeness, or wildness, either, on some of the gents who are gallantly riding their O'Sullivans over the highways of this particular segment of the Buckeye State.

❖ ❖ ❖

Dope favors the White Sox but gives the Reds a great chance. Baseball dope is about as much of a sure thing over at the Latonia track. Ask any of the lads how sure most of them were over there today.

❖ ❖ ❖

Not much betting. Cincinnati folks want odds. Sox folks don't want to give odds, Local quotations about 7 to 5, but very little doing.

❖ ❖ ❖

Grover Cleveland Alexander of the Cubs went out to the ball yard this afternoon, put on a uniform and hurled to the Red batters in their final practice. Last time Grover pitched against the Reds in a league game, which was only a few days ago, they couldn't hit him with a board.

❖ ❖ ❖

Who should also be throwing then at the home boys but (former

Reds' pitcher) Jack Pfiester, the old "Giant killer" who lives near Cincinnati. Jack went out to the yard with Joe Tinker, and both put on uniforms and worked with Moran's men. Jack had that same old southpaw dink curve that used to have the batters shaking their heads.

❖ ❖ ❖

Dutch Ruether, the Red sidewinder, is picked to start tomorrow. Eddie Cicotte, the right-handed shineballer, is expected to be Kid Gleason's series opening pitcher. There seems to be an idea 'round that the Sox can't hit left-handers. J. McGraw thought as much in 1917.

❖ ❖ ❖

Every seat at Redland Field is sold. There will be about 30,000 present, with many more than that in with a shoehorn.

❖ ❖ ❖

The Gibson and Sinton Hotels are the headquarters for the bugs and what-nots. Both have good rooms. Try and get one.

Cincinnati is a dry town. As dry as the Atlantic Ocean. Kentucky is even drier. It is almost as dry as the Black Sea.

❖ ❖ ❖

But they don't offer you that Humpty-Dumpty beer around here, unless you ask for it. Gotta give 'em credit. The reticence is out of respect to the memory of that dear departed beer for which Cincinnati was once noted. They feel that it would be sheer desecration to hand out the clown stuff.

❖ ❖ ❖

Sox got in this morning and went to the Sinton. Local fans viewed them with great curiosity. They know the American League here only by heresay, and a Cincinnatian doesn't believe everything he hears.

❖ ❖ ❖

Sox worked out at Redland Field soon after their arrival. We say "worked" as a matter of courtesy to baseball form. It reminds us of Jess Willard in the last stages of his training.

❖ ❖ ❖

Some of the Cincinnati papers were so explicit in their tales of the series that they mentioned what the players ate for breakfast. Good job Jim Thorpe (is) not on the Sox because it would waste a lot of space describing (his) mutational food inhalations.

❖ ❖ ❖

Great weather. Warmish-like. Local weather shark says tomorrow will be grand. Hope he's a better picker than we usually are.

❖ ❖ ❖

"You rather lean to the Reds, don't you?" asked a gent who burst in on us out of the parched night. Well, we may lean some, but don't nobody get to pushing.

———

RUETHER STAR IN REDS' ROUT OF SOX, 9 TO 1 (OCT. 2, 1919)

Cincinnati Pitcher Baffles Opponents and Leads Victors in Hitting with Two Triples and a Single; Cicotte, Hurling Ace of Chicagos, Driven from Mound in 4th When Moran's Men Score 5 Runs

CINCINNATI, OCT. 1 — Dreams do come true. Little dreams and big dreams come to pass, however some deny it.

Here on the banks of the old town on this night is a whole city happy in the realization of a big dream—really happy, hoarsely happy.

The Reds won the first game of the World's Series! The Reds beat the Chicago White Sox, and score was 9 to 1.

So off with you skeptics now! Be gone with you! Cincinnati's dream came true! Let those who hold there are brighter dreams than a dream of baseball greatness gaze and listen to this sturdy Midwestern town tonight, to their own confusion.

Doesn't everybody say the dream is nonsense? Didn't everybody say the Reds couldn't possibly win? Experts, ballplayers, and fans— didn't they all laugh at Cincinnati's fall pretensions as they have laughed every year for many years? Cincinnati will tell you they did.

Didn't they tell you that Pat Moran's ball club was made up of castoffs of baseball, and that it was just a sort of a baseball joke compared to the million-dollar club that represents Chicago?

Cincinnati will tell you they did. Cincinnati never tires of the telling, in fact. But all the time they were telling these things about the Reds, Cincinnati was secretly dreaming a great dream that was realized at Redland Field this afternoon, with 30,000 pop-eyed breathless Cincinnati people looking on.

Cincinnati whoops tonight, and Cincinnati sings. It may not have happened right, but this night belongs to the Queen City, and to the Queen City's Reds.

It happens that much baseball language is a bit extravagant. Yet old-time baseball language which usually speaks of "slaughter" and "annihilation" with reference to one-sided baseball defeats, best describes the realization of Cincinnati's dream today.

I'll use the world "slaughter." It was baseball slaughter of Chicago's White Sox. A baseball fan does not have to read the score to know that.

Drove Cicotte from Box

In the fourth inning, the Reds battered Eddie Cicotte, the star pitcher of the American League, for five runs. They drove him from the box. After that, the White Sox were never in the game. You have seen better baseball played in the town lots.

The fact that this game was the realization of a grand magnificent dream lifted it above the very commonplace of baseball things. There have been few games in the fall-time series that has been a baseball classic, half as lopsided as this game.

From the standpoint of baseball, that is. Not tame from the standpoint of Cincinnati. Anything but tame for Cincinnati. It may have bored the baseball writers, sitting high up on the grandstand, and it may have been most distressingly weird, and inartistic, to the veteran baseball people, but it was a highly hectic and thrilling event to Cincinnati.

It was one of those games, which in the run of baseball seasons, would be styled "just a ballgame" by the critics—a matter to be treated lightly and as of no great consequence. But this was a World Series game—a game on which hung the civic pride of two great American cities.

The score was tied 1 to 1 when the Reds went to bat in the fourth inning. They did their scoring after two were out. And it seemed to us as we sat watching the rise and spread of Cincinnati's magnificent dream, and, listening to the steady thud of bats and to the roaring of the crowd, that across the background passed a dark shadow that was the shadow of a great pitcher moving into that baseball oblivion where they all must go.

Cicotte Had Nothing

Cicotte "had nothing," as they put it in baseball language. The magic of the right arm that carried the Chicago club through to a pennant in the American League, had vanished. The spell of the so-called "shine ball," of which Cicotte is supposed to be master, and which seemed to enthrall the batsmen of his own league, was impotent before the Reds.

And while the veteran seemed to pass and go his way, a youngster was coming on to claim his own—to assert his inalienable right to that heritage of sport which is the heritage of youth.

Walter Ruether, a young left-hander for the West Coast, pitched against the 35-year-old Cicotte. And it was his first game in a World Series too. After one brief, nervous flurry, the young-ster settled down, and held the Sox safely.

If we were picking heroes in this first chapter of the World Series of 1919, we might pick Ruether. Besides pitching with great skill, he hit a three-bagger into the crowd in centerfield in that tur-bulent fourth, and drove in two runs.

He had great support. The Reds played with a rush and dash that must have surprised the White Sox. It was all the more sur-prising because, in practice, the Chicagoans seemed much faster. In the game, however, their work was drab and colorless as com-pared to the Reds—but that's always the way a baseball club seems behind poor pitching.

Cicotte can blame himself for some of the disaster of the fourth. He was very slow in making a play that would have ended the inning before any runs had been scored. Maybe it wouldn't have made much difference, however. Maybe it would have but delayed the inevitable.

The Sox couldn't hit Ruether. The Reds could hit Cicotte. There's the story in a nutshell.

Now, we'll drop completely into baseball vernacular, and tell the story of the fourth inning.

Ruether Raps a Single

Roush is out on a fly to center—Eddie Roush, the wide-ranging, hard-hitting outfield star of the National League. Pat Duncan, just "up from the sticks," as the ballplayers say, and, like Ruether, playing his first World Series game, singles smartly to center.

Larry Kopf, the short fielder, who was once traded to Brooklyn, and whose refusal to report there practically forced Moran to keep him, hit a ball to Cicotte. It looked as if the pitcher had plenty of time to wheel and throw the ball to second and start a double play which would have ended the inning; but instead he waited that fatal few seconds that are often the difference between victory and defeat in baseball.

He finally did make the throw to "Swede" Risberg, but late for

Risberg to relay the ball to Gandil and double Kopf. "Greasy" Neale followed with a single, and a moment later Ivy Wingo, the red-headed Carolinian, who did great work behind the bat for the Reds today, stepped up and slashed a hit to right, scoring Kopf and putting Neale on third and himself on second on the throw. The slaughter was on and the crowd was in a veritable frenzy.

Ruether Crashes a Triple

New came Ruether, always such a good batsman that he has often hit in the pitches for the Reds this past season and subbed in the regular lineup to give additional hitting power. He smashed the ball into the centerfield crowd, almost on a line, and Neale and Wingo scored.

There was no luck or accident about these hits. The Reds simply stepped forward and banged Cicotte's delivery. (Morrie) Rath, the second baseman, who was with the Sox years ago, crashed a double over third, scoring Ruether.

"Swede" Risberg went from his position and talked to Cicotte as the veteran moved around in the box, apparently somewhat dazed by the sudden onslaught. Jack Daubert was the next batter, and when the party between Risberg and Cicotte ended, Daubert slugged out a double, scoring Rath.

"Kid" Gleason, the 55-year-old leader of the White Sox, had been watching the furious attack, his wrinkles forming a study. Over at first base Pat Moran, the grizzled Irishman, who was released by Philadelphia after winning the city's first National League pennant, only to come to Cincinnati and win the first flag for this town too, was doing a sort of jig as he bellowed at his men.

Wilkinson Relieves Cicotte

Gleason motioned to Cicotte after Daubert's hit, and the stocky pitcher slowly walked from the box. Wilkinson, a tall young recruit from the American Association, who has been with the Sox only a short time, took his place. Groh raised a fly to "Happy" Felsch out in centerfield and the inning was over.

So, too, were the hopes of the White Sox for the world's championship unless they can produce much better pitching than they displayed today.

After that, the Reds made more runs — two in the seventh when Daubert tripled to the crowd in right-center and scored on (Heinie) Groh's single, and when (Buck) Weaver's bad throw to Gandil on (Edd) Roush's bunt was followed by an infield out which let Groh score, and one more in the eighth.

But even the crowd was satisfied with runs and with the discomfort of the White Sox. It wanted, more than anything else, after that fourth inning, to get the rest of the game over with, and to hurry away to places where it could talk about it all over again, and whoop a little for Cincinnati and for Cincinnati's Reds.

Now let us go back and begin at the beginning. Let us start from the Hotel Gibson, which splits with the Hotel Sinton, the financially satisfactory distinction of being baseball headquarters.

It is now a slow march to the lobby to the cabstands at the curb. The crowd coagulates in the entrances. It is a crowd in which soft hats predominate. It is a Midwestern and semi-Southern crowd. The hard-boiled derby of the Easterner appears only on the heads of Abe Attell, the former featherweight champion, and the sporting writers from New York, Philadelphia and other Atlantic ports.

Stand in Line All Night

The streets of old Cincinnati are packed. They have been that way for hours. People get up before breakfast in these parts. The thoroughfares leading to Redland Field have been echoing to the tramp of feet, and the honk of auto horns since daylight. It is said that some people keep watch and ward the ball yard gates all night long.

As a rule I take those stay-up-all-night-to-get-in stories with a cellar of salt. They sound too stereotyped from year to year. It may have been in Cincinnati, however. A person might as well have stayed up all night at the ball yard gates as anywhere else in the city, as long as they were going to stay up all night. They would have had the same amount of excitement.

Flocks of jitneys go squeaking through the streets. This is the heart of the jitney belt. A drink is next, because this is a dry town. It is so dry that even veteran tipplers have to wear wading boots, the easiest thing obtainable in Cincinnati.

There is no great crush at the gates to Redland Field. The early crowd is already inside. The holders of reserved seats are taking their time getting there. Cops keep the loiterers at the gates moving around. The war cry of the Cincinnati cop always seems to be "Move on, there!"

Old Frank Bancroft, the veteran business manager of the Reds, stands at the press gate beaming benignly on all comers. Forty years in baseball, this is "Banny's" second experience with a pennant winner. Away 'way back in the long ago he piloted the Providence club to a championship. A good old scout is "Banny," even if he did invent the doubleheader.

Fine Day for Battle

Noontime, and hotter than the wrath of a disappointed ticker-holder. The fans sit shirt-sleeved and sweltering. The rightfield bleachers, already packed, looks like a bank of snow. The sun blazes out of a clear sky. The smoke from scores of grimy stacks hangs lazily over the little valley in which Redland Field is situated, 'mid shops and factories. Beyond the sooty haze rise walnut hills, topped by dwelling houses.

Right- and leftfield pavilions are filled and people are commencing to blot out the vacant spaces in the lower stand, although a circle of brand-new yellow folding chairs halfway around the field in front of the grandstand boxes is still empty.

On top of the two-story grandstand is a pavilion which hangs out over the edge of the roof like an eyelid. It is here that 300 baseball writers are stationed, with as many telegraph operators, all perspiring freely as they spread the news of the day over the world.

There is a refreshment room downstairs for the writers and operators. Hot coffee. Sandwiches. A species of beer. Cigars.

Garry Hermann, President of the Cincinnati club and Chairman of the National Commission, comes in, his features aglow, and his whole being radiating in the glory of gray-checked suitings, diamonds, and a bright-red boutonnière, to see how his guests are getting along.

Sousa Attends the Game

There was a band out on the field. It played "Mammy o' Mine." Then it reminisces and drifts off into the remote musical ages. John Philip Sousa, the old march king, came in, and the band played "Hi Captain" in honor of the event. A lot of middle-aged memories go two-stepping back into the '90s.

At 12:30, the Reds came out on the field. Much cheering! The band goes over in front of the leftfield pavilion and plays accompaniment to set off organized rooting that reminds one of a college football game. The name of every member of the Reds is uttered by the rooters to music. Sounds fine.

Presently the Sox emerge from the seclusion of their dressing room beneath the stand.

There is not so much cheering. These Cincinnati fans are a curious bunch in several ways. They take their baseball seriously, and to heart. They are not much given to applauding the other fellow. In the old days, their habit was to heave empty beer bottles at him.

In those days, there was a bar right under the old grandstand. A gent would inhale his portion of brew which made Cincinnati a great place to visit, and would then occasionally chuck empty bottles out at the bean of some visiting ballplayer. It was simply a matter of habit, but strange, ballplayers never could understand it. If it hadn't been for the beer, they would have hated to come to Cincinnati.

New Uniforms for Reds

The Reds are wearing brand-new uniforms—white with their usual red-topped stockings and red monograms on the left breast.

The Sox uniforms are either new or have been so freshly laundered that the lads looks strangely clean to one who has never seen them except in their dirty old traveling uniforms.

The Reds take the field for preliminary practice and get another cheer. The Sox line up in front of their bench and start tossing the ball about. The crowd watches them curiously. The American League is a foreign country to Cincinnati. It knows of the organization only by way of rumor, although naturally some of the natives have been looking it up since it became apparent that it would be the enemy.

The batting cage is set up and Ray Fisher, the sturdy Vermont schoolteacher who used to pitch for the New York Yankees, pitches to the Red batters. Each Red get a cheer as he steps to the plate.

One o'clock, and the stand is filled, with the boxes also gradually disappearing behind the front piece of some of the most prominent people in this part of the country. There are many women present. In fact, this takes on the aspect of a social event in Cincinnati. Old-time Cincinnatians who haven't been back to town in years, returned for the series.

"Cap" Huston on the Job

Among these are Julius Fleischmann, the Yeast man, and Colonel Tillinghast L. "Cap" Huston, one of the owners of the Yankees. Ban Johnson, President of the American League, and John Heydler, head of the National, are in a box.

The band gets frisky and plays "Hail Hail, the Gang's All Here," as the Reds take the field. It is noted that many of the box occupants have opera glasses, which they are leveling about very recklessly. Such is baseball in Cincinnati.

An airplane flies over the field, and lets loose a batch of advertising material for a theatrical event. The aviator scores a clean miss on the field, at his first shot, but puts it in on the second, and suddenly the neat green yard with its clear-cut infield is blotched with masses of white.

A crowd of men and boys are rushed out to clear the stuff away, and if that aviator could be captured he would probably think Omaha, Nebraska, a delightfully quiet and restful spot compared to Cincinnati, Ohio.

Now the White Sox do a little batting practice in the cage, and the crowd is silent as the men from the shores of Lake Michigan step up one after the other and slug the ball. They watch Joe Jackson and Eddie Collins with particular interest.

Snappy Practice by Reds

Next comes the infield practice of the Reds and then the crowd has a chance to cheer. The Cincinnati men seem very lively as they skip across the field, and they put on a snappy practice, but it has none of the dash of the Sox who come on a few minutes later. Buck Weaver, at third, seemed especially filled with a wild animation that fairly startles the onlookers.

Young Ruether warms up on one side of the field and nearby the stocky Cicotte is pitching to Lynn, the White Sox second-string catcher. The youngster works with what seems to be almost nervous rapidity. There is the leisure of experience on the method of the veteran Cicotte.

A young woman rushes out and presents Pat Moran with a big batch of flowers. The band strikes up "The Star-Spangled Banner" as two o'clock comes on, and the crowd stands, bare-headed. Ruether tosses his cap aside and keeps on tossing the ball while the band is playing, but Cicotte stops work. Finally the Reds' youngster also pauses.

Now a pudgy man walks out in the field in a blue uniform, takes the baton from the leader of the band, makes a few preliminary motions that suddenly awake the memory, and band swings into the greatest march tune ever written: "The Stars and Stripes Forever."

The crowd rises with a yell, for the identity of the man is immediately established. It is John Philip Sousa.

Now Pat Moran and Kid Gleason, the rival managers, face each other at the plate, surrounded by the four umpires to discuss the ground rules. Heinie Groh and Eddie Collins, the team captains, were in the group, and the swarm of photographers on the field centered their shutters actively there.

The field is cleared, a one-armed man equipped with a megaphone dashes out to second base and in thunderous tones which can be heard all over the field, roars the stations of the umpires: "Mister (Cy) Rigler at the plate; Mister (Billy) Evans at first base; Mister (Ernie) Quigley at second, and Mister (Dick) Nallin at third."

Then the batteries.

———

The White Sox lethargy continued in game two, with the normally accurate Lefty Williams virtually unable to find the plate. Like Cicotte, he would plead guilty to intentionally losing.

GIANT CAST-OFF HERO OF REDS' TRIUMPH, 4–2 (OCT. 3, 1919)

*Roush's Sensational Fielding and Timely Hit Feature of Sox's Defeat—
Kopf's Triple Settles It; Sallee, Although Tapped for Ten Hits, Hurls Well
in Pinches; Williams Wild, Allows but 4 Hits*

CINCINNATI, OCT. 2—Turn the light on in Oakland City, Indiana—preferably and approximately a big red light. A citizen of Oakland City is at the center of the sporting stage tonight, and his name is Edward Roush.

His occupation is center fielding for the Cincinnati Reds. He pursued that occupation to such effect this afternoon that the Reds took the second game of the World Series of 1919 from the Chicago White Sox by a score of 4 to 2.

Wherefore is Oakland City, Indiana, now a sort of little sister to the grand old Queen City of Ohio, linked by the bond of the baseball greatness of their favorite son.

This tale might have been quite a different thing had it not been for Eddie Roush. It might be a narrative of Chicago triumph, instead of a repetition of the story of yesterday. Cincinnati owes much to Oakland City, Indiana, and something to Bristol, Connecticut.

Roush started the Red rush upon the White Sox this afternoon, and Roush stopped a fierce counterattack by the Chicagoans that seriously threatened the peace of mind of 30,000 Cincinnatians.

New Bristol, Connecticut, gets into the picture for William Larry Kopf, a son of that city, finished up the charge led by Roush, and put over the knockout for the "one-armed Reds."

In the fourth inning, that has become so fatal to the Sox, Kopf slugged a three-bagger onto the centerfield crowd, scoring two runs. One run had already been knocked in by Roush.

Refuse to Join Dodgers

Baseball is a queer old game. It is ruled by a fate which loves to play odd pranks. Kopf got out of the way and back into the Red lineup last spring. He was traded to Brooklyn, but refused to play there. Pat Moran was practically forced to keep him. Thus Pat Moran is going into Chicago tomorrow morning with his Reds with two games of the World Series won.

There's Eddie Roush too. Some time ago, "Sinister Dick" Kinsella, hunting for new material for the Giants, heard of a great hitter at Evansville, Ind. He dropped into town and happened to visit a barber before he saw the slugger.

"Hear you've got a swell ballplayer in this town," remarked Dick, by way of making conversation.

"Yes," said the barber. "He's all right. The only trouble with him is he broke his right arm not long ago and he's trying to learn to throw with his left."

"Sinister Dick" took the next train out of town without going near the ball yard. He didn't want that kind of ballplayer.

Old Ted Sullivan, snooping around the "bushes" for Charley Comiskey, comes along and bought Roush for quite a chunk of money. "Sinister Dick" laughed when he heard of it. Commy didn't laugh when he saw Roush because Roush had cost him too much money to be a laughing matter, but he sent him away.

This afternoon in the sixth inning, with Buck Weaver on third base, Roush went straddling back almost to the centerfield wall in Redland Field and pulled down a blow form "Hap" Felsch's bat that had all the symptoms of a home run. It would have counted heavily in the final summing up.

Baseball players say Roush is a dour figure. "They tell me there's some Indian in him," one of them was remarking the other evening. "I guess that's so. He's a funny duck in a lot of ways. Never says 'hello' when he meets you on the field no matter how long it's been since he's seen you. Always playing his head off to beat you."

Maybe Roush's experience in baseball has made him dour. They shunted him around quite a bit before he finally wound up in Cincinnati, where tonight he is a species of king. He held out on Cincinnati last spring, only to join the club at a time when there was the talk of trading him back to John J. McGraw and the Giants, who had traded him to Cincinnati.

Sweet Revenge for Sallee

Roush and Kopf were born the same year—'93. They are the youth that was served, but more particularly which served this afternoon behind the pitching of Harry Sallee, the veteran left-hander of the Reds. But old "Sal" would have the same fate he met at the hands of the White Sox in 1917, when he was with McGraw's Giants.

It was sweet revenge for Sal to get home ahead today, but he was very lucky. The Sox pounded his southpaw crossfire for 10 hits, while the Reds were getting but four off the delivery of Claude Williams, the young sidewinder of the Sox.

But Williams was very wild. He gave six bases on balls, and nearly all figured in the scoring. The Reds had little attack, but the Sox had no pitching defense. Williams is apt to do better his next time out.

It was Old Sal's weather. Hard-boiled by his years of service in St. Louis, the lean left-hander loves the heat. It was too cold for him in Chicago in '17, especially in his second game. Today he was at ease in a temperature that had everyone else dripping.

He was leisurely, and deliberate, as is his custom, and he pitched with the care of long experience, but the Sox seemed to have no great trouble hitting him. Great support, and some of the breaks helped the veteran, along with the ragged pitching in front of the Sox.

It struck some of the "grandstand managers"—the chaps up yonder in the seats—who always have their say about the way baseball should be played, and generally pay their way in to say it, which is why we have baseball—who thought "Kid" Gleason, the Sox manager, overplayed the play called the sacrifice.

Gleason can probably tell them why they are all wrong, but in the National League the sacrifice is not used as often as in the American League. National fans were the spectators and the critics this afternoon. Maybe that's why they thought Gleason should have put on a different line of strategy.

It is all history now, along with the rest of the game. Reckless souls are tonight taking those 100-to-1 shots that the Cincinnati club will take five straight from the Sox, as the series moves over to the shores of Lake Michigan.

Errors by the Reds late in the game today gave the Sox two runs, and it looked for a moment as of they were going to put on a last-minute rally. The flurry soon passed, however. For three innings the Sox made it a battle, but after that the Reds were always in front, and always looked entitled to be in front.

———

Of all the unlikely heroes, the wisp of a left-handed rookie, 26-year-old Dickie Kerr, would pitch the White Sox to their first Series win. In addition to taking game three of the Series, the 5'7" and 155-pound, 13-game winner would take game six as well, creating the high spot for the Sox in their otherwise dismal performance. Kerr would go on to win 21 games in 1920, 19 in '21, and run afoul of management, after which he'd never win another big-league game.

WHITE SOX IN FIRST VICTORY BY 3–0 SCORE (OCT. 4, 1919)

Kerr, Recruit Hurler, Baffles Reds, Allowing but 3 Blows, While Fisher Is Hit in the Pinches; Victors Score Twice on Gandil's Timely Single — Risberg's Triple and "Squeeze" Produce a Tally

CHICAGO, OCT. 3 — When "the fancy" are pawing over the litter, they always disdain the runt.

Too small! Sell for a lead nickel! Give him away! Drown him! Anything to get rid of him!

The littlest of the family always has a mighty precious existence.

Take Dick Kerr, now a wee-hop of my thumb, not much taller than a walking stick and tiniest of the baseball brood.

"Won't weigh 90 pounds, sopping wet," an astute scout once reported to his employer after a look at Dick. "Too small for a pitcher, especially a left-handed pitcher. Too small for much of anything, except maybe a watch charm."

Most of the baseball astute said much to the same effect about Kerr, but this afternoon little Dick proved too big for the Cincinnati Reds. He grew, in front of them, to the proportions of a baseball Goliath, and stopped the rush of the Ohioans toward the word's championship with a sudden shock.

They were shut out in the third game, which was the first game played in Chicago, by a score of 3 to 0, after taking the two games in Cincinnati in a manner which caused the most ardent supporters of the Sox to dolefully wag their heads. Chicago is back in the fight. The littlest of the family is the biggest man on the shores of Lake Michigan tonight.

Long, and long ago — back in what now seems the very dark ages of baseball, in fact — there was another pitcher who people said was too small when he first came into the game, but who eventually was acknowledged a giant of his kind.

Gleason Always for Kerr

His name was William Gleason, and his size immediately prompted the nickname of "Kid." Today, "Kid" Gleason is a grizzled fellow of

54, no higher than when he first broke into baseball, though twice as wide, as the manager of the White Sox.

He never agreed to the theory that Kerr was too small. He rather inclined toward little pitchers, probably feeling that the little fellows ought to stick together. He said that Kerr was going to make a good pitcher, and he was vindicated this afternoon when little Dick held the Reds to three hits.

He pitched one of the classiest games ever seem in a World Series. Behind this sort of pitching, and on their home grounds before nearly 30,000 of their home people, the White Sox were not the White Sox who played before the hostile Cincinnatians.

They were again the White Sox who rushed through the American League last summer to a pennant with a dash that sent them into this series overwhelming favorites over their National League opponents.

Fisher's Own Error Costly

They were opposed this afternoon by the first right-hander they have seen in the series. Ray Fisher, the schoolteacher from old Vermont, who pitched for years for the New York Yankees of the American League, was started by Moran. Fisher was supposed to have lost his effectiveness when he was released by the Yanks some time ago, but he has pitched some good games for the Reds. He is a spitball pitcher, and the Sox had no great trouble with his delivery this afternoon. A bad throw by the schoolteacher contributed to his own defeat.

Kerr pitched with surprising coolness. He fires the ball with a quick sideways' jerk of his left arm, and it shoots over the plate with terrific speed. He also has a great curve. It was his curve that bothered the left-handed hitters of the Reds more than anything else.

Little Dick comes from St. Louis, and when he was a kid he had prize-ring aspirations. He turned boxer, but at the same time he also turned to playing baseball on the sandlots. He became a better ballplayer than a boxer. The White Sox got him from Milwaukee of the American Association, and this is his first year as a big-league regular.

Had to Pitch Kerr

Had any of Gleason's old staff come through, it is doubtful if Kerr would have had much of a chance this season. Until the disaster of the Sox in Cincinnati, few expected him to start in the World Series. But Gleason was in desperate straits with Cicotte and Williams beaten, and had to call on what he had.

One of those almost fights between the ballplayers enlivened the game today. The Reds did not relish the licking that was being administered to them, and began snarling from their bench — not a bad move for a ball club in a big series, at that.

It finally wound up in an open jam between Eddie Collins of the Sox, and Jimmy Smith of the Reds, but hostilities ended almost as soon as they began.

So far as Chicago is concerned, the series just began today. The game was splashed high with all the vivid color of an opening session. Of course, the local fans had heard of the happenings at Cincinnati, but, judging from their enthusiasm, they did not credit the news. Thousands of them were lined up at the ball yard gates before daylight. Some of them had been there all night, according to the statements of veracious witnesses. The hotel lobbies were jammed this morning.

———

After the Reds' Jimmy Ring closed down the Sox in game four, pitching a three-hit, 2–0 shutout to put Cincinnati up three games to one, it rained, causing Runyon to pen one of his colorful rainout stories, complete with everything from baseball news to the latest gossip.

RAIN HALTS TITLE SERIES; WILLIAMS TO FACE ELLER (OCT. 6, 1919)

Runyon Declares Sox' Batting Is "Tip Off" on the American League Pitchers

CHICAGO, OCT. 5 — Luck broke against the proprietor of Cincinnati's Hotel Gibson this afternoon, and the guy who runs the

Blackstone-on-Boulevard win the first off-day of the World Series of 1919. It was about time someone in Chicago won something in this series.

Rain caused a postponement of the fifth game. Under the Marquis of Cincinnati's rules, the White Sox and the Reds stay over here until tomorrow for the playoff. The old Mark himself, otherwise known as Garry Herrmann, gave out the news early on behalf of the National Commission.

No one was very sorry. It gave some of the folks a chance to go to church, and offered others an opportunity to locate another bottle.

There was no great amount of rainfall today, but there was a spill last night heavier than a Blackstone breakfast check. Comiskey Field was dressed in its pajamas right after the game yesterday, but it seems the downpour was so profuse that it sweat right through the blankets.

After tomorrow's game, the series moves back to Cincinnati for another pair. Before the end of the month it may be decided to load what's left of the series on wagons and barnstorm the rural districts.

The Sox say they are still confident of winning out, but even a condemned guy generally tries to make the best of things. It's a dollar to a dime that every member of the local club has by this time figured out the amount of the loser's end to the fineness of a hair on a frog's back.

If the Sox win tomorrow and then get as good as an even break in Cincy, the weary old series loads its aching bones back on the cars and returns to Chicago. The Reds can do a lot of people a great favor by starting Ruether tomorrow and Ruether the next day.

It is considered illegal as well as injudicious to sell or lead a Chicago hotel or café keeper a rope, knife or pistol as they sit contemplating what they would have done today to the loyal fans in the pre-2.75 percent era.

Gibson will probably start Claude Williams, the sidewinder again tomorrow. Pat Moran may stick in Hod Eller, the shineballer. Garry Herrmann can use the money.

The glory that was the American League seems to be drifting down the far horizon, but don't let anybody tell you that there are any second Tris Speakers playing the outfield in this series. Some of the outfield plays must have made Tris bust right out laughing.

Harry Fitzgerald of New York's Fifty Club, bobbed up at the headquarters of the Tillinghast L'Hommedieu Huston Marching and Flam Bray Association this morning. The association held an indoor session with Colonel Huston in the chairs. The chairs are correct.

George M. Cohan and his faithful confederate, Steve Reardon, are still pursuing the series, but you can buy Mr. Cohan's bets on the White Sox at a reduction this morning.

Cincinnati fans are still willing to bet even money on their ball club. After the Reds win five games it is believed the odds will go to 6 to 5 in the favor of Cincinnati.

Lots of guys who always thought the Reds would win the series are now coming up for air. There were about eight of them in the whole country before the series started, and there are now about eight million.

Suicide "Harry" Felsch probably appreciated the off day more than anyone else. He didn't have to sacrifice himself for several hours.

Kid Gleason got one laugh out of the lads anyway. He is quoted as saying that he feels ashamed of losing to a ball club that will not tale a chance, meaning the Reds. Having witnessed Mr. Gleason's now-celebrated sacrifice play with no one out, a guy on second and a big hitter up, the bugs feel that the Kid's assertion is a funny crack.

This series so far has been something of a tip-off on the American League pitchers. The Sox hit a million on the run of the season against their own ilk and can't do a thing about the hurling of the National Leaguers.

Lots of guys are around speculating on the squawk that will go up from Cincinnati if the Reds win four games and then blow the title.

———

Much as Ring Lardner did with his Alibi Ike series, Runyon uses the vernacular for some observations on the Series as it

heads back to Cincinnati with the Reds leading . . . and needing
just one more victory to take the title.

SERIES OF QUEER RECORDS; LARDNER
A STATISTICIAN (OCT. 7, 1919)

Gleason Made Fatal Errors in Using Pitchers with Plural Names,
Says Humorist—Final Game an Exhibition

CHICAGO, OCT. 6—Gents: The special train for Cincy will leave tonight at 11:30, new time, and I would advise everybody to be there with their toothbrush and typewriter. The train will leave out of Pennsy Station and immediately on arriving in old Cincy, it would be a great idea to try and get a room somewheres so as you can get shaved.

The game tomorrow will be the crucial game of the serious, and it looks to me like it would be between Grover Lowdermilk and Rube Bressler. Neither manager dared to pitch anybody else.

Today's game here was just an exhibition between the White Sox and Reds and believe me it was some exhibition. It looked like both sides was having a battle to see which could get three men out the slowest. Finally Joe Jackson hit a pop fly into the rightfield seats and broke up the game as far as I am concerned.

The first two White Sox pitchers were Williams and James and I can't tell you why neither of them is plural, and if I were running it I would call them William and Jane. I wouldn't trust neither one of the both of them. If I was manager, I would pitch a guy with a singular name like Lowdermilk. Another thing Manager Gleason did today was to change the outfield around to deceive the newspapermen. The scheme worked perfectly and I do hope he is satisfied. I know I am.

Joe's the Statisticiano

Speaking about this World Series I will have to join the statisticiano and tell you the different records I seen here. It was the first world serious that Morris Rath ever broke a bat in. It is the only world serious, which Sherwood Magee ever got a base hit. It is the only world serious that Umpire Nallin ever called a strike on Jake Daubert. It is probably the only world serious I will ever see. So much for the records.

Now to get down to facts. Here are quotations from a letter received just before the game by a Chi baseball reporter. "I have been a follower of athletics and have taken part on athletics in my younger days. I have been greatly amused during the present series in reading the 'ifs' and the 'buts' explaining Chicago's defeat from day to day. It looks like a case of sour grapes to me. In fact it borders on rowdyism. I suppose if you lose another game or two you will mob the Cincinnati team."

Well, I know this here Chi baseball writer that the letter come to come to and he never mentioned sour grapes in his life or ordered them neither, and as for mobbing the Cincinnati ball club, why this same baseball writer was standing with me when the clubs come out of the clubhouse and Sherwood Magee came up and spoke to the both of us. If that don't prove how stand I don't know what will or care neither one.

Johnson Suspends Players

Now personally I don't think there will be a game tomorrow, and if there is I don't know who will pitch, as I seen Ban Johnson after today's alleged game and he said he had suspended all the pitchers on both clubs.

While being exhausted at the game, I finely set down and read the following in the afternoon papers: "The names of the early dukes of Normandy as well as their family history are known but very dimly, and it may be as well that it should be so, for their descendents do not seem to have been as orthodox as it might. This William I of England, a.k.a. William II of Normandy, was the illegitimate son of his predecessor."

How can a man pay attention to a ballgame like that when theys such good stuff to read in the papers?

—

REDS CAPTURE TITLE, ROUTING SOX, 10 TO 5, WITH ELLER PITCHING (OCT. 10, 1919)

New Champions Drive Williams from Box in First Inning — James and Wilkinson Also Hit Hard — Late Rally of the American Leaguers Fails to Turn Tide of the Game

CINCINNATI, OCT. 9 — It's a long time between baseball championships in Cincinnati, but after 50 years of waiting one landed there this afternoon.

The old town on the Ohio can now start the festivities in honor of her beloved Reds that were suspended in mid-air, so to speak, last Tuesday, when the vague possibility of final defeat cast a sinister shadow across the waiting banquet board.

In the eighth and deciding game of the World Series of 1919, the National Leaguers won their final victory from the Chicago White Sox, champions of the American League. The score was 10 to 5.

Only the fact that the closing innings found the White Sox ripping holes through the delivery of "Hod" Eller, the burly "shineball" pitcher of the Reds, prevented it from being as dreary a finish to the Sox and to the fans too, for that matter, as the beginning of the series when Eddie Cicotte was beaten by a lopsided score.

Even at best the game was a sort of burlesque touch to a show that for a couple of days gave signs of becoming quite a drama.

Eller, who last Monday, in the language of baseball, stood the Sox on their heads, was weakening fast at the close. He went into the eighth inning with a nine-run lead and the Sox piled up four runs. A marvelous tumbling catch in deep center by Eddie Roush with a Sox runner on first gave him a lot of trouble.

Rings Starts Warming

Pat Moran, the red-muzzled leader of the Cincinnati club, was several times minded to remove Eller in the last two innings. He had Jimmy Ring warming up in right field, and every time a Sox crashed across the diamond or to the distant outfield, Ring looked around at Moran, expecting the signal.

The Red infielders were constantly closing in on the "shineballer," giving him advice and encouragement. But for the fact that the Reds had an overwhelming lead Eller would not have lasted past the first couple of batters in the eighth. It was well for them that they had piled up so many runs early in the game.

Eller's weakening came very suddenly, because up to the eighth he had been pitching well. A home run by "Shoeless Joe" Jackson into the rightfield bleachers in the third inning was the only real heavy blow made off his delivery, although he was nowhere near the sensational form he displayed in his first start.

Eller's Second Triumph

It was Eller's second triumph in the long-drawn-out series. Under the old conditions of the World Series, which were changed for this year because some of the baseball magnates saw an opportunity to engage in the popular pastime, the affair would have ended there with the Reds victors by four games to one.

The elaboration of the series to nine games, an idea with originated with Garry Herrmann, president of the Reds, proved the undoing of the Cincinnati club. The Sox rallied and won two games. The series stood four games to three when the clubs returned to Chicago this morning an many fans seemed to believe that the Reds were on the run.

They quickly erased this notion this afternoon by a first-inning rush, which drove Claude Williams, the Sox left-hander, from the box. The Reds batted through their lineup in that inning and scored four runs. It was a disheartening blow to the Chicagoans right off the reel. Williams had already been beaten in two starts against the Reds. He "had nothing" today, which is to say the ball refused to answer to his hand.

"Couldn't break an egg," remarked one of the ballplayers, describing the lack of speed behind the ball as delivered by Williams.

Big Bill James, a righthander, took the southpaw's place. The seat of Bill's white trousers were sadly discolored from long sitting on the Sox bench. "He didn't have much more than a prayer" is the ballplayers' report on James.

After James came Wilkinson, a recruit. The Reds' massacre of pitching continued.

"Nothing but his glove" was the base-ballic summing up of Wilkinson's efforts.

It is going to be a difficult matter to pick the baseball "heroes" out of this series when the winter gossip begins. Cincinnati has Eller for its bright star, of course, but he will have to divide the limelight with Maurice Rath, Eddie Roush, Larry Kopf and several others.

On the Sox side, Tiny Dick Kerr is the biggest of them all. He pitched two of the three games won by the Chicagoans, and had the Sox been able to put over a victory today he would have been pitching for them in the final at Cincinnati tomorrow. Ray Schalk and Buck Weaver are the other two members of the Sox who stuck. Schalk caught every game with the exception of a few innings of one game from which he was expelled by (the) umpire. He made a few mistakes, but in the main he played good ball and renewed his hold on the title of best backstop in the game.

———

Although rumors and some news stories about the Black Sox scandal started appearing as early as October 1919, the details of the scandal became public in September 1920—flooring Runyon and the rest of America with its extent and scope. With details emerging throughout the month, Runyon still had a hard time believing that a fix of such enormous proportions could be engineered. He wrote several pieces in an attempt to sort things out, but the scandal permanently soured the game for him.

"TOSSING" GAMES IS NO CINCH (SEPT. 7, 1920)
Baseball Plotters Would Have to Get Too Many Men into Scheme to Insure Success

Once upon a time, somewhere out in "The Sticks," as the underbrush of baseball is called, eight members of a ball club got together, and conspired to "throw" a game.

That is to say, they schemed to lose this game. They were to receive a consideration for their dirty work from a clique of the town gamblers.

The eight men represented every position on the club with the exception of the centerfielder. He was a green Swede (Risberg), and the crooked eight decided that he was such a fathead that they might as well save his end of the money for themselves.

When the game was played, the Swede, knowing nothing of the plot, hit five home runs out of five times up and won the pastime, despite the efforts to lose on the part of his companions.

This yarn is by way of preamble to the statement of several well-known ballplayers with whom we have talked the last few days that it would be very difficult for one or two players to "throw" a game.

There have been rumors of gambling scandals in baseball for some time now with the hint that players conspired to lose games.

Cooperation Necessary to "Throw" Ballgame

These rumors began last season, and were connected up in the public mind with the failure of several big-league players to continue in the game. They have been recently revived by stories from Chicago.

"I doubt if any one man, alone and unaided, could arrange with any guarantee of absolute success to lose a game," said a player yesterday. "He would have to have much assistance. Of course if the fall of the play was such that an error, or a bad throw on his part, or even a deliberate strikeout in the pinch, would toss the result the other way, he might succeed."

Of course, the fact that one man in the lineup of a club stood ready to commit a crooked error if he got a chance would be a certain percentage in favor of the people betting on that club to lose, but suppose opportunity never came his way?

"A pitcher might agree to 'throw' a game; that is to say, to try to lose it and might lob the ball up for the opposing batters at the right time. He might thus give them a lead that his own club could not overcome, but in nine cases out of ten his manager would yank him out of the box before he had gone very far."

Timely Batting Often Offsets Fielding Errors

"Even if crooks succeeded in bribing a couple of infielders to do the dirty work, their efforts might not be of any avail. They might make numerous errors, but the other members of the club might offset the breaks in fielding with their hitting.

"Of course, what the crooks are looking for is that percentage of just enough guilt to bend the thing in their direction. You know that when there was talk of an attempt to bridge the umpires in a certain series years ago, they say all the plotters wanted were the close decisions.

"With the close ones in their favor they would have the advantage. I doubt a lot of this talk of attempts to corrupt ballplayers and I know any effort to guarantee a ballgame one way or the other is bound to fail because you'd have to let too many in."

Here, Runyon takes the unusual technique of delivering a "sport" editorial to deliver his briefest, but strongest remarks on the ongoing investigation.

Sport Editorial: Read This Story! (Sept. 27, 1920)

Read this story, which appeared exclusively in the *New York American* October 30, 1919, nearly one year ago.

Rothstein Admits Receiving Offer to "Buy" World's Series; Spurned Overtures of Man Who Said He Could Fix Certain Party for $20,000, Who Would See That the White Sox Would Lose
By W.S. Farnsworth

Baseball will be shocked to learn of a plan to bribe a man connected with the Chicago White Sox is the reason the World Series was captured by the Cincinnati Reds . . .

Arnold Rothstein, the man mentioned in this story, has just been summoned to appear before the Grand Jury in Chicago, which is investigating the baseball scandal.

What did baseball do about the matter at the time this story was printed nearly one year ago?

Not a thing.

Here was something for the league officials to work on. Here was a report that justified the greatest activity and closest investigation on the part of the men supposed to protect the great national game.

What did (National League John) Heydler and (American League President Ban) Johnson, and all the rest do?

They did nothing. They kept quiet.

Prompt action on their part at the time this story was published might have averted the plague of scandal, which now affects the game.

We believe in the integrity of baseball. We believe that it will all be the better for the cleansing it is now undergoing.

But we believe that the "shush" policy of the league officials has been very damaging to the best interests of the game.

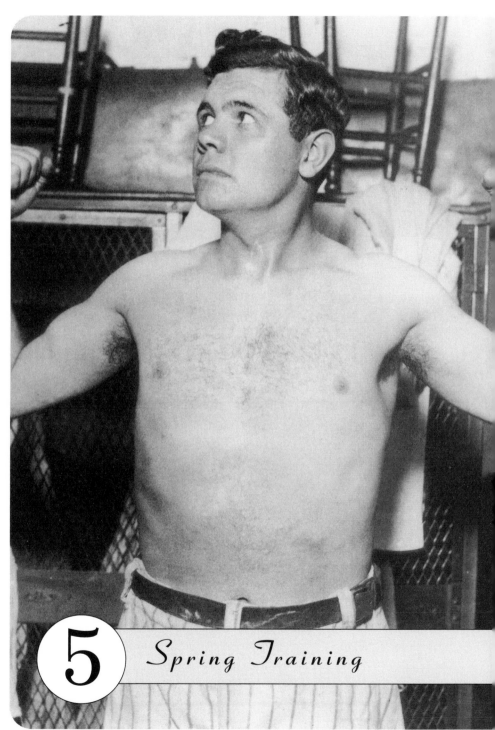

5 *Spring Training*

George Herman "Babe" Ruth

For writers, spring training was a time to get some sun and pick up a paycheck while filing articles back north that provided little insight beyond who looked good, who didn't, and who won the games. Runyon's reports from Yankee camp at Jacksonville in 1920 threw all that out the window—and were mostly a vehicle for his own brand of gentle humor that mixed in some limited reporting about Babe Ruth, the new slugger from Boston that the Yankees had just acquired for $125,000, an occasional quote or two, the saga of his pet alligator, Aloysius, and the ramblings of Yankee outfielder Ping Bodie, the Yogi Berra–style linguist of his day. Remarkably, Runyon spent all of March in Jacksonville with the Yankees while continuing to write his regular columns, "Just a Mugg" and "Th' Mornin's Mornin'," as if he had never left Broadway.

YANKEES SPEND FIRST DAY AT TRAINING CAMP ON GOLF LINKS (MAR. 2, 1920)

Crimpy Weather Interferes with Practice at Jacksonville; Babe and Rube Contrast Baseball Eras

JACKSONVILLE, MARCH 1—There was an historical meeting on the golf links of the Jacksonville Country Club this afternoon.

The eras of baseball came together, bridging a span of 11 years in time and $126,000 on the hoof. And isn't this widely known that eons ago—or anyway, 11 years—Richard De Markee De Marquard was bought by the Giants for $11,000?

Well, then, these relative voices in the high cost of baseball duked one another with their right maulers today, their more-or-less famous left hands being in the act of clutching golf shillelaghs. It was purely an accidental meeting. It stands to reason no left-hander would meet another "cock-eye" save by accident.

Folks gathered close to the noble grouping and inclined attentive ears to hear what burning words as might fall from the mouths of these parties.

291

"Lo, Rube," said Babe.

"Lo, Babe," said Rube.

It was over in a second. The illustrious Babe hauled off and socked a golf ball three miles, or more, to hear the witnesses tall, and moved off it, while Richard De Markee De Marquard faded into the obscurity of his absurdly low price of many, many years ago.

Overshadowed by Ruth

One would scarcely see him behind the parapet of figures, which divided the period of baseball-frenzied finance from Babe's sector.

Yet there was a time when people turned to look at Richard De Markee De Marquard, too, and mumble his price in awe-struck tones. There was a time when Richard, too, cost what then seemed enough money to satisfy getting the leading paragraphs in a training camp story, even though he did no more than paste a golf ball around all day.

But that was before Richard went to Brooklyn. Ah yes, most of the Yanks went a-golfing today in the wake of the ponderous pounder from Boston. It was too crimpy around the edges of the Jacksonville weather for an auspicious opening of the training season, although a few of the lads went across the river to the ball yard and hurled the pill around to some extent.

Young Dan Murphy, a kid catcher from Toledo; (Fred) Hofmann, another catcher; and (Bob) Rice, a rookie infielder, were among those present in the baseball orchard, and Ping Bodie wagged his head a many a wag as he saw them letting their arms out to the last notch.

Young guys," said Ping, in a melancholy tone, as he devoted himself to milder calisthenics. "Very young guys, throwing that way."

———

The cold weather and languid pace of early spring training gave Runyon his first themes for the month—an obsession with weather and what the players were eating.

BABE RUTH BATS OUT A FEW ON FIRST DAY OF YANKEE PRACTICE (MAR. 3, 1920)

Huggins to Direct Men Today; Plenty of Sun for New York Squad in First Workout

JACKSONVILLE, FLA., MARCH 2—Old Sols were beaming all over Jacksonville today.

Old Sol Weinstein, the clothing salesman from New York, beamed somewhat on customers at the baseball arbor in South Jacksonville.

Old Sol outbeamed his rival by two beams and a mote. He played both morning and afternoon. Old Sol, the Sun, appeared only at a matinee, but he drew a large attendance in South Jacksonville at that. Babe Ruth and Colonel Til Huston were there. They are both large.

It was high time that old Sol, the Sun, showed something around here. Folks were getting pretty much disgusted with his actions. Lou Paley was in the act of boarding a train back to New York to get warm when the beaming began. Lou is an inmate of Jack Doyle's eggery on Broadway, and he came to Jacksonville in a pair of knee pants to play meadow snooker, and to watch the Yanks go through the preliminaries to drawing these large salaries.

Up to this afternoon all Mr. Paley had seen of the Yanks was a mighty exhibition of eating, and yawning, and some of the eating was so voluminous that Mr. Paley didn't believe it, anyway.

Waiters Leg Weary

Samyewet Wick (Sam Vick) has joined on, and the table tournament between him and Babe Ruth already has the waiters at the Burbridge run flatfooted. This Sam is a plumb throw-off. He doesn't look as if he could eat his weight in cream puffs.

On the other hand, Babe looks the part. That's why he is carrying most of the money in the betting. But in the cool of the evening, when the eating begins, Sam will be there.

Anyway, the Yanks' 1920 training season was auspiciously and suspiciously opened today. Babe Ruth waggled a wicked stick.

That made it auspicious. Ping Bodie remarked that he wouldn't give a nickel for all the steam beer in the world. That was the suspicious feature. But, maybe, Ping meant it, at that. All the steam beer of the kind now left in the world really isn't worth a nickel.

Miller Huggins hasn't arrived as yet, so the opening was managed by a company. Bob Connery was president, Joe Kelley was vice-president, and Charlie O'Leary was secretary and treasurer. Phil Schenck, the groundskeeper, gave the correspondent a wide berth as the officers smiled approval on the efforts of young Danny Murphy and Bob McGraw.

No Real Slugging Yet

There was no excessive Babe Ruthing during the afternoon. Nothing was knocked over the fence except a few foolish fouls. The distinguished young man who cost the Colonels so much that they have sympathetic pains whenever they think about it stepped to the plate a couple of times in batting practice and loosened the covers on a couple of pills, but his efforts were not unduly thrilling.

However, it was no little satisfaction to Colonel Huston to note that Babe hasn't lost an arm or a leg since he was purchased. The Colonel doesn't want to see Babe lose even flesh. He cost too much per pound.

The only sensation of the afternoon was the appearance at the baseball vineyard of Samivel Newhall Crane, the dean of the baseball writers, who took his first slant at a crowd of Yanks in training in 14 years. So far no one has mentioned to Samivel the fact that he is with the Yanks for fear that he has absent-mindedly come here under the impression that he is with the Giants.

Fewster Has Cold

Chick Fewster was the only member of the crowd who didn't fondle a baseball today. He has a cold. Chick has been placed in nomination for Frank Baker's (third base) position. The Yanks have to have a Marylander at third: (Fritz) Maisel, Baker, and now Fewster. If Chick won't do, Joe Kelley will try to make the grade just to keep the job in the Oriole state (all were from the Baltimore area).

———

MILLER HUGGINS ARRIVES IN CAMP, AND REAL "BOILING OUT" BEGINS (MAR. 4, 1920)

Ruth Favors Center Field

JACKSONVILLE, MARCH 3—M. Huggins, in a jolly-looking little cap and a bored expression, went over to South Jacksonville today and took personal command of the Yanks, "including," as Harry Sparrow's new one-sheets advertising the Brooklyn series, say, "Babe Ruth, the Home Run King."

M. Huggins's first official motion was to flatwheel himself twice around the busting behemoth, admiring the graceful proportions of the Babe from his belt down, which was as far up as M. could see without getting a crick in his neck. Then he sent the Babe up to belt a few for him.

Bob McGraw, the Pearl of Pueblo, Colorado, slung one at Babe with a nice, easy second day of training motion, and Babe knocked it in the direction of the St. John River. It would have gone in the water had the river been half-a-mile nearer, or the blow half-a-mile longer.

After that, the rest of the lads took a turn at slugging the old orange. It was very exciting. It was almost as exciting as watching the grass grow. The second day of training is always like that. So is the third. And the fourth. And the fifth.

Ward at Third Base

Ping Bodie, Sammy Vick, Del Pratt, Walter Pipp, Aaron Ward, Muddy Ruel, Fred Hofmann, Danny Murphy, and various and sundry pitchers took their turn at bat, passing before the insipid slinging of (Bob) McGraw, J. Picus Quinn, Walter Smallwood and Harry Biemiller, the infielder from Jersey City, who knocked so many first basemen over with his throws last season that (former Yankee manager) Wild Bill Donovan turned him into a pitcher. So far Harry has knocked over few catchers, but it is said he can bounce a baseball off the boys' bats as far as the next fish.

After batting practice, there was some infield stuff. Pipp went to first, Pratt to second, Aaron Ward to third and "Zip" Rice to short. "Zip's" ticket of admission to the baseball park is signed by Bob Shawkey. "Zip" and Bob have a common sorrow—they both live in Philadelphia.

"Zip" was full of speed, and was snapping his arm like a buggy whip at the start, but toward the finish his throws were getting shorter than our last answer to Mexico. 'Twas ever thus in the gentle springtime.

Charley O'Leary hit to the infield, and Joe Kelley ran right out from under his cap while instructing the outfielders, displaying an island of baldness in a lagoon of dandruff.

While the delegates are in convention assembled and balloting on a successor to Frank Baker, with Wilson "Chick" Fewster and Bob Meusel as candidates, don't be surprised if a sorrel horse slips through and gets elected to that third-base office. This Aaron Ward is a jaunty-looking proposition. He "handles himself," as the saying is, around that peevish post very pleasantly indeed.

It was noticed that Babe Ruth planted himself in center field during the fielding practice. Babe has been declaring himself in on center field ever since he was bought by the Yankees. The consensus of opinion is that he ought to be playing right field, where he will not lose any more home runs than he makes—but who are we to be arguing with a fish who cost more money than we can even think about without getting a headache?

Crowd Attend Practice

And maybe Babe's self-appointment doesn't go anyway. Maybe they are just letting him stand out there in the sun until they can find a way of grafting him into right field. Meantime however, there is the danger of his legs warping under the strain of shagging high flies. Fortunately, Ruth doesn't have to chase his own punches or he would be bowlegged in a week.

Quite a number of Jacksonvillians assembled on the sunny side of the hard and dusty board at the baseball arbor this afternoon to see what was what. When Babe muffed one swing at a pitch with such vigor that he almost yanked himself out of the district, they said they told you so.

——

When Runyon's friend and mentor, the great New York newspaperman Irwin Cobb, appears in Jacksonville, the real business of spring training—seeing how much people could eat—goes center-stage.

RUTH AND IRWIN COBB TOP-HEAVY CHOICES IN FEED STAKES (MAR. 5, 1920)

Recruit Catchers Make Hit; Yankees Have Promising Young Pair in Hoffman and Murphy (and) Lefty O'Doul Reports at Camp

JACKSONVILLE, FLA., MARCH 4—Entries for the great All-American tables stakes closed today with the filing of the name of Irwin Shrewsbury Cobb, the famous eating-author, as the representative of the journalistic fraternity.

The newspapermen with the Yanks had been making an effort to bring Colonel Boseman Bulger on from New York to bear their colors on the gustatory grapple, which will bring together such stars of the culinary campus as Babe Ruth, Sam Vick, Ping Bodie, Colonel T. L'Hommedieu Huston and your Uncle Wilbert Robinson, when it was learned that Mr. Cobb will be in Jacksonville next week on a lecturing expedition.

This news was in the nature of a windfall for the journalists, for while Colonel Bulger is undeniably a mighty trencherman, and would have done them proud, he has neither the experience nor technique of Mr. Cobb. Therefore the scribes entered into communication with the great eating-author and, by offering him the inducement of a 12-course banquet immediately following the running off of the table stakes, his presence was assured.

Spot Rivals One Ham

It was decided that Mr. Cobb should start from scratch with Ruth, and that they shall spot their competitors one Virginia ham each, and a double porterhouse. George Mogridge, who is managing Ruth, insisted on a rule that Mr. Cobb shall not be permitted to tell any stories during the encounter, as George says his man cannot do a menu justice if he has to stop and laugh and eat at the same time is well-known. He can emit a raucous guffaw and chamber a Dill pickle simultaneously.

This, of course, is due to Mr. Cobb's greater experience at house parties, dinner and the like where a gentleman has to listen to his host or hostess, and protect himself, too, as the butler slides the tureens past his server. Ruth has always knifed and forked with airy persiflage barred.

There was something of a surprise in the opening betting today when a wad of quiet money came on your Uncle Wilbert Robinson, manager of the Brooklyn Dodgers. It was traced to the waiters up to the Hotel Seminole, where the Dodgers are stopping, and they took advantage of your Uncle Wilbert's opening price of 2 to 1. They gradually hammered him down to even money.

The help around the Hotel Burbridge, home of the Yanks, are betting their tip money on Colonel T. L'Hommedieu Huston to show, but since most of the tip money comes from the baseball contingent the play on this entry has not been very heavy. However, this one will bear watching. Ruth and Cobb are both held at the prohibitive odds of 1 to 10 and out.

Vick Not in Shape

Sam Vick is really not in condition as yet, and his admirers are sorely disappointed. He warmed up last night on a side of bacon, a few dozen oysters and other odds and ends in the way of the chops and hot cakes and ice cream, but he showed little form. It is doubtful he can beat out either Ruth or Cobb unless he improves.

As for Ping Bodie, the mighty eater of other days, the course is really not suited to him, and it would be no surprise if he finished in the ruck.

"If it was spaghetti, I'd show them something," Ping says, "but after I get through one of these hotel menus my appetite is dead for half an hour. Maybe it's the climate."

Business of shifting the subject: There was more baseballishness over in South Jacksonville, morning and afternoon. It was a gray, tweed-colored day. But M. Huggins had the lads working briskly. Any man who can tell anything about baseball recruits at this stage of the training season is a better man than we are.

P.S. — Babe hit a two-miler today. Knocked ball into lap of small boy sitting on rightfield fence. Boy stuck ball in pocket and ran all way to home two miles off with it. Broke Babe's bat. Broke Harry Sparrow's heart. Harry pays for both balls and bats.

Players Work Out on Links; Babe Ruth Defies Cold and Shocks Natives When He Appears in White Flannel Pants

JACKSONVILLE, MARCH 5 — Having stared the typewriter keys in their respective faces for 15 minutes without developing any thought other than that the "J" key is somewhat on the squeegee, it suddenly occurs to us that we have written nothing whatsoever today about Babe Ruth.

Did you ever sit looking into the faces of dull, unresponsive type-writer keys for a quarter-of-an-hour on a cold Friday in Florida? It's very monotonous. But the alternative in this case is going down-stairs to the lobby of the Burbridge, and gasping at the maps of the baseball players. So here we are at the old Underwood.

This Florida weather has so far been greatly misrepresented to a large number of patients. At the current period of the year, the ther-mometer is supposed to be almost as high as the hotel rates. You are supposed to be able to send picture postcards to your friends back yonder in the icebound North, showing you in linens and the straw hat, with writing on the margins of the card as follows: "Look at me, you poor simp."

Cold Wave Hits Jax

But you are able, at this time, to engage in these Florida frivolities, for which you paid all that dough to the railroads.

The local postal authorities are complaining bitterly about the sudden decrease in the picture-postcard business, but condones it on the ground that, doubtless customers are unable to get as far as the mail box without incurring the risk of chilblains.

Pieces of the cold spell, which is bounding up and down in the West, flew off and hit Jax today, and most of the Yankees hung around the hotel lobby all day, dripping intermittent and clammy conversation as an icicle drips perspiration. It was not desperately cold, but it was cold enough to freeze up all of those Huggins ideas toward a workout. A snappy wind was blowing.

Thus, by working along the wind, we have arrived at a topical subject for a nice chat. We have arrived at Babe Ruth, the Billion-Dollar fish. If we seem to speak of Babe more than somewhat, we trust the reader will bear with us. All our life we have been poor, and Babe cost so much money that even to talk about it gives us a wealthy feeling.

If we had enough money to buy a ballplayer as expensive as Babe, you know what we'd do? Neither do we, but we would not buy a ballplayer.

Anyhow, the diamond-studded ball-buster broke out in a rash of white flannel pants this morning, and announced that he was going to play a few pages of golf. He said he had put on his white flannel pants because he had been informed that Florida is productive to white flannel pants at this season of the year, and he'd been dog-goned if he was going to be shut out of wearing his white flannel.

"Trousers," interrupted Bob Shawkey, with a pained look. "Trousers, my dear fellow."

"Mines pants," said Babe, firmly. "When it gets to such a thing as the weather can tell me what kind of pants I gotta wear, I'm going to quit."

Shawkey and some of the other athletes accompanied Babe to

the golf course, and brought back the usual tales of his tall driving—or maybe they are tall tales of his usual driving. Babe is just naturally addicted to swinging a club at something or other, though whether this habit overtakes the form of work, such as aiming the old ax at the kindling, we do not know.

Ping Declares

Ping Bodie was declaring himself this morning. "When I hit those 30 homers out on the Coast (in the Pacific Coast League in 1912)," said Ping, "I was using a batting style like this Ruth's. I'd take the bat close to the end of the handle and haul off and let go at the ball. When I got to the White Sox, (manager) Jimmy Callahan made me change my style, and he finally had me choking the bat so far up that I only had about an inch to hit the old huckleberry with.

"I'm going back to my first style this year," Ping said. "I'm going to take my Moriarity whether I pop up, or what. You hear me. I'm going to have my natural smash at the old apple."

He raised his voice. "I'm going to swing, and keep swinging," vociferated Ping. "Whether I stay in New York, or whether they send me to Kanakee, I'm going to swing. Yes sir, swing."

In the distance, Miller Huggins, sitting in a chair, stirred slightly. Maybe he heard.

"Swing," roared Ping, as he started for the elevator almost knocking over the latest arrival in camp, Roger Peckinpaugh.

———

Runyon uses a slow news day to kick off his annual spring-training diatribe against golf.

YANKEES' "SUNDAY TRAINING" CONSISTS OF GOLF AND FISHING (MAR. 8, 1920)
Players Cheered by Check; Receive Share of World Series Prize
JACKSONVILLE, MARCH 7—Of a Sabbath it is the Yanks' custom to commit such mild misdemeanors as golf. Thus they observe the day, and keep it. Barely do we escape a miserable pun by writing it "holey."

This golf is the ostensibly innocent Sunday indiscretion of many persons other than baseball players, though it is our firm belief that a man who will play golf on Sunday has stud poker or maybe pinochle in his heart. A man who will play golf on Sunday is apt to play it on Tuesday or Wednesday or any other day if he gets a chance, and thus he gradually becomes irretrievable.

Not all the Yanks went golfing today, however. Some did worse. Some went fishing. Of these the less said the better. A Sunday fisherman is hopeless. It begins with week-day fishing, and gradually the little brain cells become a tangle of bait and sinkers. A man's willpower is destroyed, and mid-day fishing follows.

The family of a Sunday fisherman is entitled to the sincere sympathy of the entire community.

Three Go A-Golfing

Bob Shawkey and Derrill Pratt were among the first to break out their while flannel pantlings and hasten golfward. Babe Ruth was already there in the hands of his keeper, a caddie. The subsequent proceedings beggar description.

Bob Shawkey, who is a real dude at golf, says if they ever lay out a golf course on his bias Babe is going to be one of the greatest liabilities the country has ever seen. He is not the worst golfer in the world right now, according to Bob, because John T. Doyle is around swinging a malicious stick.

Shawkey says that Babe is one of the few living golfers who can skim a golf ball in the direction of Key West and hit himself on the flask pocket with the drive. He is ambidextrous, amphibious and ambiguous in his game, and in addition to that Babe's style is never hampered by the rules.

There are two strikes on him anytime he picks up a golf crutch, but nonetheless, the old boy is a terror to pitchers when he steps up to that home tee, especially to pitchers who trundle the white marble around the course with him. They never know what moment he is going to assassinate them with a screaming triple from behind.

But Babe certainly loves his golf. We once knew another great genius who was very peculiar.

The names of the Sunday fishermen are withheld. Enough scandal is being printed in the papers as it is. An aroma of finnan haddie was traced to Roger Peckinpaugh, but he swore he had not been fishing. He said he had merely dined up at "Cutie" Pearce's. "Cutie's" is the local Shanley.

The stronger willed and more virile in the Yankee camp, such as the baseball writers, passed the first Sunday at Dominick Mullaney's Brunswick-Balke gymnasium, quietly hardening their muscles and arteries at the manly sport of Kelly pool.

Check Finally Arrives

Veteran baseball writers have long since learned the lesson of caution in spring training. They know that a man might easily contract a severe cold in his middle typewriter finger by exposing himself to the fresh air at this season of the year.

Harry Sparrow, business manager of the Yanks, was around the Burbridge like the town crier, squalling the happy news that Colonel Jacob Ruppert, president of the Yanks, had sent him a check for the Yanks' World Series dough. Next to the arrival of Colonel Jake, nothing could have been more pleasing.

The Yanks get this dough for finishing third in the American League race and as it means a "baby grand" each, which is to say five hundred bucks, all the unmarried boys were vastly delighted. The married ones were as morose as usual, because they have to spend the money in the same old way.

———

Leave it to Runyon to devote most of his column to bad weather.

BAKER WILL RETURN TO THIRD BASE, SAYS RUNYON (MAR. 9, 1920)

Practice Game on for Today; Huggins Will Give His Yankee Veterans and Yearlings First Real Workout in Jacksonville

JACKSONVILLE, MARCH 8—The Yanks had one of the stiffest workouts of the incumbent spring today. A stiff breeze was blowing over the field, and the baselines, which have been hanging out in the stiff weather of the past few days, were still as stiff as a 1920-model hangover, but nonetheless the practice was very stiff, and also stiffening.

George Mogridge unbent his south arm at the northeast corner and displayed a stiff curve, while Babe Ruth hit a stiff foul with a stiff bat so far over Joe Kelley's head that the old scout was limping stiffly after it for 10 minutes. When he returned, he was mumbling something about a big stiff glass of liniment.

Yes, sir, it was certainly a stiff day, take it all around like a stiff collar. It was as stiff as a prohibitionist's principles. However, nearly everything is stiff nowadays — practice, precepts and prices, and many necks.

Too Much Wind

There is no doubt the weather they are now enjoying hereabouts at the current typewriting is unusual for Jacksonville, but that fellow hasn't been around yet to mention that this is the first time in 20 years they have had such weather. You know that fellow. Every town has him. Possibly the reason he hasn't been around to speak to the Yanks so far is because he has had a tip they are laying for him with murderous intent.

The sun shines all right, as it has a contract with Florida to that effect, but the wind she blows, and even the natives, who are commonly supposed to affect little more than palm leaves at this season of the year, concede that the atmosphere is percolative.

Of course it cannot last this way. The weather is just naturally bound to get warmer around here, toot sweet, as the French say, because it is against the law in this state for it to get any colder than it has been.

M. Huggins is so Pollyannaish about the prospects that he intends inciting his athletes to regular baseballing tomorrow. He will present a mob scene in seven innings, featuring everybody, including those who are doomed to Toledo, and other outlying posts on the bleak desert of baseball.

Regulars Are Yannigans

The regulars will probably compose one team, and we have already thought up a name for it, in accordance with the time-honored custom of spring. It is our intention to call this team the "Regulars." The youngsters will doubtless make up the other team, and after giving much thought to the matter, we have decided that the name "Yannigans" will be most appropriate.

What a Yannigan is we do not know, but generally it is something that sooner or later causes Roger Bresnahan, or some other manager down in the junipers to use a lot of cuss words. A Yannigan is a Yannigan, and always has been such as far back as we remember, and the only distinguishing feature of a Yannigan that we can think of at the moment is a Badger haircut.

M. Huggins says he does not know how he will line up his two teams, and if Mr. Huggins doesn't know, we would scarcely have the temerity to suggest. However, you can look into the files of last summer and find out how the Yankee regulars generally line up, and they will probably line up the same way tomorrow with the exception of third base, and a couple of spots in the outfield.

Baker Coming Back

Ruth will be out there, and probably Vick and Bodie in the absence of Duffy Lewis (who was a late arrival to camp, but would report a few days later). At third, M. Huggins will likely play Ward or Fewster. If Frank Baker doesn't return, Fewster will undoubtedly be Huggins's third base choice, although he had not been able to show as much so far this spring as Ward.

It pains us no little to break this news, after having so adroitly figured Ward in as the regular third baseman, but that's the way the wind is blowing. In fact, the wind is generally blowing in the direction of third base around here. However, the very surest bet we know right now is that Baker will return. So nobody will get the third base job but Baker.

(In fact, 33-year-old Frank "Home Baker" Baker, just widowed with two

young children, wouldn't return until the following season—and play two more years before retiring for good. The onetime Philadelphia A, a three-time deadball-era A.L. home run champion—his best year was 12 homers—was elected to the Baseball Hall of Fame in 1955.)

———

This just in: "The Bacon and the Eggs played their first legal baseball game of the season this afternoon," Runyon writes of the Yankees' first intrasquad game.

YANKEE RECRUITS WIN, 3 TO 1 (MAR. 10, 1920)

Mays in Box for Regulars; Allows Four Hits Which Yield Rookies Three Runs

JACKSONVILLE, MARCH 9—The Bacon and the Eggs played their first legal baseball game of the season this afternoon. Thus spring is surely here, if you have a swell imagination, for did not an editorial writer recently denounce the baseball players as the harbingers of spring?

He did indeed, much to the indignation of Ping Bodie, who says that any man who will call an honest pastime such a name is probably no better himself than he should be.

The Bacons, who are the Yankee freshmen, licked the stuffing out of the Eggs, otherwise the Ruphuggins regulars, in a seven-inning séance over the South Jax, and great was the astonishment thereat. The score was 3 to 1 and perhaps the feature was the fact that Babe Ruth failed to knock any home runs, thus distressing the publicity department no little.

However, Babe made a noble effort at that. He got one unadulterated two-base punch, and then tried to knock Long Bob Meusel into the State of Georgia with another shot.

Bob Spoils Homer

Bob was playing first base, where he will probably usually play when he plays with the Yanks, if he doesn't play the outfield, or third base, or some other place, and he opened out his full length like an accordion and speared Babe's drive with one duke.

It was quite a catch, but Harry Sparrow, the business manager of the Yankees, is thinking of taking Bob to task. The Yanks are paying a lot of money to have Babe knock home runs, and here Meusel goes and ruins the prospective headline: "Ruth Knocks First Homer of Season."

Mr. Sparrow says these fresh kids better not get too gay around here.

Babe played centerfield with the old heads. It looks as if his personal nomination of himself to that job has carried the convention. Bodie was in left and Sammywell Vick in right. Young Fewster played third, and led the regulars' batting order, while Peckinpaugh, Pipp, Ruth, Pratt, Vick, Bodie, Muddy Ruel and the pitchers followed him.

Carl Mays pitched four innings for the Eggs, and the Bacons plastered him for four hits and all their runs. Walter Smallwood allowed them three hits in three innings, and no runs. The Irish were too much for the opposition, if you want to figure a guy named Picus an Irishman because he goes by the name of (Jack) Quinn. Both (Bob) McGraw, the Pearl of Pueblo, and Burly Jack flung, as the saying is, for the freshies, and they allowed but two hits each.

Quinn pitched three frames, and the Eggs got their only run off him. McGraw worked four innings, and showed fine form. Quinn is ready right now, and so is Mays, despite the fact that the youngsters hit fairly freely. Mogridge is another regular on edge, so to speak, wherefore M. Huggins's pitching staff is right up to snuff.

———

The Babe's "home-run valet directed the wrong bats to the big slugger"? This sounds made up, but who cares?

RUTH'S HOME-RUN BATS FAIL TO ARRIVE IN JACKSONVILLE (MAR. 13, 1920)

Serious Blunder of Valet; Noted Slugger Fears He Will Be Handicapped in Opening Game Against Dodgers This Afternoon

JACKSONVILLE, MARCH 12—A horrible error by Mr. Babe Ruth's bat valet in Boston came to light this afternoon. It was one of those inexplicable lapses in a usually most intelligent fellow, and it grieves Mr. Ruth a heap.

Mr. Ruth had wired to his bat valet to express him at once his entire wardrobe of bats, including his full-dress and tuxedo bats, and the cut-away bat. Mr. Ruth had been around here for a couple of weeks trying to wear strange bats two and three sizes too small for him, and wholly unsuited to this climate, and as a result he could not even fit himself to the curves of a right-hand recruit.

It was a situation wholly foreign, and highly distressing to Mr. Ruth. The very largest bat Harbinger M. Huggins could find in the Yankee closet was much too small for Mr. Ruth. They loaned him one of Frank Baker's old bats, but Mr. Ruth was so uncomfortable and ill-at-ease in it that once he absently stuck it in his mouth and tried to inhale it, as it is about the same size as the cigars Mr. Ruth smokes.

Bat Valet Blunders

Last night, however, there arrived at the Hotel Burbridge, fresh from Boston, a bundle consigned to Mr. Ruth—and Mr. Ruth slumbered happily, dreaming of how he was going to look on the morrow with his good, old stylish bats.

The excruciating blunder of the bat valet did not become known until this afternoon when Mr. Ruth opened the package, and tried on a bat in the first full nine-inning game of the incumbent season between the Haig and Haigs.

These are the Yank regular and recruit ball clubs, Ruth being a member of the former, of course. Mr. Ruth is nothing if not regular.

The first bat Mr. Ruth tried on today proved to be a high-fly bat. He hastily donned another, and this one proved to be a higher-fly bat. Mr. Ruth made an examination of his walloping wardrobe, and the horrible mistake of the bat valet came to light. The poor simp had left out the home-run bat. He had stuck in the grounder pajamas and the long-foul waistcoats, but he certainly omitted the four-ply flogger.

It was indeed a disgusting situation for Mr. Ruth, the beau batsman of the world. Four times up today and nothing to wear but those high-fly bats and one ridiculous sacrifice-fly hickory. No wonder Mr. Ruth is clothed this evening in chagrin.

The Yanks meet your Uncle Wilbert Robinson's Brooklyn Dodgers in the first game of their spring series tomorrow, and Mr. Ruth says he'll put on a telegraph pole if he can find nothing else.

Harbinger M. Huggins did not insist on the kiddoes spotting the old boys any first baseman or other impediments today, so the young squirts won their third game in four by a score of 8 to 3. Bob Meusel was back at first for the youngsters, with Biemiller on second, Rice at short and Ward at third, and that combination could win a pennant in almost any league, especially the League of Nations or the Epworth.

Shore and Quinn in Box

(Ernie) Shore and (Jack) Quinn pitched for the regs and (Herb) Thormahlen and (Bob) Shawkey for the kids. Frank O'Dowd got three hits, among other things. The kids scored five runs off Shore in four frames, and a pleasant time was had by one and all in giving Joe Kelley's decisions the old cantaloupe.

A fellow arrived there today from Winston-Salem, the double-jointed town in North Carolina, where the Yanks and Dodgers are to commit an exhibition en route home, and he had news of great importance. He says they are going to lock up the town for the day—and even the Reynolds' tobacco factory, with its 16,000 employees, will be closed to give the boys a chance to go to the ballgame.

Harry Sparrow, the business manager of the Yanks, could have kissed the messenger on receipt of these tidings. Harry boxes at

Winston-Salem, for a guarantee, with a privilege. It is ever Mr. Sparrow's dream of some day having the privilege of taking advantage of privilege down in the junipers.

Winston-Salem is Ernie Shore's home town, and much of the to-do is on account of Ernie. In fact, they are calling the day "Shore Day," and it is going to be a large day, Shore enough. There will be shore dinners, and after the pastime, the hands will doubtless be given shore leave.

Shore, by the way, looks very well indeed this spring, and more like the late (boxer) Jess Willard every day. It is to be hoped, however, that he can pitch better than Jess can fight. In his last argument, Jess was more of a catcher than anything else.

(The imposing 6'4" and 220-pound right-hander, Ernie Shore, would make the Yankee team, but win only two games — never regaining the form that he had him a Red Sox mainstay and a three-time World Series winner. A look at his stats suggests he had been overworked and probably injured permanently in four years with Boston. After 1920, he'd never again pitch in the major leagues.)

———

The Yankee trip to the Palm Beach Country Club to play the Reds before the kind of crowd not usually seen at the Polo Grounds was wonderful fodder for Runyon—and with Ruth starring, just the kind of publicity the Yanks needed to build interest back north.

BABE RUTH STARTS BATTING RALLY THAT WINS FOR YANKEES (MAR. 18, 1920)
Champion Reds Lose by 7 to 3; Two-Bagger in Eighth That Nearly Breaks Daubert's Legs Paves Way to an Easy Victory
PALM BEACH, FLA., MARCH 17—Totally surrounded by billionaires, Mr. Babe Ruth felt more at home here this afternoon than at any time since he joined the Yankees. It was an atmosphere to

which his price tag has accustomed him. He realized that he cost almost as much as a white chip at Bradley's, or one of the Pomeranians in the arms of a lady fan.

Wherefore Mr. Ruth made a noise like real money. He broke a baseball game between the Yankees and the Cincinnati Reds, and at the same time almost broke up two legs for Jake Daubert, the vintage first baseman of the Reds. In the eighth inning, with the score a tie, (Wally) Pipp doubled to center, and Ruth then bounced the ball off Jake's creaking shins with terrible violence.

Before Jake could get his shin readjusted, and retrieve the ball, Pipp has scored, and Ruth was raising a cloud of vulgar dust from around second over the elite of these premises.

Babe Ruth Fans

This incident started a flurry of run making on the part of the Yanks, and the game wound up 7 to 3 in their favor. It gave the Yanks two out of three games (against the Reds).

Prior to the eighth, however, Ruth's manifestations caused a lifting of the winter resort brows, which are already the highest brows south of Boston. He was called out on strikes on his first appearance at the plate, after receiving what you might call a salve of applause due anyone or anything that cost as much as Mr. Ruth.

(Umpire) William Dinneen did the calling in a suave tone and Mr. Ruth gave him one of those looks. On his two succeeding appearances, Babe was thrown out on easy rollers, which caused one of the fashionable spectators to murmur in polite tones: "He ain't worth the money."

When he finally broke up the game, however, he went back to par. The billionaires realized that a man who can half-kill the opposition is of no little value, even though he picks out old ballplayers like (35-year-old) Jack Daubert for the slaughter. If you could wear a $137,500 ballplayer on your neck like a lavaliere, Babe would undoubtedly be bid in one of the locals before morning.

Much high-class stuff came off here today, even though it

wasn't in the baseball that was played by the Reds and the Yanks. This was the first-ever big-league game played ever played here according to the oldest inhabitants.

Good Old Summertime

The field where the game was played was surrounded by waving palms and much climate. It was weather such as you think of when you read the society journals about the "goings on" in the far south. It was so warm that we hate to tell you about it for fear you may become imbued with murderous envy.

The diamond was a sweep of grass lawn tinted by the sparkle of the sun. Not far away, the green-blue waters of the Atlantic licked lazily at the warm sand. And so forth. And all that sort of thing.

The audience was fashionable, exclusive, rich, and no doubt intelligent. You couldn't tell exactly. The beauty and luxury of the season were marred only by the action of Wild Will Phelon, the raving Cincinnatiac, in removing his coat and exposing his suspenders. They didn't fit in with the palm trees and green grass, and all that dough.

All the Bills were present, of course. So was (Yankee official) Will N. Fleischmann, of the exclusive Roaring '40s set. Will sat with E.R. Bradley and rooted for the Yanks, while Mr. Bradley cheered for Cincinnati. This Will had much the best of Mr. Bradley on the ball game, but afterward Will went over to Mr. Bradley's well-known club, and late reports seemed to offset the advantage. Everything evens up in the long run in this life.

Harry Sparrow contributed the Yanks' social tone to the occasion by chartering a deep, seagoing wheelchair, and getting himself rolled out to the ballgame. This was one of the most impressive scenes ever presented on a spring-training trip. Everybody bowed to Mr. Sparrow en route, thinking he must have money.

Battle of Southpaws

At the ballgame, Mr. Sparrow collected $1,264 as his bit on the pastime. It was almost sufficient to pay Ruth's café checks had there been any café checks of Mr. Ruth's for Mr. Sparrow to pay. The Reds got the same amount.

The American Legion, which staged the game, and which collected an admission fee by tagging the people with St. Patrick's Day tags, got $843.

George Mogridge and Rube Bressler gave a left-handed aspect to the opening proceedings. Heine Groh and Larry Kopf were both out of the Reds' line-up, but that made the Yanks' victory nonetheless decisive.

They got two runs in the first on Fewster's double, Peck's single, Pipp's sacrifice and Ward's smash down the third-base line. It was in this inning that Ruth was called out by the thoughtless William Dinneen.

Bressler's double in the fifth, Rath's sacrifice and Daubert's double gave the Reds a run. Rath's single, Daubert's double and Roush's out produced the tying marker in the seventh.

Young "Rip" Collins, the Texas "steer," was pitching for the Yanks at the time, and he was pretty wild, although he had plenty on the ball when he got it over.

(Reds' manager) Pat Moran put in Linwood Smith to succeed Bressler, Linwood Smith being not a typewriter, not a shotgun, but a right-handed hurler, and it was off Linwood that the Yanks did their heavy scoring in the eighth. After the doubles by Pipp and Ruth, Ward sacrificed Ruth to third, and Vick scored him with a single.

Roush's Error Costly

A single by Bodie off Rapp's shins, and a single by (Muddy) Ruel through both Rapp and Crane scored Vick. The Yanks were not hitting Linwood as much as they were hitting the infielders. Roush muffed Fewster's fly and Bodie and Ruel scored. Fewster pulled a delayed steal, but Peck was an easy out.

The Reds stole several of these bases, which no longer count in the box score during the ninth inning. Collins was taking a windup and letting them steal. It is a lot of work for nothing under the new rules.

After the game, the boys went over and sat under the trees in front of the hotel and felt rich. It was pleasant function in every respect, and Colonel Tillinghast L'Hommedieu Huston, vice president of the Yankees, was so pleasured up that he is now thinking of moving the club over here to train next season.

(In fact, the club did not move to Palm Beach the following season, nor would visit the town again for decades after Ruppert and Huston received reports of the Yankees' and Reds' wild night out on the town in which Ping Bodie fell into the ocean and Runyon purchased a baby alligator he would named Aloysius. Tales of Aloysius would emerge in the coming weeks.)

—

Babe Ruth Drives Ball So Far it Cannot Be Found (Mar. 20, 1920)

Clean Hit of Nearly 500 Feet; Sphere Clears Center-field Fence and May Have Been Lost in the St. John River at Jacksonville

JACKSONVILLE, MARCH 19—At 6:30 P.M. tonight no word had been received from Samivel Newhall Crane, the dean of the press corps, who set out at 3 o'clock this afternoon to pace off the length of a hit made by Babe Ruth in batting practice.

The last seen of Mr. Crane, he was swimming down the St. John River in pursuit of a bootlegger's barge on the chance that the baseball might have landed in the boat and was being carried to some remote port. Searching parties are being organized to put forth at dawn in the hope of finding Mr. Crane or the bootlegger's cargo.

Ruth hit the ball over the centerfield fence at the Yankees' training yard in South Jacksonville. Yes, sir, clean, over, right over. My what a swat it was. My! My! My! My! My! My! My! My! My! My! My! My! My! My! My! My! My! Plumb over.

"Get a tape!" screamed Harry Sparrow, business manager of the Yanks, with rare presence of mind, while everyone else was staring in dumb amazement. "We've got to get this in the papers."

Measuring Off Distance

Phil Schanck, the Yankee groundskeeper, rushed forward with a measuring line, which he fortuitously carried in his vest pocket for just such an occasion, and started to measure the length of the blow. But in the meantime, Samivel Newhall Crane and J. William MacBeth of the *Morning-Sun* had arrived in the scene as a committee representing the Baseball Writers' Association of America and the Postal and Western Union Telegraph companies.

They set out side-by-side to pace all the distance from the point where Ruth had first cocked his bat to that spot somewhere off in the dim distance beyond the wall, where the ball had presumably landed. No one actually saw it land, but following the lines of old Doc Newton's theories with reference to the laws of gravity, it was believed that the ball had eventually landed all right although Ruth himself was by no means convinced on that point.

"Don't lose an inch," implored Harry Sparrow anxiously as the dauntless pair set forth. "Let Sam do most of the pacing, Mac, as his legs have got more length in them than yours."

So they marched away and presently they were merely specks against the far horizon of the centerfield while Phil Schenck followed with the slower tape. An admiring babble came from the Yanks as they halted their practice for the day to watch the adventurers.

Mario De Vitalis, the young Jerseysite who was doing the practice pitching when Ruth hit the ball, gazed at the great slugger with doubt in his eyes. Mario had plainly seen the ball as it left his hand traversing toward Ruth and then suddenly he saw it no more.

It was in Mario's mind that perhaps Ruth might have caught it and stuck it in his pocket just to baffle the rising young pitcher, but this suspicion was most unjust.

Long Way to Fence

At 4 o'clock, J. William MacBeth was seen falling in his tracks from sheer exhaustion. He had gone as far as he could, and could go no further. An expedition was sent to bring him in and they reported that Samivel Newhall Crane was still marching doggedly across the stilly wastes of centerfield grass toward the fence.

Half-an-hour later, the form of Mr. Crane was silhouetted against the distant skyline as he topped the fence and dropped on the other side.

Phil Schenck came in shortly afterward and reported that it was 428 feet to the fence by his tapeline and Mr. Crane's left foot, and that 50 feet beyond the fence they had discovered a suspicious-looking hole in the ground, which had been dug either by a base-ball or a ground squirrel. It was Mr. Schenck's belief that the ball had alighted there and then scuttled on into the grass, seeking shelter.

Unlike a quail or a grouse, however, a baseball gives off little scent, and Mr. Schenck said he had been unable to find the ball, but that Samivel Newhall Crane was beating the cover toward the river, confident that the pill could not escape him.

The additional 50 feet beyond the fence added to the 428 feet already discovered by Schenck gave the blow a total length of 478 feet from tip to tip.

"If I'd got a good hold on that ball, I'd a sure knocked it good and far," commented Ruth when he heard the report. "I hit it too near the handle."

"How much do you think this will get in the newspapers?" asked Harry Sparrow anxiously. "Get these figures right and don't lose an inch."

Some Comparisons

It is something like 365 feet from the fence to the centerfield bleacher wall at the Polo Grounds as the crow flies. Ruth's hit today would have cleared the bleachers, crossed the Harlem River, gone up through the Bronx an circled over Grant's Tomb.

Two punches such as this placed end-to-end would reach from Montreal, Canada to (newspaper cartoonist) Tad Dorgan's house in Great Neck.

It was certainly quite a paste and it is a good thing for us it happened because otherwise there would have been nothing for us to write about today, what with there being nothing but perfunctory practice hereabouts.

Some say the lick is a record but that does not bring Samivel Newhall Crane back to our waiting midst any sooner. Harry Sparrow is particularly worried for fear Mr. Crane may not get back in time for next Monday's edition. If this news doesn't get in the paper, Harry Sparrow is going to be a much disappointed man because it is what everybody has been waiting for Ruth to do for several weeks.

Late tonight, Colonel Tillinghast L'Hommedieu Huston, vice-president of the Yankees, had sent for an expert accountant and the sheriff. He wants the sheriff to locate Sam and he wants the expert to tell him where he stands on the following proposition and problem.

Proposition:
A—Babe Ruth costs $137,500.
B—Springtime hits over the centerfield fence are worth 30 cents a bushel.

Problem::
How far is it to the principal and interest?

—

Fewster's Condition Serious; Accident May Affect Brain (Mar. 26, 1920)

JACKSONVILLE, MARCH 25 — Wilson Fewster, the Yankees' young infielder, will be out of the game for some time as a result of the blow on the head received by one of Jeff Pfeffer's fast-pitched balls in the game here today.

Dr. J.B. Black considered his condition so serious that he called Dr. Frederick Bowen, a specialist, in consultation late tonight. The medical men decided that, while there were symptoms of hemorrhages, there is nothing really alarming just at present.

"Chick" is conscious, but can't talk. He was hit just above and back of the ear. There is no fracture and, unless it turns out that the brain is injured, he should recover rapidly. The Yankees are all anxiously awaiting the doctor's decision tomorrow.

———

By "slider," Runyon isn't referring to the modern-day pitch, but a welt from sliding into base.

BABE RUTH LEARNING HOW TO PLACE HIS HARD WALLOPS (MAR. 31, 1920)

Slugger Shortens Punches; Beat Reds Twice with Two-Baggers; "Slider" Keeps Big Swatter out of Practice for First Time

JACKSONVILLE, MARCH 30—A "slider" may or may not be news. It is largely a matter of geography. It depends on the location of the "slider." For instance, a "slider" on the person of George W. Hoosis, the well-known average citizen, would scarcely be worthy of comment.

He already has so many other "sliders" in the way of income taxes and rent, and what-not, that another more or less would make no difference.

A "slider" adjacent the hip pocket of Herbert Hoover or Leonard Wood, might be considered a topic for a column in these days of anatomical investigation and discussion of presidential candidates, yet it would hardly justify a position in the paper next to pure reading matter.

Located a point and a half south of the King of England's coat tails, a "slider" might conceivably achieve attention in *The London Times*. Situated one degree west of J. Pierpont Morgan's rear suspender buttons, it would have certain effect on the stock market, but even so a "slider" would not be worth more than an editorial.

Definition of "Slider"

When the "slider" pitches itself upon such as Babe Ruth, however, the proposition takes on the aspect of vast importance. It is something to talk about. It is worthy of intimate discussion. Babe Ruth has a "slider." Hence these words.

A "slider" is a devilish contrivance, which is the result of sliding. It is almost exclusively a masculine affectation. We have seldom, if ever, heard a lady speak of having a "slider."

A man hurls himself at a nearby base, striking the ground with great concussion, and a segment of his epidermis is lifted, unveiling the red flesh underneath. Vulgarly, the process is known as being "skunup." Generally, it takes place in the vicinity of the vestibule. Presently, a scab forms over the divested region, and this is a "slider."

It is at once painful, and annoying. If a man skids again, the scab is apt to be creased, and unless the flesh is extremely fertile, it takes some time to replenish the goose pimples.

Babe slipped out from under $64.45 worth of cuticle the other day while hurling the entire $137,500 worth of himself at a base, and as a result he was unable to practice this morning.

It was the first practice he has missed, but he will not be away long. A "slider" that would keep you walking knock-kneed for a month cannot upset the curriculum of Ruth.

One thing about the great swatter, he has been one of the most earnest laborers in the vineyard of M. Huggins over in South Jax since the beginning of the spring training.

Paves Way to Victory

We violate no confidence when we tell you that this fellow can hit. If winning the 1920 pennant were contingent on Babe busting the ball up around .335, it would be all over but finding out how Abe Attell is betting in the World's Series.

In the game against the Reds here yesterday, and in the game against the same club at Palm Beach, it was Ruth who started the Yanks to victory with his smashes. He has hit many a ball this spring that would have gone into the stands at the Polo Grounds, or into home-run territory on almost any other big-league grounds.

The Yanks' training field is extremely large, and the outfielders play back almost to the walls for Ruth. As a result and as an indication that he is anything but a "sucker" hitter, Babe has shortened up his punches, and is trying to place the ball.

Both of his blows that beat the Reds were two-baggers. He has not lessened the force behind his drives, but he is not trying to knock the ball over the wall. He has hit both right- and lefthanders. Like every great hitter, he is apt to look almost foolish when he misses a swing, but after striking out he is apt to come back and break up the game in the same sort of pitch that fanned him.

It is our opinion that Ruth looks immense. There is no question about his hitting. We are not saying he will be a great centerfielder. In fact, it may finally develop that he can do better in some other district.

He did not get one fly yesterday that a faster man might have gathered in, but the field underfoot at the South Jax grounds is heavy. None of the outfielders were doing any too well with fly balls. But Babe will hit. You can bet on that.

———

As the Yankees prepared to break camp and head north by train, playing games against the Dodgers along the way, Runyon introduces his readers to the life and times of his new pet, a baby alligator, Aloysius—named in part for his friend, cartoonist Tad Dorgan.

YANKEES AND DODGERS TO LEAVE JACKSONVILLE FOR NORTH (APR. 5, 1920)
Meusel's Swatting Pleasing; Californian Sure of Regular Berth; If Baker Returns, Recruit Will Be Shifted to Right Field

JACKSONSVILLE, APRIL 4—The great Robinson–Huggins three-ring circus moved out of winter quarters tonight with all the animals and performers in good condition except little Aloysius Dorgan, the baby alligator.

Little Aloysius joined the show yesterday in the best of health and spirits. Out this morning, the infamous Yankee jinx overtook him. He was playing among some toothbrushes and shaving utensils on a bureau, and in his childish glee, he ventured too near the edge. He slipped and fell to the floor and was knocked stiffer than a poker.

When he regained consciousness, little Aloysius was at first highly indignant, as he thought one had pushed him out of a three-story window. He is resting easily tonight in the wash basin in Colonel Tillinghast Houston's drawing room, but is still very low in his mind. The rumor that little Aloysius attempted suicide on learning that he had to travel not only with the Yankees, but with the Brooklyn Dodgers, too, is without foundation.

Little Aloysius is now about six months old and displays such great intelligence that it is predicted he will grow into a very fine valise, or hang bag, if not a suitcase. He is descended from one of the oldest alligator families in Florida. His grandfather, Elmer, is over two-hundred years of age, and well remembers when Sam Crane played in the league.

In Columbia Today

A stop will be made at Columbia, South Carolina, tomorrow to get a fresh consignment of malted milk for little Aloysius, and incidentally to enable the Yankee and the Dodgers to put on their first open-air performance.

There are about 75 members of the Robinson-Huggins troupe and they are traveling in three private Pullmans. At least they are as private as Pullmans can be, which is about as private as a post office, what with the floating Democrats of the solid South passing through at intervals paging the dining car.

Babe Ruth, the ferocious curve killer, is located in two lowers, one for each half of him. Doc Woods, the trainer, has personal charge of Babe's Terrible 54-ounce bludgeon, and Harry Sparrow stands guard to keep the insurance agents from pestering the great slugger.

"Rip" Collins, the untamed Texas steer, is confined to an upper. His wide-brimmed George Pattulo, or sombrero, fell off a hook as the train was pulling out tonight, and almost brained Sam Vick, the famous Boscoe of the Yanks, who eats beefsteaks alive.

"Ah despise civilization," says Rip.

Robbie Reduces to Ton

Your Uncle Wilbert Robinson is in personal charge of the cages in his section of the train. Your Uncle Wilbert Robinson has trained down to a ton this spring.

Hennery O'Day, the iron umpire, is on the train wearing his well-known countenance. Little Aloysius, the baby alligator, trembled like a leaf when the Hennery passed his wash basin, for the fame of Hennery extends even unto the alligator incubators of Florida. It is the first time the Yanks have ever been so closely associated with Hennery, and they too, were a bit restless for a while.

With Bill Dinneen, representing the gesticulatory authority, and dignity of the American League, Hennery will adjudicate the games among the Yankees and the Dodgers. The iron umpire has never before been personally exhibited on the Juniper wheel of baseball. It will be a rare treat for the inmates. Once seen, Hennery is never forgotten.

Harry Sparrow was not feeling chipper last winter when he laid out the coming tour, and he displayed little or no facility or ingenuity in finding new towns. He merely closed his eyes and stabbed a finger into a map, and every place the finger lit, he booked a game.

However, he fell out of the beaten track only in a couple of spots. The route is well-nigh prosaic. Hapgood of the Braves, or Bancroft of the Reds, could have found at least 10 or 15 places twice as uncomfortable as the points Sparrow has booked. It is feared that Harry is losing his cunning. The trip promises to be almost pleasant.

Huggins will use about the same line-up on his journey north as he has presented the last few days. He will continue exhibiting Long Bob Meusel at third base, and if Bob keeps plucking the ball as he has lately, he may man the petulant post all season.

Meusel Hitting Hard

However, we still present as our one best bet, the return of J. Franklin Baker. Huggins wants to shift Meusel to right field. The Californian has developed more hitting ability than (Sammy) Vick or (Frank) Gleich. With Baker back at third and Meusel in right, Huggins is our belief that Baker will be induced to return.

Huggins finally took the blankets off Hoffman, his third catcher, yesterday. The young man displayed a lot of ability, and opened a can of sprightly conversation that seemed well-nigh unconventional coming from a Yankee lineup.

"They're half-gone," was Hoffman's comforting comments to Bob Shawkey and Ernie Shore when one Dodger was put out.

Added to Hoffman's chatter was a line of verbiage from Meusel at third and Ward at second that didn't sound much like the old Yanks. Conversation doesn't win pennants, to be sure, but it keeps the baseball players from going to sleep.

GROUND RULE ROBS RUTH OF LONGEST HOMER; YANKS WIN, 3–0 (APR. 9, 1920)
Wallop Is Scored 2-Bagger; Ball Would Have Cleared the Centerfield Seats at Polo Grounds, Says Damon Runyon

WINSTON-SALEM, N.C., APRIL 8—Babe Ruth today hit a baseball 850 feet. If any of these other baseball chroniclers who are going to tell you about the matter can beat that statement, why let 'em? That's all. Just let 'em.

Down at Jacksonville, when Babe hit a pill over the centerfield wall of the Yanks' training camp, we said it traveled a distance of 475 feet. We figured that the record for the Brown Derby, with something to square, but what was our great mortification and chagrin on reading the New York papers to learn that no less than three of our fellow historians had beaten us by four inches.

This time, after secretly ascertaining their mental measurements of the blow, we are confident that our 850 feet will be at least a length-and-a-half ahead of the next-best try. Anyway, we tacked on the extra 50 feet to make it doubly sure. It is in winning the game for the Yankees by a score of 3 to 0.

Across a Racetrack

Babe hit the ball across a half-mile racetrack. We might have said he hit it around the racetrack, but we want to be conservative. The incident occurred in the sixth inning of the 12th game between the Yankees and the Dodgers, and assisted in winning the game for the Yankees by a score of 3 to 0.

The ball was delivered by a lefthander named Conlon, who was delivered by your Uncle Tim L. Huston, vice-president of the Yanks. Your Uncle Wilbert is a kindly soul, and he just couldn't bear gazing at the Colonel's map any longer. So he put in Conlon to pitch against the Yanks.

He first tried young John Miljas with the best intentions in the world, but John wheeled springtime curves at the Yanks with such abandon that your Uncle Wilbert's kindness was frustrated. Conlon saved your Uncle Wilbert' great heart from breaking.

Conlon is about the size of Jimmy Wilde, and weighs little more than the bat of Babe Ruth waved at him in the sixth after Peckinpaugh had doubled and Pipp had sacrificed. The home plate was located, appropriately enough, in the home stretch, and Babe hit the ball from there over into the track on the other side.

On the Polo Grounds, the ball would have landed in groundskeeper Hennery Fabian's backyard, behind the centerfield bleachers, or thereabouts. It was longer than a peace treaty; it carried longer than Al Mamaux's singing voice. If you don't think this is far, ask the top-floor tenants when Al is singing in a hotel lobby.

Counts as Two-Bagger

The field was surrounded by folks who had turned out to honor Ernie Shore of Yadkin County, North Carolina, which is hard by Winston-Salem. A ground rule had been applied that when a ball was hit into the crowd, it only went for two bases. This ball did not go into the crowd.

It went away beyond it. Some think it even passed the boundaries of population in this state, but when Ruth plodded on past second base, umpire (Bill) Dinneen called him back. He said it was just a two-bagger. He admitted that it was perhaps the longest two-bagger in the world, but he held to the theory that it was nonetheless a two-bagger.

Ruth collected himself around Dinneen and pleaded at the top of his voice, for his rights. Will was obdurate; he hated to seem small and petty about such a matter, but he said a rule is a rule. A rule is made to be enforced, said Will, although he did not necessarily have in mind the new pitching rules. As near as can determined at this stage of the proceedings, these rules were made just for instance.

Ruth finally got home on Duffy Lewis's single, and Lewis eventually reported on Hoffman's double, but Babe never quite got over that squeezing up of his punch. Afterward, little Conlon struck him out while Babe was still brooding over his wrongs. Conlon may yet prove another Dick Kerr.

This day was called "Ernie Shore Day" in Winston Salem, and the town closed up so all hands could see the game. Ernie's pa, who is bigger than Ernie, came over with a big Yadkin County delegation, bringing a bucket of Yadkin County soil, with which the pitching mound was fertilized for Ernie's feet.

It was poetic sentiment to have Ernie's No. 14's planted in the old home dirt, barring the danger that he might root and sprout there. A lot of soil indigenous to Winston Salem blew up in a windstorm during the afternoon and frescoed the other players, who did not see the romance of it.

Ernie worked five innings, and was so inspired by his surroundings that the Dodgers were unable to score off him. They have been unable to score off him in the entire series; in fact, Ernie looks very well indeed this spring. His "sinker" ball needs only the coffee habitually associated with "sinkers" to make it a thing of beauty and a joy forever.

Visitors Entertained

About 4,000 people were parked in the grandstand, and around the diamond. The game was presented by Robert Dull, a local newspaperman, and all Winston-Salem helped him make it a success. This is one of the liveliest towns in all the Southland, and the visitors were taken in hand and royally entertained.

Major Frank C. Page, formerly of the Aviation Corps, and son of the late Walter Page, Ambassador to England, is running the *Winston-Salem Journal* and he looked after the newspapermen with the Yanks and Dodgers. A luncheon at the Country Club today, and a dinner tonight were among the festivities.

"Andy" Anderson, the old Federal League and Giant pitcher, who is now practicing dentistry here, bobbed up as a member of the committee in entertainment. The great tobacco factory was closed for the afternoon so the thousands of employees could see the game, and they were apparently all present.

—

YANKS AND BROOKLYNS COME HOME TODAY TO FINISH SERIES (APR. 10, 1920)

Dodgers Beaten; Score 5–2; Huggins Uses O'Doul in the Box; Triples by Ruth and Lewis and Homer by Pratt Win

LYNCHBURG, VA., APRIL 9—This was the last stop out of the Grand Central in the Pullman peregrinations of the Robinson-Huggins barnstormers. They arrive in New York tomorrow morning. A shipwrecked mariner afloat on an empty oil can could be more pleasured up over the sight of a rescuing canoe than the Yankees and the Dodgers over the idea of seeing Manhattan Island. Yi, cowboy!

They have traveled much. They have passed through the dangers of the cafeteria belt and have been mistreated by the ferocious tonsorialists of the tall junipers who lurk behind their painted poles to give the unwary sappyolas from the large cities those high-tide hair cuts.

They have lived for some night in dimly lighted kip-cars and have had to learn to tell a pair of openers by the feel. It has been a terrible experience, but now it is about over, and tonight the sentiment of the party is reflected by that tuneful voice of (Dodgers' pitcher) Al Mamaux, the singing kid, as it resounds along the right of way in melody.

"Rip" Collins Morose

Just two members of the big party failed to find exhilaration on the thought that they will soon be in the big town. Back in a remote corner of the good car, Fairbrook, "Rip" Collins, the detective from the perilous Big Bend district of the Lone Star State, morosely polishes up his wide-brimmed George Battulo or sombrero, and mutters: "Ah despise civilization."

Little Aloysius Dorgan, the child alligator, sniffs the changing breezes with dire forebodings and draws further back into his refuge in Colonel Tillinghast L. Huston's wash basin. The Colonel inadvertently washed his hands in the basin this morning while little Aloysius was present and the brand of soap used by the good Colonel made Aloysius ill.

Little Aloysius wishes most fervently that he was back in Florida, the land of eternal sunshine and Canadian Club at $12 per quart. This morning when he opened his eyes on the proud old soil of Virginia, it seemed to be snowing exteriorly; and little Aloysius felt that it was no place for him.

M. Huggins and your Uncle Wilbert Robinson felt that it was no place for them either, and they tried to call off the game scheduled for these parts. The local promoters couldn't hear a word they said, however, and late M. Huggins and your Uncle Wilbert were glad of it. The weather cleared, the sun came out, and they parked a pastime at the Lynchburg Race Track under the most salubrious climatic conditions yet encountered.

Chance to Tie Series

The Yanks win this game. The score was 5 to 2. M. Huggins's outfit has now taken five out of 13. They still have a chance to tie the series, beginning tomorrow afternoon at Flatbush.

M. Huggins started Frank O'Doul out on his career as a left-handed pitcher today, after weeks of thought on Frank's case with reference to the outfield. Frank was originally purchased as a pitcher, but his hitting manifestations became so violent that he was spoken of as an outfielder.

Some folk have gone so far as to pronounce Frank another Ty Cobb. That was when he seemed to be an outfielder. Now that he is a left-handed pitcher, he will have to be pronounced a second somebody-else. It was the first time he ever pitched for the Yankees and after he got himself heated up, he did very well.

The Dodgers belted him for two runs in the first frame, and thereafter were unable to score. Triples by Babe Ruth and Duffy Lewis in the third assisted the Yanks in front. The boys were playing on the infield of a racetrack and there was so much territory behind the outfielders that Babe couldn't shove the ball over their heads.

He hit one across the track in practice, but when the game started (Dodger outfielders) little (5'7" Bernie) Neis, Hi Myers and Wallace Hood mounted their horses and rode so far back when Babe came up to bat that they could barely be discerned with the naked eye. Del Pratt whacked a homer in the third, and finished under whip and spur.

All this hitting was off Jeff Pfeiffer, who was subsequently relieved by Rube Marquard. O'Doul pitched five innings during which he lived up to the Ty Cobb part of his reputation by getting a couple of hits, and Bob McGraw, the Pearl of Pueblo, finished up.

Fewster Improving

Word from (Chick) Fewster (who was seriously beaned March 25) is that he has recovered the power of speech and is improving right along. No news has been received of Ward, who was sent to New York, but Huggins expects to start the season with the youngster at second.

The Yanks have been training five weeks. Some of the players do not seem to be in exactly the condition that five weeks' work justifies, but in the main the club looks well. It has commenced to hit. The strength of this club must be its hitting, and it seems to be arriving at the top of that strength.

Huggins will show the New York fans one real good new hitter in Meusel. He may not be the fanciest third baseman you ever saw, but he can hit. And Babe Ruth now appears to be have attained the slugging form that has made him the batting sensation of the age.

(Frank O'Doul's big-league career was brief: 11 games and no record with the Yankees, before being traded to the Red Sox and pitching all of one year, and compiling a 1-1 record. The prognosis for Chick Fewster wasn't as rosy as Runyon predicted; the young second baseman would never fulfill the promise Huggins saw in him, and go on to be a utility player for several teams. Meantime, Ruth and the '20 Yanks would win 95 games, sticking in the A.L. pennant race until mid-September, and finish third behind Cleveland and Chicago. Ruth's 54 home runs would break his own big-league record by 25, and help the Yanks become the first big-league team to draw more than 1 million at home.)

6 Around the World

1914 around-the-world tour

With the world on the cusp of a global war—not to mention the beginning of the spring training—Runyon was dispatched in mid-February 1914 to Paris and London, where he caught up with the end of an around-the-world tour by the New York Giants and Chicago White Sox.

TOURISTS INVADE PARIS WITH PROFIT OF $75,000 (FEB. 18, 1914)

PARIS—Covered to all over with foreign labels and all chattering away like Baedekers, the Giants–White Sox party of sixty-seven—count 'em yourself—breezed into this sedate little village tonight with the firm and determined intention of playing a five nights' stand.

This is quite a condescension to the residents of this somnolent city, but duty is duty all over the world, so nothing is going to stand in the way of this formally scheduled five-night stand.

Slightly in the rear of the advance guard, but losing nothing by his slow progress, came one gentleman known the world over as H. Arry Sparrow, Jawn McGraw's traveling audience, and also first member of Jawn's kitchen cabinet. H. Arry was puffing under an attack of la grippe and excess baggage of $75,000, representing the profits of the trip to date.

Mons. McGraw was here in advance of the party, and in his entourage was little Tad Sloane, who rode the gallant steed in the days before Charles E. Hughes started something, and Sammy Nicklin Strang, who is over here with the intention of making Caruso look like a movie picture tenor. Needless to mention, Jawn has by force compelled Sammy to entertain him during his stay on the Seine.

Charles Comiskey, who owns the White Sox among other things, is also among those present, feeling much improved, but still a sick man, thank you. The "Old Roman" is going to stick around and will make the return trip with the bunch.

George Kessler, who believes firmly in champagne (as he sells it for a living), is going to entertain the bunch during the stay, feeding them regular food with the bubbles on the side. He also is framing up several sightseeing trips, of which we may speak later. The regular dinners will strike Mike Donlin as being something "recherché," for it will give the noble Spartan an opportunity to wear his full dress suit, which Michael says, is just like a tuxedo except the coat has long tails. These events will never be forgotten by Michael, believe me.

Jim Thorpe, the bosom friend of the King of Sweden, had a great exhibition of throwing the javelin at Nice yesterday. Now that he has reached this spot, Jimes will give the citizens a chance to watch him toss the bull.

McGraw says Thorpe has developed into a corking player, both from a hitting standpoint as well as fielding. Jawn says (Bob) Bescher or anybody will have a hard time beating (Fred) Snodgrass, ("Red") Murray and (George) Burns out of their regular job in the outfield at the Polo Grounds, New York, U.S.A. on the Harlem River.

Vive la France!

———

NAPOLEON PAYS VISIT TO TOMB OF BONAPARTE (FEB. 20, 1914)

"Jawn" McGraw Compares His Career with That of the Famous Warrior—"We Both Met Wellington," Says Giant Manager

PARIS, FEB. 19—John J. McGraw, the Little Napoleon of baseball, today paid his respects to the tomb of the man whose name the Giant chief made famous in America, the same being Monsieur Bonaparte, the deceased promoter of the Federal "outlaw" league of his time.

Mr. Bonaparte probably felt highly honored—though he did not say so. After giving the coop where the Great Troublemaker is benched forever the "once over," McGraw said he knows just how the old Nap feels about it all.

"I, too, met the Duke of Wellington," said McGraw, "only his name was Connie Mack instead of Arthur Wellesley."

Jimmy Callahan says it must be great to live where Napoleon does, as the walls are plenty thick enough to keep out the sound of the French language.

Met Mona Lisa

A tour of the city was first made. Automobiles carried the sightseers to every point of interest, including the Louvre, where Joe Benz met Mona Lisa face to face. The crowd then went to George Kessler's magnificent home for dinner.

It was a great day for Bill Klem, the Beau Brummel of the umpires and champion movie film filler. According to the ballplayers, a million feet of film have been taken on the trip and Bill has not missed an inch.

The cameras have been idle since the arrival in Paris, but resumed operations today and Bill immediately went back to work with triple fervor. He played himself across the board in every book—straight, place and show.

Mr. Kessler made a speech of welcome to the noble athletes and their fellow pilgrims. To Little Napoleon fell the honor of a reply, and he acquitted himself as grandly as on the field of battle.

The spirits of the tourists triumphed over a rather melancholy rain, which fell steadily all day.

"Joy Ride" to Japan Impresses World Tourists (Feb. 21, 1914)

Members of Giants-White Sox Bands Vividly Recall That "Pleasant" Sea Journey to Beautiful Land of Nippon; American Ambassador to Paris, Myron Herrick, Gives Afternoon Tea and Reception; Comiskey Is Rapidly Recovering

PARIS, FEB. 20—After infinite labor and overworking all our persuasive powers, the New York American field correspondent has secured an individual and separate interview with each and every member of the Giants–White Sox party regarding the trip around this big world.

The same is hereby presented in composite form to save valuable space, and we guarantee this article to be the first detailed and authentic description of what each member of the party saw or remembered of the foreign lands in which he and they dropped for various space of time.

Now we will begin:

"Well, the boat trip to Japan was something terrible, terrible, terrible. We received a wonderful reception in Nippon, but honestly, the waves we encountered on our trip to Japan were, well, about ten or twenty times as high as the Metropolitan Tower. That's some high.

"Manila is certainly a remarkable spot, but we surely thought we were going to sink along with the ship on our glide over the ocean to Japan. Australia is a big, open-faced country but water that our ship sailed on going to Japan was so rough that Harry Sparrow, leading member of Jawn McGraw's kitchen cabinet, fell and sprained his appetite very badly.

"India is absolutely and irrevocably a quaint land, as you can tell by reading Kipling, but we can never forget that boat trip to Japan.

Italians Inhabit Italy

"Much to our surprise and amazement, when we reached Italy we discovered that the country was heavily populated by Wops (say Italians?), but they—poor but lucky folks!—can never realize the dangers of boating to Japan.

"France is beautiful country barring the Frenchmen, but Bill Klem, that Beau Brummel of an umpire, couldn't eat a mouthful going to Japan, and it certainly causes a ballplayer much anguish when he knows an umpire cannot eat. Yes, it does.

"It's been a wonderful trip, but—phew!—that journey to Japan was something terrible and scandalous."

Myron Herrick, who holds down the position as American Ambassador in this fair town, gave an afternoon tea, a reception and a party at the Embassy today to the mob.

It is my duty to relate that the ballplayers are so accustomed to such functions that it is easiest effort possible for them to drink tea without the aid and assistance of noiseless spoons.

You learn a whole lot circling this little globe of ours.

Party Free of Speeches

Hon. Ambassador Myron Herrick comes from the state of Ohio, noted for Garry Herrmann and many baseball managers, but out of respect to the ambassadorial feelings nothing was said about the Reds during the reception, which was notable and memorable by no speeches rending the atmosphere.

There is great unrest in the Hibernian contingent over the rumor that Fred Merkle, Hans Lobert and other "Germans" had voted to cut out Dublin and descend upon Berlin. Joe Mullins and Father McNamara, of Chicago, favored holding an indignation meeting immediately until they found out that the cruel and baseless scandal was spread by Steve Evans.

Charles A. Comiskey continues to improve and is up and around daily, for this is no town to be sick in. The "Old Roman" plans to go to California, where his team will train, if he can possibly do so.

Jimmy Callahan has received a cablegram from Ed Walsh, the big moist ball deliverer, announcing that he will win fifty out of sixty games this year (he would go 2–3 in 1914). Some of the band think that Edward is somewhat of a Mexican athlete.

Same Lineup for Giants

McGraw intimates that the Giants will start off with the same lineup as last year, unless a few phenoms are developed in the meantime. Larry Doyle, a member of the bridegroom detachment, has received a big offer to join the Kansas City Feds, but Larry only hee-haws, as he has already signed with the Polo

Grounders for three years. Tris Speaker has heard nothing more from the Feds.

The first game in this village will come o' to-morrow, with (Jim) Scott and (Hooks) Wiltse doing the twirling for the Sox and Giants respectively.

James Thorpe, the dear friend of the King of Sweden, will give an exhibition of throwing the discus and javelin. (Boxing manager Daniel) McKettrick (and Runyon's friend) will toss the bull.

PARIS GETS ITS FIRST DOSE OF RAIN CHECKS (FEB. 22, 1914)

Incessant Rain Necessitates Postponement of Game between World Tourists—Players Spend Time in Fanfest and at Fight; Johnson-Moran Fight Comes in for Much Discussion—American Colony in France Believes Moran Will Be Champion

PARIS, FEB. 21—There is gloom in dear old Paris, for the first baseball rain checks ever dished out in old Europe were handed out this afternoon by Harry Sparrow. 'Twas a hard duty for 'Arry to perform, but when in Paris you must do as Polo Grounders do.

A heavy downpour of wet rain caused the postponement, and 'tis said in the States that the same brand of water causes postponements on the other side of the pond.

There was every indication of a big crowd—a mob that would tickle (Polo Grounds concessionaire) Harry Stevens simply to death. The gladiators were gaily attired in their faded star-spangled "My Country 'Tis of Thee" costumes, waiting the order to invade the field, but "Tip" O'Neil took soundings and reported that if there was a bottom to the field he couldn't discover it.

Rather than to cause thousands of Parisians to fight duels and other things it was announced that a game would be played tomorrow if possible.

The battalion will leave France flat on Monday morning and brave the terrors of the Channel to descend upon London.

McAleer Misses Record

The most disappointed member of the bunch was Jim McAleer, who intended to break his record of not having witnessed a game on the trip between the rivals. The players, strange to relate, were not so downcast, as viewing the sights of Paris is very hard on the eyes.

Baseball has received an amazing reception here. All the papers carried columns of stuff, numerous paragraphs, and diagrams explaining the fine points of the game to the proletariat. Reporters and photographers of both the Paris and London papers follow the players liked hardened creditors.

Ted Sullivan gives out an interview every few seconds, and every one is different.

The game tomorrow will be the first big-league exhibition in France since the Spalding tour of 1889, when (former Pennsylvania) Governor (and current baseball executive John) Tener was here. Little did the Governor dream when in this sizzling place that twenty-five years later he would be wrestling with Charles Webb Murphy, of Chicago and other parts, trying to convince the latter that everything was all right but to please take a long vacation.

There are several amateur clubs in Paris through the efforts of Spalding's agents, but their game is not very well understood.

Scores of the members of the American colony gathered at Milton Henry's café and held a fanfest while the drops were pitter-patting on the ground.

Charles McCarthy, the author of the famous $30,000 check for the (Jack) Johnson-Moran fight, a dozen jockeys, horse owners galore and a few expatriates are all touting Moran as the next world's champion on account of the speedy life of the black title-holder. Everybody believes the fight is on the level, but kind of back up on the dough part.

Johnson is now in Scotland living like a king but is sadly yearning for Chicago, a village situated on the Wabash. Henry's is the only place where Johnson is barred from spending money. The players attended the boxing show this evening between Joe Jeannette, of Hoboken, and Alf Langford, a new culled battler, of somewhere.

The game tomorrow will compete with the gee-gees at Auteil. The tourists are in love with Paris and hate to tear away. The condition of the players is remarkable and the players can leave no bad effect on account of long rests between games.

After leaving for America both the Giants and the White Sox will do light training on the *Lusitania*. They need little real work. It is expected that Mike Donlin will sign a contract with McGraw before leaving here.

———

A baseball coach for France? If it were to be anyone, it would be the eccentric "Turkey Mike" Donlin. Psst . . . It didn't happen.

FRENCHMEN OFFER DONLIN POST AS BASEBALL COACH (FEB. 23, 1914)

Gauls Awaken to Possibility of Our National Pastime, Having Read So Much about It. Comiskey Fully Recovered from Recent Illness

PARIS, FEB. 23—All that this staid country of France has learned about American baseball is that the noble representatives of the national pastime of the United States wear moonlight apparel well, and that the players are willing to risk at least one eye on anything.

The Frenchmen, who for the most part make France their habitat, know what is contained in the introductory paragraph because the Giants and White Sox closed their visit here tonight without having played a game, as rain again prevented the pastime today.

The globe-girdling party departs for deah ol' Lunnon, y'know tomorrow morning, leaving grief among the French; also considerable money. A large crowd, including the American Ambassador and other celebrities, gathered on the field this afternoon, expectant of seeing a good old game of baseball as it is played by the leading exponents of the world.

But the rain came down in such gobs that the game was finally called off. The players did not even leave their hotel, as peering through the windows they saw that a game was not even a remote possibility.

Interest in baseball has become so great here that Michael Donlin, pinch swatter extraordinary, has been tendered an offer to return here and organize and coach a team.

The Chicago of Europe

The Chicago wanderers are especially sorry to leave Paris. They say this is the Chicago of Europe. McGraw and Callahan are already talking of their proposed trip to South America next year.

Charles A. Comiskey has fully recovered and is taking interest in life sufficiently to buy a French chapeau.

The Frenchmen could not understand the postponement today. They have been reading up baseball for weeks and were wild to see at least one game. The visit of the Americans proved a big boost for the sport.

Most of the touring party spent the Sabbath at the Louvre, passing judgment on the pictures. "Buck" Weaver, White Sox infielder, reports that they are not up to the standard set by "Bud" Fisher.

Washington's Birthday was celebrated last evening at Milton Henry's café, where the American colony gathered in force. American millionaires, aviators, fighters, managers, actors, jockeys, trainers, ballplayers, bicyclists, artists and writers were among those present. All jammed into a compact room, singing and talking like a Babel.

Players See Prize Fight

The players who attended the Joe Jeannette–Alf Langford fight got the best laugh of the trip so far. Langford (not Sam) proved a huge joke. Bit his awkwardness bothered Jeannette. Alf butted Joe in the first round, opening a gash on the forehead. Finally, in the seventh round, Langford missed a random swing and flopped on his jaw, knocking himself out.

Jeannette was so enraged over the butting incident that he

kicked the unconscious battler on the head, then picked him up and kicked him around the ring.

In the meantime, the referee disqualified Langford for having fallen without being hit. Some decision!

Langford was out for more than an hour. Everyone thought his neck was broken.

Jeannette to Fight Carpentier

Daniel McKettrick, Jeannette's manager, has matched the big man to fight Georges Carpentier, heavyweight champion of Europe, here on March 21. The Frenchmen will receive $7,500 for his end, regardless of the outcome.

Jack Johnson returned today from Scotland. The conqueror of Jeffries actually blocks traffic when he goes about. He is apparently rolling in money. He has a valet, secretary, chauffeur and three new cars. His new wife, who is constantly attended by two maids, has Jack completely under her thumb, for she will not permit him to make a move without her consent.

It was learned today that Charley Murphy had told friends abroad last winter that he intended firing (Johnny) Evers, and that he was considering appointing (Hank) O'Dea, (Tommy) Leach or (Roger) Bresnahan. Murphy is said to have admitted that he made a mistake in not naming (Joe) Tinker as manager.

———

The prospect of baseball players mingling with British nobility! This was delicious stuff for Runyon.

"DOOKS" AND "LUDS" WILL BE RECEIVED BY BALLPLAYERS (FEB. 25, 1914)

Tourists Condescend to Mingle with Heavyweights of Burke's Peerage; Nobility Delighted—Thorpe to Wear Trained Hat

LONDON, FEB. 24—Baseball bumps into British nobility tomorrow. But all patriotic Americans may rest assured that it will not be baseball that recoils from the shock.

The national obsession has been taking on titles at all weights on its travels 'round the world, so is in the pink of condition for the encounter.

Lord Lonsdale, the famous patron of pugilism; Lord Guernsey, Lord Desborough, Sir George Riddell and numerous other heavy hitters in *Burke's Peerage,* are under contract to appear and will be cordially mitted by Sam Crawford (of the Tigers), the Marquis of Wahoo; Larry Doyle, Duke of Harlem; Louie Comiskey, Count of Chicago, and Ted Sullivan, Barnacle of Baseball.

Thorpe to Stage Hat

Jim Thorpe will positively appear in his self-cocking plug hat, especially trained for this occasion. Bill Klem, the celebrated film filler, is bordering on nervous prostration over the prospect of meeting so much real claws. Bill is very despondent over not having a claw hammer coat for the afternoon function, but will do his best to horn into every available inch of the films in plain clothes.

Over 150 Americans are giving the luncheon. J.L. Griffiths will preside. H. Gordon Selfridge, the famous American merchant, is taking an active part in the arrangements. The American Consul-General will be present. This will be the biggest event given in London in honor of visiting Americans of any kind in recent years.

Mike Donlin says he will have a talk with any lord who crosses his path if it costs him the Irish vote of Philadelphia. The spectacle of Joe Benz mingling with the muckmucks is expected to be extremely impressive.

Nearly all the theatres of London have been thrown open to the tourists. Larry Doyle is sincerely regretting that his days of burlesque patronage are over. Many American actors and actresses are here, and all are praying for good weather Thursday and Friday, when the teams are scheduled to play.

English sportsmen, too, are deeply interested and all the old comparisons with cricket naturally are being made. But cricket takes none the worse of the comparison in the English papers.

Sun Was Somewhere

The weather today was grand. The sun could almost be seen several times, which is said to be a record in this vicinity. The party spent the day prowling about London. Fred Merkle says he has finally located the habitat of Harry Stevens when he lived in London. The name of the place, according to Fred, is the Tower of London.

Steve Evans is a steady patron of Ye Cheshire Cheese, an inn where Ben Jonson hung out. It is believed Steve either confuses Ben Jonson with Ban Johnson or likes the place because the name is strongly reminiscent to him of the home club.

Last night some of the crowd saw a fight at the National Sporting Club for the middleweight championship of England. Report has it that the British middleweights are almost as bad as the American "White Hopes." Tonight the bunch attended the Broadway.

James Callahan is still in Ireland. Several other members of the party rushed over today. John McGraw is in the center of the most entertaining London hands — his American friends. He seems to stand well the temptation of the proximity to the Emerald Isle.

Charles Comiskey is going about a great deal. He seems entirely recovered, but it is plain to see he is not yet a wholly well man. He has lost a lot of weight.

Some of the players came up today with heavy colds, the result of sleeping in the terrible draught, which was created by the news that the hotel charges extra for heat.

The hotel also charges extra for room and board. Harry Sparrow is developing a great English accent from listening to British explanations when he kicks about extras.

Jim McAleer had ordered a dozen dress shirts of the latest cut to take with him to Youngstown. There, he says, he will spend the summer.

—

KING GEORGE TO SEE WORLD TOURISTS IN A BIG CLASH (FEB. 26, 1914)

The Ban Johnson of All England Will Give the Gallivanting Ball Tossers One Glare, with Bill Klem Officiating—Donlin Excited over Event

LONDON, FEB. 25—His Gracious Majesty, King George, the Ban Johnson of all England, will give American baseball one glare tomorrow afternoon, according to an announcement made today at the luncheon tendered the globe-gallivanting Giants and White Sox at the Savoy Hotel by the American businessmen of London.

John L. Griffiths, the American Consul-General, who presided over the luncheon, made the announcement after the guests had arisen to drink the healths of King George and Woodrow Wilson. The news was received with great applause, especially from Harry Sparrow and "Tip" O'Neill, the business managers of the tour. The presence of the King means a big crowd. Where the King goes in London so goes everybody else who can horn in.

George will be admitted to the game free of charge. He will be given the seat of honor in the vicinity of the home plate, for the purpose of keeping Bill Klem somewhere near the pastime. If George should happen to get into the rightfield bleachers, for instance, Bill would never be able to see a single play on the field, for the film snatchers will naturally be following the King while Bill will just as naturally be following the film snatchers. You can't lose Bill, boys, even in a great wicked city like London.

Englishmen seem to think the decision of the King a high compliment to baseball, not realizing that Louis Mann, George Cohan and Joe Humphreys sometimes go to ball games several days a week in New York. Mike Donlin is greatly elated over the chance to play before the King, however. For although Mike has worked out often in the presence of queens he has never had a regular king in his audience.

One Hundred at Luncheon

Over 100 prominent Americans were present at the luncheon today. Mr. Griffiths made one of the those "hands across the sea" addresses to welcome Lord Desborough, the famous English sportsman; Sir George Riddell and others. Both of these celebrities addressed the pilgrims. "Dutch" Schaefer was greatly disappointed because Lord Desborough did not wear his coronet or whatever goes with his title.

Responses were made on behalf of the globe gallivantors by Joe Farrell, of Chicago, and Jimmy Callahan. Old Ted Sullivan closed with an oratorical effort that sounded like a combination of "The Star-Spangled Banner" and Marc Anthony's outburst over the late J. Caesar set to tango music. Only it was longer. Neither McGraw nor Comiskey could be present. Both were sick in bed.

McGraw's doctor advised him against going out. Pneumonia is feared, as McGraw contracted a cold some time ago and has been getting worse since his arrival in London. Comiskey had a relapse from his old illness, but it is not believed to be serious.

Unearths Murphy's History

Jimmy Callahan returned from Ireland this morning. It seems he spent most of his time digging up the history of Murphy. And he claims he has the complete dope on the "Weskit King." Cal claims the Irish deny Murphy was ever in Ireland unless it was in the extreme north.

The game tomorrow will be played on the field of the Chelsea football team. The weather today was very promising. (Red) Faber will pitch for the Giants. He is a young recruit who belongs to the Sox. He looks like a mighty good man. Every move reminds one of "Red" Ames. Jim Scott will do the tossing for the White Sox. Callahan thinks Scott should have a great year. Jimmy said today the only man belonging to the Sox that he really wants is (Eddie) Cicotte.

The Cunard office here says the *Lusitania* will arrive in New York next Thursday night, as the result of a new schedule. All of the passengers will be debarked the same night.

KING AND 20,000 BRITONS SEE SOX BEAT GIANTS, 5 TO 4 (FEB. 27, 1914)

Monarch Calm as Foul Ball Smashes Window of the Royal Box —
Picks up Piece of Shattered Glass as Souvenir of the Game; M'Graw,
Comiskey and Callahan Introducedt to Ruler by Page

LONDON, FEB. 26—Across an English football field, in the heart of historic Old Chelsea, boomed the weird war chant of the American, while His Majesty, King George of England, and 20,000 of his subjects sat listening today. They saw the White Sox beat the Giants 5 to 4 in an eleven-inning game.

The royal box was an enclosure in the centre of the grandstand just behind the catcher's position. It was fenced off from the rest of the stand and decorated with the royal colors. A screen had been placed along the front of the grandstand to protect the spectators.

The King was a trifle late in arriving, but the stand was packed when he finally appeared about 3 o'clock. He came in an ordinary limousine with Ambassador Page, and with only a couple of equerries.

In place of a royal crown the royal dome was topped by a plain derby hat. As His Majesty entered the enclosure the crowd rose, bared heads and remained standing until the King was seated. Then Jawn J. McGraw, Charley Comiskey and Jimmy Callahan appeared in the royal box escorted by H.C. Bunnell, the advance agent of the tour. They were introduced one by one to the King by Ambassador Page.

King George shook hands with each man, said he was glad they were here with the ball clubs and hoped they were enjoying the visit.

King Starts Game

Bunnell then handed the King a baseball. His Majesty handed it to Callahan, which amounted to the ceremony of the King pitching the first ball. That ball was put into play at the start of the game, but was then given to Comiskey as a souvenir. McGraw and Callahan were both in citizens' clothes and did not appear on the field.

Leaning over the railing of the royal box, nervously tugging at his short brown beard, the ruler of Great Britain smiled with pleasure as Ambassador Page explained points in the day.

So entranced was His Majesty that he did not even dodge when (Dick) Egan's foul broke a window in the Royal box, and the glass fell all about him. In fact, he captured a piece of the glass and is keeping it as a souvenir.

King George was generous in his applause of all the brilliant field and battery plays. In one inning when Faber, twirling for the Giants, had only one out and the bases full, and then managed to keep the White Sox from scoring. His Majesty acted like a real rooter. He was just as liberal in applause and wore just as happy an expression as would any bleacherite at the Polo Grounds.

Again when Daly swatted out the winning homer in the eleventh inning His Majesty clapped his hands vigorously and the spectators imitated his example.

A Distinguished Gathering

His Majesty cancelled half a dozen engagements in order to be present at the game. Mr. Church, King George's second valet, was really responsible for the royal presence. It appears that Church, while on a holiday visit to Chicago a year or two ago, became infatuated with baseball. Upon his return he informed the King that it was much more spectacular than football.

Cabinet Ministers, leaders in society, diplomats and members of the nobility followed the royal example. Members of the American colony were present to a man.

The Earl of Chesterfield, one of the royal party, tonight was mourning the loss of a tiepin valued at $2.50. It was stolen by someone in the valet crowd.

Bill Klem, who umpired, did not announce the batteries and did not introduce each player, as has been the custom everywhere else. This omission was at the request of Ambassador Page, though for what reason is not known. The managers and umpires were carefully versed in the etiquette necessary in the conduct of the game, as well as in being introduced to the King.

What had been going along as a purely perfunctory exhibition of America's national pastime up to the ninth inning to be politely explained to curious Britons at one's elbow, suddenly took on an aspect of a real baseball battle and several thousand temporarily expatriated Americans, wedged in among bewildered Englishmen, let their voices drift out into the haze.

———

CRAWFORD'S HOME RUN DIVERTS AMERICANS' INTEREST FROM KING (FEB. 27, 1914)

LONDON, FEB. 26—The majority of the spectators, especially the Americans, had up to that time been more interested in the King than in the game. But with the Giants two runs ahead, two out in the last of the ninth, Sam Crawford, the great slugger of the Detroit Tigers, slammed out a home run into the centerfield bleachers, driving home Buck Weaver from second. That was when those Americans really began to cut loose with some home-like enthusiasm.

Even the British seemed to sense the tense excitement of the situation. One could close his eyes and easily imagine himself in any stand in America at the critical moment of the game.

Daly's Homer Ends Tour

Tom Daly, the White Sox youngster who has been playing first base on the trip, smashed another homer into the bleachers in the eleventh inning, giving the White Sox a 5 to 4 victory, ending not only the game, but the world's tour. 'Twas a fitting finale.

Chelsea Field is a great oval enclosure that is supposed to seat 90,000 people, but the British must have queer ideas of figures, for after the 20,000 got into the stands this afternoon it would have been impossible to get 10,000 more in with the aid of shoe horns. Yet one of the newspapers here placed the attendance at 85,000.

Americans can now understand about those crowds of hundreds of thousands they have been reading all their lives about attending football matches here.

At the end of the eighth inning, which came about 4 o'clock, hundreds of spectators arose, left their seats and went out to an institution known as a team bar to get their tea. By the time they had had their tea and returned the game was over.

The crowd seemed to gather in the points of the game very quickly and were all struck by the rapidity of the plays. Mike Donlin had the spectators in the centerfield bleachers acting for all the world like Yankee bleacherites before three innings were over. They applauded every move Mike made. Between innings Sir Mique smoked cigarettes.

Red Faber, a youngster belonging to the White Sox, but who has done about the only effective pitching McGraw has secured on the trip, worked for the Giants, and was opposed by Jim Scott. Later, "Death Valley" James was succeeded by Joe Benz, with Andy Slight, who belongs to Des Moines of the Western League, back of the bat. Otherwise the lineup for both sides was the same as other games on the trip.

Before the pastime started the spectators were greatly amused by shadow practice, which is just ordinary infield practice without the use of the ball. Little Danny Callahan made a tremendous hit in his miniature uniform.

"Germany" Schaefer was singularly silent and composed throughout the game all for fear of being offensive to the King.

Has Lobert drove in two Giant runs by a homer in the fourth. Buck Weaver chased in two for the White Sox in the second by singling with the bases full. The English were duly impressed by the exhibition. The *Daily Mirror* tomorrow morning is saying that Londoners succumbed to the magnetism of the game. All the papers are enthusiastic in their praise of the spectacle.

Bill Klem, standing back of the bat, unterrified by whizzing balls, attracted special notice. Now and then during the game some American would forget himself far enough to suggest killing Bill in true Polo Ground style, while other comments that he was "rotten" seemed to give our cousins quite a laugh.

The fielding stunts were the biggest hit of the whole game, two double plays by the Giants getting a big hand.

It was decided not to play any more game, and the party will sail for America on the *Lusitania* from Liverpool Saturday afternoon.

BASEBALL TOO SLOW FOR OUR "DEAH" COUSINS (FEB. 28, 1914)

Vastly Inferior to Cricket, They Declare, but Still Has Some Good
Traits — Place Pastime in the Class with Rounders; Praise,
Throwing and Fielding of Both Teams — Tourists Leave
for Home Today and Will Arrive Thursday Night

LONDON, FEB. 27 — Too much happens in baseball that counts for nothing, according to several British newspapers this morning, and their reference was to the game played yesterday and not to a National League meeting.

Another terrible charge brought against the national pastime is that it is too slow and now Mike Donlin says he sincerely hopes and prays that the writer that pulled that charge did not base his judgment of the performance of the Giants' centerfielder, who, by the way, happened to be Sir Mique.

The British will have it that baseball is merely glorified "rounders," speeded up considerably, deah fellah, but still retaining the form of the game that is popular with school children. As a novelty our cousins on this side of the deep blue say the game was bally interesting, but, really was no challenge to their sense of superiority of cricket. Fair enough.

Will Admit Something

They admit, however, that cricket players have something to learn from baseball in regard to fielding, but complain because in our game only a few runs were made in over an hour. They also acknowledge that the throwing was amazing both as to speed and accuracy, and if it were as good in cricket, and the catches were made with the same certainty as in baseball, why, fifty runs would be knocked off every inning, which is undoubtedly the tip off on cricket.

The Americans here say the fact that the game did not stop for tea upset the Britons' whole order of things and spoiled the afternoon. Some of the papers even contended that the game lacked excitement, although it was exciting enough for the Americans that were present.

Bill Klem, the fay-muss umpire, declares that a good deal of the atmosphere was removed from the pastime because he was prohibited from exercising his voice in introducing the players. It is believed now that the hint to cut out introductions and comedy was the notion of our Ambassador Page, on his volition, which shows that it takes all kinds of people to make ambassadors. If the ambass ever runs for office in Bill Klem's district, we know one vote he won't receive.

Inferior to Cricket

In short, London sporting writers generally and smugly contend that baseball is inferior to cricket, so that ends it. The members of the Giant–White Sox party got many laughs this morning reading accounts of the game.

Only seven days' seasickness now lies between the tourists and home. They are all packed up, as far as luggage is concerned, ready to leave tomorrow morning for Liverpool, where they will board the *Lusitania,* which is due in New York Thursday night under the new schedule of the Cunard line.

Most of the globe gallivantors are not sorry to be leaving for home. Callahan and McGraw are especially anxious to get to their teams to see what they have, though from remarks dropped by McGraw it is a safe bet he will start the season with the same old lineup. McGraw has been curious to learn of (whether) Shaefer has reported, but has not commented one way or the other on rumors that "Tillie" intended to retire from the game.

Last night, the members of the party attended a beefsteak supper that lasted until breakfast this morning. Some of the numerous American actors infesting London, including Joe Coyne, were present at the feast and entertained all immensely.

———

WORLD TOURING TEAMS "SAFE" HOME; GREAT RECEPTION FOR GLOBE TROTTERS (MAR. 7, 1914)

Major League Magnates Outwit Federal Agents
in Signing up Their Star Players

Umpire Bill Klem, alert and assertive, was the very first man to gallop down the gangplank when the *Lusitania* creaked wearily into her berth in the bleak North River yesterday morning.

Behind him Bill heard a wild clatter of feet, while a bleacher cheer swept the pier where guards were holding a big crowd in leash. An instant before he was enfolded by the throng, Bill paused and autocratically dropped his hands, palms downward, and fingers wide. His lips moved. He half sputtered. It was a force of habit.

"Safe," said Bill.

The Giants and the White Sox had crossed the home plate.

Schaefer a Close Second

"Germany" Schaefer, a trifle portly from the profuse provender of the ports of the world, and a trifle balder than common, was close behind the famous umpire in the dash down the plank, but for once in his life—and only once—the Washington comedian overlooked a chance to protest a decision.

He did not even wait to have his broad back hammered by the well-meaning fists of a few thousand baseball fans; he did not stop to listen to the importunities of his cellmate, Nick Altrock, who was sent posthaste by Clark Griffith to save "Germany" from the clutches of the Federals. He tossed a few "hellos" here and there and then disappeared beyond the hillocks of snow that lay outside the Cunard piers.

He was a man of single and singular purpose yesterday was "Germany" Schaefer, sometime fellow traveler of John J. McGraw, Charles Comiskey and James J. Callahan, and that purpose, as he later explained when he was in a calmer mood, was to head to a Broadway café, where the great world's first started as far as he was concerned, and to sit in that Broadway café and think, and think, and think of the places he has been in and the sights he has seen.

He was so anxious to get ashore that he sat up most of the night when the *Lusitania* was hunting for the lady with the lamp down the bay, and he was the second object to be seen on deck by the cargoes of New Yorkers and Chicagoans who ferried out to quarantine to yell across several knots of Atlantic Ocean at the voyagers. He was not the first object because the first object was indubitably Ted Sullivan, patrician of our national pastime.

"Old Glory" Greets Boats

Old Ted has been waiting mighty patiently for this very event—this homecoming of the Giants and the Sox, so when the ferryboat *Niagara*, listing slightly under a load of shrieking fans and breathing ragtime music from every porthole, crept up out of the haze, its passengers saw a short, pudgy old gentleman leaning far out over the rail of the *Lusitania*, one hand clamping his derby hat to his brow and the other swinging an American flag.

That flag was given to the Giants and the Sox away up in Portland, Oregon, just before they left America last December, and it has been flaunted along three or four continents since then. Mostly it has been flaunted by Ted Sullivan.

He was still flaunting it yesterday long after the crowd on the *Niagara*, which included a bunch of boys of the interscholastic league, had fractured their throats in yelling, and had given way to vocal reinforcements from the tug *John A. Booker*, bearing the official reception committee, and still another boatload of newspapermen.

A green-badgered delegation of official greeters, including Harry Hempstead, president of the Giants; Ban Johnson, president of the American League; Charles Ebbets, president of the Brooklyn club; Frank Farrell, president of the Yankees; and Joseph Lannin, head of the Boston Red Sox, rushed aboard the *Lusitania* and sought out McGraw, Callahan and Comiskey, and announced that all hands were glad to see them home.

M'Graw Center of Crowd

Muffled in a new fur overcoat, McGraw, the stocky boss of the Giants, stood in the center of a group of newspapermen and answered a rataplan of questions, while Jimmy Callahan, the picturesque leader of the Sox, bronzed and burly from his trip, was fenced off in a corner by another squad of interviewers.

Comiskey forgathered with his friend, Ban Johnson, but from time to time he had to step out on the deck and wave his hat to some Chicago friend on the surrounding boats. Several hundred people came from Chicago to greet the return wanderers, and considerable neighborhood news was wirelessed into the *Lusitania* during the stay at quarantine. Most of the party of sixty-five that made up the world-touring crowd, outside of the ballplayers, are Chicagoans.

Meantime, the baseball players themselves were coming in for a lot of attention, from the reception committee. Magnates who had an interest in the men on the teams that composed the Giants and the Sox got busy right away, but it developed soon after the opening flurry that none of the crowd intend jumping to the Federal League.

Players Stick to Majors

The outlaws have been in touch with (Tris) Speaker of the Boston Red Sox; San Crawford of the Detroit Tigers; Mike Doolan of the Phillies; Lee Magee, Steve Evans, Ivy Wingo, of the Cardinals; and (Walt) Leverenz, of the St. Louis Browns, but by the time the rush had subsided statements began popping out right and left that all was serene.

President (Jim) Gilmore, of the Federals, was unable to secure a pass to get aboard the *Lusitania,* so he could do any missionary work in person, but his visit would probably have been fruitless anyway. It is said that President Lannin, of the Red Sox, handed Tris Speaker a blank contract and told him to fill in the figures himself, which may, or may not be true.

When the official boat first drew up alongside the big liner, several newspapermen and others were allowed to board the *Lusitania* by way of a frail plank, then the permission was suddenly rescinded, and Ban Johnson and the magnates left staring blankly up at the steep sides of the ocean express for quite some time until the medical taboo was lifted.

This was a most unwarranted blow to the dignity of organized baseball, if the quarantine authorities only knew it. When Mr. Johnson finally entered the liner, there was stately repression in his manner. Obviously, he had been offended.

Anxious to See Comiskey

The American Leaguers seemed more anxious to see Comiskey than anyone else, and Johnson had a great deal to say to the "Old Roman." Pale, and thin, and showing in every way the effect of his recent illness, the Chicago magnate listened quietly. He had at no time take the Federal League very seriously, but he has not given out his personal opinions on the subject, and it is doubtful if he approves of the fluent conversation of some of his associates.

Tommy Ratty, and numerous other personal friends of the Giants, were in the crowd that went out to quarantine, and little reunions were going on all over the boat.

Larry Doyle, Jim Thorpe and Hans Lobert, and their brides — sole survivors of that famous honeymoon special that went as far as the Pacific Coast at the start of the tour carrying half a dozen pairs of newlyweds — were the objects of considerable attention.

Little Danny Callahan and his sister, Margaret, the children of Jimmy Callahan, were surrounded by admirers, while Mrs.

Callahan and her mother, Mrs. Dan Harden, stood in the background watching them.

Offers $80 for Speaker

Danny was the mascot of the Sox on the trip, and was zigged out in a miniature uniform during the games. He cried bitterly whenever the Giants got ahead. Tris Speaker is his particular pet, and Danny declares he has $80 of his own saved up which he is willing to pay the Boston Red Sox for "Spoke," as he calls him.

Little Margaret was quite seasick on the last voyage, and was greatly downcast because it shattered her record of not having been sick at any other stage of the journey.

Curiously enough, many members of the party were ill on the way over from Liverpool despite their past experiences on the water. The *Lusitania* had fair weather, but was bucking cross-seas constantly, and Larry Doyle, Joe Farrell, of Chicago, and many other hardy mariners took the count. Sam Crawford, world's champion sea-sicker, according to the players, escaped entirely, however.

Reception at Pier

The real reception yesterday took place when the *Lusitania* docked. The pier was jammed with cheering people and every player got a yell as he marched down the gangplank. George Wiltse was among the first recognized, as he debarked with Mrs. Wiltse, and the willowy sidewinder of the Giants was warmly greeted.

Mike Donlin drifted onto solid land with that old familiar swing of his, and the crowd roared. Mike has signed with McGraw to take Harry McCormick's place as a pinch hitter. On the way over, Mike was billed on the program of a concert for the benefits of the widows and orphans of seamen, to do the "Bolivian bomb dance" with Miss Maizie King, the famous toe dancer, who is returning from an engagement in England.

The Bolivian bomb dance may be quite a contortion for all

anyone knows, because it was never performed by Michael J. At the last minute he sprained his eyesight and refused to go on, though Miss King was not only ready, but willing.

It was during that concert that Ted Sullivan told Irish stories to the populace, and was so pleased with them that he went over and did it to the second cabin passengers the following night.

Slight Sings at Concerts

Andrew Slight, a young catcher, who was with Des Moines of the Western League last season, and has been purchased by the White Sox, sang at both concerts. While in Paris Slight had his voice tested by M. Bowes, instructor of Sammy Strang, the ex-Giant, and it is said the young backstop was informed that he has quite a musical future if he cares to take it up seriously.

After the customs inspectors had worked them over carefully the Giants' party went to the Imperial Hotel, while the Sox went to the Biltmore. Broadway traffic was blocked for some time in front of the Imperial by the crowd waiting to see the Giants.

Last night the entire party attended the Palace Theatre, which was especially decorated in their honor, and where the ballplayers attracted as much attention as the performers. Tonight there will be a big banquet at the Biltmore, and Sunday evening the party leaves for Chicago, where another banquet will be held.

Giants Going to Chicago

McGraw, (Hooks) Wiltse, (Bunny) Hearn, (Jim) Thorpe, (Larry) Doyle and (Mike) Donlin will go with the Chicago party, and journey on to Marlin (Texas) after the banquet. (Jimmy) Callahan goes to Paso Robles with (Buck) Weaver, (Red) Faber, (Jim) Scott, (Joe) Benz and Tom Daly, all under contract with the Sox. Comiskey will repair immediately to Excelsior Springs, Mo., to recuperate.

The players belonging to other clubs will attend the banquet before reporting to their respective commands. Dick Egan has signed with Ebbets, and may play the Brooklyn short field.

While the party received wonderful receptions in Manila and Australia, the big event of the trip was undoubtedly the game played in London before the King of England. Twenty-five years ago, when A.G. Spalding conducted his tour of the world, the teams played before the Prince of Wales, afterward King Edward, but it is doubtful if that game impressed the English people as did the game played a game ago.

"I believe we could make a real fan out of King George if he saw a few more battles like that one," said Jimmy Callahan yesterday. "He was certainly deeply interested as is shown by the fact that he sent us word through Ambassador Page after the game that he had enjoyed it very much."

"I was absolutely amazed at the interest displayed in our national game all around the world," said McGraw. "I do not mean interest in the individuals playing the game but (in) the game itself. I was surprised to find an intimate knowledge of baseball in the most remote places where you would least expect to find it.

"Naturally, we were greatly gratified by the presence of the King at the game in England, and we were deeply interested in the way it was received by the English people. We went there merely to show the people the American national game. I would not be at all surprised to see baseball taken up quite generally, not only in England, but in France."

John McGraw

See a dozen baseball games in a season, and probably eight of them are pretty ordinary. So goes the challenge of a baseball beat reporter who sees a lot of baseball, and endeavors to make the average game seem interesting, not to mention the days in between. But it was during the ordinary and the "in between" that Runyon soared—enlivening a dull day at spring training with a talk with the old-timers or writing about a slugest from the perspective of . . . the ball.

Runyon kills time on a slow day at spring training with John McGraw and other old-timers.

McGraw amd Other Old-Timers Believe Game Has Not Advanced (Apr. 3, 1911)

Billy Hamilton, Jim McAleer, Arlie Latham and Wilbert Robinson Have Old-Time Fanfest

ATLANTA, APRIL 2 — We are here today and gone tomorrow, as the fellow says. The Giants left at 8:40 o'clock tonight for Greensboro, N.C., where they play Monday afternoon.

Sundaying in Atlanta is not without its compensation, however, it may sound away off yonder. For instance, one may sit in the rotunda of the historic old Kimball House and listen to much conversation, interesting and otherwise, concerning the game of baseball from the lips of its most famous exponents, past and present. Then again, one may go out in the streets and watch Atlanta, arrayed in its newest spring satirical scenery, taking the soft Southern sun of this peaceful Sabbath.

Either occupation is diverting, although some consider a much more engrossing spectacle to be Arthur Bell, as he adds and two and two and subtracts 16 in the business of weighing the financial damage of the Atlanta engagement.

Manager John J. McGraw of the Giants, Manager Jimmy McAleer of the Washington American League team, and Billy Hamilton, the old Boston player who is now scouting for (Braves' manager) Fred Tenney, foregathered in the hotel lobby today, along with Arlie Latham and Wilbert Robinson, and many a tale was narrated of deeds done and well nigh forgotten on fields of baseball glory. Luminaries of today, like "Germany" Schaefer, "Gabby" Street, and Walter Johnson of Washington, and (Christy) Mathewson, (Art) Devlin, (Larry) Doyle and (Chief) Meyers, of the Giants, were scattered about the corridors and there was but one topic of common interest.

Baseball Is Same as of Yore

McGraw and Hamilton agree on the proposition that there is little to the game today that can be called "new"—that the baseball, which is instilled into the youngsters of the present, is the same baseball that was played a couple of decades back. McGraw declares, however, that his present club ranks with the greatest clubs of the past in point of "scrappiness." He says that the Giants may be mentioned in the same breath with the old Cleveland, Boston and Baltimore clubs in that respect.

McGraw and Hamilton were talking about the base stealing of today as compared with that of the old days, and both assert that the men who were playing the game when they were in the spangles themselves would be the same sensations now that they were then. Speaking of Mike Kelly, the wonderful old catcher, McGraw described a play that he thinks is the greatest example of quick thinking that ever came beneath his observation.

"Kelly was essentially as instinctive player," said McGraw. "He was not so remarkably fast, but he always knew exactly what to do at exactly the right moment. One day there was a man on third, and it was this run, which the other fellows needed to win the game. The batter hit to an infielder, and the runner was coming home. The infielder made a bad throw to Kelly to cut off the runner, and here is where Mike showed his amazing rapidity of thought and action.

"The throw was far to his left. He knew he could not take it on his glove and he knew if he shifted his position to use his right hand in making the play that the runner would be under him safe; in other words, he would be leaned too far over to recover in time to put the ball on the man. He shucked his catching glove as quickly as you bat an eye, took the ball with his bare left hand without changing his position and whipped it around in time to tag the runner at the plate. How many players of today would have that presence of mind?"

No Patience with Sore Arms

McGraw has no patience with sore-arm pitched or with twirlers who lack control. "I don't understand why a man cannot put the ball over that plate," he declared. "The trouble with most of them is lack of confidence. They get up there on the rubber with everything, and then they suddenly commence to think that maybe they can't get it over — with the result (being) they don't. I cannot understand these sore arms either. I never had a sore arm in my life."

Wilbert Robinson is another old-timer (and teammate of McGraw's on the 1890s-era Baltimore Orioles) who says he never had a sore arm. In practice, Robbie's whip seems as strong as any youngster's. When he was catching McGraw's famous "peeve" ball delivery during the horseplay against Atlanta the other day, the old Oriole displayed real form. McGraw developed a spitball, and without signing Robby, he turned one loose, which broke in the dirt at the plate, and stood Robinson on his ear as he went after it.

Robbie promptly spoke slightingly of his pitcher's control. On another occasion, McGraw tossed the ball under his leg. He had tipped Robbie off and told the catcher to turn his back and permit the ball to hit him somewhere in the region around his belt, to aid to the gravity of things. However, he intended to cross his catcher, and when Robbie turned, he shot one over with whiskers on it. He told some of the players to watch for the play, and Robbie caught on.

❊   ❊   ❊

McGraw has an ambition to take a team to Cuba some of these days. He was there 20 years ago with the first ball team that ever invaded the island, and established a fielding record, which the natives still remember. In those days, the Americans piled up scores against the Cubans.

❊   ❊   ❊

Christy Mathewson has cleaned up all the local checkers' champions and is searching for laurels in the three-cushion billiard field.

❊   ❊   ❊

Harry Sparrow (the Yankee business manager) is now an exponent of the early-to-bed, early-to-rise doctrine. He is rooming with (pitcher Ed) Hendricks, the quietest man in the United States, and, as Hendricks goes to bed with the chickens, Sparrow is ashamed to get in late.

———

Although most of Runyon's pieces were game stories, he occasionally penned a feature story, making him among the first, if not the first sportswriter of the era to do so. This story, written on a Giants' road trip to Pittsburgh in the midst of a dogged race for the National League pennant, provides both a rare, behind-the-scenes look at the lives, character and training habits of big-league deadball players as well as insight into the motivations of Giants' manager John McGraw. The article is interesting as well in light of the sad tale of Bugs Raymond, the alcoholic pitcher who by then had left the team, and, as Runyon writes, was "persona non grata" for his wayward ways.

McGraw Not a Strict Disciplinarian; That Is Reason Giants Lead in Pennant Race (Sept. 17, 1911)

Manager of New York Nationals Let Players Do as They Please, but Bans Drinking and Gambling

PITTSBURGH—Over in one corner of the hotel café Josh Devore, we will say, is calmly eating lobster salad, with a cup of strong black coffee on the side.

The hour is 11:15 P.M. The eye of the diminutive outfielder casually notes the clock as he consumes his weird repast. Perhaps he has George "Hooks" Wiltse, the somber visaged left-handed pitcher of the big-town club as his companion, also partaking of strange nocturnal diet.

At 11:30 they light their cigarettes; in five minutes more they push back their chairs, and nod at one another.

"It's that time," says Wiltse, and they are on their way to bed.

Let not the dyspeptic shudder at the thought of sleeping upon such a night-time supper. The two ballplayers—boy and veteran—will slumber as soundly as children until 9 o'clock the next morning, and at 10 they will be back in the café for their ham and eggs and wheat cakes, just as surely as the dining room doors remain open.

And perhaps "Hooks" will pitch the next day and shut out the opposing club with two or three hits, while Devore will assist in the victory by a sensational batting and fielding streak.

Thus are the theories of diet for athletes all shot to pieces.

Perhaps, while they are dining a la midnight, John J. McGraw, manager of the Giants, passes. His quick eye may note the culinary display laid before his men; certainly he cannot fail to observe the cigarettes, but food and smoke will bring no comment from the chief.

Is Interested in Bedtime

The fact that the pair will be headed for what Josh calls "the hay" at 11:30 is of more interest to McGraw.

Over in a nearby drugstore, Otis Crandall, the solidly built Indiana farmer boy whom the players call "Old Doc," because he is the pitching physician of the emergency case, is permitting ice cream sodas to seep into his system; Big Chief Meyers, the good-natured Indian catcher, is drinking some strange concoction of syrup and carbonated water; down in the poolroom, Al Wilson, young Gene Paulette, Fred Merkle, Leon Ames. Christy Math-ewson and Bert Maxwell, the new pitcher, are clicking the balls about, while Arthur Devlin. Louie Drucke and Grover Hartley are idling in front of the hotel.

Beals Becker and Fred Snodgrass have gone to a theatre; the others are scattered over the town. But by 11 o'clock, they come trooping into the hotel. They stand around talking and "joshing" a few moments, then hands slip to the watch pockets, and soon they are filing into the elevator. By midnight they are in bed and asleep.

"I suppose," says the layman, "that the rules of conduct for members of a club like the Giants, especially when it is making its final fight for the pennant, are very strict."

He supposes wrong.

There are rules of discipline, of course, and they are rigidly enforced, but they are rules which would be observed by the average citizen of average habits in his ordinary life, and they are little different now, when the club has settled down on the drive to the wire, than they were last Spring when the season opened, with perhaps the single exception of the 11:30 retiring hour.

Two Rules for Giants

McGraw makes a point of two rules in particular so far as the conduct of the players off the field is concerned.

They must not drink intoxicating liquor. They must not gamble.

It so happens that at this time McGraw has not a single man on his club "addicted to the use of liquor," as the temperance orators say, but liquor has made this pennant race harder for the Giants to win than any other one thing, just the same.

Had "Bugs" Raymond, the eccentric right-hander, continued in the narrow path as he started last Spring, the Giants believe they would have been ten games ahead of their nearest competitor, and the race would be over. "Bugs" is now around Chicago, pitching semi-professional ball, and yet he might have had his fellows and himself in a position to play the World Series, with all its attendant glory and money, long before this. He might have been drawing as much salary as any pitcher in the world—not excepting Mathewson.

The days of detectives and keepers for Raymond are over; he has undoubtedly pitched his last game for the Giants, and probably for any big-league club. As a general thing, "Bugs" was persona non grata with most of the players anyway. The liquor rule is now almost unnecessary, but it goes, just the same, probably by way of reminder, and a player found taking a drink would draw a stiff fine.

Gambling is ranked next to liquor in the McGraw category of sins.

During the Spring training season, and in the early part of the playing year, the men had their poker games and other forms of card playing. First McGraw put the ban on poker, and then he abolished all games of chance, no matter what form they might take.

Gambling Has to Go

Now it is not to be assumed that any great moral purpose was behind the McGraw orders. They were issued to preserve the morale and not the morals of the club. McGraw delivers no lecture on the subject. His ground is that gambling is just naturally bad for the players, the same as liquor is bad for them. It is liable to create dissensions and bring on quarrels; it is conducive to late hours, and the men cannot afford to lose the money they so hardly earn. So gambling had to go.

It is understood that McGraw even frowns on betting. He doesn't want his men thinking about matters of that kind when they can just as well think about the pennant.

A baseball club is like a big family, and naturally there are apt to be little internecine squabbles. Next to gambling and drinking, the quickest way to incur the McGraw displeasure would be by fighting. That is to say, by the men fighting among themselves. If players Smith and Jones have a quarrel, they had better keep it secret. McGraw will not stand for dissentions. An open fight between two would doubtless mean fines and suspensions.

Rowdyism is, of course, tabooed, but McGraw wouldn't have to put the ban on this sort of misconduct. It goes without saying that the manager expects his men to conduct themselves as gentlemen off the field, and they would be expected to do that whether they were ballplayers or not. Men of the stamp of Mathewson, Merkle, Snodgrass, Ames, (Larry) Doyle and the rest are not likely to need rules in that respect.

If a crowd of players are together talking, in a Pullman, for instance, and a woman enters, the men nearest the door who sees her first warns against conversational accident by a cry of "heads up!"

Don't Need Diet

There are no rules, which obtrude themselves into the dining room, as stated. McGraw takes it for granted that the men know what to eat and when to eat it, and the fact that there has not been a case of illness this season, and that the players are all in great health right now, indicates that a prescribed diet is wholly unnecessary.

They eat what they please, and when they please, and incidentally they go right through the bill of fare when they sit down to the table. Most of the men eat but twice a day—a light breakfast around 10 o'clock and a heavy dinner after the game. And the testimony of the hotel chef who has had experience with them is that they are "right smart feeders." Some of them eat again during the course of the evening and most of them can go right to sleep after coffee.

Nearly all of them smoke cigarettes, and some cigars. Mathewson occasionally affects a pipe.

Of course, if a man was overdoing his eating or smoking, and was affecting his health, or his work, McGraw might take a hand in the matter, but he assumes that they are old enough to know how to take care of themselves.

Anyone who thinks that the older men like Mathewson or Wiltsie or Devlin would be given more leeway than the youngsters on the rules is very much mistaken. McGraw looks to them, in fact, to set the example for the younger fellows. If Matty, for instance, should violate a rule of discipline, the manager would very likely give him a "call" quicker than he would a newcomer, for the reason that he figures the "old heads" should, of all others, know better.

However, it is rarely that a reprimand is necessary for violation of rules of conduct off the field.

Dislike a Tale-teller

While McGraw does not mingle to any great extent with the players off the field, he has a way of knowing just what is going on. He particularly dislikes a tale-bearer, and no player would think of carrying stories to him of infractions of the rules. The manager would express his opinion of the storyteller first, before taking cognizance of the reported offense.

That he is almost as patient with human frailties off the field as with shortcomings on the diamond is indicated by efforts to reform Raymond. He believed that "Bugs" was a great pitcher when he was right, and he gave him every chance. There was a selfish interest, of course, but the advantage would have been all Raymond's in the end, rather than McGraw's.

A ballplayer does not have to keep himself in the same course of training that other athletes do. A prizefighter, for instance, or a foot racer, is working up to a certain event, while the ballplayer has to keep himself in the same condition for months. The prospect of big money and much glory at the end of the season is sufficient incentive to make them careful of their living.

The day of the hard-drinking roistering player has departed. A big-league manager nowadays does not care to be bothered with them. Occasionally a character of that sort bobs up who has such phenomenal ability in his particular line that the manager must overlook his private life for the time being, but the way the great players of the past have come and gone along the primrose path seems to have served as a warning to the boys now breaking into the game.

——

When an old Pueblo friend contributed some baseball poetry at a Yankee–Red Sox game, Runyon made it the centerpiece of his game story the next morning. Note how little of the article has to do with the game itself, and the reference to one George "Baby" Ruth, the Boston lefthander already being noted for his unusual ability to hit home runs.

RED SOX WALLOP YANKEES, 7 TO 1 (JUNE 3, 1915)

There's a Boston young fellow named
   Ruth,
Whose manner is very uncouth.
He slings with his left,
And there's a whole lot of heft in his
   war club.
Now ain't it the truth?

*   *   *

That limerick there was composed for us on the spur of the moment, and also on the back of an old envelope up at the Polo Grounds yesterday afternoon by Mr. Lemuel J. Finch, of Pueblo, Colo., who is visiting in this city, and who sat through one of the coldest days of the current Winter to see the Yanks defeated by the Boston Red Sox. The score was 7 to 1.

Mr. Finch is a fellow townsman and boyhood friend of Mr. Jim Flynn, the well-known old gentleman who recently engaged in a hand-breaking contest with Mr. James Coffey out at Brighton

Beach, Mr. Flynn losing the match by one hand. Mr. Finch came on to see that affair, and is staying on to view the other sights of our city, including the Yankees' baseball playing.

Mr. Flynn's Townsman

Mr. Finch and Mr. Flynn were charter members, in their younger days, of a celebrated social organization of Pueblo, which was euphoniously named "The Boo Gang" and which had its head-quarters at a bathing pool, or swimming hole, in the Arkansas River up above the county bridge. The swimming hole was popularly known as "The One-Armed Minnie." However, that's a very long story.

In his home town, Mr. Finch has a wide reputation for his proficiency in the use of the limerick form of expression, being in fact, sometimes called "Limerick Len." He wrote one yesterday about (Yankee pitcher) Cy Pieh, which ran:

> There was a young fellow named
> Pieh,
> Who was often heard uttering a Cy.
> It dented his crust
> When the ball they would bust,
> And he pitched on a very cold dye.

Of course it really doesn't mean anything, but it goes to show you how handy Mr. Finch is with pencil. He wrote that one about Pieh, when Pieh went in to pitch in the sixth inning. Pieh relieved Jack Warhop at that time. Mr. Finch did not write a limerick about Warhop, because he said Warhop didn't deserve it, and besides that, Warhop is a very hard name to rhyme.

Jack left after the Sox had scored five runs. The Bostonians had no trouble in seeing through Jack's underhanded subterfuges. In the sixth Harry Hooper singled with two aboard the bridges and only one down, scoring another tally to add to the four already credited to the account of (Red Sox owner) Joe Lannin's payroll annoyances, and (Yankee manager) Wild Bill Donovan waved Jack aside. Cy did just so-so after his advent, just so-so.

Mr. Finch's opening effusion was incited in the second frame, when Along Came Ruth, and belted a home run into the rightfield stand. We are referring to George Ruth, the left-handed pitcher and batter. George did the hurling for the Boston delegation yesterday, and he was strangely diffident about allowing our boys any runs. When he hit his homer Chet Thomas was on first base, having been plucked with a pitched pellet by J. Warhop. It was immediately recalled by many persons that George had whacked an h.r. into that same stand off that same pitcher on or about May 6, 1915, which is the same year that is now going on. However, these statistics are wholly immaterial.

The best limerick that Mr. Finch wrote during the afternoon was in the subject of Fritz Maisel. Fritz compiled a triple in the first frame, and scored on a wild pitch emitted by Ruth, whereupon Mr. Finch said:

> There's a fast young fellow named
>   Maisel,
> Who is just as slick as a waisel.
> He's the size of a match,
> But very hard to catch,
> And out on the bases he can be
>   raised.

"Of course," explained Mr. Finch, "waisel" is simply another way of spelling "weasel." A weasel is an animal, but if I spelled it "weasel" in my limerick, it would not rhyme with Maisel. So I spell it "waisel." It means the same thing.

Mr. Finch Refuses

We endeavored to get Mr. Finch to write something about the weather, but he declined to do so, on the ground that three limericks per diem is enough for any man to write. It was quite a lot of weather, just the same. The winds—pronounced "winds," as in winding a clock—did blow, and the atmosphere was colder than (umpire) Bill Klem's stare when someone yells "Catfish!"

The audience was very incipient. Those present felt very conscious of their feet. Someone remarked that it was football weather, but that is not true. The football people always close their playing season before it gets that cold.

Speaking of football, Roy Hartzell booted Dick Hoblitzel's single out in left center after Wagner and Speaker had extracted passes from Warhop, and while he recovered the ball quickly and hurled it on to Maisel ahead of Speaker, Wager went on over the plate and registered a tally. There were two out when Hobby hit the ball, and many present held that the play on Speaker at third came off before Wagner's foot landed on the plate, and that therefore the side should have been declared retired, but it appears that Messrs. (Bill) Dinneen and (Dick) Nallin (the umpires) had their respective gazes riveted on third.

You Can't Beat 11 Men

They did not time the arrival of Wagner at the home dish, or platter. They had eyes only for that third satchel, and so Heine's run counted. Wild Bill Donovan became more than ever convinced that it is next to impossible to defeat 11 men.

In the fourth frame, with one out, Scott Gardner and Thomas singled one after the other, filling the bases, but Ruth forced Scott at the plate on a tap to Peckinpaugh. It should have been mentioned here that Ruth is sometimes called "Baby" Ruth. 'Arry 'Ooper, as 'Arry Stevens would doubtless call him out of his name altogether, singled and Gardner scored, but Wagner fouled to (Les) Nunamaker. Nunny was doing the catching for our side yesterday.

That's about all that one can conveniently say about the ballgame in the space allotted to the subject by the sporting editor. Mr. Finch thought it was a pretty good game, but then Mr. Finch is a stranger in our city. We have requested him to return in the Summer and see a regular pastime.

—

Runyon covers a Yankees-Browns doubleheader from the perspective of . . . the ball.

AUTOBIOGRAPHY OF A HOME RUN BY ITSELF, IN COLLABORATION WITH DAMON RUNYON (JUNE 15, 1915)

I AM a Home Run.

If I wanted to be right chesty about it, I might tell you that I am THE Home Run, and you would never know any better, but I am an honest Home Run, and as modest and unassuming as Ed Sweeney's batting average.

Besides that, there are some Home Runs that I wouldn't want to be for the price of two week's board and room at Long Beach; disreputable and characterless Home Runs that are always running around in loose box scores, never caring who hits 'em, and bringing odium upon a good old family name.

I believe some of these profligate Home Runs claim to be distant cousins of mine, but I deny the relationship. There used to be one that showed up around this city every few years, which was hit by (Giant pitcher) Red Ames, and which presumed upon a similarity in name to allege connection with our branch of the Home Runs, but everybody knows it was an imposter.

Anytime you see a Home Run letting pitchers hit 'em, you can wager there is something wrong somewhere. I do not even except these Home Runs that are being hit by this (Yankee pitcher) Ray Caldwell, although we are giving them the benefit of the doubt until we make a thorough investigation. They are either spurious, or this Caldwell is an outfielder at heart, and not a pitcher at all.

Figured in Doubleheader

If you will pick up your favorite newspaper this morning you will find that I figured largely in the doubleheader that was played at the Polo Grounds yesterday afternoon by the Yankees and the St. Louis Browns, and you will further ascertain that the Yankees were victorious at both ends of this doubleheader and have elbowed their way back into the first division, which is a very pleasant place to be in this hot weather—coolish-like and free from care.

The score of the first game was 12 to 7, and the count in the second pastime was 5 to 4 in 10 innings. I was largely responsible for many of those tallies, just as your paper states if it tells the truth about me and five other Home Runs. All of my associates were blood relatives, and with the possible exception of one—free from taint in the scoring, but several of them spring from the scorer and more reduced branches of our family, and for that reason are found consorting with the St. Louis Browns, as you can see by an examination of the genealogy of the pastimes herewith attached.

Home Run's History

Now then, before I go any further, I suppose you would like to learn a little about my history. Well, I was born in Section 1, of Rule 48, of the Official Playing Rules, and I have been around a long time. My habitat is the leftfield bleachers, the rightfield stand, or the remote corners of the baseball yard, and I am often indigenous to the pitching of Grover Lowdermilk, Harry Hoch, Ray Keating, Lefty Weilman and even Ray Fisher. If you want to get me when I right good, however, drop in when Rube Marquard has left the hop on the fast one in his apartment. I can bounce mighty far off a hickory stick those days, I tell you what.

I was the more prominent of the Home Runs yesterday. I say that without undue arrogance. I am not going to tell you which one I was, but if you will pick out the cleanest cut, handsomest Home Run that you find in the tally sheets, that will be—yours hastily. I was most certainly not that one sponsored by Ray Hartzell in the fourth frame of the first game, which hit the outer rampart of the upper rightfield stand—not that one, indeed.

That Home Run would have had no social prestige whatever in the National League, where any decent, self-respecting Home Run is worth $5 on the hood, from the Suffragists—but it is admitted without question in the inner circles of the American League, where Home Runs are ranked at only one dozen pairs of sox.

Walker's Homer Second-Rater

I was not Clarence Walker's homer into the leftfield stand in the fifth inning of the second game, nor was I (Ivan) Howard's whack to the rightfield stand in the ninth. I might have been Walter Pipp's (off Harry Hoch) pelt into the leftfield bleachers, 'way down yonder back of the auto sign, with two aboard in the fourth inning of the curtain-raiser—mind, I say I might have been that one; but then again I might have been Fritz Maisel's four-sack smack to right-center in the sixth inning of the second game.

These were both very nourishing knocks—but I am not committing myself. I might have been either. I am not saying for certain. My assistant, this Runyon—a windy fellow, withal—is for restraint, and self-repression, but I was the Big Home Run of the day. I must give it to myself for that.

I was not Clarence Walker's second circuit clout into the left-field bleachers in the ninth inning of the second game with a runner aboard, although I don't mind saying that I am a full brother to that Home Run, and taught it all it knows. It was right after that whack that Gus Williams got to first on (Roger) Peckinpaugh's fumble and took third of (John) Leary's single, then scoring with the tying run on (Doc) Lavan's lick to Peck, and sending the Yanks over into the ninth inning.

I have scant patience with singles, as a rule. They are puny things, always begging at the doors of us Home Runs and never having a nickel, but I must say that Luther Cook's single in the tenth, after one was out, seemed mighty self-reliant and self-supporting. It was followed by Peckinpaugh's out, which put Cook on third, and then that long, left-handed fellow Weilman, who is one of the Home Run family in the league, passed Fritz Maisel intentionally. Otherwise Fritz would have secured another Home Run as we are becoming very friendly to him.

(Yankee manager) Wild William Donovan sent up Birdie Cree to bat for Walter Pipp, and I don't mind confiding to you here and now that I was lurking in the background ready to do my duty for Birdie had I been needed. I would have been that Home Run that Birdie would have busted had I been called upon, but he used one of those weakling singles to the rightfield wall, and the game was over.

———

You can sense Runyon didn't give two hoots about the Yale-Princeton game he was undoubtedly told to cover. So he wrote about everything but the game.

YALE TAKES DECIDING GAME FROM PRINCETON AT POLO GROUNDS, 4–3 (JUNE 17, 1915)

Scene — The press box at the Polo Grounds yesterday afternoon. A game of baseball is in progress between the Yale and Princeton teams, a game that was eventually won by Yale, the score being 4 to 3, giving the Bulldogs two out of three on the series.

Mr. (W.O.) McGeehan, of the *Evening Journal* (dictating to a telegraph operator) — "In a riot of color, and assorted noises, Yale and Princeton clashed here this afternoon — got all that?"

Mike Donlin, the former Giant, now an actor (entering twirling a cane) — "Hah-do, ev'body. Certainly a lot o' swell dolls here. Glad I came. Who's that fellow warming up there? I'm for his side. He's got a pile o' stuff on 'at ol' pill. Yale, eh? All right, I'm for Yale."

Henry Fabian, the groundskeeper (mournfully) — "Lookit what they're doing to my ground awready. Ain't it terrible?"

Harry Sparrow, business manager of the Yanks (approaching all out of breath) — "Well, they pulled it on themselves. I just wanted you people to know I didn't do it. What? Why, don't you see the Yale rooters are back of the Princeton bench, and the Princeton crowd is behind the Yale coop? I didn't do it. Give me credit for that. They gummed it on themselves."

Mr. Donlin—"What'd you say this bird's name is? Whay? Oh, Way? He's got a pretty good fast ball. I'll say that for him. Yes, I'm for Yale."

Billy Fleischmann, a Yankee official (critically)—"Not much of a crowd, Harry. Not more than five or six thousand, eh?"

Mr. Sparrow (indignantly)—"Not MUCH of a crowd? Not MUCH of one? Say, do you know what they get for seats around here? One buck and a half for the stand and a buck for the bleachers! Think o' that? Just think of it awhile! Oh, I wish we could only do that to 'em every day! One buck and a half! Say, boys, don't forget I didn't pull that one about switching the seats around."

Mr. McGeehan (dictating)—"In Yale's half of the first Middle-brook was safe on Douglas's error. Milburn smashed a double to left, scoring Middlebrook. Milburn took third on Legore's out, but Hunter raised to Law. One hit, one run, one error."

Mr. Donlin (cheerfully)—"Well, us Yale boys are out in front, and—say, who's that ump, anyway? He missed that one! Yes, he did! It was right over the old oyster! Right over! What! That batter isn't going to do anything to him? Well well! Funny kind of a game."

Paul Armstrong, a visitor (entering with apologetic air)—"I had to come. My children wanted to see the game."

Henry Fabian—"Ain't it awful what they've been doing to my ground?"

Mr. Donlin—"What'd you say ump's name is—the one behind the plate? Stafford? I don't know him, but I'll remember the name. I may meet him some day. So that's old Jack Egan out there on the bases? Well, well! Not a bad fellow, Jack, for an umpire."

Mr. Donlin—"Say, do you fellows see that bird over there without any coat? The one with the megaphone? He's leading his gang in yelling all alone, and this fellow over in front of the Princeton bunch has two assistants. That don't seem right."

An Obliging Spectator—"That's Aleck Wilson, the Yale football captain. He's acting as cheer leader."

Mr. Donlin — "I think he'll outlast those other fellows at that. He seems to have more stuff."

Mr. McGeehan (dictating) — "The Tigers forged ahead in the third. With one down Deyo was safe on Way's bad throw, and Hanks singled to left. Gill forced Hanks at second, and Deyo took third. Deyo tallied, and Gill stole third, scoring when Driggs hit a hot shot at Way, which was deflected by the pitcher's glove."

Mr. Donlin (excitedly) — "Hi, there's a fellow kicking to Jack Egan! He thinks he beat that throw. What's his name? Douglas? You're all right, Doug! Tell him about it!"

Mr. Fabian — "I don't know how I'm ever going to get it in condition again. I mean my ground."

Mr. McGeehan (dictating) — "The New Haven boys tied it up in the fifth on singles by Long John Reilly and Vaughn. Way's sacrifice and Middlebrook's infield out. In the sixth, Gill doubled to right, and Driggs sacrificed. Green drew a pass and Scully hit to Legore, Gill being effaced at the plate. Scully took second and Green third on the play, and Green scored on Douglas's single, but Scully was out at the plate. The Princeton boys started an argument over this last play — getting that?"

Mr. Donlin — "Now, we're going to have some real nice trouble. Talk to him, boys! I don't like his face myself. What! Is THAT all they're going to say to him? Funny game."

Mr. Armstrong — "Gentlemen, what's that Yale shortfielder's name, did you say? Legore? Pretty good hands. What league does he play in regularly?"

Mr. Donlin (very suspiciously) — "Say, is this game on the level? Are they playing to win? What's the infield doing in with two out? And didn't somebody hit with (the count) three and nothing a little while ago? I don't know about this game. I like that Princeton catcher myself. What's his name? Kelleher? I like him all the better now."

Mr. Fabian — "Just lookit! Lookit what they're doing!"

Mr. McGeehan (dictating) — "Way got Kelleher's drive in the seventh and stumbled and fell in the path of the runner, who sprawled over the pitcher and reached first. Egan called him safe, and the play aroused much discussion—got that?"

Mr. Donlin—"There's another good chance for an argument gone. The decision was all right, but Yale ought to have said something about it. I certainly like that catcher. Name's Kelleher."

Mr. McGeehan (dictating)—"With one down in the eighth, Driggs walked, and stole second, taking third on Hunter's bad throw. Green hit to Legore, and Driggs was out at the plate, Hunter making the star play of the day, blocking his man off."

Mr. Donlin (positively)—"There's a regular catcher! I like him even better'n the other fellow. Did you see him stand in there and take that bird's cleats? Ty Cobb might have left him a little marked up."

Mr. Armstrong—"I call your attention to Legore."

Mr. McGeehan (dictating)—"With the score tied in the eighth, and one out, Legore was safe on Scully's bad throw, and stole second, Scully dropping a perfect throw. Hunter singled, and Legore scored with the winning run—get that? In the Tigers' last inning, Kelleher was hit by a pitched ball, but Stafford refused to let him take his base on the ground that he had not tried to avoid—getting that?"

Mr. Donlin—"Say, don't they give a man no credit in this league for stepping into a fast one?"

Mr. Donlin—"Hey, look! What did I tell you about that Yale cheer leader? He's gone right through the nine innings. He just naturally outgamed these other fellows."

Mr. Fabian—"I hate collegers. I hate 'em."

———

The Giants were well off the pace in 1916, when on Sept. 7, they beat Brooklyn's Nap Rucker to begin an improbable 26-game winning streak that would only end with the doubleheader split with the Braves that Runyon describes below. Winning every game the rest of the month, the New Yorkers would finish fourth, seven games back of the Dodgers, and enter with the record books as the longest modern-day winning streak of all time; the Dodgers, meanwhile, went on to lose the World Series in five games to the Red Sox.

Only a writer of Runyon's skill could compare a baseball game to a Texas train. He knew Corsicana, the classic Texas boom town, where oil was discovered in 1894. The town is approximately 50 miles north of Marlin, then central Texas's Mecca of mineral baths and spas, where the Giants journeyed for spring training.

GIANTS HALTED BY BRAVES; WIN 26 IN ROW; THEN LOSE (OCT. 1, 1916)

Tyler Masters Sallee in Second Game, 8 to 3. Benton Yields One Hit in Opener

Just as the celebrated Giants' Unlimited reached the railroad yards on the outskirts of Corsicana, Navarro County, Texas, and was whistling for the switch that would have put it on the 27th straight siding yesterday afternoon, a Boston bandit by the name of George Tyler crawled aboard the blind baggage, tossed a left-handed money wrench into the doodad, and help up the train. He robbed the Giants of a tie for the world's record for consecutive baseball victories, which is treasured in Corsicana, leaving them flat at 26.

The Giants reached the latter station in the first game of a doubleheader with the Boston Braves before the sinister Tyler crawled aboard, the noble Rube Benton jamming the caravan through with one hit. The score was 4 to 0.

Then, when all the train crew and passengers were smiling and chatting and enjoying the scenery as they rushed into the second game, there was a sudden jar, a gritty, grinding of brakes, a hoarse cry of "Hands up!" and George Tyler—for it was indeed he—came through the cars holding a southpaw in people's faces.

The stuff was off. The long ride was over. When the tourists crawled out from under an 8 to 3 wreck, the train was a mess. It may get started again this season, but it cannot get very far as the right of way peters out presently.

The travelers heard rumors last night to the effect that they were burning red fire in the streets of Corsicana, and that the Mayor was making speeches, which gives rise to the suspicion that the people of that town never really wanted the unlimited there, anyway.

Sallee Assists Tyler

It is believed that George Tyler had inside assistance in his nefarious exploit. It is whispered that Sheriff Slim Sallee, who was supposed to convey the train with a posse on into Corsicana after the 26th point was reached, worked in cahoots with Tyler and slowed down enough for the bandit to get aboard.

The Sheriff denies the charge, but the left-handed monkey wrench found in the doodad is accepted in many quarters as evidence of collusion. "Slim" is left-handed. So is Tyler. So was the monkey wrench. Things look dark for the Sheriff.

Now that it is over, some folks are saying that the Giants' Unlimited never was going anywhere anyway, and that Corsicana was just an excuse for a joyride; but nevertheless, over 30,000 people were out again at the Polo Grounds yesterday afternoon to watch them travel. Attendance records at the Polo Grounds have fallen lately along with the baseball records.

The world's record for consecutive victories still stands at 27, but the Giants have hung up a run that will probably stand as a big-league mark for years. They went through every other club in the league during their drive.

Konetchy Spoils Record

For seven palpitating innings of the first game, Rube Benton held the Braves without a hit. One man got to first on him in that time; he passed Hank Gowdy in the sixth. Dick Rudolph followed Hank and stumbled into a double play.

In the eighth, Ed Konetchy, the first man up, pelted a hot drive over second for a safe hit. He was forced by Red Smith at second base on a roller to (Heinie) Zimmerman. Sherry Magee fanned and (Art) Fletcher tossed out (Dick) Egan.

Meantime, little Dick Rudolph was pitching a crafty game.

There is no wiser noodle underneath a baseball cap in the big leagues than the bald bean, which belongs to the Bronx boy.

(George) Burns tripled in the third, but was smothered at the plate trying to stretch the blow, and thereafter until the seventh, Rudolph held the Giants in the palm of his oily old glove. (Benny) Kauff singled in the second, (Lew) McCarty singled in the fifth and (Buck) Herzog singled in the sixth, but they got nowhere.

Giants Win in Seventh

In the seventh, with one out, Fletcher hit a terrific drive to right center, the ball rolling down in among a bunch of extra players and just ordinary citizens who were watching the pastime from that point. It might have been a homer, but (John) McGraw stopped Fletcher at third. Kauff brought Fletcher in with a rap past (Rabbit) Maranville.

There was no luck about these smashes. Kauff pasted the pill with the count two balls and no strikes on him. Kauff stole second and (Walter) Holke got an infield hit of the lucky variety after Rudolph worked him down to three and two. Holke reached out and tapped a ball that would have walked him, and hit just out of Rudolph's reach.

McCarty fouled out and with Benton at bat, Holke was caught flat-footed off first by Rudolph as the Giant first baseman was about to leave the bag on his end of a double steal. Kauff started home and Koney fired for the plate, the throw being wide. Kauff scored and Benton then fanned.

In the eighth, the Giants added two more. Burns was safe on Smith's low throw of a grounder, and Herzog singled, Burns stopping at second. (Dave) Robertson sacrificed the runners along and Zim lifted a sacrifice fly that scored Burns with his 100th run of the season. George is the only man in the league who will have that number of runs to his credit this season. Fletcher singled, scoring Herzog, while Fletcher himself was being erased in a run-up.

Braves Finally Score

The Braves scored for the first time in the series in the fourth frame of the second game. Fletcher made a two-base bad throw on Maranville.

He remained on second while McCarty was throwing out (Ed) Fitzpatrick, but "Rabbit" stirred his stumps and scored when Konetchy singled to right. Koney got to third on Smith's out and scored on Magee's single. Magee was out trying to take second on the play.

Robertson got a double in the Giants' end of the fourth, but Zimmerman raised a fly to right, Maranville made a great catch of Fletcher's short fly to left and Kauff fanned.

In the fifth frame, Holke was safe on Konetchy's bad toss to Tyler, who covered first, and McCarty walked. Ol' Slim Sallee gritted his teeth and bunted to Koney, who made a play to third on Holke and lost him, filling the bases.

Burns singled to right, scoring Holke. Herzog hit a sharp grounder over second and Maranville made a good play getting the ball, a double play resulting. McCarty scored and Sallee took third, but Robertson picked one over his head to complete a strikeout.

In the seventh, Red Smith hit a homer into the leftfield stand with Koney on base ahead of him. Koney had singled to center. The Braves had been pasting the ball hard on Sallee from the start, and it was only smashing fielding behind him that kept many of the licks from going safe.

Sherry Magee stepped up in the wake of Smith and knocked another homer into the leftfield stand and away went Sal, reaching for his tobacco. Sallee had been out once before during the Giant drive and while he won, he did not look any too good on that occasion. His attack of "ptomaine" recently seems to have left the Sheriff a little weak.

Jeff Tesreau took the mound with none out and Egan singled. (Earl) Blackburn bunted and all hands were safe when no one covered first. A wild pitch advanced the runners, and Egan scored on Tyler's short hit to Tesreau. Larry Chappell batted for (former Giant Fred) Snodgrass and singled, scoring Blackburn. Jeffy Tesreau rode away on that lick and in came Andy Anderson.

Andy started several games during the streak, but failed to finish one. He finally managed to get the Braves all out in that seventh, but the old train was beyond all repairs.

But 31-year-old Slim Sallee, who had joined the Giants in midseason after eight strong seasons with the Cardinals, was far from finished. He'd go 14-9 with a minuscule 1.37 ERA in '16, and play another five seasons in the big leagues, winning 172 lifetime games.

———

In mid-1919 for no apparent reason, Runyon abandoned his tra-ditional game story, turning his coverage into virtual short-hand—loosely connected observations that took in the game, who showed up in the press box, and whatever else struck his fancy.

SHOCKER KALSOMINES YANKS; BROWNS IN 1 TO 0 VICTORY (JUNE 16, 1919)
Quinn Loses Pitching Battle When He Wings Demmitt and Jacobson Follows with Triple

A chicken came home to roost up at the Harlem hennery yesterday afternoon.

❊　❊　❊

Urban Shocker, who was peddled to St. Louis by the Yanks a couple of seasons back, returned to the old farmyard with "Goose-Hill Jimmy" Burke's Browns, and knocked our flock right off their top perch. White Sox now lead league.

❊　❊　❊

Closed the gate on 'em with five hits.

❊　❊　❊

Final score: Browns, 1; Yanks, 0.

❊　❊　❊

387

Hit batsman and "Baby Doll" Jacobson's three-bagger did it.

＊　＊　＊

Yanks scared 'em in the eighth, at that.

＊　＊　＊

Two out, Baker doubled. Lewis beat out a poke. Pipp couldn't help. Easy bouncer to (Joe) Gedeon.

＊　＊　＊

Jack Quinn pitched well for us, but not well enough.

＊　＊　＊

Yanks don't beat Urban since he went away from here.

＊　＊　＊

The firm of Colonel & Colonel, Messrs. Ruppert and Huston, sat together in a box for the first time this season. Colonel Ruppert was somewhat embarrassed by the fact that Colonel Huston wore the old iron boiler.

＊　＊　＊

Harry Sparrow's eagle-eyed cops created a diversion before the game by making a collar of a "gam(bler)" in the stand back of third. After a while, all of Harry's old acquaintances of the Criterion days will stop speaking to him.

＊　＊　＊

George Sisler's "shiner" is still keeping him out of active service.

* * *

Ol' Lefty Leifield, an echo of the Halcyon days of the Pittsburgh Pirates, was out on the coaching line.

* * *

Ollie Chill, the limited edition of umps, worked behind the plate yesterday. Ollie is about as high as (catcher) Truck Hannah's belt buckle. Quiet day for Ollie.

* * *

Colonel and Colonel, (Ruppert's friend) Bill Fleischmann, and the Yanks, are entertaining the officers and men of the Leviathan at the P(olo) G(rounds) Tuesday.

* * *

Crowd was around 25,000. That was some crowd for the St. Louis Browns.

* * *

Jimmy Austin made a nice play pulling Peck's foul out of the boxes back of third in the first.

* * *

Ray Demmitt was hit by a pitched ball in the second. Nobody was out. "Baby Doll" Jacobson smacked a three-bagger to right-center and Ray reported.

❊ ❊ ❊

An attempt was made to squeeze Jacobson home, but "Baby Doll" was eradicated at the pan.

❊ ❊ ❊

In the Yanks' end of the second, with one out, Lewis singled and Pratt was sale in Gerber's error, Lewis taking third.

❊ ❊ ❊

This looked like a great chance for a little business, but Bodie and Hannah were easy.

❊ ❊ ❊

Lower stand packed. Upper stand fairly well filled and both bleachers nicely populated yesterday. The firm of Colonel & Colonel did a lot of loose beaming.

❊ ❊ ❊

With two spitballers in, the game dragged.

❊ ❊ ❊

Quinn isn't as much of a spitballer as he used to be, at that. He bluffs it a lot.

❊ ❊ ❊

Third inning, Austin doubled to right. He had to dive for second to get in ahead of Lewis' great throw. Play was close, and in hustling up to give it a look, "Brick" Owens, the ump, went down in a bunch.

✿   ✿   ✿

"Brick" twisted his knee, but kept on working. He once broke a leg in a similar fall when he was in the National League.

✿   ✿   ✿

Good ump, "Brick."

✿   ✿   ✿

Austin didn't get beyond second. Two were down when he hit his lick, and Quinn whiffed Gedeon.

✿   ✿   ✿

Lieutenant Mike Clofine, late of the 79th Division, looked in from the press pavilion.

✿   ✿   ✿

Austin put too much on his throw of Peck's bounder in the third for no good reason, and Jacobson couldn't hold it.

✿   ✿   ✿

Two were out at the time. Shocker made a dozen attempts to catch Peck napping and finally Roger stole second while Urban was holding the ball.

✿   ✿   ✿

Urban is one of those slobbery spitballers. He almost eats the old apple while he is wetting it up and is very deliberate.

❀   ❀   ❀

He deliberately fanned Baker with one of the most deliberate balls the world has ever seen, after Peck's steal.

❀   ❀   ❀

Baker skidded on his chin going after Tobin's short push at the beginning of the fourth, but Demmitt promptly staggered into a two-ended play, Peck to Pipp.

❀   ❀   ❀

"Goose Hill Jimmy" Burke, manager of the Browns, wears a uniform and coaches off third base in a loud voice.

❀   ❀   ❀

Shocker singled in the eighth and Austin walked and Hannah went and had a talk with Quinn about Gedeon.

❀   ❀   ❀

Decided to let him bunt, and get Shocker at third, then Quinn pitched too high for a bunt. Great strategy.

❀   ❀   ❀

Gedeon finally became an infield out, on which Shocker took third, but Peck made a great play getting Tobin's fly, and Pratt tossed out Demmitt.

❀   ❀   ❀

Austin, who seemed to be constantly on the bases, got as far as third in the sixth on a single, Gedeon's sacrifice and Gedeon's passed ball, but Tobin lined to Peck and Demmitt was easy.

✿　✿　✿

That one run commenced to look mighty formidable along about the fifth.

✿　✿　✿

Still looked formidable in the ninth.

———

Well, why not? About five weeks later, Runyon uses the observations of a young boy in reporting on a Giants' doubleheader split in Pittsburgh.

GIANTS SPLIT WITH PIRATES: TONEY PITCHES 3–0 SHUTOUT (JULY 30, 1919)

Benton and Dubuc Falter in Second Game and Pittsburghs Win Out, 7 to 6

PITTSBURGH, JULY 29: Little Wilton Sapp, favorite nephew of A. Mugg, is making the big swing with us. It is the little fellow's first trip away from home, and he is having a lively time. Lovely.

✿　✿　✿

"Why do they call this place Pittsburgh?" he asked this morning. "Why don't they call it something else?"

✿　✿　✿

Well, of course we don't know about that, but it shows the childish boy very bright and very observing. Very.

❉ ❉ ❉

This afternoon Little Wilton saw the Giants split up a double-header with the Pittsburgh Pirates, and that was something for anybody to see. Saw Fred Toney, the Tennessee dinosaurus, blank the homeboys with three hits by a score of 3 to 0 in the first game.

❉ ❉ ❉

Saw the Giants drop the second pastime in the ninth inning after they had a four-run jump on the Pirates, the final accounting in that scene being 7 to 6, and it was just that sort of a game.

❉ ❉ ❉

"What's a Pirate?" demanded Little Wilton, but of course we dunno that, as it's been a long time since Honus Wagner was around.

❉ ❉ ❉

Still, even the brightest of little children are sometimes more or less trying. Little Wilton was found with his tiny hand in a gentleman's pocket in the hotel lobby this morning.

❉ ❉ ❉

Gentleman seemed disposed to make a fuss about the matter. Trouble is, Little Wilton didn't know the gentleman.

❉ ❉ ❉

In the closing stages of the second game today, the Giants underwent some slight preliminary training for the expected 2.75 beer bottle barrage over in Cincinnati later on. Inmates of Pittsburgh got greatly agitated, and hollered around at our boys and all that.

✿　✿　✿

They waited after the game was over to drape themselves over the ramparts of the grandstand as the Giants marched toward the exit, and they hollered and hollered.

✿　✿　✿

"My, what funny noises they make out of their mouths," commented little Wilson.

✿　✿　✿

But they didn't throw any of the furniture at our folks, which is more than can be promised of Cincinnati. Our scouts, who are in contact with the enemy on the Rhine, do say that the populace there is much smoked up about the coming of the Giants. They have already hired 50 extra cops to do duty during the race rioting between our people and the natives of Fountain Square.

✿　✿　✿

One cop to guard the Giants, and 49 to restrain Wild Will Phelon, the leading Cincinnatiac, when he starts to boil over.

✿　✿　✿

First game today: Burns, the first man up, busted a single on the aged Babe Adams. Fletcher doubled after Young had gone out, and Doyle scored 'em both with a single to right. Enough.

✿　✿　✿

"Why do the Pirates keep away from third base?" asked Little Wilton Sapp.

＊　＊　＊

Well, we dunno that either, but the fact remains that none of them got there during the incumbency of the ponderous Mr. Toney. Off-stage, the massive (6'1" and 195-lb.) moundsman is the very next-to-last person you would pick out as a ballplayer. The last one, of course, is Marie Dressler.

＊　＊　＊

In the second game, after getting an earlier run on Snyder's single, Benton's sacrifice and Young's single, the Giants grabbed a handful in the fourth. Doyle singled and Kauff's clout got through Stengel for three satchels, Doyle scoring. Zim tripled to left, Chase walked and Snyder tripled.

＊　＊　＊

That ought to have been at least three more than enough. John Calhoun Benton was left-handing of it very nicely, and our men were cracking Wilbur Cooper's side-winding right on the coco.

＊　＊　＊

But look, look here. With two down in the eighth, Pittsburgh scored two runs off a pass to Stengel, a triple by (George) Cut-shaw and a single by Sallee. John Calhoun Benton was thereupon ingloriously ousted from the premises by John J. McGraw, and Jean Dubuc tried it.

＊　＊　＊

Jean stopped the scoring in the eighth, but in the ninth there was heaps of trouble. Lee was safe on Doyle's error, which was the first of the game, and Cooper and Bigbee singled, filling the bases.

❈   ❈   ❈

With the count three and two, Barbare walked, forcing in Lee and forcing out Jean Dubuc. "Shufflin Phil" Douglass, who worked in Brooklyn yesterday, came aboard. Southworth lifted a fly to Burns and Cooper scooted home with the tying marker.

❈   ❈   ❈

That brought Casey Stengel up and Casey smacked a single to left, scoring Bigbee with the winner. And there you are. There you certainly are.

❈   ❈   ❈

Young got four blows in the second game. The club looked grand in the first pastime behind Toney's twisting. Grand.

❈   ❈   ❈

"What makes the people in this place the way they are?" inquired Little Wilton Sapp, with childish naiveté.

❈   ❈   ❈

But, of course, we dunno that.

———

YOU'VE GOT THE "BIG ONE" LEFT
(AUG. 18, 1920)

When there are two strikes on the batter, you hear the coaches yelling, encouragingly!

"You've got the big one left!"

He means that the batter has a final chance to hit the ball. The players call this chance the "big one." The batter has swung twice and missed, or has had two strikes called on him by the umpire. But the batter has the "big one" left.

A good hitter is little disturbed by two misses. The "big one" still remains; he is all the more keyed up by his failures. Sometimes he may have a fleeting regret for letting a couple of good opportunities go by without offering at them, only to hear then called strikes by the umpire, but the "big one" is left.

There is a whole sermon in the expression.

Many a man steps up to the old home plate of life and takes a couple of heavy wallops at what he considers good chances and misses 'em. Maybe he stands idly by, and lets them be called against him. In any event he finds himself in the same situation with two strikes on him.

Only too often a man in that situation becomes discouraged. He feels that the pitcher has him "in a hole." He either takes a half-hearted swing at the next offering, or again stands there glum, and downhearted, without moving a muscle while the umpire yells: "You're out!"

He might better take courage, and remember that he has the "big one" left.

Another opportunity is coming over, and if he keeps himself keyed up, stout-hearted and expectant, he may hit it into the stands for a home run.

Timid batters, in life, as well as in baseball, are always at a disadvantage. If they permit themselves to become discouraged over a couple of failures, they will never be ready for the "big one."

Take a tighter grip on the bat, crowd the plate a little closer, watch the pitcher carefully, and try to determine whether the next offering is going to be to your liking. Never mind the two strikes . . .

"You've got the BIG ONE left!"

———

Clearly, Runyon was a tad bored with the proceedings of this meaningless late-season Yankees–Washington game at the

Polo Grounds. So he presents a dated tale of explaining the game to women through a running conversation that may or may not have actually happened.

NO BOTHER TO ENTERTAIN LADY (SEPT. 27, 1920)

He Keeps Away from Baseball Technicalities while Yankees Are Beating Grifters, 9 to 5

While the Yankees were giving the Washington Grifters a 9 to 5 plastering up at the Polo Grounds yesterday afternoon, we thought of a new system of entertaining a lady at a baseball game.

Ladies, in their naïve ignorance of baseball, are apt to ask questions which greatly amuse all hearers, and bring a brush of embarrassment to the leathery cheek of a veteran baseballist.

Technical explanations of plays to a female mind are difficult. Yet one must assuredly say something to one's company, if only to make conversation. We thought of a new line of chit-chat, interesting and informative, but at the same time avoiding the intricacies of the pastime.

"This man," we remarked, as Will Evans walked across the field, "is said to be the handsomest umpire in the business." However, we added hastily, "a man does not have to be excessively handsome to be the handsomest umpire in the business at that."

"Yonder," we said, pointing to Colonel Jacob Ruppert, who sat in the press box, "is one of the owners of the Yankees. You should be worth his dough. The gentleman sitting behind him in his short sleeves is Harry M. Stevens (the concessions' director at the ballpark). The other gentleman is the group is probably just some other millionaire."

Pipp Runs Billiard Room in the Winter

"The man throwing the baseball," we said, "is Jack Quinn. He has been around some time. The man who just caught the baseball is Walter Pipp. He comes from Grand Rapids, Michigan. In the winter-time, he runs a billiard room, and does very well."

"Here," we remarked, "is Babe Ruth. He is a well-known hitter.

Possibly you have heard of him. He is married, and owns a new
Packard car. The band over there in the grandstand is from the
school at Baltimore where Ruth was educated.

"This is a very large crowd for this late in the season," we continued. "The New York club is not going to win the pennant this
season, and generally people are not interested in a club that has no
chance to win. The Washington club is not going to win the pennant
this season either, or next season, or the next season after that.

"The reason so many people are here," we hazarded, "is that
there is no other place to go. The gentleman in civilian clothes on
the Washington bench over there is Mr. (Clark) Griffith, the Washington manager. He is sitting so far back in the corner because he
does not want to appear to be with the Washington club.

"The man who just came into the press box," we chatted, "is Mr.
(Henry) Fabian, the groundskeeper. He takes care of these
grounds and sees that there are no pebbles left on the field to furnish excuses for shortstops. This man just walking into the New
York bench is (rightfielder) Sam Vick, and the people you hear
talking about killing him are mad because he let that ball get away
from him for a home run for Mr. Shanks, of the Washington club,
scoring two runs."

Zachary's Pitching Not O.K. for Griff

"The Washington young man now throwing the ball is (Tom)
Zachary," we said. "You see he throws it with his left hand. He is
now leaving because he does not throw it to suit Mr. Griffith, the
manager, although it is very satisfactory to the New York boys.

"The young man who is taking Zachary's place is named (Joe)
Gleason," we said, after we had gathered the rest of the
announcer's remarks. "We don't know where he comes from, or
where he is going, but Mr. Griffith probably does.

"Yonder sits (veteran sportswriter and onetime big-leaguer)
Sam Crane," we said. "He has been with the Yankees most of this
season. He is thinking just now, and maybe he is thinking about
the Yankees. If so, you could not print his thoughts."

Thus we whiled away the afternoon with pleasant discourse. Not once did we leave an opening for one of those fatuous questions that would bring the glance of amusement in our direction.

"This chap at bat is Aaron Ward," we finally announced. "He is said to be one of the best dancers in baseball. The ballplayers claim that Aaron can certainly shake a wicked French, Shriner & Urner. He is playing his first year as a regular, and—"

"Yes," interrupted our company, "and he ought to make a great ballplayer next year. He's got a great pair of hands, and I like the way he hits the ball. That home run into the leftfield bleachers in the fifth and that other homer to right-center in the sixth were as nice hits as I ever expect to see.

"How many does that make him this season—10?" she asked.

"We dunno," we said glumly.

———

The retired ballplayer, in need of a buck and missing the old days, was a common sight at big-league ballparks in Runyon's day. That was particularly so at the Polo Grounds, where former greats like Dan Brouthers and Amos Rusie worked as beneficiaries of the otherwise hardbitten John McGraw, who could be a real soft touch to old baseball friends. So who was the "Old Guy" as depicted in Runyon's poem? Probably a composite of Brouthers, a watchman; Rusie, a ticket-taker; and a couple of other of colorful Giants of the 1890s who wound up at the Polo Grounds: "Smiling" Mickey Welch and Joe Hornung. The hard-bitten Hornung, nicknamed "Ubbo Ubbo" for the curious remark he'd make every time he cracked a base hit, held forth with tales to anyone who cared to listen about the old days when "men were men and not pampered and spoiled like modern ballplayers." Ubbo Ubbo didn't even care for baseball gloves that came into vogue in the late 1890s; wearing a glove was "sissy" in his view.

The Old Guy's Lament (Oct. 5, 1921)

I.

The Old Guy stood in a corner,
        'Tending a bleacher stile,
And the fans rushed in by thousands,
        But gave him never a smile.
Never a glance or tumble,
        As he gathered their duckets in,
And they hurried into the ball yard
        To root for their club to win.

II.

Well, the Old Guy twisted his moustache,
        And wrinkled his mug in a smile,
A wry, dry, facial contention.
        As he 'tended his bleacher stile,
And he said, as he turned down a coupon
        That came with a nickel cigar,
"There's nary a soul that knows me—
        And I was once Murderous McFarr!"

III.

"There's nary a soul says howdy,
        Or dukes me in passing by,
And they all used to swell with pleasure
        If I give them a friendly eye.
And after the game was over,
        Thousands would stand out and wait
Just for a glance at my figure—
        'Hey, Mister, you can't crash this gate!'

IV.

"Look into your baseball figures,
        Your history, and such as that,
Turn to the name I have mentioned,

And see what I done with my bat.
You talk of your Ruth, and your Meusel,
     And Kelly—don't make me smile!
Them guys hit 'em a furlong,
     Where I sued to hit 'em a mile!

V.

"When I stepped up in the pinches,
     I'd blow on m'bat with my breath,
And you'll find it set down in the record
     How I scart ten pitchers to death!
And no one knew how to run the bases,
     And no one could field 'em like me—
Hey, Mister, this ticket's for Tuesday,
     And I never let no one in free!

VI.

"I broke out early in '80,
     In the days when they played the real game.
And I was a riot to start with
     And Murderous McFarr's my name.
Them was the days of good pitchin',
     Them was the days they played ball!
Nowadays guys they git famous,
     Who can't play the old game a-tall!

VII.

"Half of 'em nothin' but boneheads,
     And the other half worse than that;
Look up my moniker, Mister,
     And see what I done with my bat!
But think of the dough that they're grabbin',
     Guys that can't hit a balloon—
I can see where my parents where crazy
     By havin' me born so soon!"

VIII.

The Old Guy stood in a corner
   'Tending a bleacher stile,
And watching the rushing thousands
   And smiling that wry, dry smile.
While I thought as a I heard the turnstile
   Playing its whining tune,
That most of is, when we are Old Guys,
   Learn we were born too soon.

—

*Ever wondered who the fat cats are in the fancy seats? Sure you
have. So did Runyon, writing during the the 1926 Yankees–
Cardinals World Series.*

STRANGERS GETTING IN. WHO ARE THESE BIRDS? ALWAYS HAVE BEST SEATS. (OCT. 7, 1926)

Regulars Are Rushed Back. A Plea for "Old Guard"

I often wonder through these great sports assemblages, just as a
matter of curiosity, to peer into the open faces of the occupants of
those vastly coveted and much debated first-line chairs. I mean to say
the desirable seats from the first on back to the 10th or 12th rows.

It is these seats that always somehow unaccountably disap-
pear—vanish as if into thin air—about two minutes after a great
sports event is announced. I never hear of any of them being on
sale, and I never chanced to meet anyone who had any of them. To
me, they have always been a dark mystery.

I know that there are such seats, to be sure, because I see them
occupied, but I rarely know the occupants. I often find myself wondering who they are. They seem to be well-dressed, substantial-
looking citizens, most decorous of behavior, but who are they? I
pride myself on a fairly wide acquaintance of faces in the world of
sport, but it seems to me that aside from a familiar countenance here
and there, I rarely see anyone I know, never any of the regulars.

❀   ❀   ❀

I mean the men, and women, too, who are regular patrons of the different sports. You see them in the most expensive seats day after day, and night after night in the baseball orchards and the pugilistic emporiums, always willing to buy the best. And the management is always delighted to sell them the best.

But the instant that a large sports event is in on the tapis, the best seems too good for the regulars. At all events, I see few of them in those desirable seats. They are father back. The best seats are held down by the strangers.

I suppose the management figures that the regular will take what he can get rather than miss the event but that they must cater to the strangers, bankers, brokers, merchants, political bigwigs, and the like, who may see one big sports event once in their lifetime, then never attempt to see another.

I have no specific event in mind, my friends. It happens not once but every time, whether the event is a heavyweight championship fight, or a World Series, or some other desirable attraction. Nor am I complaining. I am merely wondering who those eggs are that get the good seats.

❀   ❀   ❀

Through the lean periods of sport, the regular chips in his regularity. He is the old anchorman against adversity. You might think that the managers and promoters of these big sports events would think of the old boy when prosperity rolls around, and some particularly juicy melon is about to be opened. But they never do.

The managers and promoters would get fat, as the saying is, if they depended on the strangers for all-the-year-round support. They would be in the bands of the receivers in no time. It is the steady grind that keeps them alive.

I suppose the most astute promoter in the pugilistic racket is

Mr. George "Tex" Rickard. Yet Mr. Rickard seems to gloat more over the presence of a few odds and ends of bankers and society loogans, as we say in Chicago, at his ringside, than over the tens of thousands of common, or garden ringworms who are packed in back beyond the bug guns.

Yet, how much money would Mr. Rickard draw in the long run with his pugilistic performances if he depended on the bankers and society boys for the patronage to the exclusion of the everyday worms.

The same thing is true of the baseball magnates. I seem to find numerous celebrities—social, political and otherwise—in the boxes and the front-row seats during a World Series, but where are they during the run of the season?

❅   ❅   ❅

This world, as I have long since discovered, is arranged all wrong. I do not know just how I would rearrange it if they left the job to me, but I would certainly make some provision for the regulars getting the best seats when the best seats are really worth having.

I have no doubt that Mr. Rickard's immediate ringside at the Sesqui-Centennial Stadium to mention an instance that still sticks in my craw, was made up of representative unknowns at that, but I must confess I never saw a more anonymous bunch of citizens in my life.

I am talking about the very first rows—the first 10 or 15 of them. Everyone you know seemed to be crowded back into the offing. It is a mystery to me where those unknown lads come from, and how they got their tickets. I presumed they were friends of somebody influential.

I took a peek at the more consequential chairs at the first World Series game in New York, and I didn't seem to see many familiars even there. Of course it might be argued that I do not know enough persons of consequences to be a good judge, but foreseeing that criticism both at the Sesqui-Centennial Stadium and at the Polo Grounds, I enlisted experienced cooperation.

"Who is that?" And that?" And that?" I asked over and over again, pointing out pans protruding above the choice chairs . . . and the answer invariably was, "I don't know."

※　※　※

I believe that some pugilistic entrepreneurs like to "dress up their ringsides on important occasions," as they call it, by installing celebrities in the best seats.

This is all right with me, but I claim that the regulars look just as well as anyone else, and there are a lot more celebrities among the regulars, at that. It makes things more homelike for me if I am able to look around and see the smiling faces of the old guard close at hand.

It is certainly more comfortable than walking through a (stand) peopled only by strangers, and they occupy the seats that you know ought to belong to the supporting taxpayers of the game.

But maybe I am out of order again.

———

In the wake of the St. Louis Cardinals' six-game World Series triumph over the Yankees, Runyon holds forth on an idea that would catch on: minor-league clubs owned by big-league teams.

CHAIN-STORE BASEBALL. THAT'S ST. LOUIS IDEA. CARDS OWN FIVE CLUBS. AND 200 PLAYERS. (OCT. 13, 1926)

The chain-store idea brought into baseball is really responsible for the St. Louis Cardinals as the new champions of the baseball world.

The originators of the idea, as applied to what we call the National Pastime, are Mr. Branch Rickey, vice president and business manager of the Cardinals, and Mr. Charles Barrett, scout for the club.

In all the talk about the late World Series, I heard no mention of the name of Mr. Rickey nor of Mr. Barrett. Yet they are indubitably the master-minds of the outfit. But for their master-minding, which gave birth to the chain-store policy, there would be no St. Louis Cardinals save those that annoyed the baseball customers along the Big Muddy for lo these many years.

Mr. Rickey was once a baseball player, and a very terrible baseball player, at that, as those who witnessed his efforts on behalf of the New York Yankees years ago will testify. He gained far more fame later on by his introduction of the tenets of the Y.M.C.A. into baseball, which some held was a serious mistake. It is not of record that baseball suffered, however.

❁ ❁ ❁

When Mr. Branch Rickey took hold of the St. Louis Cardinals the club had no money in the treasury, or anywhere else, for that matter. It could not pay those fancy prices for baseball players. It had enough trouble paying its laundry bills.

Mr. Branch Rickey and Mr. Charles Barrett, his scout, set about forming affiliations with different clubs in the small leagues for the production of young baseball players.

Eventually, Mr. Rickey began taking over clubs in the small leagues on behalf of the Cardinals until today the St. Louis club controls five different clubs—Fort Smith, Ark.; Austin, Tex.; Syracuse; Houston; and Danville, Ill. It owns most of them outright and has first calls on all their players.

Some of these clubs are very valuable property. Houston, in the Texas League, for instance, is held to be worth $230,000, counting the franchise and real estate.

❁ ❁ ❁

The St. Louis club appoints the officials of the minor league clubs, and takes care of any deficit where they fail to prove self-supporting.

They can write off a pretty heavy loss against a club if that club develops one good big-league player, for big-league players nowadays cost anywhere from $4,000 on up into six figures.

Take the Fort Smith club, for example. It gave St. Louis Chick Hafey; Taylor Douthit; (Bill) Hallahan, a left-handed pitcher; Flint Rhem; (Ed) Clough; and Hank Mueller.

Hafey and Douthit cost St. Louis $500 each before they were sent to Fort Smith; the price paid the men who originally tipped Mr. Barrett to the players. Hallahan cost $500, Rhem $3,000 and Clough and Mueller nothing.

Mueller was picked up from the sandlots by Mr. Barrett, then traded even up to the Giants for Billy Southworth, so Southworth cost the Cardinals nothing. On that batch of ballplayers, the Cardinals could write off a tremendous loss on the operating expenses of the Fort Smith club.

❀ ❀ ❀

Austin sends its players to Houston, and Houston recently sold a player named (Harry) McCurdy to a big-league club for $25,000 and two ballplayers. The Cardinals could have had McCurdy, of course, but for some reason didn't want him. Another Houston player, (Ray) Benge, was sold for $6,000 to another big-league club.

From Houston the Cardinals get such players as (Ray) Blades and others, and from Syracuse, in the International League, came (Tommy) "Thames" Thevenow and "Sunny Jeems" (Jim) Bottomley, worth $100,000 apiece of they are worth a dime under the present scale of prices for baseball players.

Now the Syracuse franchise is commencing to be a valuable property, but even if the club was a loser, the St. Louis Cardinals could afford to carry it on the strength of Thevenow alone. Certainly it might as well be spending $100,000 there with the chance of first pick on a score of players and sinking the same amount in some individual prospect with a club in which it has no interest.

❈ ❈ ❈

As it stands the St. Louis Cardinals control from 175 to 200 baseball players, and of its five clubs only Fort Smith and Austin are what are known as draft clubs. That is to say other big-league clubs have the opportunity of picking from them, but by the time they are ready to pick really available prospects they are probably well covered up by the Cards.

Syracuse is a non-draft. One man who might be taken from Houston in the draft, and Danville is in the same category as Syracuse, although it is a Class B club. This club was recently taken over by the Cardinals.

Some many argue that the Cardinals' system, generally practiced, would eventually result in all the clubs in the land being controlled by the big leaguers, but that would not be as bad as it sounds. The little leagues nowadays need the support of powerful allies, unless baseball is to dip out altogether outside of the larger cities.

There is no denying that interest in the game isn't exactly what it used to be in many spots. Golf and other games have made serious inroads upon the baseball following. It is a hard struggle for the little clubs, and few of them are able to show a profit. With a big-league club behind it, a little club has a chance.

And in keeping the little clubs alive the big leagues will be fostering and preserving that interest in baseball that is necessary to the game.

———

Runyon reveled in his dislike of golf and fishing. He really wanted to add softball to his list, but admitted here the game was more popular than he realized.

RUNYON LEARNS MORE SOFTBALL FROM DEVOTEES (SEPT. 26, 1933)
Many Thousands, Young and Old—Play Game in New York
It appears that I have been living on woeful ignorance of what's going on.

Some time ago I wrote about the prevalence in Canada of a diversion called softball, a species of indoor baseball played outdoors, and wondered why the games had not found favor in these United States.

I am at this writing peering over a stack of communications from all parts of the NRA taking me to task, informing me, and in general putting me right on the subject of softball.

I am feeling somewhat abashed at the widespread exposure of my lack of knowledge on an important sport, but am at the same time experiencing a flow of pleasure over the proof of the vast circulation of this column. Furthermore, I am arranging for an intensive course in softball study.

It seems that this game is far more generally played in this country than in Canada. It numbers *millions* of followers. It is played to a considerable extent right here in the Greater City of New York. And yet so little of it is known to the sportswriters of the big town, I think I was the first to speak of it at any length—and I knew practically nothing about it.

Three Leagues Here

Among the letters I have received on softball is one from Albert B. Hines, director of the Madison Square Boys' Club, who says:

"When I saw the game played in Miami I felt it was something we could do in New York. Last year I had to force it on the boys in the playground, but after a few weeks they became so interested that they are now keen on it. You may be interested to know that in our playground we now have three softball leagues, one for the boys 6 to 10 years of age, one for the boys 12 to 14, and one in the evening for the boys up to 16, playing two games every night."

Now I didn't know that. Nor did I know that over in New Jersey there are numerous softball leagues, especially around Jersey City and Elizabeth. The newspapers carry columns of softball box scores.

I have a letter from Harry Wolfe of 225 East 2nd St., Brooklyn, who has been visiting out in Lansing, Mich., and who tells me that the game is extremely popular in those parts, especially among the girls. It is called "diamond ball" in Michigan, Mr. Wolfe says, and down south they term it "kitten ball."

Punch Ball

L.D. Robins of 450 7th Ave. claims that the game has been played in the streets of New York for the past 15 years under the name of "punch ball," which I admit is news to me.

"If you were to take a trip around the New York streets, you would see the game being played between passing automobiles, with the players dodging in and out," says Mr. Robins.

I do not doubt Mr. Robins' statement, but I am inclined to think that softball, as I viewed it in Canada, requires more space than is permitted, by a New York street. However, as proof of his assertion that softball isn't new to New York, Mr. Robins cites a tournament promoted some years ago by the defunct *Evening Graphic* in which teams from all over town took part.

Popular on Coast

I have learned that one seat of softball activity in this country is California. I might have suspected that. California is nearly always first with any sport that requires plenty of good weather.

They play softball in nearly every town in Southern California. They play it mostly at night, with the fields illuminated by elaborate lighting systems, and they play it with great seriousness. I have a raft of letters from the land of Mark Kelly to prove it.

A lot of the old-time professional ball tossers are taking part in the newer pastime, so I am informed. Among them are "Wahoo" Sam Crawford, who could pelt that old orange about as hard and as far as any man who ever lived.

It's a Fast Game

Oddly enough, as one of my correspondents, Mr. Lisle Sheldon of Long Beach, Cal., informs me, the old hardball players are not always satisfactory as softball pastimers. It seems that the softball game is *too fast* for them.

"This statement is no exaggeration," says Mr. Sheldon. "I have seen many men try to hit this big ball, who can (figuratively speaking) knock the cover off a hardball, and they say they didn't even see the pitcher throw the softball."

Mr. Sheldon is certain that a new national game is coming over the hill, and after another peek at that stack of correspondence that lies before me, I am inclined to think he is right.

———

Runyon ruminates on the All-Star game, kicked off the year before in Chicago, as it prepares to take place at the Polo Grounds—and is not impressed.

BOTH BARRELS (JULY 10, 1934)

This writer sees as the main purpose of the All-Star baseball game at the Polo Grounds today the fact that the proceeds go to a quite meritorious cause.

They go to an association devoted to the relief of sick and distressed veterans of baseball. Any effort that contributes in the slightest to the amelioration of human suffering and distress, the writer deems worthy of his support.

The game itself means nothing to competitive sport. It is merely a novelty parade of many of the star players of the American and National leagues. Neither club selected as representative of its league headliners (who) could beat any second-division club in the two leagues in a best five-of-seven series.

But as a spectacle the game should be worth seeing, and the writer sincerely hopes that the fund for which it is played will be enriched by many thousands of dollars.

❋   ❋   ❋

Years ago the writer often suggested that the big-league ball players, while in their playing prime, make some provision for the upkeep of the aged and infirm of the game.

This was long before the organization of the association, which now carries on that very work. Among the ideas advanced by the writer was taking some small percentage each year off the World Series receipts.

The active young players of the day laughed off these suggestions. They did not need assistance. Why should they provide for improvement old-timers who had failed to save their money when they were going (well)?

Many of these then-active young players in later years found themselves in the very predicament of the old-timers whose cause they had spurned. One of the greatest all-time stars of baseball, now long since dead, who criticized the writer's suggestions, saw the day when he was glad to accept the proceeds of a benefit game.

❊ ❊ ❊

There is something of his attitude, the writer is told, among some of the baseball stars of today with reference to the All-Star game. They are said to be lukewarm toward this game, for which they do not receive any immediate reward.

They should reflect that their reward is the consciousness of a kindly deed, of effort toward a worthy cause. In the years to come, some of them may be very glad that they assisted in the building of this fund.

The baseball magnates, it is said, are not particularly enthusiastic toward the All-Star game. The magnates never have done much to help their players. Yet they should welcome the game as solving one of baseball's oldest problems, the care of the sport's human relics.

❊ ❊ ❊

This All-Star game originated in Chicago, the parent of the idea being Archie Ward, splendid Chicago sportswriter and editor. Incidentally, the idea of the association that administers the funds raised by the games was western (in) birth — California, if the writer does not err.

Thus the East has had nothing to do with it so far. The game today seems likely to fall short of the tremendous success of the first contest in Chicago last year. A thing of this kind usually goes biggest when it is first launched because it then has the added attraction of novelty.

❊   ❊   ❊

However, it seems likely that upwards of 40,000 spectators will be in the Polo Grounds today, not a complete sellout, but a fine crowd.

Bill Terry, manager of the Giants, and Joe Cronin, manager of the Washington Senators, are the opposing managers of the All-Star clubs, Some old-time fans yearned for the management of their favorite club leaders of another era.

Since this game is supposed to typify the highest development of baseball with its greatest stars as exponents, the writer thinks it is quite proper that the young managers lead. After all, on the record, they are foremost among their kind.

❊   ❊   ❊

The greatest touch of sentiment in the game will be the presence of Babe Ruth, who won the game with a home run for the American Leaguers last year.

The baseball glory of the mighty Ruth is fading. This may be his very last big-league year. It is unlikely that a baseball manager, organizing a club to win a pennant, would stake his chances on Ruth as a regular.

Among the young fellows who will surround him this afternoon, Ruth is an old man, both in age and time of baseball service. But, even so, the fans would have laughed at any All-Star American

League line-up that did not have Ruth. Some of the American League fans are criticizing Manager Joe Cronin's selections, as it is.

Had he omitted Ruth—but Manager Cronin is too smart for that. The writer expects to see the great Babe, always rising to every big occasion, again steal the limelight today, and more power to him.

Babe Ruth did not hit any home runs in the 9–7 A.L. 1934 All-Star win. Stealing the show was Carl Hubbell, who struck out Ruth and four other Hall of Famers in order, over the first two innings; Lou Gehrig, Jimmie Foxx, Al Simmons and Joe Cronin were the others.